Don Roberto
Stanford, 1994

Also by
James B. Twitchell

The Living Dead: The Vampire in Romantic Literature

Romantic Horizons: Aspects of the Sublime in English Poetry and Painting, 1770–1850

Dreadful Pleasures: An Anatomy of Modern Horror

Forbidden Partners: The Incest Taboo in Modern Culture

Preposterous Violence: Fables of Aggression in Modern Culture

CARNIVAL CULTURE

The Trashing of Taste in America

JAMES B. TWITCHELL

Columbia University Press
New York

Columbia University Press
New York   Chichester, West Sussex

Library of Congress Cataloging-in-Publication Data

Twitchell, James B., 1943 —
    Carnival culture : the trashing of taste in America / James
Twitchell.
        p.   cm.
    Includes bibliographical references and index.
    ISBN 0-231-07830-7
    ISBN 0-231-07831-5 (pbk.)
    1. Mass media — United States.   2. United States — Popular culture.
I. Title.
P92.U5T88   1992
302.23'0973 — dc20   91-32227
                                                                   CIP

Book design by Teresa Bonner
Printed in the United States of America
c 10 9 8 7 6 5 4 3 2
p 10 9 8 7 6 5 4 3 2 1

For
Pam and Gary

Contents

Everything in this world has turned into show business. Politics is show business. Running Chrysler is show business— look at Lee Iacocca trying to get the attention of Congress by running full-page ads in the newspapers. When I keep trying to keep New York City out of bankruptcy, there's a lot of show business involved. Sports is show business, and Henry Kissinger is show business, and when they popped two million dollars for his book they had to recoup it by throwing a big number on television, with his world-statesman posture and all the rest. You package all these things. That's the reality of the marketplace. And then you have this appetite for vulgarity, which seems limitless—as witness what the paperback houses are bidding millions of dollars for. Those are the realities of the marketplace. So, as I've said, everything in this world has turned into show business. And if you're not in show business, you're *really* off Broadway.

—Felix Rohatyn of Lazard Frères & Company
(as quoted in Thomas Whitside,
The Blockbuster Complex)

Introduction

There's no business like show business. —Irving Berlin, *Annie Get Your Gun*

But then, for vulgarity, there's no business like show business. —Joseph Epstein, "What Is Vulgar?"

This is a book about show business: about which images are shown, about the industries that transport these images, about the audience that makes up the traffic, and about the critics who comment on the process. The industries I concentrate on are publishing, motion pictures, and television, and I contend that Irving Berlin and Joseph Epstein had it right. These businesses are unique: there *is* no business like show business. Worldwide industries produce and exhibit sequences that even they don't understand, and show them again and again until, as Irving Berlin says in a later verse, "the customers won't come." Although they may not know exactly what they show, these industries know how to calculate the exchange with precision: profit and loss, box-office receipts, rates for advertising time. The *New York Times* bestseller list, *Variety* reports, and the Nielsen ratings are weekly referenda on what "the traffic will allow." Joseph Epstein also had it right. If these conglomerated industries are successful from the point of view of shareholders, they will produce entertainments termed "vulgar" by high-culture critics.

So, in a sense, this is also a book about an aesthetic category, the vulgar. This category is rapidly disappearing because of the relentless economic demands of show business. In fact, taste has shifted more dramatically in the last two decades than in the entire century. In a world now consuming images as never before, what will be shown is what most paying customers want to see. What most customers want to see is, almost by definition, what a generation ago would have been labeled common, unwashed, scumular, barbaric, or *vulgar*. It is no happenstance that as we lose "ordinary" as a pejorative classification, we also give up the extra-ordinary as praiseworthy. In show business everything — and, therefore, nothing — is unique. *Derivative, repetitive*, and *imitative* are not terms of opprobrium but of praise. "Imitation," says Mighty Mouse on the *New Adventures of Mighty Mouse*, "is the sincerest form of television." When we no longer classify certain entertainments as vulgar, we will also be unable to classify their opposites as art. If the vulgar is the anticanon of high culture, then as we lose the power to recognize it, we also lose the ability to isolate, or "privilege," its counterparts. The current academic debate over what really belongs in the *Norton Anthology of Literature*, or in museums, or in the curriculum, is really a minor movement in the rapid tectonic shifts of modern taste. And those shifts in canonicity are being wrought daily by the most important industries in American culture: show business.

An apt analogy for American show business might be the Holy Roman Catholic Church of the early Renaissance. The Church's great power was its willingness to pay attention to its audience and to provide a steady stream of images that were comforting and inspiring. It never forgot that every act was an exchange: audience attention and support were traded for the promises of purpose and hope. But even the Church pales in comparison with modern mass media. Perhaps a better analogy might be that institution which grew up alongside the Church and both subverted and reinforced its doctrines — the Carnival. Here the barter is simpler: pay up and see what you want. Redemption can wait. If modern culture may be seen in terms of a competition for audience between high and low entertainment, between art and vulgarity, between the Church and the Carnival, then the Carnival is having its day. Mardi Gras is less and less dependent on Lent. The paperback book, the Cineplex 16, the audiocassette, the videocassette, the compact disk, and the coaxial cable have allowed a huge audience to attend the ceremonies of entertainment, and a huge amount of money to be made by those who can gauge what the mass audience desires. In the twentieth century, especially since the 1960s, the gatekeeper/cleric has wandered away and the carnival barker/programmer has taken his place. "Step right up, folks, right this way and see . . . " In the beginning was the Word, but in the end it will be the Image.

And what are the images? We have seen Geraldo Rivera, *USA Today*, professional wrestling, Stephen King, *Nightmare on Elm Street*, Mort Downey, Jr., Motley Crüe, Jacqueline Susann, the *Gong Show*, Harlequin Romances, Andrew Dice Clay, *Love Boat*, the Home Shopping Network, Public Enemy, *Porky's Part II*, a revival of comic books, *National Enquirer* headlines ("Hitler Found Alive in Florida," and "Son Kills Father and Eats Him"), Madonna "vogue-ing" in executive pin-striped suit with holes cut in the jacket for torpedo brassiere, novels by most of Morton Janklow's clients (Judith Krantz, Barbara Taylor Bradford, Danielle Steel, Sidney Sheldon, Jackie Collins), Prince, Andy Capp, plastic fruit, the garbage pail kids, Roseanne Barr singing the national anthem while scratching her crotch in baseball player's style, graffiti on everything, Andre Agassi in Day-Glo spandex, heavy-metal music, the *Dating Game*, Sam Kinison, the omnipresent raised middle finger, Conan the Barbarian, cubic zirconium, Jimmy Swaggart, Teenage Mutant Ninja Turtles, rap videos, Mick Jagger, single entendres, Eddie Murphy's "concert film" *Raw*, *Married . . . with Children*, New Kids on the Block, *America's Funniest Home Videos*, Freddy Krueger, soap operas, *Rambo*, 2 Live Crew, *Entertainment Tonight*, Uncle Buck. . .

Although I am going to concentrate on the production, transmission, consumption, and criticism of images, I would be remiss not to mention the dominance of music in the trashing of taste in America. In fact, in the spirit of the vulgar, I have shamelessly lifted the subtitle of chapter 1 from a book on popular music, Robert Pattison's *The Triumph of Vulgarity: Rock Music in the Mirror of Romanticism*. This book, along with works by Andrew Ross, Lester Bangs, Simon Frith, Jim Collins, George Lipsitz, Jon Pareles, Ann Kaplan, Greil Marcus,

Mr. T and Nancy
Reagan, Associated
Press (Wide World).

Arnold Shaw, Dave Marsh, Steve Chapple, Fredric Dannen, Reebee
Garofalo, Paul Hirsch, and Marc Eliot (to name only a few), studies
popular music as it electrifies, synthesizes — and especially ampli-
fies — lowbrow concerns. Because popular music hovers on the bor-
derline of acceptable taste, the study of it offers invaluable insights
into the ingredients of toxic pop culture. Heavy metal and especially
rap music do indeed prove, as Amanda offered in Nöel Coward's
Private Lives, "Extraordinary how potent cheap music is." This po-
tency is never more impressive than when a "boomcar," driven by a
teenage male and outfitted with huge speakers, pulls up next to you at
a stoplight and literally sets *your* entire world vibrating. And certainly
there is no better epitome of the vulgar than the band Milli Vanilli,
which lip-synched not just their "concert" performances of the
Grammy-winning "Girl You Know It's True," but the recording ses-
sion as well. However, I am going to ignore pop music until the

Model 2600, 1962. "As an option you can have a single button that actuates the top ten tunes for a 50 cent coin" (The Wurlitzer Co.).

conclusion for a rather embarrassing reason — I cannot listen to most of it. Lord knows, I have tried. I have two teenage children. Instead, in *Carnival Culture* I am going to focus on what can be shown — shown in ink, shown on celluloid, and shown in pixels.

But I must mention two aspects of the music business now because we will see how they are repeated in the production of images. First, a machine is at the center of the entertainment. From the 1920s to the 1950s, the jukebox did what all popular-culture media must do to succeed: it continually registered desire in terms of economic choice. You put your money into this bizarre-looking creature with its blinking lights and eerie record-changing mechanism bathed in fluorescence, and you heard your song. Sinatra? Jo Stafford? The Beach Boys or the Ink Spots? Elvis? Johnny Mathis? The Platters or the Supremes? It was your nickel, then your dime, then your quarter. You chose. The jukebox made one person's taste a group experience. CNN recently has applied the jukebox formula to the news. It broadcasts *Newsnight* from 12:00 midnight to 1:00 A.M., stopping on the half hour so that viewers may call a 900 number to request that certain stories be repeated. The only difference between the jukebox and "user-friendly news" is that the majority rules. The majority currently likes stories from Hollywood. Second, a song does not get into the machine — be it the jukebox, MTV, the record store, the FM dial, the cassette, LP, CD, or the movie soundtrack — by magic. A multibillion dollar industry is dedicated to making money from that choice. As with books, movies, and television shows, the most money in the music industry is to be made by producing a "hit," now called "going platinum." Gold is already passé. Those industries seeking platinum are conglomerated behemoths merchandising sounds all over the world. We will see them again, the usual suspects. Six large corporations account for more than 90 percent of the sales of recorded music. They are Time Warner's Warner Records, Matsushita's MCA Records, Sony's CBS Records, Bertelsmann AG's BMG unit, N. V. Phillips' PolyGram, and Thorn EMI's Capitol-EMI Records. Although pop music has engaged the wrath of everyone from Theodor Adorno and Marxist grumps to "Tipper" Gore and the Parents' Music Resource Center, pop music is so potent, and the profits so lush, that this *reductio ad obscenitatem* of adolescent concerns promises to grow still more important in the Carnival.

Let the Germans and Japanese produce objects; we in the United States will produce shows. "Entertainment products" are now our number-two export item, right behind military hardware. In fact, when these entertainments succeed, they are as powerful as military ordnance. The term to describe them comes out of World War II. They are "blockbusters," explosions able to knock down every standing thing. They capture not physical territory but audience attention. In the battle for consciousness, American popular culture may carry the day and the world. This culture has built an empire with motion pictures and television (and music), an empire in many ways like that of ancient Rome with legions sent out into the hinterlands. These modern legions descend from orbiting transponders and turn any iron curtain into chicken wire. American popular culture, for better or for worse, for richer and not for poorer, is already world culture. On the Day Glo yellow cover of the 1989 annual report of Time Warner is a single word in massive block letters: WHY? On the flyleaf, superimposed over an image of the world is the answer: GLOBALIZATION.

Time magazine, the vade mecum of middle America and now a minor subsidiary of a global conglomerate (along with HBO, Atlantic Records, Bugs Bunny, *Entertainment Weekly, People*, Warner Bros. Productions, *Mad Magazine, D.C. Comics*, Warner Books, two of the largest cable companies, and the Book-of-the-Month Club), knows from experience whereof it speaks:

> Pop culture is, after all, the culture of the free market: Heather Locklear and Prince and Chuck Norris are all laissez-faire by-products. Only in a wildly unregulated society could such beings have a ready means of becoming rich and famous. As a practical matter, too, only capitalists have both the necessary cash and the unembarrassed eagerness to please. It is expensive to produce convincingly slick records or movies. More than any other commodity, pop depends on blockbusterism. People listen to Michael Jackson's music in part because he has sold 69 million albums. Boffo begets boffo. Sustaining such a modulated mob psychology for profit requires an elaborate system of distribution and promotion, the pop equivalent of military command-and-control, and here the U.S. is absolutely without peer. (Anderson 1986:69)

In 1990, Time Warner reached agreement with Sovexporfilm to build multiplex theaters in Moscow and Leningrad. Pizza Huts and the golden arches are already in Moscow. The first American television program to be broadcast daily in the Soviet Union? *Geraldo*. First complete series? *Love Boat*. Rock and roll is played throughout the world, everyone wears Levi's, Americanisms like "OK" and "no problem" are part of the international Esperanto, as are "leveraged buyout" and "merchandising." Coca-Cola signs are all over Morocco. When the Berlin wall was torn down in December of 1989, representatives of Harlequin Romances were at Potsdamerplatz, Invalidenstrasse passing out 720,000 copies of their slender paperbacks. Michael Jackson makes more money touring in Japan than in the U.S. Nikes are worn by cannibals. As I write this, the most popular series on British television are American imports: *L.A. Law, thirtysomething, Cheers*, and *Roseanne*. On BBC-2, *Golden Girls, Lost in Space*, the *Waltons, St. Elsewhere*, and *Oprah Winfrey* are in the top 20 shows. To be candid, this is not a one-way street. In 1989, Japan-based Nintendo Video Entertainment grossed $2.3 billion. One toy amounted to more than one-quarter of the entire American book trade.

Although *Time* may be positively gleeful with the prospect of worldwide commodification of culture, others are not. To many people the notion that American popular culture is becoming the lingua franca of the world is the Orwellian nightmare come true. What has happened to Matthew Arnold's "best which has been thought and said," F. R. Leavis's "great tradition," T. S. Eliot's "ideal order," and all the other dreams of an enduring Eurocentric culture beloved by the intelligentsia? Is there a Gresham's law in cultural as well as in monetary circulation: bad stuff drives out the good? Or perhaps some application of the second law of thermodynamics could explain the modern entropy of taste. How long can a culture live on Ritz crackers spread with Velveeta and topped with Bacos? Must images always trump words? Must Bart Simpson always elbow aside Allan Bloom? The California Raisins and the Ninja Turtles *uber alles*?

It would be nice to think that we could open up the canon — in the sense of what Dante sought to do in writing an epic poem in the vernacular, or what Wordsworth attempted by using everyday language — and let just a little bit of this vulgar culture in. But this has not happened. Commodified culture is rather like zombies shuffling at the door. It is difficult to let a few of them in for a short stay. Once inside, they like to stick around. When a Coke advertisement featuring Mean Joe Greene is such a success that it becomes a network Movie of the Week, one knows that something has gotten stuck inside. When "Did you read?" becomes "Did you see?" or "Have you heard?," the markers of a shift in dominant taste are in place. The mere fact that in 1990 the department of painting and sculpture at the Museum of Modern Art, the sanctum sanctorum of high modernism, voluntarily assembled an exhibition like "High and Low: Modern Art and Popular Culture" means that even the avant-garde is losing its edge. The "great divide," as Andreas Huyssen calls it, has been crossed. John Silber, Lynne Cheney, William Bennett, and even Jesse Helms may still know which works automatically deserve to be studied, and known, and revered, but those in the trenches, who hear and see the blockbusters exploding around them, are not so sure.

The traffic flow from art to popular culture has already reversed, and postmodernism (whatever that may finally prove to be) promises still more of the autocanonization of the vulgar. The *Tyndall Report*, a newsletter that monitors the evening newscasts, reports that the three nightly network news shows spent an average of 68 minutes a month on showbiz stories in 1990, up from 38 minutes a month for both 1988 and 1989. More than 25 percent of ABC's "Person of the Week" choices are from the entertainment world. On the day the U.S. and the Soviet Union signed a pact to reduce the number of nuclear weapons (May 16, 1990), the lead story on ABC and NBC was the death of Jim Henson. Showbiz even has its mythology carried in the fastest-growing sector of the entertainment industry: information and gossip about showbiz. Called "entfotainment," this grist is the result of the surge of new delivery systems of entertainment in the 1980s: home video, cable, compact disks, and an audience eager to know not merely "what's on" but "what's in." We have television shows about television shows (*Entertainment Tonight*); television shows about movies (*Siskel & Ebert, Sneak Previews, Showbiz Today*); low-priced videocassette "magazines" sold at supermarket check out stands (*Persona*), and even an entire cable network broadcasting puffery (*E!*). Throwaway print magazines about show business (*Premiere, Movieline,* and *Entertainment Weekly*) are dedicated to "what's on *right now.*" *USA Today*, "McPaper," not only has an entire section dedicated to entfotainment but is itself an entire entfotainment approach to the "news." *Time* and *Newsweek* have vastly expanded their show business coverage as have national newspapers. When *US* magazine clamors for advertisers in *Advertising Age* (January 7, 1991), it trumpets this simple fact in boldface: "Entertainment covers on *Time* outsell all others." Even the formats and subject matter of the *New York Times* and the *Wall Street Journal* have been influenced by the tabloid style of electronic entertainment. When the *Times* runs a front-page story about Kitty Kelley's unauthorized biography of Nancy Reagan and treats its old muck as breaking news, one knows that the supermarket "tabs" have shown that muck still sells newsprint. The irreverent monthly *Spy* demonstrates such an overweening dedication to cataloging what used to be called the vulgar that it runs a pseudonymous column titled simply, "The Industry." As Elliot Mintz (a Hollywood "media consultant" for entertainers such as Melanie Griffith, Don Johnson, Diana Ross, Bob Dylan, and Yoko Ono) comments, the "enfo proliferation is almost carnivalesque" (Gold 1990:7). Why "almost"?

Historically, there have been three ways to deal with carnival culture once you isolate it: (1) You can pretend that it really doesn't need to exist, so when you find it you can excise it (as did Mrs. Grundy or Thomas Bowdler). (2) You can hope the dominant culture will pass it by once you have isolated and named it for them (as Dwight Macdonald, Clement Greenberg, and most critics of the twentieth century have done in the manner of the high Victorians, such as Ruskin and Arnold). Or (3) you can acknowledge that not only does it exist but that it is worthy of attention simply because it is so popular. You can argue that the vulgar is powerful because it takes very simple ideas very seriously, earnestly and energetically; that its predictability is strength; that derivation and repetition are signs of success; that it is authentically democratic and classless, and that it is infinitely tolerant, viciously cheap, and ultimately adaptive. It doesn't go away because our need for it remains intense, especially in adolescence. The vulgar is not "the best that has been thought and said" because it is too important to be thought and said. It comes to us in formulas and force fields because this is the stuff to be remembered. In short, the vernacular contains the enabling language of a culture.

Clearly, I am in this third camp. However, I have no interest in "recovering" the vulgar in the sense of recovering slave narratives or women's diaries. I have come not to celebrate popular culture (well, okay, a little) as much as to answer some of the questions about it. A few of them might be: Was there ever a time in the modern world when intellectuals would have said that vulgarity is not encroaching? What is the relationship between machine-made entertainments and aesthetic values? Why do certain stories get told, and why do certain stories get told too much? What is the role of class and leisure in making judgments of taste? Why do highbrows suddenly lose interest in certain stories and start calling them *trash*? Why do certain vulgar stories drive art stories out? Why do certain images travel between mass culture and elite culture, stuck in first one, then in the other? Why are the most powerful industries in our culture those that transport vulgar stories? Why, even though there are over 30 stations on my cable-equipped television set, are there so few different shows ("umpteen channels and nothing to watch")? Why do I have so much trouble finding high-culture music on the FM dial when it is supposedly "demonstrably superior"? How can high-culture taste be so whimsical that one prestigious publishing house will give up a $300,000 advance rather than publish a book (Bret Easton Ellis' *American Psycho*) it finds "in bad taste," while another equally prestigious house will find the project deserving of immediate publication? Why are today's "A" movies really yesterday's "B" movies dressed up in $50 million budgets? What is the relationship between the rise of the professoriat and the myth of cultural decline? Is vulgarity the result of repression or of freedom? Does television carnivalize or exalt cultural norms? What is the process by which we exclude stories from the canon as well as from study, but not from transmission? Does vulgarity depend on a high-culture canon and vice versa? But, most of all, I am interested in how the organizations of production and transmission evolved into their current conglomerated forms and what this portends for the future. So, I am especially interested in what might be called the economics of the carnival, the business of show business.

one

Untended Gates: The Triumph of Vulgarity in an Age of Show Business

Is not every civilization bound
to decay as it begins to
penetrate the masses?
—Michael Rostovtzeff

Hey, hey, ho, ho, Western Civ
has got to go.
—Stanford students, 1988

When I was growing up in the 1950s I was acutely aware of a distinct aesthetic category: the vulgar. There were vulgar words (those spelled with *'s in the middle), vulgar amusements (the sideshow at the fair), vulgar humor ("dirty jokes"), vulgar noises (air escaping the body or being expressed as a "raspberry"), vulgar gestures (an Italianate grammar of finger positions), vulgar foods (chewing gum, Devil Dogs, and Cokes), vulgar clothing (angora for girls, pegged pants for boys), vulgar dancing (the twist, the frug), vulgar jewelry (chandelier earrings, diamond pinky rings for men), vulgar hairdos (beehives and ducktails). You name it — if I liked it, it was sure to be vulgar.

Now that I am a parent, I try to

pass on this taxonomy of taste to my kids. "That's so vulgar," I say, shaking a finger at whatever they are enjoying. "What's so vulgar about that?" they ask. "How come you decide what's vulgar?" I tell them that Madonna videos are vulgar, as are Stephen King novels, *Screw* magazine, Van Halen, John McEnroe, Las Vegas, the Trump Tower, dances like the Lambada, Mr. T., professional wrestling, Batman, Opal Gardner, "graphic novels," Velcro, Cher, costume jewelry, almost anything reported on in *People*, Joan Rivers, clothing with someone's name on it, Geraldo Rivera, anything that the adjective "loud" can be used in front of, Rupert Murdoch, Richard Simmons, Houston, Texas, Joan and Jackie Collins, Benny Hill, the late Billy Martin, *USA Today*, confrontainment television with Mort Downey, Jr., paintings on velvet, electrified musical instruments, monstrous bodybuilding, Barry Manilow concerts, Ed Koch's campaigns (when he was running for mayor of New York City), political advertising in general, the second edition of the *Random House Dictionary*, Brian Bosworth, Mick Jagger, Donald Trump, any Aaron Spelling production, men's suits that shine, the Philip Morris Company trucking around the Bill of Rights, Countess Mara ties, Rodeo Drive boutiques, almost all Top 40 music and rap music, diamond jewelry for men, any movie with a sequel, music by Michel Legrand, Forest Lawn, paintings by Leroy Neiman, full-length leather coats, George Steinbrenner, Larry Flynt, Jerry Falwell, Hawaiian shirts, Tammy Bakker, Disneyland and World, Chuck Barris, anything on prime-time television with a market share of more than 10, any large building by John Portman, belt buckles that look like silver dollars, roller derbies, anything that shines. . . "Everything fun is vulgar to you, Dad," they say, as I continue listing away.

They are right, I guess. Is this because I am forty-eight years old and the vulgar is a category of intergenerational reproach, or is it because, whatever vulgarity is, there is certainly a lot more of it around? After all, weren't Elvis, Lenny Bruce, Annette Funicello, Ilie Nastase, the 1956 Cadillac, beefcake centaurs with blushing nymph girlfriends prancing to Beethoven's "Pastorale" in Walt Disney's *Fantasia*, Seagram's 7 and 7-Up, Jell-O, Nehru jackets, red tulips, Formica, the Three Stooges, Wonder Bread, Dean Martin, miniskirts, LBJ showing off his abdominal scar, wide-eyed Keane children, Liberace, diet drinks, Corfam, Jayne Mansfield, and Milton Berle also from Upper Vulgaria? And before them John Martin, Richard Wagner, Charles Dickens, Frederic Church, Honoré de Balzac, Frans

Hals, Tchaikovsky, Eugene Sue, Franz Liszt, anything published by Arthur Harmsworth . . . ? Riding a bicycle at Oxford in the 1890s, Max Beerbohm reports, "was the earmark of vulgarity." A century earlier Lord Chesterfield had warned, "Never walk fast in the streets, which is a mark of vulgarity . . . though it may be tolerable in a tradesman." Who now is able to make a taste judgment about the speed of transport? Who cares about recognizing the fish knife at dinner? Who still covers the piano legs? True enough: tastes change. Manet's *Déjeuner sur l'herbe*, now one of the Louvre's treasures, was considered indecent when first exhibited in 1863. Aristophanes' *Assembly of Women* was judged to be so disgusting that the English translator of the play preferred to remain anonymous. In the 1740s George Washington wrote his "Rules of Civility and Decent Behavior in Company and Conversation" to remind himself to emulate the "language of persons of quality" like Addison, Hume, Locke, and Johnson and to eschew the language of "the vulgar." In the 1984 presidential campaign George Bush commented after a debate with Geraldine Ferraro, "We tried to kick a little ass last night."

In these pages I am going to argue a difference in degree and kind. We live in an age distinct from all other ages that have been called "vulgar" because we are so vulgarized that we have even lost the word in common use, and, in a sense, the aesthetic category. It is not that we think it bad manners to criticize someone else's taste, as much as it is that we have lost the concept of taste as a measure of criticism. While the vulgar is usually pleasurable to those experiencing it, the greatest pleasure intellectuals used to have was to call someone else's behavior or taste "vulgar." No more. When an interviewer for *Playboy* commented to Mel Brooks, "You've been accused of vulgarity," Brooks retorted, "Bullshit!" Instead we say that certain words, clothing, or actions are "inappropriate," preferring a vague psychological category to an aesthetic one. Or we apply standards of "political correctness" as if they were aesthetic criteria. They often are, to be sure, but not to the exclusion of other concerns. In public discourse, we have adopted the quasi-legal term "obscenity" to disguise taste. When the National Endowment for the Arts is hectored for spending public monies on private follies, few critics are willing to invoke standards of taste. The only standard seems to be what a local jury can agree on in a court of law. This standard, which came down from the Supreme Court in *Miller v. California* in 1973, reveals much about our unwillingness to assert taste as a judgment. What is "obscene," and hence unacceptably vulgar, under the *Miller* test is any work that meets each of three different criteria: the "average person" must find it appeals to "prurient interests"; it "depicts or describes in a patently offensive way sexual conduct"; and, taken as a whole, it "lacks serious literary, artistic, political or scientific value." What is modern about these criteria is that the judging body is composed of "average" people — exactly those people who, according to high-culture standards, should not be making taste judgments. The high-culture standard would be that of the late Justice Potter Stewart, who said he couldn't define hard-core pornography but knew it when he saw it.

In fact, if you search electronic databases like Nexis for the most recent uses of "vulgar" in the popular press, you will find that, if used at all in print, it is used by food critics to describe certain foods such as garlic, black beans, kidney beans, and navy beans; in the fashion industry to criticize designers like Mary Quant; in political tracts and in literary criticism to denigrate a particular kind of literal Marxism (called "vulgar Marxism"); in agronomy to classify certain kinds of wheat; and in geology to mark certain quartz intrusions called "vulgs." The one place it is not commonly used (with the rare exception of critics like John Simon, Miss Manners, Jonathan Yardley, William Buckley, and Allan Bloom) is where it used to belong: in cultural criticism. This is not to imply that we blithely accept what is broadcast our way. Certainly Andrea Dworkin and Catherine McKinnon have railed against pornography, Tipper Gore and Thomas Radecki have lobbied against depiction of gratuitous violence, and the attorneys general of most states have a docket full of pending cases against various rap groups. But since the 1960s, the argument of good taste as a basis of evaluation is rarely invoked.

Strangely enough, the most realistic media are the only ones left that can convey sufficient violation of taste to warrant the trespass of the vulgar. We don't expect good taste in movies down at the Cineplex 16; we have been assured that cable television is beyond questions of aesthetic value; and popular music since the 45-rpm disk has conveyed reproductive rather than artistic rhythms. But the photograph, the basis of much modern show business, is still a generator of anxiety. In 1971, at a retrospective of Diane Arbus in the Museum of Modern Art, the custodial staff ended each day wiping spittle from the glass covering her images. And in 1989 the Corcoran Gallery of Art in Washington raised a hornets' nest of concern by canceling a show that included photographs of homoerotic images by Robert Mapplethorpe, most notably one of a standing black man urinating into the open mouth of a recumbent white and another of a bullwhip inserted in the artist's anus. At the same time, the sacrilegious images of Andres Seranno, especially one called "Piss Christ," showing a submerged crucifix in a beaker of the artist's urine, were being shown in photographic exhibitions. These outrages in the name of art were front-page news in large part because both photographers had been subsidized by government monies. Senator Jesse Helms, prissy worrywart and general obstructionist to the public funding of private art, had the gumption to call the works of both artists "vulgar." But when he brought forward legislation to constrain the National Endowment for the Arts from funding such displays of tastelessness, his emphasis was not on bad taste but on offending minority rights. Had his amendment passed, it would have restricted federal grants for works that "denigrate, debase, or revile a person, group or class of citizens on the basis of race, creed, sex, handicap, age or national origin." A hundred years earlier, when Edouard Manet painted his naked Olympia staring straight out to the audience with no hint of embarrassment, his audience blanched. For shame. This was disgusting, in bad taste. The Corcoran's response to the Mapplethorpe hubbub? The director was asked to resign and the trustees apologized. Admittedly, the Mapplethorpe show was removed for political reasons (what if Senator Helms and his colleagues had just happened by the gallery? a possibility analogous to a visit from Martians), but it was also, alas, in bad taste.

We live in a culture that still reacts to bad taste but refuses to admit it as such. If we want to remove Richard Serra's *Tilted Arc*, a twelve-foot-high steel fin almost a block long, from in front of the Federal Building in Foley Square, we have to say it is a traffic hazard. Until quite recently, we thrived on condemning bad taste. Now, we don't just say *"Chacun son goût"* and *"De gustibus non est disputandum,"* we believe it. "Isn't that creative? — from a political point of view of course," we are supposed to say as Karen Finley spreads herself with chocolate while reciting lines that would cause the Playboy bunny to blush. "This must be performance art. Thank goodness, it's art." Yet, from the eighteenth century to the 1960s, cultural education sought to undermine exactly this anarchy. Taste was an aristocratic privilege parceled out to the socially acceptable and aesthetically docile in dollops of art. Taste *had* to be exercised to become "taste," and certain groups *had* to be excluded. Then about 1960 the situation changed abruptly. Tom Wolfe understood what was happening. He called the interaction between the bourgeoisie and the artiste the "Boho dance." The artiste frantically shuffles to stay just at the edge of his audience while the audience cha-chas frantically to keep up. The key is never to embrace. "Art," said dancemaster Andy Warhol in the platinum wig, "I don't believe I've met the man."

We don't need Marxists to tell us that much of what constituted taste was based on the separation of classes in a society. Jean Lorrain, with no political ax to grind, understood the dynamics of taste when he answered the rhetorical question, "What is a vice?" with "It is a taste not shared." Of course, aesthetic evaluation is partially social oppression, a refusal to share. When Voltaire wrote in his *Philosophical Dictionary*, "The connoisseur in music, in painting, in architecture, in poetry, in medals, etc., experiences sensations which the vulgar don't suspect. The man of taste has different eyes, different ears, and a different touch than the coarse man has," or when Montesquieu commented in his *Essay on Taste* that "those who tastefully judge works of talent have become used to an infinity of sensations that other men do not have," they were sharing a hauteur that covers a festering sense of class separation. The "philosophes" of the eighteenth century who were so keen on reviving what they took to be classical systems of value were able to distinguish two natures. To them, there was *la belle nature* and there was "vulgar nature." When Addison notes in the *Spectator* that "there is not a Common-Saying which has a better turn of sense in it, than what we often hear in the Mouths of the Vulgar, that Custom is a second Nature," he is asserting a doctrine of taste, yes, but he is also accepting a social striation. We now have in their place the decidedly nonplatonic Rosanne Rosannadanna (Gilda Radner), the nose-wiping arbiter of the contemporary scene, and her colleague Leonard Plinth Garnell (Dan Aykroyd), host of "Truly Bad Art" on *Saturday Night Live*. Ms. Rosannadanna and Mr. Garnell are sendups of the connoisseur of taste because connoisseurship can no longer be taken seriously. A century ago Mr. Punch was laughed at, but he was also taken seriously. We no longer believe in the categories of taste. Diderot, it was said, "shuddered at any theory that would justify a peasant's taste as well as his own." We don't shudder at all. In the modern world of showbiz, we believe it. In the art world of postmodernism we canonize it.

"Only when need is satisfied can we decide who among the many does or does not have taste," wrote Immanuel Kant in *Critique of Judgement*. It would be nice to think that our tastelessness has come from our classlessness, and classlessness from the satisfaction of need. But another alternative exists. If the etiology of taste depends on the myth of an aristocracy keeping the vulgar at bay — in effect, distancing the common herd with the wedge of art and making them think they need high culture to be fulfilled — then it may be that the vulgar has disappeared because it has triumphed. In the elite-vs.-popular-taste conflict of the last two centuries, the highbrow has not so much given up as he has been convinced that his domain is not worth the struggle. The control of show business has passed from dour sentinels to carnival ticket-takers with hardly a murmur of discontent. After all, bread and circuses are more fun than wine and the theater.[1]

More for the sake of example than of argument, I present here a taxonomy of taste — a sample of the taste spectrum of middlebrow America from the vantage point of academia. In order to set this taxonomy in our time and on more or less familiar ground, I have settled the center of popular taste inside the Trump family. Although we may have to wait until her three ghostwritten novels are published to be certain, it does seem that Ivana is more highbrow than The Donald. Meanwhile, at the top of the table, matters are self-explanatory (biased, naturally, by my own personal values some of which are clearly murky) but I think generally representative of academic culture. Essentially, modernism mixed with a good measure of classicism, still dominates my cultural outlook. Occasionally, there are rogue entries such as Andy Warhol and "punk" which, I think, prefigure the transformation within modernism toward acknowledging the power of the vulgar. Also in the table, at the boundary where high culture meets popular culture, I denote the presence of the

1. The establishment of cultural hierarchies is still one of the enduring legacies of the nineteenth century. The pseudoscience of phrenology with its racial stereotypes claimed even to be able to locate and ascertain levels of taste by forehead size. Thus, "highbrow" was first used in the 1880s to describe intellectual or aesthetic superiority, while "lowbrow," first used after 1900, meant someone not highly intellectual or aesthetically refined. Presumably, since this kind of cataloging is usually a concern of popular culture, "middlebrow" was not too high, not too low — just right. Creating taste structures is a central articulation of class striations although, as Paul Fussell contends in his insightful *Class: A Guide Through the American Status System*, it can never be admitted as such. "What's hot, what's not" and "Who's in, who's out" delimit not just the insecure parameters of adolescence, but also the process of induction into what is sometimes called "maturity" — though it is more appropriately as an aspect of "one's class."

Value Terms

HIGH
CULTURE

"beaux arts," elite, highbrow,
good taste, "fine arts," unique,
critic-demanded, inventional, self-
conscious, adult, transcendent,
literature, "classical," minimalist,
silent, nonreproducible

presence of
gatekeeper
and
creation of
canon

POPULAR
CULTURE

LOW
CULTURE

vulgar, junk, "mere," "only,"
"just," lowbrow, bad taste,
audience-demanded, orality,
juvenile, escapism, carnival,
blockbuster, excessive, formula,
repetition, mass-produced, loud,
freakish, sensational

People/Ideas/Specific Works, in Descending Order

Abstract expressionism, Kant's sublime, quantum mechanics, JeanLuc Godard, James Joyce, deconstruction, Wallace Stevens, modernism, "Le Sacré du Printemps," Blake's Prophetic Books, some French philosopher you've never heard of, Ingmar Bergman, Henry Moore's "Family Group," Martha Graham, Grecian urns, Rheims Cathedral, Ezra Pound, "new wave," stream of consciousness, New Music, *film noir*, cubism, Ruins of ancient Rome, Manet, Elgin Marbles, *The Divine Comedy, The Sound and the Fury*, Ruskin, Harold Acton, Mozart, Arnold Schönberg, Dada, Igor Stravinsky, Emily Dickinson, Edith Wharton, Lacan, Henry James, *New York Review of Books, King Lear*, impressionism, the waltz, Gustav Mahler, Shelley, *New York Times* before the 1970s, postmodernism, the uncertainty principle, French philosophers you have heard of, *Heart of Darkness*, Matthew Arnold, Verdi, biography, *New York Times* since the 1970s, jazz, Sigmund Freud, "The Nutcracker Suite," "camp," Andy Warhol, George Bernard Shaw, *Catch 22*, romanticism, "punk," green-bottle beer, Madonna (for a few), Maria Callas, Fred Astaire, Hemingway, Laurence Olivier, Cole Porter, *Frankenstein*, gourmet cooking, the martini, PBS,
Ivana Trump

Donald Trump,
musical comedy, Mickey Mouse, *Cosby Show*, rum, Phil Donahue, *I Love Lucy*, ESPN, Countess Mara ties, the Oscars, soap operas, *People's Court*, The Super Bowl, "kitsch," disco, Stephen King, Jerry Falwell, Marilyn Monroe, Elvis Presley, the Coke bottle, spaghetti westerns, HBO, "I Want to Hold Your Hand," designer jeans, New Age music, Alf, country music, Geraldo Rivera, MTV, "schlock," Dr. Joyce Brothers, *National Enquirer*, Tarzan, Dracula, books of "gross jokes," Disney World, *USA Today*, Aaron Spelling productions, "The Sound of Music," Wonder bread, Muzak, Madonna (for the rest), McDonald's arches, Tammy Bakker, Sylvester Stallone, the Coke can, *Dallas*, Richard Simmons, the happy face, Joan Rivers, Punch and Judy, 2 Live Crew, Kung Fu movies, Las Vegas, roller derby, Chuck Barris productions, Thunderbird wine, Mort Downey, Jr., Mr. T., splatter movies, Jacqueline Susann, slam dancing, professional wrestling, truck/tractor pulls

gatekeepers.[2] By this I mean to indicate that here some external arbiter is usually necessary to explain to the uninitiated the importance of the loftier levels. A key to understanding high art is understanding that understanding requires a key. In high art this is achieved by the construction and establishment of a canon — that is, a collection of special works grouped together under some rubric such as "literature," "the repertory," "classical music," "Renaissance painting," "modern dance," and the like. In the left column are included some of the more common terms that have been used to describe or categorize these works.

Below Mr. Trump is outlined what I take to be descending levels of taste as perceived by my academic community. The lower one goes on the chart, the more vulgar, the more base the taste, the more adolescent (not necessarily younger) the audience. Most of my colleagues would, I think, judge slam dancing, Mort Downey, Jr., big-tired tractor pulls, professional wrestling, and most rap music to be about as low as this culture has yet fallen. At this level there is no gatekeeper class with keys, only CPAs with spreadsheets. What is consumed is what is demanded and what can be profitably broadcast and/or merchandised. Here, to update Santayana, the dictum is that unless you remember the past you can't possibly repeat it at the box office. Again in the left column is included another vocabulary of terms, one that describes this low culture from the point of view of the high culture.

Still farther to the left is another cultural diagram done in interlocking circles, again in stated and implied elevations. Above is the circle of art culture, below is the circle of vulgar culture, and joining them is popular culture — the infamous "norm." Above is Yeats's world of Byzantium, below is the world of "mackerel-crowded seas." Above is Wordsworth's "sense sublime," below the "world of getting and spending." Above is Arnold's "best that has been thought and said," below is barbarianism. Above is Pericles, below Arnold

2. Although Kurt Lewin first coined the term "gatekeeper" in the 1950s, it has now become a commonplace in sociology (see works by Lewis A. Coser, Charles Kadushin, Walter Powell, and Michael Lane). Essentially the term refers to the role played by editors, gallery owners, music critics, literature professors, and the like, who decide what will be printed, shown, played, and studied. A Cerberean membrane between the creator of an entertainment and the consumer, the gatekeeper decides what gets in and what is kept out. The gatekeeper controls the canon. He holds the keys. In the following chapters I will focus on the declining roles of the editor, studio mogul, and television producer as they have been replaced by the agent, studio producer, and programmer. The triumph of the vulgar reflects the fall of the gatekeeper and the rise of the accountant.

Paul Klee, *Vulgar Comedy*, 1922 (Museum of Modern Art: Gift of Victor S. Riesenfeld).

Schwarzenegger's Conan. You choose, we tell our students. Class dismissed.

Not to put too fine a point on it, the thesis of this book (and of most social commentators since the 1832 Reform Bill) is that the center of gravity — the "norm" — in Western culture and world culture is dropping. What marks our times is that the speed of descent has increased dramatically. Is this because the next generation is choosing unwisely because they have not been taught well, as many melancholy but best-selling authors now tell us, or is this descent also the inevitable and ineluctable result of the worldwide conglomeration of show business that has taken place since the 1960s? The transformation in what we call "the entertainment industry" promises still more profound, although not necessarily destructive, shifts in what is understood as the dominant culture. We are rapidly approaching the point where there will be no border between Lower Aesthetica and Upper Vulgaria. The gatekeepers can't find the gates. On the way to the Philharmonic in our Nikes we see nothing amiss in dining at the sushi bar, while listening to Pink Floyd in the back-

Left: Horace Vernet, *Carlo Alberto*, 1834. *Right:* Anthony Van Dyck, *Thomas de Savoie-Carignan on Horseback*, 1634. (Both from Galleria Sabauda, Turin.)

ground and drinking Bass ale. After all, greeting cards are becoming our epic poetry, MTV our heroic opera, and Walt Disney our Michelangelo.

While the term *vulgar* now has only heuristic value (and in the postmodern world it will be lucky to keep even that), it was accepted as a designate of specific and locatable taste in the nineteenth century. Consistency was all. One did not mix and match. Culture was not a salad bar. John Ruskin consigned works to this category with the wiggle of a finger. Here he is pontificating in "On Vulgarity" in *Modern Painters:*

> The so-called higher classes, being generally of purer race than the lower, have retained the true idea, and the convictions associated with it; but are afraid to speak it out, and equivocate about it in public. . . .

The lower orders, and all orders, have to learn that every vicious habit and chronic disease communicates itself by descent; and that by purity of birth the entire system of the human body and soul may be gradually elevated, or, by recklessness of birth, degraded; until there shall be as much difference between the well-bred and ill-bred human creature (whatever pains be taken with their education) as between a wolf-hound and the evilest mongrel cur. And the knowledge of this great fact ought to regulate the education of our youth, and the entire conduct of the nation. (1905:344–45)

Art, for Ruskin and for his colleague Matthew Arnold, is that which allows us to separate the wolf-hound from the mongrel cur. Our task is to be sure to breed to a higher evolutionary strain. We may well find this eugenic argument shocking enough after the events of our century, but on a less apocalyptic level "the best which has been thought and said" is a tidy demarcation line to separate who is in from who is out.

Now that we know the stakes, Ruskin presents a taste test in the manner of competing comestibles. On pages 24 and 25 are two paintings — one high culture, the other low; one elite, the other vulgar; hound and cur. Realizing the future of civilization depends on it, make up your own mind. For Ruskin the painting on the right has a "grand quietness" and "nobility." "The other is, on the contrary, as vulgar and base a picture as I have ever seen, and it becomes a matter of extreme interest to trace the cause of the difference" (1905:359). Indeed. And here is the difference: The gentleman on the right is shown in rusty armor that is not too shiny; the saddle cloth is only flecked with "sparkles of obscure gold." The knight seems to be preparing to leave his castle of which he is clearly the master. Note well, continues Ruskin, "the rich, light silken scarf, the flowing hair, the delicate, sharp, though sunburnt features, and the lace collar, [which] do not in the least diminish the manliness, but *add* feminineness. One sees that the knight is indeed a soldier, but not a soldier only; that he is accomplished in all ways, and tender in all thoughts." Not so his counterpart on the left. This man is vile. "In the first place, everything the general and his horse wear is evidently just made. It has not only been cleaned that morning, but has been sent home from the tailor's in a hurry last night." All his equipage looks "as if they had just been taken from a shopboard in Pall Mall." Worse yet, "we are shocked by the evident coarseness" of the horse's mane "which hangs indeed, in long locks over the bridle, but is stiff, crude, sharp, pointed, coarsely coloured." Notice also, says Ruskin, the context. The general is out reviewing the troops. How parvenu. "All which reviewing and bowing is in its very nature ignoble, wholly unfit to be painted: a gentleman might as well be painted leaving his card on somebody." The scene is so base that "one does not know whether most to despise the feebleness of the painter who must have recourse to such artifice, or his vulgarity in being satisfied with it" (1905:359–60).

Vulgarity has not always been pejorative. For instance, the Vulgate was the Latin version of the Bible for the Roman Catholic church and comes from "vulgata editio," simply meaning the edition in general circulation. Why then should the term *vulgar*, which meant "of the common" in the time of Horace, have been transformed in the eighteenth century to mean something coarse and lacking in refinement? In 1797, the *Monthly Magazine* notes the shift: "So the word 'vulgar' now implies something base and groveling in actions." After the turn of the century, William Hazlitt tempers this in his essay "On Vulgarity and Affectation": "A thing is not vulgar merely because it is common, but there is no surer mark of vulgarity than thinking it is." By the time Ruskin inherits the concept it implies the incipient rebarbarization of the species. The word has become a veritable club. And Ruskin is not alone. Herbert Spencer also feared the retrograde influence of a surging popular taste. After a while, even satirists had become serious in confronting the menace. "Death and vulgarity are the only two facts in the nineteenth century that one cannot explain away," says a despondent Lord Henry in Wilde's *Picture of Dorian Gray*. The usually jovial Mr. Punch comments in his 1876 Almanac, "It's worse than wicked, my dear, it's vulgar." So while an Augustan Lord Chesterfield had warned his son that "vulgarism in language is the distinguishing characteristic of bad company, and a bad education," or Alexander Pope had commented in *Thoughts on Various Subjects* that "to endeavor to work upon the vulgar with fine sense, is like attempting to hew blocks with a razor," the lightheartedness was short-lived. James Russell Lowell spoke for many Victorians: "Vulgarity is the eighth sin . . . and worse than all the others put together, since it perils your salvation in *this* world" (*On a Certain Condescension in Foreigners*).

The Victorians saw what the eighteenth century had missed. The mob had its own culture, and that culture was not only raw and vibrant, but was becoming too powerful to be contained. The very word "mob," a Victorian coinage, carried the threat within its etymology. "Mob" was a slang version of *mobile vulgus:* the rabble on the move. Cultures must be kept separate, and the aspiring middle class had the most at stake. The battle must be joined in earnest. Nowhere is this conflict more easily observed than on the untrammeled grounds of American cultural soil. Here the "vulgi" could really be mobile. Although Alexis de Tocqueville had predicted that the ultimate culture of a democratic system is a mass culture leveled to the demands of the jamboree, he had no idea that the driving force would be economic, rather than political. The same middle class that so valued the promise of high culture was the same class most rewarded by the industries of entertainment. American cultural history is the condensation of contrary Western forces focused with great intensity. The battle between highbrow and lowbrow, between High Church and Carnival, is nowhere more evident than in the literal conflicts waged for entertainment space in the nineteenth century. That battle is now all but over. The Carnival now controls the show; the High Church is the sideshow.

In *Highbrow/Lowbrow: The Emergence of Cultural Hierarchy in America*, Lawrence Levine, a MacArthur fellow at Berkeley, traces the transformation of three disparate entertainments: the dramatizing of Shakespeare, the production of opera, and the institutionalizing of collections into museums. These were not the only sites of competitive values in the nineteenth century, but they were representative of how competing audiences marked out the territory of taste. Let me briefly recapitulate Levine's separate histories, for we may see in them the construction of the cultural hierarchies we all recognize. Ironically, however, what the Victorians separated and ranked with such passion, the modern world is rapidly (and mindlessly) putting back together.

The history of "appreciating" Shakespeare is essentially one of audiences competing for the "text." In the early nineteenth century, Shakespeare's plays were performed as an integral part of popular entertainment. His works were so popular in nineteenth-century America that the participatory audience would yell for — and often get — instant encores within a favorite scene. As television viewers use the videocassette player to repeat favorite sequences, or as the remote-control wand allows them to watch different shows simultaneously, the theatrical audience moved easily from text to text. Mark Twain's Duke and Dauphin performances were remarkably accurate representations of what happened. Not everyone, as Twain pointed out, was pleased. Playbills assured that the audience would be controlled, but often to no avail. "The public in the final resort govern the stage," said one homegrown American critic in 1805 (Levine 1988:29).

He was soon to be proven wrong. The stage was becoming the property of a different audience, an audience that did not want to change channels, an audience that could pay to hear the "right" version, the "authentic" version. Just as "fine arts" separated from the general arts, so too did "legitimate theater" separate from popular entertainment. This transformation of Shakespeare occurred coincidentally with the rise of the university and the need to provide a pure text suitable for study. Let hoi polloi have their oral culture complete with audience interaction; this new print culture wanted integrity. So Shakespeare, who had been rewritten over and over by the Colley

Cibbers and the Nahum Tates, became standardized. By the end of the century, parts of the audience would attend the show with the complete printed text (available by 1895 from Montgomery Ward) and complain at moments of subversion. Critics like the noted A. C. Wheeler even argued that Shakespeare should not be performed at all because performance "materializes" the Bard and in so doing "vulgarizes him." When Edmund Kean was chided for performing a bogus version, he said he had tried "to do right," but "when I had ascertained that a large majority of the public — whom we live to please, and must please to be popular — liked Tate better than Shakespeare, I fell back upon his corruption; though in my soul I was ashamed of the prevailing taste, and of my professional condition that required me to minister unto it" (Levine 1988:73, 44).

Shakespeare did not disappear; he switched audiences. While the Bard was being expropriated by a nascent elite, the mass audience turned to other diversions such as vaudeville, boxing, burlesque, and especially the silent movies. The only vestige of his previous presence in America is the Central Park summertime productions of Joseph Papp, underwritten by large corporations eager to be associated with literary prestige. But the segmentation of audiences, which we now accept without question, was not achieved without some effort and pain. In the Astor Place Riot of 1849, the aristocrats down in front and the modern groundlings up in the cheaper seats finally had at each other. Each audience wanted its own version performed, and the militia had to be called to calm the ensuing melee. Although Henry James claimed that the Astor Place Riot represented "the instinctive hostility of barbarism to culture," it would be more accurate to say it represented the anger of an audience denied entertainment that it had assumed was part of its culture. Levine notes that, "The Astor Place Riot, which in essence was a struggle for power and cultural authority within theatrical space, was simultaneously an indication of, and a catalyst for, the cultural changes that came to characterize the United States at the end of the century" (1989:68). And, as we will see, this conflict has begun to be played out in reverse in the electronic theater as the mass audience marginalizes the elite.

As Shakespearean drama was being divided between the authentic and the corrupt, between Aesthetica and Vulgaria, so too was music being sectioned off into serious and popular. Like Shakespeare, the opera was simultaneously common and elite in the early 1800s. The libretto and score were not "sacred texts" but were performed by

Riot at the Astor Place Opera House, 1849 (*London Illustrated News,*
June 2, 1849).

artists who felt free to embellish and alter, add and subtract, according to various audience tastes. No one thought it amiss if "Yankee
Doodle," "Hail Columbia," and even occasional local parlor songs
were inserted into the overtures to Italian opera. And no one complained if sword fights were a little longer and more prominently
staged than in the original. Songs and dances were often transposed
with abandon into other operas. Rather like modern-day movie
scores in which Mozart, Wagner, and Pachelbel mingle with the
Temptations, the Mamas and the Papas, and Roy Orbison, opera
was more a free-for-all than a true-to-the-text experience.

As Levine claims, "It is hard to exaggerate the ubiquity of operatic
music in nineteenth-century America" (1988:97), but already the
shifting audiences were marking out their proprietary claims. Sight-
ing down the transit of taste, the new class of the cultivated attempted
to excise the dross, the common, the vulgar, and leave the pure and
intended art behind. The maestro, the connoisseur, the academician,
the classicist, and the antiquarian were now keeping the gate, deciding what should be on stage, how it should be performed, who should

be in the audience, and how that audience should behave. Soon the voices of those shoved aside could be heard. In May 1853, *Putnam's Magazine*, a weekly pulp, proposed that P. T. Barnum be named the manager of New York's opera because "He understands what our public wants, and how to ratify that want. He has no foreign antecedents. He is not bullied by the remembrance that they manage so in London, and so in Naples, and so in St. Petersburg. He comprehends that, with us, the opera need not necessarily be the luxury of the few, but the recreation of the many." Increasingly, however, opera was performed in isolation for those who could afford not only the increased price of admission but also the rituals of privilege. "Going to the opera" became a ceremony of display and hence an announcement of exclusion. To be sure, individual performers escaped then as now to perform for the public (viz., Caruso and Pavarotti), but they were the exceptions. By the beginning of the twentieth century, opera had become sacramentalized and privatized—literally a privileged site.

As a cleavage developed in the theater between legitimate and popular, as opera was dividing between grand and operetta, so too orchestral performances were being torn apart by competing audiences. At mid-century John Philip Sousa, then called a "bandmaster," could say of his programming: "I have no hesitation in combining in my programme tinkling comedy with symphonic tragedy or rhythmic march with classic tone-picture" (1928:275). Even Theodore Thomas and his upper-crust orchestra thought nothing of playing polkas, waltzes, and other light pieces as well as his "educative" ones as they toured music festivals. Such eclecticism was to be short-lived. Soon well-meaning readers of John Ruskin and Matthew Arnold were insisting that music play a composed score, not vulgar tunes. Wealthy men, who wished to "repay their debt" to the society they had often pillaged, endowed symphony orchestras. Without exception, the founding of these city-based symphony orchestras was based on a quid pro quo: "I'll give you this money," said the wealthy benefactor, "if you'll play this kind of music for me." The adjective "this" was becoming known as "classical," not because it was ever called that by composers, but because it was the term preferred by this particular audience. A hint of the shift: in the early 1800s the names of composers were often omitted from concert programs in order to feature some virtuoso performer. After the turn of the century the composer's name was emphasized. As we will see, the phonograph record has shifted this emphasis back to the performer, but we would still be unhappy to hear the PBS morning "Pro Musica" program (the title itself a vestige of exclusionary tastes) mix popular and "serious" genres. Charles Ives could do it, but just barely.

The establishment of the Boston Symphony in the 1880s is instructive, for it illustrates the dynamic that characterized the shifting function of popular entertainment as it became Art. In the 1840s, the Amateur Orchestra was taken under the wing of John Dwight, who had been to Europe, had heard the "old masters," and who felt it his calling to return to his native land and educate the untutored. He did so by publishing a journal of music in which he maintained not only the acceptable composers (Bach, Haydn, Beethoven, Schubert), but also the acceptable method of play (following the score, abhorring variations), and the proper audience response (reverential and quiet). With the aid of a wealthy stockbroker, Henry Lee Higginson, he announced in the Boston papers the formation of "a full and permanent orchestra, offering the best music at low prices such as may be found in all large European cities" (Levine 1988:122). The Amateur Orchestra was to become the Boston Symphony Orchestra, and it would consist of sixty musicians with a European-born conductor, now called "maestro." There were contracts and pensions for the musicians, education and improvement for the audience. No smoking, no drinking, no carousing, no inappropriate applause, no yelling suggestions, and even a prescribed hat height for women, as well as the number of encores that could be expected. If concertgoers wanted otherwise, let them listen to the Boston Pops, a summertime diversion for those who could not stand the demands of cold winter and good behavior. Higginson would countenance no alternatives. In one of his many speeches to the orchestra he explained that his role was "to pay the bills, to be satisfied with nothing short of perfection, and always to remember that we were seeking high art and not money: art came first, then the good of the public, and the money must be an after consideration" (Perry 1921:294). This same kind of evangelical search for a perpetual memorial on the part of men who made fortunes, often at the expense of the public good, was behind the endowments of the New York Philharmonic, the Chicago Symphony, the Pittsburgh Orchestra, and many others.

The process of sacralization, of canonization, of separation, of authentication was no temporary fashion but a profound shift in culture. The High Church was in the ascendancy; the Carnival ostracized. The struggle to establish aesthetic standards and then to pretend that these had been there all along, to separate true art from the merely vulgar that had just happened to corrupt it, to dole out serious art like medicine to the sick, was conducted in all seriousness because the stakes were thought to be so high. Did we want to become curs or purebreds? After all, in an age that took phrenology seriously, the highbrow/lowbrow dichotomy was no metaphor but a genuine cultural choice. Did we want to run the risk of de-evolution, rebarbarization? If we wanted to be pure and strong then we must excise the dross. Purification was not only for the individual soul, it was for the national spirit, and perhaps even for the species. One would not get into the City on the Hill by playing in the mud of this world, and we could not create the New Jerusalem by allowing the masses to determine the moral architecture. The "mobile vulgus" must be immobilized. We must memorialize the "best that has been thought," not the most popular, or the most entertaining, or even the most interesting. Needless to say, making these distinctions stick was the triumph of middle-class authority.

The edifices of middle-class authority are museums. What goes into them and what is kept out are acts of human choice. There is nothing in nature called art, but there is something central in modern Western culture called Art. Art depends on fine-line distinctions, and we can watch those distinctions being made with growing confidence and enthusiasm at the same time music is being made classical, writing is being made literature, and theater is being made legitimate. Masterpieces depend on minor-pieces. The construction of the canon of paragons depends on the construction of the anticanon of vulgarities. Rather like the fraternity system of clubs, inclusion is never enough. Some must be excluded.

Eighteenth-century museums were a literal hodgepodge of exhibits, paintings by old masters and local talent, stuffed animals, live animals, wax figures, mechanical devices, light shows, and whatever would gather a curious crowd. As Neil Harris has observed of the first museums, "Painting and sculpture stood alongside mummies, mastodon bones and stuffed animals. American museums were not, in the antebellum period, segregated temples of the fine arts, but repositories of information, collections of strange or doubtful data" (1973:78). We can actually see this culture inadvertently portrayed in Charles Willson Peale's peek at his Philadelphia museum in 1786. At his right side are display cases of stuffed birds each in a reconstructed habitat,

Charles Willson Peale, *The Artist in His Museum*, 1822 (The Philadelphia Academy of The Fine Arts: Gift of Mrs. Sarah Harrison).

but on his left are the tools of his art: brushes and pallet. All that separates them is the tasseled curtain which Peale holds up as if to beckon us inside. This curtain is not to separate the pictorial from the natural sciences. Note that above the bird boxes are paintings, portraits of the heroes of the American Revolution. And note too that in the foreground are several mastodon bones, a skeleton, and a stuffed turkey. The visitors in the background are in both a picture gallery and a natural history exhibit. Make up your mind, the curator of the modern museum would surely say to Peale, your museum needs some "de-accession." Museums need themes the way literature needs genres, the way an orchestra or an acting company needs a repertoire. Specialize. Exclude.

While the Amateur Orchestra was being transformed into the Boston Symphony Orchestra, the Boston Atheneum was being transformed into the Boston Museum of Fine Arts. The concept of "fine" art as opposed to "coarse" art, as well as the current academic favorite — the "liberal" arts — is yet another instance of a linguistic elevation (this one coming from the French distinction first used in 1767 of the "beaux arts") and reflects a middle-class audience yearning. Higher things depend on lower things. The "curiosities" were sent downstairs into storage with the lower things. The Atheneum's remarkable collection of casts of Greek sculpture was treated with a scorn we might today direct toward those firy-eyed tigers cast in velvet on the walls of the K-Mart. If it is not original, it is not art and these plaster "profanations," which vulgarized the originals, were not worth keeping, much less displaying. As the assistant director, Matthew Stewart Prichard, opined, "The first and great commandment is to establish and maintain in the community a high standard of aesthetic taste." These casts were reproductions, subversive, even dangerous. They were, in Prichard's words prefiguring Walter Benjamin, "data mechanically produced," no more aesthetic than motel art and Musak. They were, he continued, in a synecdoche worthy of that generation of curators and protectors, "the Pianola of the Arts" (Levine 1988:154).

Clearly, as Levine repeatedly shows with numerous apt examples, what was happening was a battle for control, for social territory, for what is now in the cant of modern criticism called "privileging." Who is going to make the decisions on what goes to the cellar: the curious onlooker, the educated patron, the new class of curators? Who is going to determine what is heard: the musician, the conductor, the audience, or the benefactor? Who is going to determine what is printed: the avid reader, the editor, the critic, the agent, or the publisher? The answer that evolves throughout the nineteenth century and remains in place until relatively recently is that in high-culture endeavors a gatekeeper is needed. From 1850 to 1950 you could have heard the same refrain again and again: Art is salvation. The Work of Art is sacred. The Artist is a god. The Critic is a priest. The culmination of this tradition was the modernist James Joyce, who made the analogy self-consciously transubstantiational. In his *Portrait of the*

Artist as a Young Man, Joyce says as much. Just as the priest consecrates the body and blood of our Savior in the wafer and wine, so the artist consecrates experience into art. To the reader, at least, the author is a once-removed Messiah. The penitential reader does not only enjoy art; he is saved by it. The cleric/critic/gatekeeper holds the wafer/text/key.

Henry James was our Matthew Arnold. Both James and Arnold would have blanched at Joyce's analogy, but both were subtly responsible for it. "I shall not go so far as to say of Mr. Arnold that he invented the concept of culture," James wrote in 1884, "but that he made it more definite than it has been before — he vivified and lighted it up." Thanks to his apostle James, and others of like mind, Arnold was more popular in the United States than in England. The Arnoldian desire to cultivate, to send the Philistines packing, and to welcome the apocalypse of "sweetness and light" is omnipresent in American middle-crust culture. The first step to salvation, however, is a clean room. So when W. J. Henderson, music critic of the *New York Times*, was asked by a reader how to improve standards of music, he replied in slightly exaggerated Arnoldian tones:

> First of all, abolish the music halls in which the vulgar tunes set to still more vulgar words provide the musical milk upon which the young of the masses are reared. Abolish the diabolical street pianos and hand organs which disseminate these vile tunes in all directions and which reduce the musical taste of the children in the residence streets to the level of that of the Australian bushman, who thinks noise and rhythm are music. Abolish the genuine American brand of burlesque . . . and the genuine American "comic opera." . . . Abolish the theater orchestra which plays the music hall stuff. . . Abolish those newspapers which degrade art by filling their columns with free advertising of so-called musical performers who are of the genus freak. (1898:4)

Little wonder that Toscanini was hailed by that same newspaper for "absolute fidelity to the score." Who would dare subvert the text when so much was at stake? Here is a man who does not "want my MTV."

Henderson was not alone. Nor is he still. But the tone has softened as the argument has grown progressively more difficult to make in a relativistic context. In fact, to a generation taught arithmetic by Count Count, the social sciences by Professor Indiana Jones, political science by Marx, and criticism by the Yale School, the high-art argument could not be made at all without risking ridicule. Yet two generations ago in the pre-show-business world one could trace an "appreciation," nay adulation, of the classics across the curriculum of American culture. "Higher education" comes into its own. Charles Eliot Norton at Harvard thought that Harvard and Yale were necessary as "barriers against the invasion of modern barbarians and vulgarity." Norton gave lectures (the series still exists, content much diluted) that were described as "fiery denunciations of vulgarity and corruption of modern society in Ruskin's best vein." While Norton was easy to parody—undergraduates would imitate his bellowing, "I propose this afternoon to make a few remarks on the hor-ri-ble vul-gar-ity of EVERYTHING"—he was equally hard to overlook (Graff 1987:83). In 1867, *Harper's* does not so much editorialize as trumpet the Nortonian prophecy that

> Certain things are not disputable: Homer, Shakespeare, Dante, Raphael, Michael Angelo, Handel, Beethoven, they are towering facts like the Alps or the Himalayas. They are the heaven-kissing peaks, and are universally acknowledged. It is not conceivable that the judgment of mankind upon those names will ever be reversed. (1867:261)

Admittedly, not all critics agreed even then. Walt Whitman fought the new cultural hierarchy, insisting in *Democratic Vistas* that culture should not be "restricted by conditions ineligible to the masses" and that "with this word Culture, or what it has come to represent, we find ourselves abruptly in close quarters with the enemy." But his "barbaric yawp" was to go pretty much unnoticed. You don't call Matthew Arnold "one of the great dudes of literature" and get away with it for long. Let the undergraduate curriculum committee at Stanford then as now pretend otherwise, those named by *Harper's* are the nonnegotiable, the demigods, the idols of the modern cave; they are, and were, and will be, the hierophants of unapprehended salvation. At least, until recently.

So what happened? Why did the Visigoths escape their exile in faraway Vulgaria and return not only to plague us, but to dominate? Who forgot to lock the gate? While it is demonstrably true that the highbrows captured "classical" music, the "legitimate" theater, the "fine arts" of museums, the "canon" of "serious" literature, to say nothing of etiquette, rare books, and horse racing, they lost the battle for separating tastes. Why is it that today, since, say, 1960, the dominant taste is not highbrow, or even middlebrow, but decidedly lowbrow? The battle for Astor Place is over, and those in the bleachers have won. The very part of the population that sought to improve taste now finds itself asking these questions: "Why is it that they don't make movies for us any more?" "Why is it that there is nothing on television for me?" "Why is there only one station on the radio that plays my music?" "Why is it that I don't recognize most of the best-selling books anymore?"

The answer is that popular culture proved not only far more powerful and resilient, but it proved far more important in doing exactly those things elite culture promised: it produced a comprehensive ideology by responding to audience desire. Mass-produced and mass-consumed American popular culture is rapidly encircling the globe because there is something in it that is transcultural, something even transcendental. In many respects popular culture resembles a secular religion promising release, not in the next world, but in this one. Wishes are fulfilled, not later, but NOW. Gratification is instant because for the first time it can be. There is so much to look at, so much to see. This is exactly the sense of the new Adam and Eve pictured in their show-business paradise by Richard Hamilton: "Just What Is It That Makes Today's Homes So Different, So Appealing?" Have a look-see.

And here in a verbal whirlwind is Tom Wolfe's intuitive realization that indeed something profound was happening to the dominant taste culture during the "purple decades" of midcentury. Although Wolfe doesn't quite realize it, he has his finger pointed to the future of carnival taste, toward postmodernism. He too knows that these modern times are "so different, so appealing."

> The old establishment still holds forth, it still has its clubs, cotillions and coming-out balls, it is still basically Protestant and it still rules two enormously powerful areas of New York, finance and corporate law. But alongside it, all the while, there has existed a large and ever more dazzling society, Cafe Society it was called in the twenties and thirties, made up of people whose status rests not on property and ancestry but on various brilliant ephemera, show business, advertising, public relations, the arts, journalism or simply new money of various sorts, people with a great deal of ambition who have congregated in New York to satisfy it and who look for styles to symbolize it.
>
> The establishment's own styles — well, for one thing they were too dull. And those understated clothes, dark woods, high ceiling, silversmithery, respectable nannies, and so forth and so on. For centuries their kind of power created styles — Palladian buildings, starched

Richard Hamilton, *Just What Is It That Makes Today's Homes So Different, So Appealing?*, 1956 (Kunsthalle Tübingen: Collection Prof. Dr. Georg Zundel).

cravats — but with the thickening democratic facade of American life, it has degenerated into various esoteric understatements, often cryptic — Topsiders instead of tennis sneakers, calling card with "Mr." preceding the name, the right fork.

Once it was power that created high style. But now high styles come from low places, from people who have no power, who slink away from it, in fact, who are marginal, who carve out worlds for themselves in the nether depths, in tainted "undergrounds." The Rolling Stones, like rock and roll itself and the Twist — they come out of the netherworld of modern teen-age life, out of what was for years the marginal outcast corner of the world of art, photography, populated by poor boys, pretenders. "Underground" movies — a mixture of camp and Artistic Alienation, with Jonas Mekas crying out like some foggy echo from Harold Stearn's last boat for Le Havre in 1921: "You filthy bourgeois pseudo-culturati! You say you love art — then why don't you give us money to buy the films to make our masterpieces and stop blubbering about the naked asses we show? — you mucky Pseuds." Teen-agers, bohos, camp culturati, photographers — they have won by default, because, after all, they DO create styles. And now the Other Society goes to them for styles, like the decadenti of another age going down to the wharves in Rio to find those raw-vital devils, damn their potent hides, those proles, doing the tango. Yes! Oh my God, those raw-vital proles. (1963:211–12)

If one were looking for a geographic analogy for this upsurging of raw vitality one could do no better than look at the self-proclaimed "Versailles of America," Las Vegas. To Lewis Mumford, squarely in the tradition of Brahmin taste, this is the ultimate "roadtown . . . an incoherent and purposeless urbanoid nonentity, which dribbles over the devastated landscape and destroys the coherent smaller centers of urban or village life that stands in its path" (1962:108). But to those like Robert Venturi, Las Vegas is urban sprawl, yes, but it is also the commercial strip in its purest and most intense form. "We term it sprawl," this onetime Yale professor of architecture contends in *Learning from Las Vegas*, "because it is a new pattern we have not yet understood" (1977:76). The city is a concrete and asphalt and, especially, neon reaction to all that zoning and controlled urban development implies. It is permissive, commercial, and irredeemably vulgar. The signifying image in Las Vegas is the signifier itself, the sign qua sign — more specifically, the big sign in front of the little building on the roadway. While these signs are an unnecessary blot to some observers, they form a medium through which we pass, a plasma, a text if you will, that can be read *only* at sixty miles per hour. The speedway is central: the median strip for turning right and left, the sidewalk and the boundaries of private and public space, a zone of the highway and a zone off the highway, continuity and discontinuity; going and stopping; cooperation and competition; the community and the individual. Las Vegas does not follow the prescriptive forms of a Eurocentric elite culture. There is no secret hierarchy of taste, but rather the competitive forces of democratic capitalism, each vying for "market share." Looking at Las Vegas is like watching television, going to the movies, or reading a bestseller: glitz, kitsch, pulp, and neon are all designed to capture attention, hold it, let it go, and then recapture it.

Yet, when you think of it, claims Venturi, this "messy vitality of forms" is rather like the agglomeration of chapels in a Roman church,

Las Vegas signs (photo: Dan Wilson).

or the sequential parts of a Gothic cathedral. After all, the Roman church and especially the Gothic cathedral can be seen as totally sign-covered too — billboards advertising for customers, steeples pointed skyward with the promise of salvation for patrons: showtime. As brilliant and glitzy as these Las Vegas signs are, the building interiors are low and dark and quiet. Like the church facades with gargoyles and reliefs, these signs are also often in mixed media — words, pictures, and sculpture. The Pioneer Club on Freemont even talks: a cowboy sixty feet tall says "Howdy Partner" every thirty seconds. Perhaps the casino also evolved to satisfy desire, and even the need for salvation, however inappropriate it may seem.

To consider popular culture as a variety of religion is more sacrilegious than most of us want to be. Although Venturi went on to win the Pritzker Prize (architecture's rough equivalent of the Nobel Prize), his arguments have hardly carried the day. More typical of our hand-wringing response is Neil Postman:

> Today, we must look to the city of Las Vegas, Nevada, as a metaphor of our national character and aspiration, its symbol a thirty-foot-high cardboard picture of a slot machine and a chorus girl. For Las Vegas is a city entirely devoted to the idea of entertainment, as such proclaims the spirit of a culture in which all public discourse increasingly takes the form of entertainment. Our politics, religion, news, athletics, education and commerce have been transformed into congenial adjuncts of show business, largely without protest or even much popular notice. The result is that we are a people on the verge of amusing ourselves to death. (1985:3)

Possibly true, but because this force is so powerful that it can erect a city of neon and glitz on a pile of sand and become a Mecca to millions of the faithful, we might reconsider not only what the force is, and was, but what it can become. What is it about show business that is so alluring that we, like the sailors in the *Aeneid*, will amuse ourselves to death? Where does the narcotic of a Las Vegas culture come from? And how does it get to us?

Before the 1960s, popular culture was usually contrasted with elite culture on the one hand, and folk culture on the other. These divisions were some of the most enduring legacies of Victorian taste. Folk culture is noncommercial, created by anonymous amateurs and circulated orally, if not materially. The "purpose," if such a concept can be used, is to improve a living situation whether it be a tool, an article of clothing, or a story. How to cook, how to hunt, how to attract members of the opposite sex, how to rear children — all are typical subjects of folk transmissions. The main audience of folk culture is unschooled in the ways of the elite or popular culture, and the only standard of success is whether or not the creation is adopted and circulated. The producers and consumers are generally unconscious of process, however. Popular culture is a result of the industrial revolution. Its products are formulaic, mass-produced, commercial, and the standard of acceptance is measured by the bottom line. Does it sell? Is it consumed? Its purpose is to entertain, not to enlighten. Elite culture, which had its roots in classical antiquity, was an eighteenth-century reaction to the rising bourgeoisie who could now read the same texts as the aristocracy. The elite-taste culture distinguished itself by subverting much that popular culture maintained. While popular culture was produced by industry, pretested for acceptability, and received by many people, elite culture was original, ironic, immediately useless, and consumed by a coterie. A work of art is serious, we assume, in fulfilling some serious authorial intention, and it is by such standards that we appraise the *Iliad*, Aristophanes' plays, the fugue, *Middlemarch*, the paintings of Rembrandt, Chartres, the poetry of Donne, the *Divine Comedy*, Beethoven's quartets, and so forth. The pantheon of high culture is built on attributed truth, beauty, and seriousness. And who determines this? The excellence of an elite production is determined by its reception by an appointed group, first of the clergy and then of scholars, whose professed purpose is to raise the consciousness of others. This class is nowhere to be found in folk or popular culture.

In another sense, these epistemologies can be seen as stages of maturation. Childhood is informed by folk culture, by a prelogical assimilation of "the way things are done." Entry into the adult stage is characterized by adolescence, by movement from an unarticulated family relationship into the larger world. This stage is naturally traumatic. Not only is one losing one's natal family, but now one has acquired the ability to reproduce, with its attendant anxieties as to how to create a new family. Here folklore yields to popular culture, the culture of the "others." Entire industries are supported by these anxieties and their hoped-for resolutions. Much of what show business shows is the popular-culture responses of adolescence. The major audience for much of the electronic media is between twelve and twenty-five years of age — the age of maturation. Since the 1950s, American entertainment has proved to be so vibrant that it is extending its domain not only across different national cultures, but deep into folk as well as elite cultures. In other words, the rituals of adolescence are becoming the central focus of modern attention.

Consider what is occurring as commercial culture encroaches on the domain of family myth. For generations, maxims, homilies, and parables have been offered by parents, especially by mothers, to their young. We all know them because they have the stamp of clichés: "Two wrongs don't make a right," "What goes around comes around," You can't do good work with poor tools," "Finish what you start," "An idle mind is the devil's playground," to name a few. Every family has its own grammar of these "momilies." By the 1980s these mother-delivered " 'cepts" were being delivered by commercial culture. "It's no use crying over spilt milk" has been rendered into Bobby McFerrin reggae as "Don't worry, be happy." While an older generation knew "A stitch in time saves nine," the current one knows the Nike shoe company's "Just do it." Clint Eastwood's "Make my day," Clara Peller's "Where's the Beef?," even *Laugh-In*'s now-ancient "Here come de judge," show an expropriation of family lore by commercial culture. True, such commercialism of folk wisdom is directed at capturing attention for reasons other than the conduction of lore, but transmission is the result. The traditional family is not just being displaced by the show-business surrogate, such as the Cosby family or Roseanne (or any of the hundreds of prime-time substitutes), but the *function* of the family to socialize youngsters into culture is being co-opted.

Equally interesting is what is happening at the other juncture, where popular culture meets art culture. Just as mass-produced scenarios are encroaching onto folklore, so too they are pushing over the edge of art. Although one could make a case that this intrusion starts with such nineteenth-century *trompe l'oeil* painters as John Haberle and William Harnett, who experimented with using vernacular objects as primary subject matter, it erupted in the mid-twentieth century as pop art. Its most famous personage, Andy Warhol, was the antithesis of the bohemian elite artist of the nineteenth century at odds with the society and its psyche. Here was an artist infatuated with the ephemera of American commercial culture and intent on capturing its fixation on repetition and glut. In his first shows in 1962 with those enormous paintings of the Coke bottle, Elvis, and Marilyn Monroe, the implied subject was vulgarity, to be sure, but the approach was devoid of criticism or anger. Warhol was not alone. Roy

Lichtenstein's jumbo cartoon panels of bloated benday dots and Larry Rivers' heraldic cigarette and cigar logos were celebrations, not censure. Painting a soup can or a beer bottle is not a radical act. What *was* radical was the adoption of mass production, turning them out en masse, and marketing, selling them to anyone. Warhol's consumer art mimicked the process, as well as the look, of consumer culture. Little wonder that he called his studio the Factory and quipped, "Being good in business is the most fascinating kind of art." He enthusiastically removed the space between high art and low advertisement.

Warhol knew that modern museums resembled department stores for a reason. An increasing number of Americans, indoctrinated by the sacralization of art, decided they needed to consume the holy wafer. As the result of his Catholic Eastern European upbringing with its iconic tradition, and from his early experience as a window dresser, Warhol knew the power of repeated images in mass media. If "art" was being usurped by television, fashion, and film, it could just as easily deal with them on their terms. Which twin has the Toni? Which is the simulacrum? If mass media were going to use art, art could use mass media. If mass culture cannibalized high culture, why should turnabout not be fair play? What characterizes pop is mainly its use of what is despised by the Charles Eliot Nortons. Like Saint Remi addressing the Frankish king, Warhol's god of pop says, "Burn what you have worshiped, worship what you have burned." This is a two-party line. After all, art is show business.

Warhol simulated the act of painting, extending Duchamp, creating rows of readymades, dissolving high art into mass media. His adulation of the once-vulgar, his studied self-effacement, his desire to become machine, his love of the vernacular, his passion for the camera, his shifting sexuality, his concentration at the margin with appropriated images from the popular (like Marilyn Monroe/Norma Jean Baker) to the elevated images of Leonardo and Botticelli, all made him a pivotal character in the transformation of modern culture. Warhol's achievement was to legitimize his love of the secular, to attach religious value to profane subjects, to make trash respectable. Was he successful? In the fall of 1990 the Museum of Modern Art, a sacristy of high culture if ever there was one, mounted an exhibition entitled "High and Low: Modern Art and Popular Culture" in which the vulgar was at last accorded equal time and better space. Although the show took a critical drubbing primarily for not representing fractional interests, the mere acknowledgment of the

Which is the advertisement? Left: Andy Warhol, *Absolut Warhol* (Carillon Importers). Right: Andy Warhol, *Soup Can with Torn Label* (Leo Castelli Gallery), photo: Eeva-Inkeri.

interaction of high and low by the panjandrums at MOMA constituted an important realization made public. (The massive catalog, however, still captive to high-culture print sensibilities, was curiously condescending to low culture.)

In his art Warhol was sending up all the dour and melancholy critics who had predicted the ruin of modern sensibilities once the machine age took hold. No Cassandra was more dyspeptic than Walter Benjamin, whose "The Work of Art in the Age of Mechanical Reproduction" encapsulates early modernist anxiety. To Benjamin, steeped in the Victorian taste culture, originality was the be-all and end-all of culture. Repetition denies the very concept of the unique. From the Greeks, who knew only founding and stamping, to the woodcut and graphic art of the Renaissance, to movable type and

lithography, to photography, then to film and sound film, the central concept of "authenticity" was being effaced. In a melancholy aside, Benjamin even notes that the worst staging of *Faust* is superior to the best film version of *Faust* in that the stage play more nearly imitates the first performance at Weimar and hence expresses Goethe's intent. Art loses its aura of ritual once secularized; its cultic value and fetishist power are depleted when shared with the hoi polloi. Mechanical reproduction means mass production, and mass distribution means mass consumption, and anything that the rabble has is, by definition, without value. Beneath this cultural Ludditeism lurks the dog-in-the-manger mentality of exactly that kind of elite that the Marxists supposedly abhor. But Benjamin has a point: if everybody hears Beethoven, then Beethoven becomes vulgar. Print the Mona Lisa on a washcloth too many times and she loses her allure. As Huysmans observed, "The loveliest tune imaginable becomes vulgar and insupportable as soon as the public begins to hum it and the hurdygurdies make it their own" (*Across the Grain*). Familiarity even breeds ignorance. We all know that the William Tell overture precedes *The Lone Ranger*, not Rossini's opera.

Another interpretation of vulgarity was being offered contemporaneously with Benjamin by other Germans equally disaffected with the turn of cultural politics. The so-called Frankfurt theorists essentially argued that what we see in popular culture is the result of manipulation of the many for the profit of the few. The manipulators, aka "the culture industry," attempt to enlarge its "hegemony," establish its "ideological base" in the hearts and pocketbooks of the mindless. The masters of the media strive to "infantilize" the audience, to make it both docile and anxious and consumptive with "reified desire." The media lords are predators, and what they do in no way reflects or resolves genuine audience concerns. Just the opposite. We may think vulgarity is "mere escapism," but this is not so. Acquiring such taste by force-feeding pabulum results in an entrapment into a commodifying system, a "false consciousness" and a "fetishism" that only the Frankfurters can correct. Not all is lost, however. Vulgarity is the last gasp of capitalism, the stuff produced before the revolution. Show business is the last business before the real business begins — the rule of the proletariat.[3]

This tension on the margin where popular culture meets elite culture has given rise to our newest articulation of separation anxiety, the high take on low culture: postmodernism. Although many critics revel in recognizing that the breach between high and popular culture is sexist and racist, a systematic disenfranchisement of women (and blacks, Chicanos, and children), a gendering of mass culture as feminine and inferior, the ramifications are startling. Is everything up

---

3. Three striking aspects of the Frankfurt school: (1) Until the 1980s their influence was profound in academic circles — hardly a day went by when one did not hear in the halls of academe such jargon as Antonio Gramsci's "ideological hegemony," T. W. Adorno and Max Horkheimer's "culture industry," Hans Enzensberger's "consciousness industry," Friedrich Schiller's "mind managers," Michael Real's "mass-mediated culture," Fredric Jameson's "use value overcoming exchange value," and the old standby, Herbert Marcuse's "systematic moronization" and best yet, "repressive tolerance." (2) Their intellectual descendants still produce the most interesting cultural criticism, quite possibly by default: witness the works of Tod Gitlin, Andrew Ross, Stuart Hall, Raymond Williams, Ariel Dorfman, John Fiske, Neil Postman, Mark Crispin Miller, as well as the numerous publications of Routledge, Methuen, Pantheon, and many university presses. And (3) most of the explanations and predictions of the Frankfurt school are now having to be reconsidered in the light of political events. In retrospect, given the political transformation of Eastern Europe, fewer books were needed on the necessity of Western socialism and more were needed on how to transform controlled economies into free markets.

for grabs? If taste is by definition oppressive, then does equality mandate tastelessness? Recall that the meaning of taste has moved from the physical sense of tasting with the mouth to something that can only be acquired by study and birth. The potential for oppression based on taste is clear. What was once a passive act became a ritual of induction. Wordsworth in his *Preface to the Lyrical Ballads* invokes taste only to dismiss it as too full of rules and mannerisms. If so, the triumph of the vulgar may be the ultimate romantic aesthetic statement. It may be "leveling down," to be sure, but at last art will be "the overflow of powerful emotion" understood by Everyman. Postmodern discourse, as it is called, is a blur, a constellation of styles, a mixture of levels, a relish for copies and repetition, a knowledge and pleasure in the play of surfaces, a rejection of history, an appreciation of all that Ruskin would abominate: Michael Graves's Portland Building, Philip Johnson's AT&T building, Rauschenberg's silkscreens, Warhol's Brillo boxes, in addition to shopping malls, mirror facades, Cinema 16 as cathedral, paperback bookcovers, not to mention television viewers equipped with remote-control devices who "zap" around the TV dial making up their own "text" as they go. The only rule: no rule. Admittedly, not quite what Wordsworth had in mind.

The high-art concept of genre has evaporated, not only because of a relaxation of taste limits, but because of the astonishing ability of modern technology to collapse distinctions. Computers, for instance, have blurred the distinction between real/natural and artificial/ human-made. Who is the composer of computer music: a programmer, the software developer, an instrument, a chip, or the player? Appropriation and plagiarism which were opprobria a decade ago have now become encomia. Twyla Tharp's "Deuce Coup" reprises the Beach Boys' classic, Sherrie Levine repaints others, rock bands like Pussy Galore remake an entire Rolling Stones album, and in movies we have one self-conscious remake after another. The ultimate in derivation is prequel- and sequel-ization. One sees and hears this transformation in popular music, especially on MTV. Instruments like electronic drums and the synthesizer can copy any pulse; music videos remake each other, mixing classics and ephemera; schlock and high art are equalized. The digital sampler, which turns sounds into number strings and can play back virtually every sound ever recorded, means that every note may be in the public domain. All of this mimicry depends, of course, on audience familiarity, and familiarity is exactly what popular culture has delivered since the printing press.

From serialized novels, to movie sequels, to sitcom spin-offs, to Mostly Mozart, to Top-40 music, the process of repetition is what drives the market. Asked to explain the lingo of his business, a young Hollywood composer of film scores explains that, " 'Give me something new' means 'Be imitative and follow current style,' 'Let yourself go' means 'Repeat yourself,' 'Do something creative' means 'not that creative,' and 'I'm not concerned with money' means 'This film must turn a profit' " (Lewis 1986:43n). When movies and television shows are "pitched," they are usually described in terms of what has recently succeeded at the box office or in the Nielsen ratings.

Repetition is of course the essence of vulgarity. Let the high-culture artist suffer the anxiety of influence, the popular-culture merchandiser prefers the balm of cash. While to Susan Sontag recombination and repetition are symptomatic of an exhausted culture, to the anthropologist they may mean the opposite. For just as the compulsion to repeat represents some unassimilated desire of the individual to revisit trauma, the repetition at the core of mass media also betokens some as-of-yet incomplete transaction with anxiety for the audience. In show business the "knock-off" is the economic ideal. Yet, it is also a sign that some important subject is being addressed. The vulgar in any culture is powerful because it takes very simple ideas very seriously—earnest and energetic, predictable yet novel, new but not surprising. As William Dean Howells wrote in *Letters Home*, "Real feeling is ALWAYS vulgar." The more powerful the feeling, the more important the message, the more often it is repeated. So, for example, "sex and violence" do indeed characterize much of mass media because sex and violence are the central concerns of our culture.[4]

What is particular about the world since the French Revolution is the speed with which the repetition occurs. Popular culture, which

4. With respect to the vulgar, the medium is not the message, the message is what drives the medium. Bruno Bettelheim demonstrated in *The Uses of Enchantment* that the function of fairy tales is always to repeat and resolve situations of anxiety. The process occurs in high art as well, although at a much-reduced speed. Leo Steinberg illustrated in *The Sexuality of Christ in Renaissance Art and in Modern Oblivion* that the burst of crucifixion images that appeared in the Renaissance was connected with audience anxiety about their own mortality. Was Christ really a God who died for us as a Man? If so, he should be pictured as a human, complete with the mark of humanity, a penis, and enduring what we recognize as the human experience, namely, pain. Once this audience anxiety was resolved, imaging both Christ's sexuality and the Passion disappeared. What characterizes any culture, high or low, is repetition. As a general rule, the more important the message, the more often it is repeated, and the more likely it is to be termed "vulgar."

depends on reproducible imagery, could only have started in the late eighteenth century as a result of mechanical devices to first print and then lithograph in quantity. In addition, however, popular culture needs an eager audience massive enough to keep these machines occupied. A lowering of the average population age as birthrates increased meant a shifting of storytelling to younger and younger audiences. The younger the audience the more insistent the demand to repeat. The speed of repetition was increased with the introduction of electronic transmission. The difference between the lithograph and the celluloid image is the speed of light. Speed is only part of the spectacle of modern life. What characterizes the condition of culture since World War II is, as Jean Baudrillard has made a career of saying, that now we have more signs than referents, more images than meanings that can be attached to them. The machinery of communication often communicates little except itself—signs just refer to each other, creating a "simulacra" of reality. We have lost the aesthetic category of the vulgar because we have been overwhelmed by it. We have ceased to recognize it because it has become the norm, in computer jargon—the default mode of taste.

To the modern Frankfurters of the social sciences, capitalism is the villain in multiplying and repeating worn-out signs. The "culture industry" is repeating entertainments until they are drained dry of audience interest and disposable income. The "masters of the media" are only scapegoats for a more profound shifting in taste cultures. Blaming the messenger for the message is not a new response. It's "them"—the media moguls who generate porn, horror, romances, sequels, sitcoms, rock 'n' roll music, and all the trivialities and soporifics that *we* would scorn if we could, but, alas, we are too weak to resist the manipulation. Not quite correct. As Leslie Fiedler writes in *What Was Literature?*:

> It turns out, however, that . . . far from manipulating mass taste, its so-called masters breathlessly pursue it, cutting each other's throats, risking bankruptcy to find images which the great audience will recognize as dreams they have already dreamed, or would if they could. No wonder they think of themselves as riding a tiger, as do the commissars of culture in societies where socialism has triumphed. What items of popular culture they have sought to ban, in the name of "progress" rather than profit—from jeans to rock-and-roll records—are traded in secret, the black market having replaced the free market as the dream machine of the masses. (1982:101)

The cultural history of the twentieth century, especially since the 1960s, is the history of the most rapid shift ever in dominant taste. Once directed by the few for the many, modern-day show business is being directed by the many for the many. The people in the conglomerated industries that make books, television shows, and movies do not say, "This is something I want to consume." They say instead, "This is for them." And if bestseller lists, box-office receipts, and Nielsen ratings are correct, they are profiting by such decisions.

To be vulgar on purpose is not easy. Uncertainty is the driving force. Fewer than half of American films recoup their expenses; of the fifty thousand books published annually less than 10 percent will appear at any particular bookstore; about 250 records are released every week, of which only three or four stand a chance of being on a national playlist, and eight of every ten new television shows will not be renewed in the next season. What this director of business affairs at CBS says of the music business is true of all mass media: "Our industry is a classic example of crap shooting. When you win, you win big. You can afford to take a 70 percent stiff ratio. On the three that make it you more than make up your cost and profit on the entire ten. If you're not willing to gamble, then you shouldn't be in the business" (Lewis 1986:31). Understandably, confected fame and the fabricated pseudoevent characterize a system where the flop is far more likely than the hit. Actors, musicians, even authors strive for the condition of being "brand names" because the star system is one of the few ways of not being shunted aside.

To approach the triumph of vulgarity in the contemporary world we need to put aside the "text," "star," and "author" to concentrate on the "reader." Vulgarity is uniformly adolescent. The term "juvenile" is central to discussion of the vulgar as it describes the audience and its concerns — the literal child and the child in us all. For adults the allure of the vulgar is regressionary and often secretly pleasurable. While the primary audience may seek education, the adult seeks release — Fiedler calls it "privileged insanity." Such unearned instant gratification or "escape" generates a sense of shame, and this sense of shame is not resolved. For refusing to "give the devil his due" and admit that we have slipped off to seek the forbidden in the mythic realm of Vulgaria, we condemn the very titillation and release we have sought. What is avidly consumed in adolescence becomes the guilty pleasures of adulthood.

We call whatever is vulgar, *junk*. We also use this term to describe the most potent narcotic (heroin) and its users (junkies), a particularly potent and annoying kind of marketing (junk mail — now junk phone calls), a favorite diet of empty calories (junk food), and even a method of risky financing (junk bonds). The current (again since the 1960s) use of the word "junk" demonstrates how ambivalent we have become. The gist of its many uses is that here is something that is "bad for you, good for us." Junk is garbage, and garbage is what we throw away *after* it is used. Here is Grant Tinker, erstwhile producer of such shows as the *Mary Tyler Moore Show*, *Rhoda*, and the *Bob Newhart Show* as well as CEO of NBC television, misunderstanding what he does, but appreciating the result: "I think what is probably the biggest sin of the medium as it exists is that so little sticks to your ribs, that so much effort and technology goes into — what? It's like human elimination. It's just waste" (Gitlin 1983:16). We may like to say we consume this or that elite entertainment, but once you hear the adjective "junk," "garbage," or "waste," you know what is really being used. "Trash TV" is television that is watched. Trash novels are read, and not only in airports. Those tabloids are taking more and more supermarket space for a reason. "I know it's trash but I like it" is a key to understanding a culture's most important commodities. Thus "mere" entertainment, "just" a commercial, "only" an advertisement, a show without "depth," "formula," "shallow," not "worthy" of consideration, are mixed protestations of use and guilt. As "garbagology" is a recognized specialty in anthropology, so should the study of throwaway entertainment be central to understanding what a culture claims to value and what it really consumes.

The most perceptive commentators on the subject of throwaway commodities are not the mini-Lacans and faux-Foucaults of academic institutions, who invariably hold it in gleefully unconcealed contempt, and not the people like Mr. Tinker who produce it and then disdain it, but those who still enjoy it. Here is the playwright, novelist, and especially the cartoonist, Jules Feiffer:

> Junk is there to entertain on the basest, most compromised of levels. It finds the lowest fantasmal common denominator and proceeds from there. Its choice of tone is dependent on its choice of audience, so that women's magazines will make a pretense at veneer scorned by movie-fan magazines, but both are, unarguably, junk. . . . Junk is a second-class citizen of the arts; a status of which we and it are constantly aware. There are certain inherent privileges in second-class citizenship. Irresponsibility is one. Not being taken seriously is another. Junk,

like the drunk at the wedding, can get away with doing or saying anything because, by its very appearance, it is already in disgrace. It has no one's respect to lose; no image to endanger. Its values are the least middle class of all the mass media. That's why it is needed so. The success of the best junk lies in its ability to come close, but not too close; to titillate without touching us. To arouse without giving satisfaction. Junk is a tease. (1965:186–87)

In the sense that junk is a tease, it aspires to the condition of pornography. Pornography is oriented toward one purpose: physical arousal. While tumescence may be one extreme of the vulgar, physical arousal is almost always involved in the experience. Generating laughter, tears, shivers, and swoons is what "junk" usually strives for. Sentimentality is the essence of the vulgar, the most enduring legacy of Romanticism. We can play along with it because we like having those sentiments, at least in controlled moderation. One of the reasons why there are so many mindless game shows on television is because the audience can participate, can feel along with the contestants. Danielle Steel makes us cry. Stephen King makes us shudder. Successful junk is escapist, of course. We escape the confines of the self-conscious self and become emotional participants.

When academics do wander downstream into the Heart of Popular Culture Darkness they almost always want to bring out their own prizes of ivory, very often just old tree trunks painted cream color. Since the derogatory label "junk" hardly seems worthy of reputable collectors, some new coinage for mass-produced, mass-consumed commodities must be struck. It is no happenstance that these coinages for disposable entertainment are relatively recent, and all of foreign derivation. The terms are certainly never used by the primary paying audience. These academic subcategories of the vulgar are: "schlock" from the Yiddish (literally damaged goods at a cheap price); "kitsch" from the German, meaning petty bourgeois; and "camp" from the French *se camper*, a phrase ripe with a history of upper-class English use even before Susan Sontag. Schlock is truly unpretentious, kitsch has pretensions toward taste and camp is just good fun. These are not fixed categories, but attempts to account for the attraction of the vulgar, perhaps even to account for pleasures still felt by the critics. To those who use such terms, schlock, kitsch, and camp are usually examples of "failed taste," junk consumed by those who should "know better," those who should not have ventured across the boundaries of official taste, and now have to account for these guilty pleasures. If taste is only possible by exclusion, here is what critics have problems excluding.

Camp, schlock, and kitsch all assert that good taste is not simply good taste, but that there exists a good taste of bad taste. Such categories, of course, exonerate the consumer. It's okay to like this trash, wink-wink. The critic makes fun of such vulgarities, to be sure, but this fun is rather like smirking at jokes you once really enjoyed but now are ashamed you laughed at. Here is the upside-down canonizing of the vulgar, protecting it from the censure we are supposed to direct toward junk. What Susan Sontag says of camp is also true of these other legitimizations, and provides an insight into elite culture's ambivalence about physical pleasure:

> Camp is a subcategory of banal and the vulgar . . . [and appreciating it] is the way to be dandy in an age of mass culture. Dandyism in the age of mass culture makes no distinction between the unique object and the mass-produced object. Camp taste transcends the nausea of the replica. The old fashioned dandy hated vulgarity, but the new style dandy is a lover of Camp, appreciates Vulgarity. The dandy held a perfumed handkerchief to his nostrils and was liable to swoon; the connoisseur of Camp sniffs the stink and prides himself on his strong nerves. (1966:289)

The nausea of the replica, indeed.

Camp, kitsch, and schlock are clearly on the edge of "good taste" and show how aesthetic categories depend on both exclusion and confusion. Keep this stuff out (but not too far out), says the critic. The margin must exist and yet it must be blurred. The canon of high culture depends on its opposite, the canon of low culture. As contemporary events show, when confidence is lost in one, it is lost in the other as well. Mr. Nice and Mr. Nasty travel together. Vulgarity exists between the acceptable and the forbidden, the normal and the freakish, the usual and the tabooed, the speakable and the unspeakable. As such, it is most often demanded by those who need instruction about behavior, namely those who are about to act on their own — adolescents — and, indeed, is very often produced by those also on the edge. Homosexuals and Jews play a disproportionate role in the production of popular entertainments, in part because they are especially sensitive to being marginalized. The vulgar crosses boundaries, simplifies the complex, mediates unwelcome contradictions of life, and provides a guilt-free release of repressed aggression that allows us to explore the verge between the permitted and the forbidden as well as to experience the limits of order in what is usually a carefully controlled way.

When you reflect on early adolescence, the vulgar first described occurrences at the margin of the body: what was excreted, and what was aroused. In other words, vulgarity occurs first with our understanding of how the body discharges waste, next how we maneuver our body in acts of aggression, and finally how we use our bodies in copulation. What is vulgarized in our culture essentially is the imagery of the transition from childhood to adulthood, from lack of control to containment. As Stephen Greenblatt has argued, this transition has numerous cultural parallels. In the modern world the codes elaborated for the management of the body's products — urine, feces, mucus, saliva, and flatulence — developed between the fifteenth and eighteenth centuries. "Proper control of each of these products along with the acquisition of the prevailing table manners and modes of speech marked the entrance into civility, an entrance that distinguishes not only the child from the adult, but the members of a privileged group from the vulgar, the upper classes from the lower, the courtly from the rustic, the civilized from the savage" (1982:2). From these early experiences, "delicacy of feeling" develops. This "delicacy" often matures into contempt, distaste, modesty, embarrassment, and other codes so powerful that they can influence the nervous system, producing blushing, even nausea, and the no-longer-fashionable rising of the gorge.

Scatology, of course, did not vanish either for the culture or for the individual in the modern world. Yet what Norbert Elias calls in *The Civilizing Process* "the threshold of shame and embarrassment" has altered profoundly. Eventually all body products except tears became unmentionable in decent society. Martin Luther's statement, "I am like ripe shit and the world is a gigantic ass-hole" simply could no longer be made by the eighteenth century. The Groom of the Stool, whose duty was to help King Henry VIII at his, was renamed the First Gentleman of the Bedchamber by 1669. What was once acceptable in the central zone of the social system, as well as what is tolerated in children, was pushed out to the periphery. What was once tolerated has become unacceptable, but it is still there on the edge. Thanks (or no thanks, depending on your sense of the proper) to the transformations wrought on storytelling by the electronic media, the thresholds of shame are shrinking and vulgarities are now coming back toward the center. The modern world has come full circle. Vulgarity, which had developed into an entire anti-aesthetic by the time of Ruskin, has now returned, in common parlance at least, to describe only dirty words and jokes.

One of the reasons Mikhail Bakhtin has become so provocative a critic of contemporary times is because he understood that the transformation into modern times essentially had to do with the repression of the vulgar. The "lower bodily stratum," as he called the vulgar, had been progressively distanced from consciousness through the Renaissance. The power of the vulgar, however, was too dynamic to be totally repressed, and so it was institutionalized at the margin. The Carnival became its celebration. Only in controlled display could what was considered the "grotesque" be acknowledged, could youth be served, foolishness indulged. Freaks were a central totem in this process. Their exhibition has certainly existed since antiquity, and, like other pagan practices, was revived in the Middle Ages. The Church recognized their allure as both a drawing card and an admonition, and displayed them on feast days. While we do not know exactly how they were displayed (probably in booths and in morality plays which included other performers), we do know they were then, as now, an eerie projection of audience anxiety and curiosity. The grotesque human body receives its fullest visual representation in the art of Bosch and Breughel, and, as Bakhtin demonstrates, its most masterful literary expression in Rabelais' Gargantua and Pantagruel. Today we open the best-selling paperback, turn on the TV set, or go to the Cinema 16 to experience the thrills of perceiving the "other."

In England freaks were displayed with increasing popularity in Elizabethan times, but not until the Restoration did they become public attractions. In 1858, a decade after the great fairs had been ordered closed, Henry Morley recalled Bartholomew Fair. Here in a week all "entertainments that at other times were scattered over town and city . . . were concentrated on one spot." As a hardly approving Victorian, he continues, "The tone of society was degraded by the Court of Charles the Second [as the] taste for monsters became a disease" (Fiedler 1978:280). Morley was certainly not alone. Here is William Wordsworth in one of the most biting elite indictments of the rising tide of popular carnival:

> From these sights [of modern London]
> Take one, — that ancient festival the Fair,

Holden where martyrs suffered in past time,
And named for St. Bartholomew. . . . What a shock
For eyes and ears! what anarchy and din,
Barbarian and infernal, — a phantasma,
Monstrous in colour, motion, shape, sight, sound!
Below, the open space, through every nook
Of the wide area, twinkles, is alive
With heads; the midway region, and above,
Is thronged with staring pictures and huge scroll,
Dumb proclamations of the Prodigies;
With chattering monkeys dangling from their poles,
And children whirling in their roundabouts;
With those that stretch the neck and strain the eyes,
And crack the voice in rivalship, the crowd
Inviting; with buffoons against buffoons
Grimacing, writhing, screaming, — him who grinds
The hurdy-gurdy, at the fiddle weaves
Rattles the salt-box, thumps the kettle-drum,
And him who at the trumpet puffs his cheeks,
The silver-collared Negro with his timbrel,
Equestrians, tumblers, women, girls, and boys,
Blue-breeched, pink-vested, with high-towering plumes.
All moveables of wonder, from all parts,
Are here — Albinos, painted Indians, Dwarfs,
The Horse of knowledge, and the learned Pig,
The Stone-eater, the man that swallows fire,
Giants, Ventriloquists, the Invisible Girl,
The Bust that speaks and moves its goggling eyes,
The Wax-work, Clock-work, all the marvelous craft
Of modern Merlins, Wild Beasts, Puppet-shows,
All out-o'-the-way, far-fetched, perverted things,
All freaks of nature, all Promethean thoughts
Of man, is dullness, madness, and their feats
All jumbled up together, to compose
A Parliament of Monsters. (*The Prelude* Book 8:675–718)

By the middle of the nineteenth century the fairs were gone. Indus-
trialization had changed the seasonal habits of the common worker.
Holidays geared to the hiring of field hands, or the reaping of crops,
had all but disappeared in a manufacturing environment where all
days and all weeks were standardized. There were no respites in
which safely to vent curiosity, bonhomie, or even aggression. Plough
Monday, Guy Fawkes Day, May Day, sheep-shearing days, and the

William Hogarth, *Southwark Fair*, 1773/4 (British Museum).

like were not part of the six-day work week. Also, such elite groups as the Society for the Suppression of Vice, and some not-so-elite groups like the evangelical Methodists, had lobbied against displays of common entertainment. Like the Puritans (whom Thomas Macaulay suggested disallowed bearbaiting not because of the pain it caused the bear, but because of the pleasure afforded the spectators), these latter-day improvers of "the human condition" could think of better things for the young to do.

This is not to say that carnivalesque recreations disappeared. Punch and Judy, dogfighting and cockfighting, bullbaiting, freak shows, and games of chance continued. But the state-sanctioned celebration of vulgarity was no more. Much the same situation was occurring across the channel in France, where the "Pont-Neuf" shows, the fairs of Saint Clair, Saint-Fermain, and Saint-Laurent, the opéra comique and opéra bouffes, and all manner of "parade" and "spectacle" were being suppressed by the Church fathers, city fathers and, most importantly, the captains of industry. Diversions corrupted the soul and, worse, took valuable time away from work.

Lithograph by Brown and Severin of Barnum's American Museum c. 1850 (Barnum Museum, Bridgeport, CT) and P. T. Barnum at the entrance to his museum (*Vanity Fair*, September 13, 1862).

Such economic anxiety and social control were not present in America. Their absence explains, in large part, why show *business* developed here. While the Church, the State, and the industrial revolution certainly existed on the western side of the Atlantic, they were neither as entrenched nor as enthusiastic for reformation. The opposite was true. The Puritans could censor John Williams and cut down the Maypole of Marymount, but the dissenters could always head for the territories. In America there was a modus operandi that was missing in Europe, a strain of frontier enthusiasm for excess, be it the tall tale or the carnival celebration of the common. Here there was no tradition to tarnish, no history to violate, no escutcheon to blot. In fact, if one could make money from entertainment, so much the better. No one exemplified the enthusiasm for displaying the outrageous for a dime more than P. T. Barnum, a figure every bit as important as Dickens, Hugo, Twain, and Poe in understanding how the demands of a mass audience created the mass media. Barnum

NO DRAFTIN' IN BALDINSVILLE.
THE FIRST OF A SERIES OF ORIGINAL LETTERS ON THE WAR, WRITTEN EXPRESSLY FOR VANITY FAIR BY ARTEMUS WARD, WILL APPEAR IN OUR NEXT NUMBER.
THEY WILL BE CONTINUED WEEKLY.

VOL. 6.
NO. 142.

VANITY FAIR

Saturday,
SEPT. 13.
1862.

MUSEUM
WALK UP.

THE RIVAL DWARFS

THE SINGING Lobster

THE Abolition Angel Fish

THE Educated Clam

Fred B. F. and young ones

H. G. H. Greeley.

PHINEAS TAYLOR BARNUM:
BLOWING, WITH ALL HIS MIGHT, FOR HIS "HAPPY FAMILY," THE CONFIDING PUBLIC.

knew what the rapidly expanding affluent populace wanted — thrills; and he knew how to provide them — in shows. His New York museum, his hoaxes, his bigtop, his sideshow, these first shifted the economic engines of modern show business into gear. Barnum understood what the publishing, film, and television industries had to realize to survive. He knew how to market wonder; how to carnivalize curiosity. He knew what we would pay to stare at, and he knew that it is the story above all that makes the object interesting.

In the 1840s, Barnum started to collect the objects and to tell the stories that would become the staples of modern media. He purchased the failing Scudder's American Museum on the corner of Broadway and Ann Street opposite the prestigious Astor Hotel, near the photography studio of Mathew Brady and the lithography studio of Currier and Ives. The museum was a few blocks downtown from

"WHAT IS IT"?

Is it a lower order of **MAN**! Or is it a higher order of **MONKEY**! None can tell! Perhaps it is a combination of both. It is beyond dispute **THE MOST MARVELLOUS CREATURE LIVING.** It was captured in a savage state in Central Africa, is probably about 20 years old, 4 feet high, intelligent, docile, active, sportive, and **PLAYFUL AS A KITTEN.** It has the skull, limbs and general anatomy of an **ORANG OUTANG** and the **COUNTENANCE of a HUMAN BEING.**

TO BE SEEN AT ALL HOURS AT BARNUM'S MUSEUM.

"What Is It?" Number 12 in the series *Barnum's Gallery of Wonders* published by Currier and Ives (Shelburne Museum, Shelburne, VT).

the current conglomerated offices of the Columbia Broadcasting System, Capital Cities Communication, the National Broadcasting Corporation, Advance Publications, Time Warner, Paramount Communications Incorporated, etc., all of which still continue the business he mastered. Plastering the facade of the museum with bright banners, Barnum transformed the building into an entertainment center — a place to exchange money for wonder. It was one of New York City's premier attractions, on the itinerary of European tourists (Dickens, Thackeray, and the Prince of Wales) and of almost every native luminary, politician, and financier. Skits, pantomimes, lectures, ballets, and dramas were presented in the lecture hall, but, more importantly, "human curiosities" were displayed in its exhibition rooms. In 1860 you could have seen thirteen of these unique, "never-before-seen wonders-of-Nature," including an albino family, the last Living Aztecs, the Swiss Bearded Lady, The Highland Fat Boys, and most famous of all, the "What Is It?" (a mentally retarded black man).

In the museum you would have been taken to the edge, been able to explore the limits of the normal. In doing so, you would have been one of the forty-one million customers, each of whom paid not ten cents (the going rate at the other "dime museums") but an exorbitant twenty-five cents. From Barnum's museum sprang a host of imitations with more prosaic names: "Hall of Human Curiosities," "Ten in One," "Kid Show," "Pit Show," "Odditorium," "Congress of Oddities," or "Museum of Nature's Mistakes." They all celebrated the Other, the what-might-have-been, the "there but for the Grace of God go I." You paid to stare. We still do. The screens are different and the method of payment more sophisticated, but the process is the same.

As the hodgepodge museum was co-opted by the elite institutions of fine arts, the freak show was taken over by the traveling circus. The freaks vacated their stable city life and went to the train station. The entire dime museum was often loaded on boxcars to be set up on the edge of the circus as the literal side show. These shows were, like their counterparts of today in the electronic media, eagerly consumed by the unsophisticated and just as eagerly criticized by those who had already seen them and "knew better." The criticism, then as now, proved ineffective. As long as there was a story, a ticket, and a turnstile, there was a market to be made. So at the edge of the Centennial Exposition in Philadelphia in 1876 was "Centennial City," better known as "Dinkeytown," which housed freak shows. Likewise, at the next exhibit of high culture, the famous 1893 World's Columbian Exposition in Chicago, the Midway Plaisance was nearby. Showmen sitting on stools spieled to the crowds of the wonders inside. Here was an image that expressed with gnomic concision the future of American culture. On one side of

Luna Park, Coney Island
(NYT Pictures).

the Columbian Exposition was the Court of Honor, or the White City, filled with works of serious art gathered from all over the world. On the other side was the midway with George Ferris's towering wheel at its center. The choice was clear: see the best which had been thought and painted, or ride the Ferris Wheel. While there were only a few exhibitions like the White City in a lifetime, the circus became an annual event. There were only a handful of circuses in 1820; by 1850 there were more than a hundred. Most of them were moved by rail and most had a boxcar filled with the "wonders of nature." By 1920 the circus was in decline, owing to the rise of vaudeville, the nickelodeon, and then of the cinema. The sideshow, however, survived.

Sometimes the show stood still and became an amusement park. The most famous of these was Coney Island, which contained three internal parks: Steeplechase, Luna, and Dreamland. Between 1910 and 1940, there were more oddities here than at any other place on earth. For many freaks this was home. When wanderlust was on them they joined the pitshow of a traveling carnival and made extra money.

In the days before television co-opted the carnival, these ever-moving festivals were the direct descendants of Renaissance street fairs and harvest celebrations, updated with games of chance, shooting galleries, mechanical rides, and the pitshows with a barker and a bally out in front. The economic dynamics that inform the electronic midway were developed here. "What do you want to see," asks the barker/movie producer/television programmer. Step this way, pay your money, and I'll show it to you. No, no, said the parents, don't go in that tent; but in the adolescents go as they have for generations. Behind the canvas, into the darkened theater, downstairs late at night to watch the television, we go to see what we could not see during the day. We have not lost our ancient need to see behind the curtain. All that has changed is that we now have industries that lift it for us, or at least for some of us, every day, for a price.

Say what you like about capitalism, its mindless and amoral drive to open up and saturate markets has ironically returned us to what in many ways is a pre-industrial culture. Lawrence Levine concludes *Highbrow/Lowbrow*: "What was invented in the late nineteenth century were the rituals accompanying that appreciation [of art]; what was invented was the illusion that the aesthetic products of high culture were originally created to be appreciated in precisely the manner late nineteenth century Americans were taught to observe: with reverent, informed, disciplined seriousness" (1988:229). To be sure, not everyone bought in. Walt Whitman demurred. In 1871 he writes in *Democratic Vistas*, "With this word Culture or what it has come to represent we find ourselves abruptly in close quarters with the enemy." And it may well be that what was reinvented in the middle of the twentieth century was the exact opposite of the Victorian legacy of modernism: a resurgence of irreverence, an uninformed populace responding with undisciplined glee to the common experience, an acknowledgment of the untranscendent joy of the senses. The "struggle for fun," as Simon Frith calls it, may well be the governing force in our carnival age. To see how that "struggle" has transformed (and been transformed by) both print and the electronic media, we now turn to examine the individual industries "at work," struggling for profits.

two

Paperbacked Culture: How Candles Became Shoes

It was at least ten years ago [in the 1960s] that I heard Charles Scribner say, "If books become obsolete, I will make candles." He didn't explain his remark, but I think he had in mind that, although the electric light has made candles obsolete, candle making today is a hundred-million-dollar industry—not large, but it casts a lovely light. And after all, books are candles.
—Herbert S. Bailey, director, Princeton University Press

We sell books, other people sell shoes. What's the difference? Publishing isn't the highest art.
—Michael Korda, editor-in-chief, Simon & Schuster

Something seems to have happened to the high-culture publishing houses of Charles Scribner's Sons and Simon & Schuster in the years between the end of Charles Scribner's management in the 1950s and the installation of new "editorial teams" in the 1970s. Candles became shoes. Candles do cast a lovely light, and they do illuminate small spaces with cozy intimacy, but books as shoes? Shoes are so common, so ordinary, so . . . vulgar.

What made candles into shoes happened on both sides of the printing presses. Although details will follow in this chapter, essentially bookmakers have gone from wide-range, short-run publishing to narrow-range, long-run publishing. In the last century, the dominant commercial publishing houses have gone from charging a high price to a small audience for many categories of items to charging a low price to a mass audience for relatively few categories. The economic equation between price and print run has been resolved: long print runs + low unit prices = maximum profit. The transformation from candles to shoes is the result of a "revolution" brought about first by literacy, then by steam-driven presses, by lending libraries, by ever-cheaper paper and nonrunning ink, by binding technology, by shifts in disposable income, by pocket-sized books, by new patterns of distribution, by electronic transfer devices, and, most recently, by the enfolding of family-held businesses into vertically integrated, bottom-line obsessed, entertainment conglomerates. This shift from private to public taste, from editor approval to audience demand, from the canonical to the carnivalesque represents a profound veering in cultural aesthetics of which publishing constitutes only one site.

Books are no longer "respectfully presented to the reading public." They are rather the results of profit-and-loss marketing decisions in which the book itself is often less important than the merchandising rights of a creative property. Books have become "deal material." To get its share of the "deals" the Walt Disney Company is starting an adult book division named Hyperion Press. (Lest the name be confused with the mythic Titans, the studio's PR release assures us that the name is derived from the street in Los Angeles where Mr. Disney built his first animation studio.) As Robert Miller, publisher of this new imprint says, "After starting new ventures for adults in music and films it was inevitable that we should do something exciting in book publishing. But most importantly, Disney gives total support on the promotional end" (*Publishers Weekly*, October 26, 1990, p. 9). What they want to do "on the promotional end" is what the other "players" are doing, namely, cross-marketing. Blockbuster Video has sold out 600,000 copies of its *The Greatest Movies of All Time*, all of which just happen to be in Blockbuster's inventory. So, too, Ted Turner has entered joint publishing ventures to produce books mostly about the TV and movie properties he owns. *Kisses*, a collection of 150 duotone clinches from his MGM archives, is published as a St. Valentine's Day gift book, cablecast on TNT with hostess Lauren Bacall, excerpted in *Life* and *TV Guide*, and used by Macy's in its window dressings. Doubtless, *The Famous Mr. Ed* is already in press. Time Warner recently achieved marketer's nirvana, the ultimate multimedia "deal." *Listen Up: The Lives of Quincy Jones* was published by their book

Paperbacked Culture

Kisses advertisement, Citadel Press/Turner Publishing
(*New York Times Book Review*, February 3, 1991).

division; the record division distributed a recording of the same title on cassette and disk, and the movie studio simultaneously released the film version. To complete the circle, Mr. Jones is a 50–50 partner with Time Warner in his new company, Quincy Jones Entertainment. As in the child's game of "Paper, Rock, and Scissors" (in which paper covers rock, but rock pounds scissors, and scissors cuts paper), in the game of publishing, shoes snuff out candles.

This candle/shoe discussion is only the most recent colloquy on the transformation of print. The "graphic revolution," as Daniel Boorstin has called it, has been going on in earnest since images could be reproduced. In fact, it is the subject of Umberto Eco's novel about publishing, *The Name of the Rose*. At the center of this medieval fable about the modern world of print stands a library. It is a maze inside a fortress inside a monastery inside a walled town. Arranged in fifty-six interlocking and adjoining rooms on the top floor of a huge tower, this library houses the greatest collection of books and manuscripts in medieval Christendom. Everything worth knowing is here. Nothing new is ever added. All truth already *is*. Yet what is, is endlessly copied. The librarian is in charge. He decides what is to be reproduced. He ferries books back and forth between the stacks and the monks who endlessly transcribe them. The monks could not get to the original books even if they wanted to for there is a coded catalog of library holdings that only the librarian knows. Additionally, although the books are shelved in rooms that are arranged systematically, the system is hidden in yet another code embedded in quotations above the library doors. To make the shelving system even more obscure, the rooms are of different sizes and shapes. Some actually have no identifying quotations. Passageways are further confused by mirrored walls. Every night the library is locked, and hallucinogenic herbs are set out by the librarian to disorient and frighten any intruder. If ever there was an apt mythologem for high-culture print, here it is. This place is a thicket of briars.

The thicket has a purpose. It protects a nest of ideas. How paradoxical that the work of the monastery should be to copy and lock away what is already copied and locked away. But no one questions that this is a noble and sacramental calling. If an object is valuable, then the more of these objects you put in the nest, the more value you control. So generations of monks protect and increase the vast store of beautiful books for generations of monks. The monks also think of the books as candles. They hoard the light. But at the same time, the monastic authorities realize that some candles are dangerous and must not be increased. The ideas expressed in them are called heretical or blasphemous. They provide not light but fire. They can burn the monastery down. One book above all others, a book hidden in a deep cell at the center of the labyrinth, is considered so incendiary that if its ideas caught fire nothing could extinguish them. The whole Catholic world would be burnt to ashes. The attempt to keep this book out of the hands of the unfit occasions a series of murders. That forbidden but protected book is the only surviving copy of Aristotle's treatise on comedy — on turning the "world upside down." The heart of its danger was that it celebrated the carnivalesque. It argued that the people should be able to decide what they want. As the monk charged with withholding this "text" says,

> Laughter is weakness, corruption, the foolishness of our flesh. It is the peasants' entertainment, the drunkard's license; even the church in her wisdom has granted the moment of feast, carnival, fair, this diurnal pollution that releases humors and distracts from other desires and other ambitions. . . . Still, laughter remains base, a defense for the simple, a mystery desecrated for the plebeians. The apostle also said as much: it is better to marry than to burn. Rather than rebel against God's established order, laugh, and enjoy your foul parodies of order, at the end of the meal, after you have drained jugs and flasks. Elect the king of fools, lose yourselves in the liturgy of the ass and the pig, play at performing your saturnalia head down." (1983:576–77)

Aristotle's treatise can't be hidden any longer. The high-culture monastery cannot keep things in or out any longer. The doors of publishing are wide open. Calvin and Hobbes (not John and Thomas) are bestsellers. *Tales from the Farside*, not Truths from the Monastery, draws readers. *The Secret Diary of Laura Palmer* and *Star Trek: The Tie-In* are what we have for Augustine's *Confessions* and Virgil's *Aeneid*. *The Best of Doonesbury*, not the Doomsday Book, is a favorite. The most sought-after book in recent memory, which set bidding records for publishing rights, was hardly the Ten Commandments. It was David Letterman's *Late Night Book of Top Ten Lists*. The printing press, like the movie camera and the broadcast spectrum, is being driven by forces of supply and demand, and those with the power are those with disposable income and the eagerness to spend it. Forget Aristotle, almost half of the trade paperback bestsellers today are cartoons. For many modern readers, it appears that All They Really Needed to Know They [indeed] Learned in Kindergarten. Just as it is carnival time on the coaxial cable, at Blockbuster Video, or down at the Cinema 16, it is a free-for-all in the once cloistered world of publishing.

It is hard to think that Eco did not have in mind a Xerox television commercial of a few years back. In the first part of the commercial we see a tonsured monk bent over his writing table inscribing the final letter. He looks heavenward with relief and then proudly carries the manuscript to the abbot who says, "Very nice, Brother Dominick. Very nice. Now I would like five hundred more copies." A dumbfounded Dominick is rescued by a Xerox machine and returns with a stack of copies. The abbot exclaims, "It's a miracle!" The anachro-

Xerox advertisement, 1977.

nism of leap-frogging over five hundred years of printing technology is as funny as it is profound. Now, however, the abbot no longer even needs Dominick. He now has an MBA and does marketing studies for target audiences.

And what is the abbot with a spreadsheet producing? Candles or shoes? Here are the top 25 of the Fiction Bestsellers of the 1980s:

1. *Clear and Present Danger*, Tom Clancy; 1,607,715 copies
2. *The Dark Half*, Stephen King; 1,550,000
3. *The Tommyknockers*, Stephen King; 1,429,929
4. *The Mammoth Hunters*, Jean M. Auel; 1,350,000
5. *Daddy*, Danielle Steel; 1,321,235
6. *Lake Wobegon Days*, Garrison Keillor; 1,300,000

Paperbacked Culture

7. *The Cardinal of the Kremlin*, Tom Clancy; 1,287,067
8. *Texas*, James A. Michener; 1,176,758
9. *Red Storm Rising*, Tom Clancy; 1,126,782
10. *It*, Stephen King; 1,115,000
11. *Kaleidoscope*, Danielle Steel; 1,065,355
12. *Zoya*, Danielle Steel; 1,000,319
13. *Star*, Danielle Steel; 1,000,119
14. *Patriot Games*, Tom Clancy; 957,400
15. *Misery*, Stephen King; 875,000
16. *The Sands of Time*, Sidney Sheldon (sales figures submitted in confidence only for placement on list)
17. *The Talisman*, Stephen King and Peter Straub; 830,000
18. *Leaving Home: A Collection of Lake Wobegon Stories*, Garrison Keillor; 817,000
19. *The Satanic Verses*, Salman Rushdie; 766,000
20. *The Icarus Agenda*, Robert Ludlum; 753,967
21. *Poland*, James A. Michener; 750,475
22. *The Eyes of the Dragon*, Stephen King; 750,000
23. *Caribbean*, James A. Michener; 749,941
24. *Bonfire of the Vanities*, Tom Wolfe; 739,862
25. *Skeleton Crew*, Stephen King; 720,000

Although this list is an eloquent gloss on the carnivalization of print, a few observations make it even more startling. First, ten of the thirteen novels selling one million or more copies were written by only three novelists: Stephen King, Danielle Steel, and Tom Clancy. Second, these novelists have only recently found their way to the copy machine. King made it to bestsellerdom with *The Dead Zone* in 1979, Steel's first bestseller in 1981 was *Remembrances*, and Clancy's *The Hunt for Red October* appeared in 1984. Whatever it is that these authors are producing, it is something for which an insatiable appetite has recently developed. Each author has staked out a distinct category (horror, romance, and the techno-thriller) and has found a mass audience that clearly wants more of the same. And this new audience is driving the machinery of publishing. No gatekeeper/monk can stand in their way. Other blockbusters have made the list for different, but no less revelatory, reasons. Jean Auel's *The Mammoth Hunters* is part of her Earth Children's saga *The Clan of the Cave Bear*. The series is so popular that the most recent entry, *Plains of Passage*, actually made the bestseller lists *before* it was published, simply on the basis of advance orders. In the late 1970s, Robert Ludlum and Sidney Sheldon gathered an audience for action-adventure genre novels which followed them into the 1980s; Garrison Keillor did radio broadcasting which appealed to a book-buying audience; Tom Wolfe was a best-selling nonfiction author before *Bonfire* and was helped by buyout mania, and Salman Rushdie's success is clearly a reflection of political events. The bestseller list, treated almost as a joke by publishers a generation ago, has now become the Holy Grail.

The fact that James Michener is the only author with a huge audience for an "educational" category (fiction-based-on-fact) shows how rapidly shifting the market for print is. As André Schiffrin learned, if you don't find at least part of that market you're doomed. Even Mr. Michener can't help. Schiffrin was the editor of Pantheon Books, a venerable firm founded in the 1940s by his father Jacques and Helen and Kurt Wolff—all of whom were refugees from the Nazis. Pantheon published elite-culture books by Boris Pasternak, Jean-Paul Sartre, Eric Hobsbawm, and Giuseppe di Lampedusa, as well as much left-leaning political commentary. In the 1980s it was bought out by Random House, itself to become a part of S. I. Newhouse's Advance Publications, a multibillion-dollar conglomerate of newspapers, cable stations, book publishing, and magazines. Although Pantheon had annual revenues of $20 million (accounting for only 3 percent of Random's total sales), it was publishing too many books at too high a cost and had been too unprofitable for too many years. Robert Bernstein, in charge of Random House, was told to bring Pantheon under control. But he was unwilling to do what had to be done: to slash the number of books published and tighten up the financial controls. He was replaced by Alberto Vitale, whom James Michener described as "an able number-cruncher, but not a man reared in the traditions of American publishing." Vitale did what he was told. He forced the resignation of André Schiffrin.

What occurred next tells much of what has happened to Brother Dominick in the contemporary world of conglomerate publishing. On February 27, 1990, Schiffrin announced his resignation, together with the now-standard severance document forbidding comment. He was followed by his other senior editors, who could see their future coming. In March there were a number of rallies in front of the Random House offices with as many as 350 writers, agents and others chanting such slogans as, "Newhouse, Newhouse, you can't hide; we charge you with bibliocide." More than 120 authors decried "an assault on editorial independence and cultural freedom" in an advertisement in the *New York Review of Books*. In a "spontaneous response" more than forty Random House staffers signed a statement regretting that their brethren at Pantheon had not been more responsible. As Mr. Vitale had said: "If you're selling 1,500 copies of a book and printing 7,500, you don't need to have been to Harvard to know you're in trouble" (Cohen, March 19, 1990).[1]

Other publishers hardly waited a shark's turn to capitalize on the weakness of one of their own. In a provocative advertisement, again in the *New York Review of Books*, we learn much about the nature of modern-day publishing. The implications of the headline "Independence is alive and well at Hill and Wang" are self-evident. In the main-body copy, Hill & Wang (an imprint of Farrar, Straus & Giroux) bemoans the "sorry destruction of Pantheon," while inviting disaffected authors to come over to their house for a while. In contrast to the anguish of publishing at Random House, Arthur Rosenthal boldly promises a "freshness of spirit, freedom from corporate constraints or a computer model making the publishing decisions, and, above all, the independence to maintain the standard of excellence . . . both in its attitude toward quality and in its close personal relationship with every author." To Rosenthal's right in the ad is erstwhile Pantheon editor Sara Bershtel, and looking on, while gently patting a stack of books, is the avuncular Roger Straus. Alberto Vitale, CEO of Random House (a subsidiary of which published *Truly*

1. In the high-culture world Mr. Schiffrin had considerable support, of course. The curmudgeonly Jonathan Yardley of the *Washington Post* demurred. In "Taming the Sacred Cow," he opined: "The assumption is that because Pantheon is ideologically pure — because it publishes, God help us, the likes of Todd Gitlin and Barbara Ehrenreich and Jonathan Schell — it is somehow exempt from the rules by which others in our (loathsome) capitalist market are expected to play; because Pantheon is on the side of the angels, that is to say, it is entitled to a free ride. Well, the truth is that it's gotten one for a long time, and it's taken full advantage." As well, George Will attacked the "hyperventilating intellectuals" supporting Pantheon "who reek of contempt for America, and bourgeois societies generally."

The business press knew what the conservative pundits meant. In an unsigned editorial in the *Wall Street Journal*, the following appears: "The protests proceeded from the premise that Pantheon's editors have a right to indulge their taste for money-losing books without any risk of losing their jobs. Still, the world's political culture seems to be passing away from a time when it was possible, if not profitable, to lionize the proletariat, advocate centralized economies and celebrate Marxist liberation movements. . . . Pantheon and its supporters may have to be dragged kicking and screaming into the present, but the fact is there are alternatives. If Mr. Schiffrin believes that people are still interested in what he and his editors are interested in, he can undertake a leveraged buyout, and own Pantheon himself" (Reuter, March 30, 1990). And the *New York Times*, which covered the story primarily on its business pages, sympathized with the plight of another publishing conglomerate unable to control its expenses.

Hill and Wang advertisement. (*New York Review of Books*, November 8, 1990).

Tasteless Jokes a few years ago), called the advertisement "in terribly bad taste" (Cohen, October 26, 1990). But what makes the ad copy especially interesting is that Rosenthal had recently come to Hill & Wang not from paperback publishing but from elite culture: he was the former head of Harvard University Press. One can only wonder how old-style bookmen like Alfred Knopf, Bennett Cerf, Harold Guinzberg, Cass Canfield, Kurt Wolff, Ian Ballantine, Victor Weybright, and Maxwell Perkins would have reacted.

The most insightful commentary on the Pantheon affair, however, appeared in "The International Magazine of Book Publishing," *Publishers Weekly*. In the March 9, 1990 issue, an impassioned and unprecedented editorial appeared. The text is full of what one might expect from a trade journal:

> Pantheon published nothing trivial or merely fashionable, nothing contemptible or money-grubbing; it was always a shining example, to those critics who complained of conglomerate publishing, of how sophisticated work could still flourish in its context. Now it seems as if perhaps those critics were right: that big-money publishing cannot tolerate important, exciting work that does not always reap instant profits. . . . In America today, the general consensus, as reflected in the media, is one of complacent, often jingoistic, enjoyment of power; the valuable task of the critic, and of the publisher of that critic, is always to question that complacency and power.

The author of the editorial has conveniently forgotten Pantheon's publication of *Lost, Lonely and Vicious: Postcards from the Great Trash Films* and *The Postcards That Ate My Brain*, but no matter. What is far more interesting is what follows the editorial. On the opposite page is a full-color advertisement for Rebecca Brandewyne's *Heartland*, featuring the requisite clinch illustration, and copy touting a "Triumphant Track Record," "a return to the territory her fans love best," and "An Unbeatable Multimedia Campaign," complete with thirty-second television spots, special mailings and bookmarks, a full-color poster for floor display, and a thirty-six-copy display rack. *Heartland* is published by Warner Books, a subsidiary of Warner Communications, itself a partner in Time Warner. Even more interesting is that following this editorial are sixteen pages touting the glories of the biggest money-making titles of 1989 followed by four pages bemoaning the 1989 titles that didn't make enough money. Tucked in between are two pages of the 1989 Literary Prizes. Need we wonder why Pantheon was, in a new publishing term, "newhoused"?

The democratization of print has occurred rapidly in the last twenty years as the mass audience was able to find a commodity — the paperback book — which could dominate the publishing of all commercial books. The transformation of print from a high-culture medium to an aspect of the entertainment industry has taken about one

EDITORIAL

A Sad Day for André Schiffrin—and for Publishing

The news that André Schiffrin is out at Pantheon and that the operations of that very valuable imprint are likely to be curtailed cannot help but appall anyone who believes in book publishing as ultimately something more than a plain act of commerce.

Virtually alone among major commercial imprints, Pantheon concentrated on publishing serious books for people seriously interested in the state of the contemporary world. It was one of the few imprints that regularly offered translations of significant fiction and political observation from overseas. And it was certainly the one house through which valuable critiques of many American assumptions, institutions and attitudes could regularly find an outlet. The compassionate documentaries of Studs Terkel, the towering anthropological work of Gunnar Myrdal, the penetrating social analysis of Barbara Ehrenreich, the significant writings of thinkers and political critics like Eric Hobsbawn, E. P. Thompson and Noam Chomsky formed a list of which any publisher could be proud. Nor was the list without humor and escape: the celebrated series of Sjowall/Wahloo Swedish detective thrillers, the poignant hilarity of Art Spiegelman's daring comic book *Maus*. Without Pantheon we would have lost significant books by major world writers like Anne Morrow Lindbergh, Simone de Beauvoir, Jean-Paul Sartre, Boris Pasternak, Mary Renault, Günter Grass, Marguerite Duras, John Berger. Currently admired novelists like Anita Brookner and Fay Weldon are among Pantheon's pillars, and the house has always been in the forefront of publishing on civil rights and minorities issues.

It is a 50-year publishing history that is, unhappily, all too rare in an American book business increasingly dedicated to the superficial and transitory. Pantheon published nothing trivial or merely fashionable, nothing contemptible or money-grubbing; it was always a shining example, to those critics who complained of conglomerate publishing, of how sophisticated work could still flourish in its context. Now it seems as if perhaps those critics were right: that big-money publishing cannot tolerate important, exciting work that does not always reap instant profits.

Robert Bernstein, who retired last year as head of Random, understood that, and was said to have made it clear that Pantheon would not be held to the same profit requirements as other parts of the company, because of the prestige its name carried throughout the serious reading world. Schiffrin's own name, a revered one in publishing through his celebrated exile father, was also one to conjure with. To see him at Frankfurt and other major world book events, engaged in earnest, often whimsically quizzical conversation with foreign authors, agents and publishers—he speaks half-a-dozen languages—was to understand the true meaning of the international fellowship of the book.

We hear that one of the complaints directed by current Random management against Pantheon, apart from its too-large list and unprofitability, was that it published too many left-wing books, and why could these not be better balanced by some right-wing ones? To suggest such a thing is to misunderstand completely the nature of the publishing act: true publishers publish what they believe in, for a readership of open-minded people. In America today, the general consensus, as reflected in the media, is one of complacent, often jingoistic, enjoyment of power; the valuable task of the critic, and of the publisher of that critic, is always to question that complacency and power. One is reminded of Harry Truman, accused of "giving the Republicans hell": "I just tell 'em the truth, and it seems like hell to them!" A great society should encourage, not seek to muffle, its critics—because it can only learn from them. And no, a true book publisher does not have to offer some spurious notion of "balance" to the customers.

It is being said, of course, that Pantheon will continue to exist, despite what we understand will be a heavily pared staff and list, and the departure of the man who has led it so inspiringly for nearly 30 years. But a house is more than just a name, it is an ethos. And the ethos that drove Pantheon, that made it a source of pride to anyone seeking to offer an example of the best in American publishing, was Schiffrin's.

We wish Fred Jordan well in his role at the head of what will remain of the imprint; but it is difficult not to feel, at this sad moment in American publishing history, that the Pantheon led by Andre Schiffrin is irreplaceable.

John F Baker

Editor-in-Chief

Publishers Weekly editorial and Warner Books advertisement (March 9, 1990, pp. 8–9).

A Triumphant Track Record:
- Rebecca Brandewyne is the author of three *New York Times* bestsellers—*And Gold Was Ours*, *Desire in Disguise*, and *The Outlaw Hearts*.
- There are 5 million copies of her books in print, including her most recent *Across a Starlit Sea* and *Upon a Moon-Dark Moor*.
- She is the winner of the 1988 *Romantic Times* award for Romantic Historical Writer of the Year and three-time winner of the *Affaire de Coeur* Silver Pen Award.
- Now in HEARTLAND, Brandewyne returns to the territory her fans love best—the American West—and creates an epic historical romance set in the lush wheatfields of post-Civil War Kansas.
- HEARTLAND has been chosen as an Alternate Selection of the Doubleday Book Club.

An Unbeatable Multimedia Campaign:
- Alluring 30-second TV spot to air in "Heartland America."
- Special publicity mailings, 4-color bookmarks (to fans and booksellers), local media, and autographings.
- 36-copy floor display with sizzling riser: 0-446-15110-6/$214.20 (In Canada: $250.20).
- Full-color poster for in-store display.

REBECCA BRANDEWYNE

IS ABOUT TO WIN AMERICA'S HEART... AND MAKE IT HER OWN

0-446-35580-1/$5.95 (In Canada: $6.95)

HEARTLAND

W WARNER BOOKS A Warner Communications Company ...THIS AUGUST IN PAPERBACK!

generation. Film and television needed only decades to become almost totally market-driven. A hundred years ago one could witness the sacralization of print in any number of places: in collections like Palgrave's Treasury, in the rising interest in collecting books as artifacts not as "investment instruments," in the defining of "proper" editions, in the rise of connoisseurs, in the hermeneutical approach of scholars, or in the professionalizing of readers into critics and of critics into academic departments. This transformation roughly paralleled the rise of "higher education," which continually provided the rationale that certain books deserved special treatment since they were receptacles of cultural wisdom.

Print was not alone, of course. The process of sacralization can be seen in music wherein certain genres became suspect while other became "classical." In painting, certain images were classed as "mauvais goût" while others became the "fine arts." Publishing was the most important form of communication, however, because it was the chief medium of shared experience before electronic transmission. The Victorian privileging of print was crucial because print constituted culture. The canon became a weapon, controlling not only what is in, but also what is out. Once "in," certain works needed to be protected; once "out," they needed to be systematically neglected. Rather like Eco's monastery, the library is a central cultural totem. It tells us what is in. And being "in," being on the shelf as it were, has both literal and figurative importance.

Two anecdotes from the end of the nineteenth century illustrate a seriousness about books as icons. Justin Winsor, a Harvard librarian, met President Charles Eliot in Harvard Yard. Eliot asked how things were going in the library, and Winsor is supposed to have replied, "All the books are on the shelf except one that Agassiz has, and I'm going after it now" (Alexander 1983:382). Or what the implications of this imaginary dialogue concerning New York's Lenox Library, published in *Life* magazine on January 17, 1884:

> *What is this?*
> This, dear, is the great Lenox Library.
> *But why are the doors locked?*
> To keep people out.
> *But why?*
> To keep the pretty books from being spoiled.
> *Why? Who would spoil the pretty books?*
> The public.

How?

By reading them.

To understand the demythologizing of print one must first realize that today the mass-market book is no longer a discrete object isolated in the hands first of the author, then publisher, then bookseller, and finally of reader, but is instead a point in the plasma mix of entertainment. In a not untypical example, HarperCollins in 1991 paid more than $20 million for all the rights to Jeffrey Archer's next three books, even though his previous books hardly warranted such an expenditure. Why? HarperCollins is a subsidiary of Rupert Murdoch's News Corporation and another subsidiary, Twentieth Century Fox, is having difficulties buying movie properties. In fact, books are called "units" by those who manufacture them, just as studio executives call their films "product" in the sense of "how much product is in the pipeline." In a reprint of his speech to book publishers, Oscar Dystel, the guiding force behind Bantam Books, first gives us the text: "Over the years the paperback revolution turned into an evolution with perhaps predictable results: Growth slowed. Annual unit sales stagnated and industry reactions to this situation were varied, to say the least." He continues the print version with a single-line footnote for the uninitiated: "1. Units are books" (1985:334).

The supreme "unit" is the "blockbuster." The blockbuster drives all parts of the entertainment machinery, be it in ink, on celluloid, or through pixels. The risks of producing this blockbuster are enormous, every bit as unpredictable as finding a movie that will gross over $100 million, or a television show that will make it into syndication. Of the 55,000 books published each year, only 200 will sell more than 200,000 copies. Only .008 percent of the 800,000 books in print are on the bestseller list at any one time. But the hunt for the bestseller is intense because success here means winning the lottery. The best-selling book, the franchise movie, the television series that makes it into reruns are the brass rings of show business. They now support the business, whether publishing house, studio, or network. Blockbuster sequences become so powerful that they float from medium to medium with no anchor except finally at the bank. Movies are made from books, books are made from movies, television makes movies from books inspired by movies. The goal of all participants is not only to get into the food chain of entertainment but to have franchise rights to part of it.

Part of the transformation of books from the private property of an elite to relatively minor aspects of show business has to do with how they are fabricated. To paraphrase Bismarck on the law, it is with books as with sausage: if you like the stuff it's best not to watch it being put together. The average novel or nonfiction book costs about $1.50 to $2.00 to manufacture. The cost of composition, typesetting, and jacket design, as well as fixed costs like office space, editorial salaries, overhead, advertising and promotion, add perhaps 5 to 7 percent. In the last decade, however, great advances have been made in typesetting and printing. Electronic devices can "capture" the author's keystrokes, and a compositor using programs like Telos can hyphenate, justify, and paginate sixty thousand of those keystrokes in less than six seconds. A 360-page book can be formatted in less than a minute. Such programs can cast off a book in half a dozen different "specs" in a few minutes: deciding page breaks; avoiding widows, orphans, and hyphenations on page breaks; and formatting final pages. All of these procedures previously demanded capital-consuming, labor-intensive typesetting.

Once the project is fed into the computers driving the printers, the speed is still more startling. Hardcover books are produced more than ten times faster than they were a decade ago. The change is still greater with paperbacks. The changeover to mass-produced books has meant that plants must be completely "conveyorized" from gathering to finishing, including trimming, staining, jacketing, stacking, and packing-off. With Kolbus Compact 2000 casing-in machines, print runs can be increased tenfold and start-up time can be cut in half. The automatic sewers are computerized, as are the guillotines, high-speed shrink wrappers, and even Printronic labelers which crack and peel labels read by optical scanners to show where they are to be shipped. Two hundred and fifty books can be produced in a minute, or 10,000 an hour and, with two shifts of eight hours, 200,000 books a day can be printed. Paperbacks are much faster. The three largest printers (Arcata Graphics in Buffalo, Offset Paperback Manufacturers in Dallas, Pennsylvania, and Drueger Ringier in Dresden, Tennessee) have Opticopy machines for automatic page imposition, Misomex automatic platemaking machines, superfast Strachan and Henshaw presses, Bickerstaff cartoners, Bobst and Kluge presses to make covers, plus Steinemann rollers for UV coating. These machines may sound like a regiment of German panzers, but they can produce up to two million books per day. From start to finish, a mass-market paperback can be turned around in five days. Little wonder we got the *Pentagon Papers* in just over a week.

Ten monks working every day, all day, could not have finished the *Pentagon Papers* — ever. They would have died first. The old letterpress clunkers printed sheets ninety-six pages on a side, 1,400 sheets an hour. The web press could print twenty-five times faster. These machines could not keep up with demand. Books took months to print. But there is a downside to current productivity. These presses work twenty-four hours a day, every day. They need continuous use to be cost-effective. To them there is little difference between a print run of 100,000 and 500,000 copies — just minutes. They can, and have, glutted the market on the production side. Books are made like magazines, but they still sell like books — slowly. As cheap as they are to make, they are expensive to sell.

The book that costs $2.00 to make is sold to bookstores and wholesalers at an average discount off the retail price of 45 to 47 percent, meaning that the retailer pays the publisher about $11.00 for a book to be sold at $20.00. The ratio between the cost of hardcover and paperback books is currently less than four to one. A few years ago it was about seven to one, so hardcover prices will certainly have to be raised to over $20.00. Moreover, since books can be returned for credit, the cover price must include this cost, because almost 40 percent of hardcover books are now returned to the warehouse. The resolution, of course, would be for publishers to refuse returns, but as Harcourt Brace Jovanovich found out when they tried precisely that, the retailers headed them off at the pass by refusing to take delivery. So with all costs subtracted, including the author's royalty (which is based on the cover price and ranges from 10 to 15 percent), the publisher is lucky to make $1.00 on each book. In fact, most books make no money on the first printing. Profit comes from subsequent printings, reprint rights for paperback editions, and especially sale of "performance rights" elsewhere on the midway.

As Richard Snyder, chairman of Simon & Schuster, recently said with no trace of irony: "In a certain sense, we are the software of the television and movie media" (Whiteside 1980:70). As compared to software in the computer industry (which can be judged by its application to a series of tasks), the software that publishing produces is judged by the number of times it can be successfully redistributed in the loop. Best-selling books have a multigenerational life: first, teasing excerpts in magazines, then hardcover publication, then film sale, possibly a tradepaper edition, then the mass-market paperback, the release of the film, then back to the presses with the publishing of the edition tied to the movie, complete with scenes from the picture, then the television series, and, if the jackpot is struck, the endless merchandising of trinkets. Exploiting niches is suitable not only for fiction. In 1978 Richard Nixon's *Memoirs* had a regular $19.95 edition, two autographed editions (one deluxe for $50 and a "presentation" copy limited to 2,500 at $250), then a trade paper at . . . and so on.

The allure of books as entertainment ventures has not gone unnoticed. As the prescient Oscar Dystel observed decades ago: "We are witnessing a melding phenomenon in trade publishing, where the industry is moving from a horizontal, stratified business into a vertical, integrated *totality;* the increase and intensity of this melding process may prove to be the greatest change of all" (1985:316). Publishing has "gone vertical." And in so doing it has changed forever what it can publish and whom it attracts as consumers. The "verticalizing" of once fiercely independent publishing houses into the "literary-industrial complex" first occurred in the 1960s and was done in the name of the then-buzzword "synergy." Between 1958 and 1970 there were 307 mergers, of which 224 were mergers among publishers. Thirty-three involved other communications companies, with only 22 others involving companies outside the industry. Book publishing companies, which never had much of a history as cash cows, were soon treated as cash pigs — fattened up quickly to be sold off.

In a sense the consolidation at the upper end of the publishing trade started in October 1959 when Bennett Cerf went to Charles Allen of Allen & Company and offered to sell 30 percent of Random House. Cerf certainly knew what "going public" meant. Of his trip to Charles Allen he wrote in his memoir, *At Random:*

> This marked a big change, since the minute you go public, outsiders own some of your stock and you've got to make periodic reports to them. You owe your investors dividends and profits. Instead of working for yourself and doing what you damn please, willing to risk a loss on something you want to, if you're any kind of honest man, you feel a real responsibility to your stockholders. (1977:277)

This statement was to prove prophetic. Soon CBS acquired Holt, Rinehart & Winston, Praeger, Popular Library, and Fawcett. Xerox acquired Ginn & Company and R. R. Bowker. Bobbs-Merrill went to

ITT and so forth. The family-owned houses became part of industrial families. To some degree conglomeration was the result of capital gains taxes and federal estate taxes, and to some degree the realization that it would take even deeper pockets to stay in the game. Ironically, the price of fending off a hostile offer was often worse than being taken over. Harcourt Brace Jovanovich was so weakened by taking on debt to keep Robert Maxwell at bay in 1987 that it was almost taken over by General Cinema in 1991 and is still perilously close to Chapter 11. Scribner's had been run by a Scribner, Putnam's by a Putnam, Doubleday by a Doubleday, Simon & Schuster by a Simon and a Schuster, and even when no immediate family was left, as with Harper & Row, Houghton Mifflin, and Little, Brown & Company, they were closely held houses. However, even they were soon tucked into the folds of larger and more powerful entities. There were exceptions, notably Farrar, Straus & Giroux, W. W. Norton, and Houghton Mifflin, but the general rule was merge, be devoured, or go under. A North Point Press usually goes south.

Industry centralization also did not go unnoticed. In a statement that indeed may prove Shelley's point that artists are the "hierophants of unapprehended knowledge," the Author's Guild voiced alarm in the late 1970s:

> We have seen mergers in every imaginable permutation — hardcover houses merging with each other; hardcover houses merging with paperback houses; the combination thus formed being taken over, in turn, by huge entertainment complexes, involving radio-television networks and motion picture companies. And in some cases, perhaps most distressing of all, we have seen the business of choosing and purveying books, traditionally the province of more or less dedicated book men with one eye on profit and the other on literary and social values, falling under the control of business men with no prior interest in books — men, it has sometimes seemed to us, cursed like the Cyclops with having only a single eye, and that eye not trained on literary or social value but steadfastly on the bottom line of a company's financial statement. (Powell 1985:214)

But their words, as Shelley might have continued, "died upon the hearth." The mergers continued apace because of a business climate free of government regulations and weakness in the dollar which attracted the Europeans. In the next consolidation the paperback houses went, absorbed into the entertainment industry. MCA, Gulf

+ Western, Times-Mirror, Time Inc., and Warner Communications soon accounted for almost 90 percent of mass paperback sales. As William Sarnoff, chairman of Warner Books, predicted at the annual booksellers' convention in 1987, "Soon the convention will be held in the office of the lone remaining publisher" (McDowell, May 25, 1987).

Why did all this consolidation happen so quickly? How did it happen that while six major houses reaped 50 percent of the adult book revenues in 1983, the same six now gather in 60 percent and the process is accelerating? By 1980, eleven hardcover trade publishers were responsible for 71 percent of sales. In both hard- and softcover publishing 2 percent of the publishers do 75 percent of the titles, and the top third of the industry is responsible for 99 percent of what is printed. The publishing business has moved closer to the Hollywood oligarchy in which a half-dozen companies hustle for the same product. Once again, Oscar Dystel was one of the first to see the future. In the Bowker Memorial Lecture on November 25, 1980, he explained the inevitable vulgarization of publishing, "Today, mass-market paperback publishing has invaded the domain of hardcover publishing" (1985:210). The paperback is driving the market. What was once a carnival attraction — the paperbound edition — now runs the bigtop.

The dominance of the paperback is attributable to such matters as changes in manufacture, tax laws governing inventories, contract shifts between author and reprint publisher, and simple economics in which marginal profit returns are higher on a $4.00 unit that costs $2.50 and sells 2 million than a $20.00 unit that costs $8.00 and sells 100,000. The paperback book has been the linchpin of most of the modern shifts in the industry, whether it be the rise of the bookstore chains, the dominance of agents, the decline of editors, the shift in formula content, or the subsuming of publishing into the entertainment industry. One can see all the forces of the vulgarizing process at work, first, in the history of the paperback industry and, second, in the fortunes of one paperback house, New American Library. For both the industry and this particular house initially did attempt to preserve high-culture standards but were soon forced by the demands of the market to mass produce books for a mass audience.

The transformation of candles into shoes could be said to have started on June 19, 1939, when Robert de Graff, an erstwhile salesman with Doubleday, placed this advertisement in the daily *New York Times*. With financial help and advice from Richard Simon, Lincoln

Pocket Books advertisement (*New York Times*, June 19, 1939).

Schuster, and Leon Shimkin of Simon & Schuster, De Graff did a market sampling with a questionnaire covering fifty-two titles. Once he had narrowed the choice to ten titles, he printed 2,300 copies of Pearl Buck's *The Good Earth*. They sold quickly. De Graff was convinced that New Yorkers, at least, would buy twenty-five-cent versions of familiar titles. So he printed ten thousand copies of ten titles that were either in the public domain or for which he could buy rights for about $500. De Graff cut production costs in half by borrowing the publisher's plates and reducing the books to pocket size. He used a new innovation, the "perfect" binding system of glues, rather than the more costly sewing to the spine. His real breakthrough, however, was that he distributed these books like magazines through the American News Company.[2]

De Graff was a visionary. Not only was he willing to let the market decide what he should publish, not only did he know that these books should be treated like magazines and not sold in bookstores, but he also recognized the interactive power of media to generate audience long before anyone could pronounce "synergy." One medium does not deplete the stories of another; it works to enlarge the audience for shared stories. Of his list of ten books, four became movies within two years: *Lost Horizon*, *Wuthering Heights*, *The Way of All Flesh*, and *Topper* (which had two sequels by 1944) and two other books, *The Bridge of San Luis Rey* and *Bambi*, would become movies after the war. *Wuthering Heights* with Laurence Olivier and Merle Oberon was a blockbuster at the box office. The movie dramatically increased print sales and showed that "you've read the book, now see the movie" could work both ways. In fact, books seemed to sell especially well in retail outlets adjacent to downtown movie theaters. De Graff also predicted the powerful allure of self-help manuals. While *Wake Up and Live* did respectably well, Dale Carnegie's *How to Win Friends and Influence People* and Dr. Spock's baby book would become money pumps. The publishing of Shakespeare in an inexpensive edition (a sop to De Graff's critics) prefigured the educational market, as *Bambi*, published to see if there was a market for juveniles, announced what is now almost a quarter of the entire book market. While De Graff had one detective novel by Agatha Christie, he overlooked the romance

2. Each Pocket Library book carried the bespectacled Gertrude-the-Kangaroo logo which De Graff had commissioned for $50 (and which would gradually change over the years). In a sign of what was to come, the eyeglasses were eliminated so no one would think that these books were too serious.

and science fiction genres. With this backlist Pocket Books was guaranteed success, and paid for it in the American way. It was bought out by Marshall Field in 1944, who then sold out to Leon Shimkin and James Jacobson in 1957, who took it public only to be taken over in 1975 by Simon & Schuster, which was itself subsumed by Gulf + Western, a hodgepodge conglomerate of companies producing inter alia auto parts, designer clothing, and cutting tools, and which has now been re-formed into Paramount Communications.

While Pocket Books was getting started in the late 1930s, Allen Lane was trying to find shelf space in the United States for his Penguin Books. Quite by accident (the wife of a Woolworth executive made the suggestion) Lane discovered that he could sell color-coded paper editions of classics in England for six pence in five-and dime stores. Would the Americans also be interested in belles lettres on the cheap? He knew he had to be careful to distinguish his high-culture books from penny-dreadful pulp and so declared his policy in promotional flyers: "The dominant motive in the firm's endeavor is to provide good reading. . . . For those who lack an habitual appetite for reading, Penguins have nothing to offer: they do not associate with those products which aim to excite and contaminate the mind with sensation and which could be more aptly listed in a register of poisons than in a library. But for each civilized and balanced person there are Penguins to suit each taste." The Penguin philosophy of "avoiding vulgarity" was touted in promotional material written by a straight-faced Gilbert Highet, who said in well-publicized praise, "Not one of the Penguin books has a cover which emphasizes the fact that human beings are mammals. On the contrary, they treat us like intellectuals." For the time being, at least.

It was those covers, however, that partially caused the rupture with the American branch started by Ian Ballantine. In England, Penguin covers were nothing if not chaste. Green covers were for thrillers, blue meant travel and adventure, cherry for biography, yellow was miscellaneous (and used carefully lest it imply pulp) and light blue for educational, especially for science. When Lane saw the American Penguins, he did not approve of either the covers or the emphasis on popular fiction. "Commodities with garish and sensational eye-appeal," he said. "The contents of the book . . . were relatively unimportant, what mattered was that its lurid exterior should ambush the customer." Lane fired Ballantine and replaced him with Kurt Enoch and Victor Weybright. But even new management could not bridge the cultural gap. You need lurid and gaudy covers if you want to sell books to Americans, they told him. Yanks were accustomed to this, what with their tradition of pulp fiction and wild west shows. Also, the war had made it expensive to ship books from England. So Lane sold out.

His protégés did remarkably well in the business. As we will see, Weybright and Enoch went on to found New American Library which itself, after a typical series of buyouts and exchanges, is again part of Penguin. Meanwhile, Ian and Betty Ballantine, fired from American Penguin, founded Bantam, initially sharing ownership with Grosset & Dunlap (itself owned by Random House), Charles Scribner's Sons, Little, Brown & Company, Harper's, and Book-of-the-Month Club, before going off to found the house that bears their name. Ballantine knew how to distribute by using the Curtis Circulation Company which handled magazines, and how to choose titles appropriate for magazine racks. Bantam published such works as the *Mad Magazine* books, fantasy literature, the Tolkien oeuvre, movie tie-in books like those of *Rocky* and *Star Wars*, and subjects often supplied by the incomparable master of the nonbook, Bernard Geis. Intext bought the Ballantines out in 1973 and then sold part to Random House, which was folded into Advance Publications, owned by the Newhouses. Bantam had also been traded around like a playground marble, finally becoming part of the Bertelsmann Publishing Group of West Germany. One can see from their corporate alliances that these softcover publishers, in contrast to their hardcover brethren, were always treated with mild disdain. They were, after all, reprint houses, vulgarizers of an elite tradition, putting the sacramental host in the palms of Everyman.[3]

---

3. The other paperback houses have had equally complicated corporate lives, although not such illustrious pedigrees. Fawcett Publications was started by Wilford H. Fawcett, who had made his initial foray into publishing with *Captain Billy's Whiz-Bang*, a collection of off-color jokes he had heard in the army, *True Confessions*, and *Woman's Day*. Fawcett had always wanted to publish books, but his contract to distribute the books of New American Library along with his magazines prohibited competition. Once that contract expired in 1950, Fawcett launched Gold Medal Books, paying top dollar ($2,000 guarantee) for long press runs (200,000 copies were standard) of "category fiction" — first detective and western stories (with glorious covers by Al Allard), then plantation romances, and the John D. MacDonald suspense thrillers. Fawcett did so well that he went from being a reprinter of jokes for soldiers to a major shareholder in CBS, which bought the business in 1977.

Dell Publishing was also started by a man once described as "the man who made money guessing what the lowbrows want." Like Fawcett, George T. Delacorte founded a magazine empire with *Ballyhoo*, a joke collection, then published such magazine titles as *Modern*

Why is it more interesting to spend an evening with this book than with a beautiful woman?

A DELL BOOK

A COMPARISON TEST CHART

BOOK ⬇   WOMAN ⬇

49%		TEXTURE		100%
100%		AVAILABILITY		2-100% (depending on competition)
60,000		NUMBER OF WORDS		11
97%		LAUGHTER PRODUCTION		3% average
0		MISERABILITY (capacity to make you feel terrible)		73%
80%		INSOMNIABILITY (ability to keep you up all night, one way or another)		79%
100%		OVERCOATABILITY (ease of placing in overcoat pocket)		11%
25¢		COST		$45 for dinner (wine and cabs not included)

Dell advertisement for paperbacks: "What a Body!" 1951.

With few exceptions, most of the publishers who followed Pocket Books in the 1940s and 1950s had experience in the magazine, not the book, business. They knew how to market the carnival of titles in the

---

Screen, Inside Detective, Looney Tunes, Walt Disney's Comics, and *Screen Romance.* He entered book publishing primarily because he knew how to distribute magazines.

Dell struck paydirt with *Peyton Place* in 1957, which allowed the company to take over Western Publishing, thereby achieving the ultimate dream of the modern entertainment industry. For a time Dell controlled production, printing, and distribution. Because of the success of Dell paperbacks, Delacorte even took the next step and founded Dial and Delacorte as hardcover outlets for paperback bestsellers. Although a big fish by midcentury, Dell itself was swallowed in 1976 by the Doubleday whale which in turn was consumed by the German behemoth Bertelsmann AG.

wire racks down at the drugstore. They knew that the profitable place to be was side by side with the throwaway magazines. Dell and Fawcett were among the largest periodical publishers, and Ace, Avon, Berkley, Popular Library, and Pyramid were all directed by men with mass-circulation magazine experience. While most paperback houses evolved from pulp publishing, they all ended up in popular entertainment conglomerates. With only one exception, they are now subsidiaries of companies managed by executives whose careers depend on quarterly reports of per-share earnings. Warner Books, evolved from Paperback Library, is now a division of Warner Communications, part of Time Warner. Ace Books was sold in 1956 to Hill & Wang, a division of Charter Communications, part of Grosset & Dunlap, a subsidiary of Filmways. Berkley, which started with pocket-sized magazines *Chic* and *New*, was purchased by G. P. Putnam's and was then bought in 1975 by MCA, where it shares space with Jove, once Pyramid, itself bought by Harcourt Brace Jovanovich and sold in 1974. The Putnam Berkley Group is now but a speck in the universe of Japanese electronics giant Matsushita, which acquired MCA in 1990. Avon, founded just after Pocket Books survived a fierce legal battle with Gertrude-the-Kangaroo (the court ordered a name change from Avon Pocket Size Books but let the style and format stay the same), was a creation of American News Company, a magazine distributor. Avon, now famous for historical romances by Rosemary Rodgers and Kathleen Woodiwiss, is part of the Hearst Corporation, which also owns William Morrow. None of these publishing histories is important in itself. But together they show that the paperback, although started as a reprinter of high culture, soon found a product so lucrative that its production was controlled not by editorial gatekeepers but by bottom-line accountants.

Certainly one of the most interesting developments of the 1980s has been the rise of Harlequin Books. Started by a one-time soap salesman for Procter & Gamble, W. Lawrence Heisey, Harlequin "did for paperbacks what L'eggs did for panty hose." Heisey established a publisher brand name over individual authorship, and that brand name was Harlequin Romances. Again, distribution was the key. The first novels were placed inside boxes of Bio-Aid laundry detergent. Then in 1973 Harlequin *gave* two million copies of *Dark Star* to dealers to be sold at fifteen cents each — pure profit. Harlequin hoped the books would be addictive; that once women started to read them, they would buy according to the number on the cover, not by the title.[4]

A standardized product is offered in the same form each week, just like a television series or a movie sequel. The key is not to offer the new, but rather to supply the known. Harlequins even come in their own racks, and so don't have to compete with secondary titles. With lower-than-usual cover prices and higher-than-usual profit margins, they were the fastest-growing paperback publisher in North America by the late 1970s. The 23,000 titles usually sell 80 percent of each 500,000 print run. Harlequin now pays about 140 women a standard royalty scale to churn out the same story about sixty times a month. A young virgin falls in love with a man of means, survives a tempestuous courtship characterized by misunderstanding and uncertainty, and is finally happily married. Sex is by implication (even the covers are subdued); in fact, there is no mention of premarital sex. Romance triumphs. As Heisey says, "We make no pretense to publishing litera- ture. We are in the light entertainment business, selling a branded consumer product to women." In 1990 Harlequin sold more than 200 million of this "branded consumer product," accounting for more than 40 percent of all mass-market paperback sales (Stanley 1991:13).

Whereas Harlequin makes no pretense "to publishing literature" and hence is at ease with its position in the "light entertainment business," the history of New American Library makes a provocative counterpart. The one thing the founders of NAL did not want was the one thing necessary for survival — a mass audience. But in the world of modern show business there are two possible routes — follow the traffic or be run off the road. NAL attempted to follow the middle course, to (as its slogan proclaimed) provide "Good Reading for the Millions," or in the words of cofounder Victor Weybright, to achieve both "lucre and luster."

In 1948 Victor Weybright and Kurt Enoch left Penguin Books to start their own firm, which they grandly called the New American

4. Almost twenty years later Harlequin's strategy remains the same. Mike Muoio, an executive, comments on their new campaign: "We can't afford to do the whole country at once, so we have to carve it up in pieces. We're going to do a bang-up job. Things like radio, television, in-store promotion, giveaways, giving books to people with a five dollar purchase, put the books in their hands, then see how they perform thereafter. You've got to let people know. Look at the way shampoo is sold — if you think you have a better shampoo, you give people a sample of it, you give the coupons, you advertise it. We're taking the same packaged-goods approach" (Jones 1990:23).

Harlequin advertisement, 1989.

Library of World Literature. At Penguin they already had experienced the hostility of hardcover house editors to publishing the classics in paperback. A particularly revelatory instance: on July 25, 1946, at a party at the Waldorf to celebrate George Bernard Shaw's ninetieth birthday, Weybright tried to distribute free paperback copies of *Major Barbara* to the assembled panjandrums. He was told not to do it or Dodd, Mead (Shaw's American hard-cover publisher) would leave. When Howard Lewis, editor of Dodd, Mead, rose to address the party, he opened his remarks, "Speaking for Shaw's conventional publishers," and then, glowering at Weybright, "not the Horn & Hardart variety. . . ." Point taken. Hardcover publishers offered haute cuisine; paperbackers served junk food. To succeed, NAL would have to be acceptable both to the stuffy publishers who controlled the copyrights and to the buying public who were not intimidated by this automat approach to bookbuying. As Kurt Enoch wrote in a brochure extolling the enterprise: "The peculiar services of the book to society have seemed to derive from the fact that it has not been a 'mass' medium. We now seek to make it one. The fundamental problem of statesmanship, from the social viewpoint, in the paperbound book industry is thus to achieve a mass audience while preserving the special virtues of books" (Tebbel 1987:429).

To achieve both the mass audience and the "special virtues of books," NAL imitated Penguin's policy of separating original fiction from nonfiction and literary classics. The Penguin series became NAL's "Signet Books" and sold for twenty-five cents, while the Pelican series became NAL's "Mentor Books" and cost a dime more. The paperback reprinters were still petitioners, bowing and scraping before the major houses, paying a one-cent royalty to be divided between author and hardback publisher. The battle for profits was acute, especially after World War II. Paper was in short supply, and NAL had to compromise its principles. To hold the retail prices at twenty-five and thirty-five cents, they cut text to stay within a 150- to 190-page limit. In typical high-culture language to describe low-culture profits, these books were marketed as "special editions abridged for the modern reader." In the Virtue-vs.-Vulgar, Luster-vs.-Lucre battle, Vulgar/Lucre was edging ahead.

There were no secrets to paperback success. Volume was crucial, and volume depended on distribution. NAL's initial strength was its ability to distribute books because of its exclusive contract with Fawcett. NAL books were simply included in the Fawcett "bundle" delivered weekly on consignment to magazine wholesalers. What the distributor didn't sell, he returned. The success of mass-market paperbacks rested on the willingness of some 800 local middlemen who supplied the 100,000 or so newsstands, drugstores, and variety stores to find retail space. The use of national distributors like Fawcett Publications to put a monthly list of softcovers into wire racks was a crucial step. In the battle for rack space, the end-of-the-line local businessman had nothing to say about what came in the bundle, but he could decide what to display. If books came along with important magazines, they had a better chance of being displayed. The more titles exhibited, the better the sales. The retailer was happy, but such bulk can be a problem for the publisher because of returns. So, in a Darwinian metaphor, publishers either produced a lot of progeny,

Delivery truck for United News Company of Philadelphia, 1948 (Thomas Bonn Collection).

many of which died unsold, or cared for a few very well and let them wait until they sold. NAL tried in every possible way to protect their products. They displayed books by title arrangement, then by publisher imprint, then by subject and genre. They experimented with letting local dealers select what to display, and even sold directly to larger retail outlets, bypassing the national and independent wholesalers in what became known as "direct sales."

NAL succeeded by producing and distributing in bulk. Although some titles might languish, others might survive, thus making it easier for the next generation. By maintaining a steady flow of books, NAL assured the retailers they could count on publishers as they counted on the producers of cosmetics or sundries. Every week there would be new product. Soon they were reprinting the works of such elite authors as Faulkner, Lawrence, and Joyce, as well as up-and-comers like Norman Mailer, James Jones, Truman Capote, Gore Vidal, William Styron, Flannery O'Connor, and J. D. Salinger. NAL made a special effort to encourage young writers by reproducing their work in a money-losing periodical, *New World Writing*, and seeking reprint rights to the works of such black writers as Ralph Ellison,

James Baldwin, and Richard Wright. Mentor and Signet were associated with the best that had been published. By 1958 they had published six Nobel Prize winners and six Pulitzer Prize winners. Weybright, true to his desire to balance "lucre and luster," was also paying a retainer to Harvard professor Howard Mumford Jones for ideas on what to print in midlist editions of seventy-five thousand copies. In 1950 the editorial headquarters moved from lower Fifth Avenue to Madison Avenue into the same building with the venerable house of Alfred A. Knopf and within easy walking distance of Random House, Scribner's, and Simon & Schuster. Tiffany's might not like to have Woolworth's next door, but proximity certainly helped the dime store.

For economic ballast NAL was also publishing Mickey Spillane and Erskine Caldwell. Soon the ballast was edging out the quality cargo. It took no close reading of the ledger to see where the money lay. You could pay the rent with the classics, but you could buy the building with a few bestsellers. So it made sense and money to pay Norman Mailer $35,000 for *The Naked and the Dead*, then $100,000 to James Jones for *From Here to Eternity*, and then hundreds of thousands of dollars for the works of writers like Mario Puzo. The point when lucre overpowered luster came when Weybright offered Irving Wallace $25,000 for two projects, *The Chapman Report* and *The Twenty-Seventh Wife*. Weybright then went upstairs with *The Chapman Report* galleys to Alfred Knopf. Knopf harrumphed. He was not interested in a preassembled nonbook on the fictional sex lives of a group of American women. After fruitless attempts to find a hardcover printer, Weybright finally struck a deal with Simon & Schuster and MGM studios. The project made a great deal of money as it passed through various media. It made a great stink as well. *Time* magazine (August 22, 1960) and Malcolm Cowley in the *Reporter* (July 7, 1960) denounced the whole enterprise as typical of the era of the "hack job." The editor thinks up a project, hires an author for the print version, sells the movie rights to a studio — everything is backward, they complained. How lowbrow. Weybright claimed this wasn't so. Wallace even wrote a book, *The Writing of One Novel*, to show it wasn't so, but who cared? Too much money had been made. NAL was now in the proprietary publishing business. The corporation would buy all the rights, farm out the hardcover, but retain paperbound as well as foreign rights. "Buying backwards" became commonplace by the 1970s. Soon NAL started a West Coast movie and television office called "Literary Projects" to dovetail with the entertainment media.

Where there is money, there is Wall Street, and where there is Wall Street, there are "deals." In 1961 Times-Mirror, publisher of the *Los Angeles Times*, wanted to add to its "book-publishing group" and bought NAL. True to form, it moved the senior editors out of their paneled Madison Avenue offices into a corporate highrise, encouraged "buying backwards" by forming an NAL hardcover division, found a new Mickey Spillane in Ian Fleming, turned away from any pretense of "Good Reading for the Millions" to "Good Bottom Line for the Shareholders," and began publishing such blockbusters as Erica Jong's *Fear of Flying*. Off went the elbow patches, on came the green visors. Then, after all the senior editors had departed in bitterness, Times-Mirror sold the company to private investors who bought E. P. Dutton to cover both sides of the backwards buy.

In 1971 Sidney Kramer, president of NAL, distributed a brochure at the annual convention of the American Booksellers Association (ABA) with a "Letter from the Publisher." He waxed enthusiastic about "the whole idea of putting expensive books into inexpensive formats and marketing them everywhere," which had "become a part of the fabric of the lives of several generations, with profound implications for the emotional and intellectual development of the American people." As he was enthusing, NAL's contribution to intellectual and emotional well-being included Erich Segal's *Love Story* at the top of its list, with Adele Davis' *Let's Eat Right to Keep Fit* close behind. In 1986 Penguin Publishing acquired NAL, folding it into the Pearson conglomerate, thus ending the thirty-eight-year separation. The house that published Erskine Caldwell, Mickey Spillane, Irving Wallace, and Ian Fleming, as well as Joyce, Lawrence, Faulkner, and Shakespeare, had learned its lesson: it now publishes the novels of Stephen King.

As NAL's history demonstrates, the more books resembled magazines, the more profitable they became. As Ian Ballantine reminisced on the fiftieth anniversary of paperback publishing:

> A sad fact that both we at Penguin and the people at Pocket had to face was that there were only some 1,500 bookstores in all the United States at that time, Of these, only 500 had really good credit ratings. Americans read magazines. Those addicted to books got their reading matter largely from public libraries and the lending libraries that rented the latest popular titles for a few cents a day. So from the start

distribution was the major problem, and solving it the key to success. (1989:46)

If the three secrets of real estate are Location, Location, Location, then the three secrets of bookselling are Distribution, Distribution, Distribution. In the "old days" of hardcover publishing when the high-culture gatekeepers were solidly in place, the bookstore owner used to call up and say to his customers, "The new John Hersey is in. I've read it. You'll love it. Shall I hold you a copy?" Now no one calls, but paperback books are all over the place — in the supermarket, the drugstore, the airport, the truckstop, the convenience store. Wherever magazines once were, there shall books now be. They are, however, all the same titles. Twenty years ago "IDs," independent distributors, did 80 percent of mass-market paperback distribution; now they do only about 40 percent. The IDs once had all their retail business in specific areas from airport to drugstore; now they service only the top of the list with brand-name products in high-volume food stores. The large warehouse wholesalers, called "rack jobbers," do the rest. As publisher Leonard Shatzkin observed:

> It was the *distribution* of books to the retail network rather than the laborious *sale* to each retailer, title by title, copy by copy, that was the magazine wholesaler's contribution to popular paperback publishing. Unfortunately, neither the publisher nor the wholesaler supplied a second ingredient. Unless the privilege to put books into retail outlets without question results in putting in the right numbers of the right titles, adjusted according to the subtle variations and changes in demand from place to place and time to time, the privilege will become a trap instead of an opportunity. The strength of the magazine distributor has been his ability to get the retail space; his weakness is that he doesn't know with sufficient discrimination what to put there. (1982:212)

As many publishers are still discovering, selling books as magazines is harder than selling books as books. Magazine inventories are easy to track. Each publication has a space in the rack and if you want to know how many of the September issue to order, you simply see how many of August are still unsold and do the subtraction. However, each book is different. The paperback must sell twice: once to the independent wholesaler or retail bookseller, and then again to the bookbuyer. As with the movie and television industry, you sell to the viewer but you must first sell through the local theater/station/bookstore. If you don't make the first sale you don't get your product on the shelf. Here is where the blockbuster, displayed in slots labeled "#1 bestseller," "#2 bestseller," and so on, resolves the problem of inventory control. Very often the labels bear no relationship to the bestseller lists of the *New York Times* or *Publishers Weekly*, but are a retailing device like the dating of magazines a month in advance. Rarely do you see an empty slot — it is filled with whatever the distributor has on hand.

The publicity surrounding large advances to authors, elaborate book covers, and movie tie-ins are for the distributor as well as for the customer. When a paperback house pays $3.5 million for *Princess Daisy*, much of this is to impress the publisher's own sales reps, the distributors, the truck drivers, and the drugstore owners, as well as the ultimate readers. Knowing that a book has received a big advance is like studios bragging about how much they have invested in a movie. Such knowledge moves the product along past people who cannot estimate its value and who associate price with worth. When total nonbooks, like the novelization of *F.I.S.T.* or *Ode to Billy Joe*, receive $400,000 and $250,000 respectively, you can be assured that part of this price is an attempt to get it on the rack. Dell, now a subsidiary of a German media conglomerate, Bertelsmann AG, paid $12 million for a not-yet-written Ken Follett novel. Assuming 350,000 sales of hardcover at $22.95 and two million in paper at $6.95, the *best* it could do is break even. Why would they pay so much? A spokesman said it was partly to be sure Dell is talked about.

If mass-market books behave like magazines, they aspire to the condition of greeting cards. Greeting cards went from a shabby display in corner candy stores to the now-glamorous display with genre categories and with ever-shifting inventory. Want to express your feelings for a friend who has broken a leg? There's a card. Broken a toe? A toenail? A happy Halloween for your stepgrandfather-in-law? Don't worry. There's a card. Once Hallmark and American Greetings had gained direct control over inventory and distribution, they could market for every situation. Like books, they are continually shifted around from niche to niche.

Such saturation of audience sectors is risky. If you don't make the sale with a greeting card, or a paperback book, the product returns to your door like a grimy teenager. As Alfred Knopf used to say of book publishing: "Gone today, here tomorrow." At the time he said this, returns were averaging about 2 percent. Returns are now the single most perplexing problem faced by the industry. About 450 new paperbacks appear each month, and few stores can display even 40 percent of these. Most bookstores receive only about 10 percent of the entire monthly run of books. Those books that make it over the threshold into the rack stay only a few months. If unsold, they are stripped and covers returned for credit. An "acceptable" rate of return is 35 percent, but for many companies it is well over 50 percent. Recall that Harlequin averages 25 percent and you see why category publishing is so attractive to publishers. In 1953, the first year paperback publishers really glutted the market, 175 million books piled up in warehouses and had to be pulped. More than twenty years later, the industry still had not learned the importance of controlled distribution of all product, not just specific titles. Over 100 million paperpacks continue to be destroyed yearly.[5]

The lesson has not been learned because there is still good money to be made by some, even considering the great waste of the whole. The key to success for some publishers is to skip the distributor. Movie studios are learning this lesson by selling videocassettes directly to customers, and television producers are almost learning it from pay-per-view broadcasting. The distributor gets a 20 to 25 percent discount, but the publisher gives 40 percent to the bookseller if they are "dealing direct." Publishers routinely give chains like Woolworth and K-Mart a 45 percent discount. So the short-run solution is to skip the middleman and lower the discount. Better yet, do what the studios did: own the outlets. Alas, however, publishers, anxious about antitrust violations, missed this step. The bookstores conglomerated not with publishers but with merchandisers. Waldenbooks, which was started by Carter Hawley Hale and once specialized in rental libraries, is now a subsidiary of K-Mart. B. Dalton, started by Dayton-Hudson, is owned by Leonard Riggio, owner and founder of Barnes & Noble discount stores backed by the Amsterdam-based retail conglomerate Vendex International. These chain stores are not at all like the bookstores of yore. They are much more like self-service shoe stores.

5. "Move 'em out," is the publisher's call. "Send 'em back," says the retailer. This "musical chairs" became like "hot potato" in 1979 when the IRS ruled in the Thor Power Tool case that books held in inventory were not entitled to tax write-downs for depreciated value until after the books had left inventory. To the tax man there is no difference between stacks of books and piles of tool parts. Many publishers would prefer to destroy their product rather than be destroyed by it.

The success of these two "book outlets" (which have more than 2,100 suboutlets between them, sell nearly 290 million books a year, and have sales in excess of $2.2 billion) rests appropriately on the cash register. The electronic cash register, called an EDP POS (electronic data processing, point of sale terminal), was brought to the market in the 1970s and has profoundly influenced editorial decisions. This machine has become the gatekeeper. These computers allow the salesclerk to sit behind a checkout platform, run an optical scanner over the bar code on the books, and pass customers through as if they were at the local A&P. Each night the figures are downloaded to a national mainframe and within hours central management knows exactly what was selling in Peoria and Manhattan. Waldenbooks has gone one step further. Their book club offers members a discount in exchange for providing information about their buying habits. When the buyer makes a purchase he presents his membership card with its customized bar code to be run through the scanner. Not only does Waldenbooks know what books are selling, they know exactly to whom they are selling. Publishers are concerned with impressing chain-store management with huge author advances and massive publicity because the chains now do the crucial bookbuying that makes blockbusters possible. They market almost half the books published in this country. Shocking as it would surely seem to Charles A. Scribner and his sons, the chief monk in publishing is a middle-level executive at a subsidiary of the K-Mart corporation looking at small blinking numbers on a computer screen. "Get me some more Danielle Steel and Stephen King," he says to the editorial departments of the publishing subsidiaries of Paramount Communications, Bertelsmann, Time Warner, News Corporation, and Advance Publications.

To be fair, the national chains have become the most recent scapegoat for what happens when the prices of an entertainment drop and new audiences shove older ones aside. Harry Hoffman, CEO of Waldenbooks, was taken to task for his comments in the *New York Times Magazine* in which he said that he wanted books that people could read in one sitting. He was correct, in a sense. Edgar Allan Poe said exactly this in 1848, and it has since been called the insight of an artistic genius. "Giving the people what they want" may make Marxists mutter, but it makes sense to mass merchandisers.[6] This leveling

6. While there have been bestsellers of approximately sixty thousand words like Hemingway's *The Old Man and the Sea*, Camus' *The Stranger*, and Koestler's *Darkness at Noon*,

of taste is the inevitable result of a literate and affluent audience and a profit-driven show business. We will see the same phenomenon as the matinee audience commandeers the attention of Hollywood studios, or when the prices of televison sets dropped and the Saturday morning cartoon watchers were able to change the afternoon programming of the television networks.

This shift in publishing toward paperbacks, the lowering of reading age and sophistication, the differential in price between hard- and softcover, and the changes in product distribution has had some disconcerting effects. Not only are the big chain stores arranged like a supermarket with "product" garishly displayed at eye level, but also there is no one in the store who knows anything about books. Salespeople are forever shifting inventory and consulting their microfiche. Noise is even encouraged to reduce the "library conditions" of old-time bookstores; silence is not conducive to purchasing. "Motivational Music" is piped in to increase "item velocity." There is no place to sit. The tale of the tape tells all, and that tape is in the electronic distribution program, in the spreadsheet, in the supercharged-turbo cash register. Books used to have a life of thirty years; now they last for thirty days. Today mass-market books are treated as perishable commodities with the shelf-life expiration of a tomato.[7]

Since only one out of every seven or eight titles ever pays for itself, publishers try to limit risk by paying big money for a few books, publicizing the advance, and hoping that the big numbers will attract readers. In the 1980s it would have been hard not to read of astro-

---

the modern fictional bestseller tends not just to go on, but to go on and on. Not only are romances interminably long, but Stephen King's *The Stand*, as big as a brick in its first incarnation, has returned in its unedited form the size of a concrete block.

7. High-volume discounters, essentially warehouses for both publishers and retailers, have helped to some extent. Barnes and Noble, Outlet Book Co., and Publishers Central Bureau sell the excess supply of successful books (to have 100,000 copies left over from a one-million-copy press run is a common occurrence) as well as the flops. They also buy the unreturnable books from stores like Rich's Department stores and B. Altman, as well as the unsold inventory of university presses.

The next generation of discounter is already on the scene. Price Club, Sam's, Costco and Pace are selling 350 million books a year, far fewer than the 2.4 billion of the big chains, but what they offer is vast floor space, exceeding 100,000 square feet, and even deeper discounts. The discounters have become so successful that they often print their own facsimile editions of, say, the Gutenberg Bible or the unabridged *Gray's Anatomy*. Ironically, while remainder houses resolve the surplus, they also help to maintain it by providing an outlet for blockbusters gone awry. As the studio executive has the video aftermarket to cushion the shock of mistakes, and network television has cable broadcasters eager for failed product, the publisher has the discounters to clean up after editorial excesses.

nomic sums being paid first to writers like E. L. Doctorow, Mario Puzo, and Colleen McCullough, and then to Judith Krantz, Mary Higgins Clark, Stephen King, Tom Clancy, Jackie Collins, and Danielle Steel. But, like show business, it only lasts as long as the "customers will come." One increasingly hears of books that have not made back their advances, or "minimum guarantees" as they are called in contract euphemisms. "Sure bets" by the likes of Debbie Reynolds, Nathan Sharansky, John Jakes, Studs Terkel, Barbara Gordon, Joseph Heller, Shana Alexander, and Jay McInerney proved not so sure. Publishers like Dodd, Mead and Weidenfeld & Nicolson learned that six- and seven-figure advances add up to millions of unrecoverable dollars and Chapter 11. While most contracts have a "satisfactory manuscript" clause, an increasing number are "cut loose" even after the advance is paid. Publishers who "sin in haste" prefer not to "repent in leisure," and these "orphan" books, as they are called in the trade, go back into the market to find another sponsor at a lower price.

While the lure of big money has showed the chains that the publishers will promote and advertise certain books, the actual figures are deceptive. Sometimes the advance includes world rights, hard/soft rights, U.S. or U.S.-and-Canada rights, English-language rights, subsidiary rights, and all kinds of show-business extras ignored by the popular press. Still, a $35 to $40 million advance for four books, as Stephen King reportedly received from Viking Penguin, or a seven-figure advance for a first novel does boggle the mind. Such sums have produced a three-tier system, with established blockbuster authors who write "brand-name product" on top, a second rung of not-yets or maybe-nevers, and a third of wannabes, usually first novelists. Since nearly 80 percent of published books are financial failures, if only five books of 100 sell in large enough numbers (usually over 100,000 copies), the rest can be carried along. No one knows how to find those five books but, ironically, the first-time novelist is in a better position than the midrange author. In 1990 not one of the fifty-four novels that sold over 100,000 was by a first novelist. Still, the wannabe is at least promotable. Blurbs like "astonishing debut," "fresh voice," and "startling fresh talent" have powerful appeal to readers who see the bandwagon passing by. "Its getting much harder to build an author's reputation in the stores," says Patrick Filley, an executive editor at Doubleday. "In fact, in some ways it's easier getting a big money first novel into the chainstores than getting in the

"But why don't you publish ONLY bestsellers?"

Mort Gerberg, "But why don't you publish ONLY best sellers?"
(*Publishers Weekly*, January 15, 1988).

latest title by an author whose previous books haven't sold that well"
(McDowell, April 10, 1989). Simon & Schuster was so excited to be
offered "Just Killing Time," a first novel "blurbed" by best-selling
authors John le Carré and Joseph Wambaugh, that they offered an
advance of $920,000. When the two authors announced they had
never heard of the novel, S&S canceled publication. The battle for
rack space has become so intense that the "frontlist" (new and forthcoming titles) overpowers the backlist. A generation ago 60 percent
of sales was backlist; now that has dwindled to about 25 percent.
While the frontlist is aggressively promoted and the backlist is kept at
a minimum, the midlist disappears. It is almost as if publishers were
saying, "We like the baby and the adult, but the adolescent is too
much trouble to have around."

In the drive to increase sales, publishers have imitated their cousins
in the entertainment business by attempting to make their frontlist
authors into media personalities. The best-selling author has to become a "star," and the book is the "vehicle." The moviegoing audience doesn't seem to care what movie Tom Cruise, Kevin Costner,
or Eddie Murphy appear in, they enjoy proximity more than performance. So too the reading public. As Stephen King has said, he

himself is a brand name like Ivory soap or a Hershey bar — the "Green Giant of horror fiction."

Although one might argue that Lord Byron was the first author-as-celebrity, the modern phenomenon of celebrity-as-author was rediscovered by publishers like Bernard Geis after the collected wisdom of Art Linkletter became a bestseller. Geis realized that just as out-and-out hacks can be made into celebrities, celebrities can be made into authors. In the late 1950s, Alexander King reappeared on the Jack Parr show to hype a book based on being on the show to hype another book. Jacqueline Susann was one of the first to gather a national audience simply by being a guest on television talk shows. Then she wrote about touring the talk shows and toured more talk shows. Now the "author tour" is a standard feature of bookselling. In one of the many "synergies" beloved by those in merger and acquisition departments, television needed talking heads as much as the book publishers needed readers. Why pay $10,000 for an advertisement in the *New York Times Book Review* to reach a few thousand readers when for the same amount an author could tour ten cities, hold his book up to the camera, and reach millions? Once the author stood to gain royalties on all aspects of the publishing process from hardcover to film, the reward for notoriety could be realized at every point of sale. Norman Mailer and Joseph Heller are performing the same media routines as Jacqueline Susann for a reason. The not-as-robust-as-they-should-be sales of reluctant colleagues like Saul Bellow, John Hersey, Philip Roth, Bernard Malamud, and Anne Tyler show what happens when you stay at home. Whereas Alfred Knopf was supposed to have said that he did not care to publish any author he could not invite over for dinner, the modern publisher is apt to say he does not care to publish any author who will not go out and talk to Phil or Oprah.

One of the more grotesque by-products of the author-as-celebrity property is that publishers are not willing to let their authors die, at least not in the minds of consumers. Although V. C. Andrews died in 1986, Simon & Schuster has published five novels under her name including the best-selling *Dawn*. The thinking seems to be that even though Colonel Sanders is no longer here, the original recipe remains forever. Louis L'Amour, who died in 1988, left enough stories to keep Bantam alive for the next decade. While Bantam does not hide the fact that Mr. L'Amour is no longer with us, they do include a new photo on each book. Most macabre of all is L. Ron Hubbard, dead in 1986, but immortal, thanks to Bridge Publications' purchase of all Mr. Hubbard's juvenilia. The jacket descriptions treat him as if he were alive and well, reporting that Mr. Hubbard "has" written hundreds of novels and "is" one of the most widely read authors. No past tense here, only intimations of immortality for the founder of the Church of Scientology. Had Ian Fleming had the misfortune to die in the 1980s we probably would not be seeing John Gardner's name on the spine of new James Bond adventures. Such posthumous ghosting has not been without contention, however. Barry Winkleman, managing director of HarperCollins in England, expressed dismay that Simon & Schuster was continuing to publish V. C. Andrews by someone who was not V. C. Andrews. He granted that part of his irritation was caused by the fact that, after publishing most of the Andrews franchise, he was outbid by S&S for *Dawn*. "We invested an enormous amount in the Virginia Andrews titles. If that canon is diluted by new titles every few months, it will diminish our assets. What about if I come to America and publish under the name Ernest Hemingway" (McDowell, March 4, 1991)? Touché.

For a living display of the vulgarizing of print, however, go into any mall bookstore. For the war, as they say, is still in the store. On the front line is the book and on the book is the cover. As in other aspects of show business, the covers are the smoke and mirrors that often determine how many paperbacks will sell. Like lobby posters for movies, the covers battle for attention. When the paperback publisher of Ludwig Lewisohn's hardcover *The Case of Mr. Crump* retitled it *The Tyranny of Sex*, everyone, including the author, understood. Like rock album jackets, the design on the 4x7-inch space must be attention-getting. Once publishers discovered they could wrap a lurid dustjacket around an unpopular book, the route to the audience was clear.

While there may be only one text editor, as many as fifteen executives may be in the decision loop for the cover of a product costing $2.95 to $5.95. Frank Metz, vice president of Simon & Schuster, comments, "It is no secret that we and other publishers are vying for face-out treatment for our lead titles. Those books must have immediate eye impact" (Frank, June 2, 1989). To get that face-out treatment publishers have gone to multiple covers for the same book or, more slyly, have created covers that fit together, expanding their display space. So a recent book on Michael Jackson has a front jacket showing the left side of his face while his right side is on the back jacket. The bookseller is encouraged to display the two books front and back, side by side, so as to take up twice the display space.

The paperback cover is a billboard, and what Americans have put on that space has been a carnival of illustrated excitement. Ironically, one of the reasons why Allen Lane sold his interest in American Penguin was that he thought the Americans wanted too much cover decoration. Americans could not figure out the simple system of different colors for different genres. In the 1940s, Dell cover art attempted to announce subject matter less delicately. So an eye in a keyhole was a mystery, a heart in a keyhole was a romance, a cow's skull was a western, an ocean liner meant an adventure, and a quill pen in an inkstand was a historical novel. But this approach proved too subtle, too English. In the last few decades, covers have gone from voyeuristic vistas through keyholes and knotholes, to realistic scenes from the movies, to spare white backgrounds, to the current tours de force of high-technology printing. American cover art is a tribute to sexual innuendo. As with movies and television which wait for a hit and then clone it into exhaustion, one good cover deserves a hundred imitations.

Whoever said you can't judge a book by its cover did not understand paperback publishing. You *must* be able to judge content by cover, and especially in category fiction, by the background alone. Some of the greatest American illustrators have been employed (at often greater expense than for the author) to ensure that those covers were not only seen but recognized. The best of these illustrators, such as Howard Pyle, Harvey Dunn, George Erickson, and Dean Cornwell, and the best of the book designers, Robert Jonas, Walter Brooks, Leo Manso, James Avanti, Stanley Zukerberg, and James Meese, are responsible for creating a grammar of cover art every bit as sophisticated as most of the internal texts. Westerns traditionally have had brown backgrounds with skyline vistas. Horror and gothic were dark blue or black with hands and skeletons. Fantasy and science fiction often had the Frank Frazetta wish-fulfillment scenes of adolescent males. Techno-thrillers portray authentic images of ordnance. Detective novels, historically the most inventive, have had, besides the requisite gun or knife, women: foregrounded women, naked and partly naked women, dead women lying on the floor, women on beds with men standing next to them, women in red dresses, women being carried by men, women being slapped and embraced by men.

However, the most distinctive of all covers currently appear on

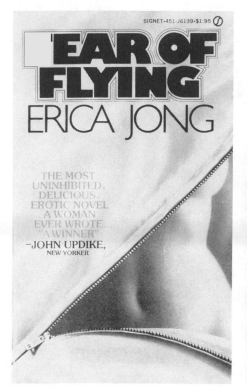

Zipper covers: Signet 1973, Warner, 1978.

books that are the least content-variable, namely, the romance. These covers in acid colors of pinks, purple, silver, and gold are on reflective foil resembling nothing so much as boxes of candy. Under titles formed with curlicues is an image featuring lovers in the clinch position. A long-haired woman is wrapped in an embrace with a darker-skinned man. The handsome rogue wears a ruffled shirt open almost to the groin. His tautly muscled arms, burnished by a life of adventure and swordplay, are wrapped around an obviously wellborn young woman whose ample bosom threatens explosion as she reclines on his lap. On the grass between their feet lies the hero's unsheathed sword. . . . Exotic backgrounds and flowered foregrounds float around the spine and onto the back cover. The romance cover, like the movie ad in the newspaper, is essentially a cartoon. Romances have titles in which jewels, timelessness, the English upperclass, and wickedness are mixed in with Rape, Passion, and Lust. The inter-

Romance covers (clockwise: Dell, Warner, Avon, Berkley).

changeable titles are every bit as much of the cover as the clinch and the author's name (which usually includes a Faith, Bright, or Goode).

In a joyful parody of both gothic and romantic covers, Signet produced a double-cover for the first paperback edition of Stephen King's *Misery*. On the front cover is a desolate-looking man in a wheelchair threatened by an immense shadow of an ax projected on the wall above him. The second cover, tipped in, is a torrid historical romance illustration featuring the standard al fresco embrace with all the motifs in place except that the male protagonist has the face not of a robust yet sensitive hero, but of the real author, Dondi-faced Stephen King.

The paperback cover is so important that the most advanced developments in printing technology are usually exhibited here. Appropriately, most of our current covers result from innovations developed in the greeting card industry. In the late 1970s, the Kluge embossers and Bobst stampers were brought on line to produce the heavily decorated cards that have become a central part of American communication. Feel an emotion? Send a $2.00 card. Want a good read? Buy a $4.00 book. Much like the use of chromakey on television or computer-assisted special effects in the movies, new developments in printing were used to startle, to capture attention. Content was secondary. Gold seals, embossing, die-cut holes to reveal an illustration beneath, step covers (the front cover trimmed short so that the right-hand margin reveals a color band or part of the inside illustration), foldouts, cover gatefolds, tipped-in gatefold, metallic inks, light-refraction techniques such as UV coating and refractive foil, and now multiple-image holography add considerable expense to the printing. For an average print run of standard length and paper quality, the cover may cost thirty-five cents. A foil cover adds from two cents on runs of a million to two and a half cents on runs of 250,000. For the same runs, embossing and die cutting each add another quarter to three-quarters of a cent. Although there was a general feeling that publishers could not push too hard on the $4.95 price, many clearly think that these covers are worthwhile. Presses like Zebra that must battle for rack space against established houses have been willing to lose large sums in the hope that it can exploit that "real estate" with other titles. Roberta Grossman, Zebra president, explains the market for her product:

> Everybody was concerned a year or two ago about breaking the $3.95 cover price. Now they've crashed through to $4.95. But it is probably one of the reasons why we've lost the multiple purchase. I've always said that if a woman goes into a supermarket and finds that she is paying the same amount for a book as for a chicken, she may well buy her books at a paperback exchange, where she can get them for a dollar or two. That will hurt us. And if it hurts us, it will hurt the finishers, the paper mills, printers and others, so someone will have to draw the line on increases if we are to operate a business in a viable way. (Frank, January 22, 1988)

The battle to get the reader under the cover continues all over the store. Only two generations ago Henry Holt condemned all book advertising as an "abandonment of morals and the degradation of activities to a lowered level of purpose," considering that the "pandering to a vulgar popular taste" was the book publishing counterpart to "yellow" journalism (Carter, June 10, 1988). Tastes have changed and pandering is now the norm. NAL, for instance, holds about twenty full-scale promotions each year, complete with floor displays, free trips, videos, and coupons in books for other books. Publishers of romances often offer free lipstick with a purchase; Vestron Video provided the visual accompaniment for Shirley MacLaine's *Inner Workout* to compete with Jane Fonda's outer one, and weekends at Trump Plaza were offered to lucky buyers of Donald Trump's *The Art of the Deal*.

A recent development, reminiscent of "product placement" in the movies and on television, has been the inclusion of brand names in fiction. Just as in *E.T. The Extra-Terrestrial*, where a cute alien gulping Reese's Pieces contributed to a sales increase of some 70 percent, so Beth Ann Herman put a Maserati, "whose V-6 engine had two turbochargers, 185 horsepower and got up to 60 in under 7 seconds," into her novel *Power City*. Her publisher threw a $15,000 party for her at the Wilshire Maserati dealership in Beverly Hills, a party covered by *Entertainment Tonight*, but not by many readers (Rothenberg 1989:31). If the electronic media are any predictors of what publishing may expect, product placements will only increase. Stephen King will mention McDonald's once too often and the commodification of books will be complete: brand names mentioning brand names in brand names.

In a neat inversion of history, Whittle Communications is attempting something similar. Whittle is commissioning books as a vehicle for advertisements. Just as television is punctuated with commercials, movies introduced by advertisements, and videotapes like *Top Gun* preceded by Pepsi "spots," so Whittle has included advertisements inside books. They call it "controlled circulation advertising." After all, Dickens' novels had advertisements in them (often for "ladies underclothing"), and some computer books, cookbooks, and travel books already carry ads. In fact, until the late 1940s many cheap paperbacks had ads. The turning point came when Dr. Benjamin Spock refused to allow cigarette ads in the baby book. Paperbackers, eager to be perceived as high culture and just as eager not to lose their fourth-class postal rates, voluntarily removed the ads. Of course, corporations have paid for private histories (which they often hope will be mistaken for the real thing), and so-called premium

Whittle Direct Books advertisement, 1989.

books (like *A Day in the Life of Australia . . . China . . . Rio*) are essentially a collection of flattering photographs subsidized by Kodak, Apple Computer, and Sheraton Hotels. But Whittle, half owned by Time Warner, has no such pretensions: it knows that its books are billboards between endboards. Whittle has contracted to pay $60,000 for 100-page hardcover books "on timely topics" which will be interspersed with ads and sent free to 150,000 prominent individuals. John Kenneth Galbraith, David Halberstam, Edward Jay Epstein, George Gilder, and James Atlas have signed up to fill up the space between the ads. As the company says, "Big ideas, great writers, short books." They mean it. They refused Halberstam's *The Next Century* because the manuscript was too long and needed more "reporting." It became a bestseller.

One of the chief reasons books have not carried advertisements is that publishers could not use the fourth-class book rate for books containing promotional material. United Parcel Service (UPS), however, has no such restrictions and, as postal rates rose, the differential between "library rate" and UPS diminished. Not only will we see more bound-in advertising, but books themselves may bypass the retail outlet. Books may achieve the ideal of every marketer: "sell-through." *The Reader's Catalog: An Annotated Selection of More Than 40,000 of the Best Books in Print in 208 Categories* is the brainchild of Jason Epstein. Epstein introduced Doubleday's Anchor books in the 1950s, which helped the trade paperback become standard, and was one of the founders of the *New York Review of Books. The Reader's Catalog* has the size and function of a telephone book. By calling an 800 number the reader can have his merchandise in a few days. Understandably, the American Booksellers Association is upset, for no sales commission is involved, yet the full retail price is charged. Whether Epstein can generate volume sufficient to justify use of storage space for warehousing remains to be seen. But the direction of bookselling, like that of videocassettes and subscription television, is clear — circumvent the store. This catalog approach will not be easy. High-culture books may be sold this way, but it is doubtful that mass-market books could be. A plan to sell books by wire, patterned after the system used by florists, cost $3.5 million and showed that while books may be shoes they are not flowers.

Another transformation in bookselling has been the return of storytelling to the spoken word. Two innovations made this possible — the Sony Walkman and the audiocassette player in the car. Audio tapes have become one of the fastest-growing and most remunerative profit centers in the product cycle. A rough figure for what is now called "spoken-word publishing" is somewhere in excess of $250 million per year. Proof of the financial value of "audio aftermarket" is that ownership is continually contested in courts. For instance, Simon & Schuster took Dove Books-on-Tape to court because while Simon & Schuster had rights to the print version of Larry McMurtry's *Lonesome Dove*, Dove had contracted for the audio portion of the television rendition. Whereas audio tapes were once introduced only

Reader's Catalog advertisement, 1989.

after the paperback edition had been marketed, they are now often sold simultaneously with the hardcover release. Readers listen to the tapes while traveling, jogging, or relaxing, mixing the audio experience with the reading of the text. The two-page advertisement from the *New York Times Book Review* on page 116 illustrates how audio is competing with visual. Not only are the works of Mr. King accorded the "boxed set" treatment associated with literary masterpieces, but at bottom right we are told that we may buy the tapes and hear "the master reading his own epic." Homer should have had it so good!

Little wonder that editors cringe and point to the merchandisers a floor below, or to conglomerate executives a floor above, as the culprits in the carnivalization of print. The days of the bookman mooching about in his J. Press tweeds with leather elbow patches,

Signet advertisement for Stephen King (*New York Times Book Review*, November 27, 1988).

sipping sherry in an oak-paneled office, puffing on his Dunhill and discussing the manuscript of some young Thomas Chatterton who needs nurturing are no more. In fact, they never really were. Max Schuster, Dick Simon, and Leon Shimkin, for instance, were hardly gentlemen of leisure, but they were close enough. No one who makes publishing decisions today in the "literary-industrial complex" is going to last very long without first paying attention to the "financials." As Gerald Howard, an editor in the trade department of W. W. Norton, one of the few independents left, explains:

> The American publishing business today is in a tremendous state of confusion between its two classic functions: the higher-minded and more vocally trumpeted *mission civilisatrice* to instruct and edify and uplift the reading public and the less loudly advertised but, in the nature of things, more consistently compelling *mission commerciale* to separate the consumer from his cash. Happy the publisher (and happy the author) who can manage to make a single book fulfill both functions! However, the two-way road in publishing from the bottom line to Mount Olympus travels right across a fault line, and that is where

the serious editor lives and plies his trade. To put it bluntly, the tectonic plates are shifting, there's an earthquake going on, and all that moving and shaking you've read about is making it hard to attend to business — or even to be certain from day to day, just what our business is. . . . The heart of darkness at the center of today's publishing world is not a jungle. Rather, it is a flashy, disorienting environment, a combination hall of mirrors, MTV video, commodities pit, cocktail party, soap opera, circus, fun house, and three-card monte game. The message one emerges with, stunned and shaken by what one has witnessed, is: "Mistah Perkins — he dead." (1989:335, 369)

The conflict between the gatekeeper of ideas and the merchandiser of printed pages is not new. It originates in the Battle of the Books in the eighteenth century and then re-appears in the mass-market publishing of the nineteenth century. But the increasing separation and tension are peculiarly noticeable since the introduction of the paperback book and the conglomeration of the entertainment industry in the 1970s and 1980s. In the Victorian term for book publishing, "commercial printing," the current emphasis is clearly on "commercial." As if to underscore the shift of editors from *litterateurs* to "procurement executives" in the late 1970s, the National Book Awards were replaced by the American Book Awards. The National Book Awards were prizes of $1,000 given to the most distinguished work in six or seven major fields as determined by a jury of eminent figures in that field. The ceremony was generally held at Avery Fisher Hall in Lincoln Center. A public figure gave an often boring speech. Many pipe smokers in tweeds politely listened. The ABA awards are granted on the basis of sales in categories that include westerns, mysteries, and current interest. As well there are prizes for jacket illustration, book design, and reprints. Booksellers' data have replaced critical judgment. No boring speeches; black tie requested; cigars smoked. The EDP POS register is the primary judge. Not even the Oscars are so crassly commercial. No wonder that the American Booksellers Association recently held its annual circus in Las Vegas.

As editors have become disenchanted with the corporate structure, publishing companies responded by creating boutique houses for books (and editors) of special quality. Almost as if to acknowledge the loss of their good name and reputation as book publishers, they give us the editor's name instead. So there are John Macrae books at Henry Holt & Co., Villard Books from Random House, Helen and Kurt Wolff books at Harcourt Brace Jovanovich, Cornelia and Michael Bessie Books from HarperCollins, Nan A. Talese books at Double-day, Del Rey books at Random House, Margan Entrekin books from Atlantic Monthly Press, to name only a few. Often the imprint hides executive shuffling. When Joni Evans was eased out of editorial power at Random House, she got Turtle Bay Books as a quittance. There are also presses inside presses like Poseidon Press (Pocket Books) or Summit Books (Simon & Schuster). Although Helen and Kurt Wolff are no longer active, the imprint lives on because, as Peter Jovanovich says, "It's not blockbuster publishing, but it's special." What is special is a sense of quality book publishing that returns to the editor a sense of personal involvement. Harold Miller, CEO of Houghton Mifflin, which has five imprints, says with equally insight-ful irony about his imprints, "They afford maximum individuality for creative editors and book publishing, after all, is supposed to be a creative business" (McDowell, December 11, 1989).

To a considerable degree, the slack in quality publishing caused by blockbuster mania is being taken up by the small independent presses and the larger subsidized university presses. In 1989 *Publishers Weekly* gave its Carey Thomas Awards for creative publishing to Thunder's Mouth Press, Curbstone Press, Seal Press, and Eridanos Press — small publishers devoted to alternative fiction, Latin American writ-ing, feminist literature, and foreign language classics. Small presses have always played an important cultural role. The Hogarth Press was more than therapy for Virginia Woolf. The press printed T. S. Eliot's *Waste Land*, works by Robert Graves, Conrad Aiken, Edwin Muir, and the first English translations of Gorky, Dostoyevsky, Bunin, Tolstoy, and Freud, because Leonard and Virginia believed the books had intellectual and literary merit. Today, however, controver-sial books about Edward Kennedy or by Salman Rushdie, or with unflattering treatments of the mass media (like Ben H. Bagdikian's *The Media Monopoly* and Thomas Whiteside's *The Blockbuster Complex*, first serialized in the *New Yorker* in the pre-Newhouse days) have trouble finding major publishers and can only find an audience via small presses. As Edwin McDowell, book editor of the *New York Times*, wonders quizzically, "Still, does it not at least suggest some-thing profoundly disturbing that some of the most successful recent books of controversy had to be published by small presses, including presses operated by a church and a university. Moreover, while the conglomerates brag that they publish more titles than ever, is it possible that many books on controversial subjects never get signed up at all" (August 7, 1989).[8]

As the high-culture editor has fallen from power, the gatekeeper has been replaced by the shill. "Call my agent," cries the distressed blockbuster author, not "Check with my editor." Book publishing changed forever when reprint contracts were sprung loose from the hardcover houses (who used to divide the royalties 50–50 with the author). Once the paperback publishers discovered they could expand the market by buying all the rights themselves and then cut whatever deal at whatever percent with the author (sometimes even giving 100 percent of the paperpack rights to the author) in order to get the subsidiary rights, it was not long before the lawyers and agents appeared. While the editor can discuss tone, characterization, and narrative flow, the agent can comment on "floor position," "preemptive bid," and "topping privileges." And the lawyer/agent many authors would like to have, especially if money is an overriding concern, is Morton Janklow. "Mistah Perkins" may be dead, but Mr. Janklow is very much alive. Janklow does "deals," knows how to "orchestrate,"

8. University presses, largely because of their favored tax treatment, low overhead, and intellectual and corporate freedoms, are now doing what the old-time family houses used to do: they print good books that may lose money. Oxford, Johns Hopkins, Columbia, Chicago, California, Yale, and Princeton, among the many established university presses, and newcomers like New England, Georgia, and Nebraska, are now publishing books once the province of Basic Books, Pantheon, Grove, and even of Knopf. Occasionally, they even behave like their big-city brethren. When I approached an Ivy League press for interest in this manuscript, I received an encouraging note with this postscript: "Would you be able to give me some idea of how your earlier books have sold in cloth?" Such a sentiment would have been shared ten years ago, but never expressed.

Still, university presses play an invaluable role in modern publishing, taking up the slack caused by the unwillingness of the conglomerated houses to absorb even minuscule losses. For instance, some of the best poetry is coming out of series published by Wesleyan, Yale, and Iowa. Unfortunately, with the exception of such wonders as LSU Press publishing *A Confederacy of Dunces*, fiction has suffered because it is still outside the academic purview of most university presses. University presses now have acquisitions editors who compete with the majors, managers who do more than service library orders, and manuscript editors who have the time and patience to nurture trade, as well as scholarly, books. They also copyedit their manuscripts, a stage in production that many of the major houses seem to have decided to forgo along with galley proofs. Admittedly, the sale of four thousand copies of an eight-thousand copy print run is no way to write a bottom line, but it does show that high-culture books make it to market. Many an "A" book has been able to carry the weaker but more scholarly "C." Sometimes those Cs are positively noble, such as the University of Chicago's *Complete Works of Giuseppe Verdi* or Yale's *Peale Family Papers*. This effort has not gone unnoticed. Since 1950, 20 percent of the National and American Book awards have gone to university presses.

to "bundle" and "unbundle" rights, realizes that "well-published" has more to do with the bottom line than with how the book looks or feels, let alone reads. After all, in the current version of publishing musical chairs, the author may not even know where his editor is, let alone who he/she is. But the agent stays put. Like his colleagues Michael Ovitz and Swifty Lazar in Hollywood, Janklow essentially acts as a producer of entertainment, not as an intermediary between author and publisher. The measure of success is based on the flow of capital, up to 15 percent of it trickling into the agent's pocket. As Laurence J. Kirshbaum, president of Warner Books, joked at a Simon & Schuster party for editors, authors, publishers, and agents in 1989, "You can tell who the agents are. They're the ones with all the money" (McDowell, January 19 1989).

Agents have the money because they understand that books are shoes (not candles) and that the demand for certain kinds of shoes — blockbusters — far exceeds the supply. While agents are often blamed for the vulgarization of the print medium, they are simply the ones who are aware of the audience demand for certain stories and have known how to barter those stories for money.[9] According to agents, huge advances make booksellers sell books in order to recoup their investments. Advances motivate publishers. When Mr. Janklow is asked to explain the six- and seven-figure advances he has wrangled for unproven clients or the record-setting $3.2 million for the paper-back reprint of Judith Krantz's *Princess Daisy*, he replies with as much insight as gusto:

> One of the reasons to drive for big advances is not to make authors and agents rich. It's to make the publisher aware of what he's bought. You've got to get them pregnant. They get up before their sales force and say, "We paid millions for this book. This is the biggest book we've got. *Drive* it into the stores." (Gabriel 1989:80)

9. The current "heavy" among agents is Andrew Wylie. He has been profiled in *Vanity Fair*, where he spat on a Saul Bellow novel to stamp out his cigarette; in the *Wall Street Journal*, where he was almost gleeful about Khomeini's part in publicizing his client's *The Satanic Verses*; in *Time*, where he was photographed with arms locked over chest in pout, and on the cover of *7 Days* under the banner "Who Killed Publishing?" In a not untypical move, he convinced his client Philip Roth to switch to Simon & Schuster from Farrar, Straus; struck a contract giving Roth $2 million for his next three books; and encouraged Simon & Schuster to market their new author primarily as the creator of *Portnoy's Complaint*. On the cover of Roth's *Deception* from his new publisher: a man's hand grasping the shapely flank of a young woman.

Agents succeed in show business because they understand that what makes the carnival a money-maker is not the unique exhibit but the naming and clustering of similar exhibits. You can show the same object again and again by changing its name and place. The crowd lines up where the crowd is lined up. Boffo begets boffo. Show it to me again. P. T. Barnum and the lesson of the "What Is It?" has not been forgotten. As they say in Hollywood, "We don't make movies, we make deals." The publisher's market became the agent's market, and the work of art has become the contract.

Allowing the agents and the national chains to make many of the storytelling decisions based on the iron laws of the spreadsheet may have shoved the editor aside. It may have depressed the quality of prose, may have coarsened the medium, but it does show us what the mass audience wants to read. Books no longer reflect "the best that has been thought and said" (if they ever did); they reflect how a literate and eager audience wishes to pass time. Entertainment, not enlightenment, is the goal. Genres that took generations to develop now change in a matter of years. Since the introduction of the paperback book, the dominant reading audience has wanted easy-to-digest formulae. While this may seem simplistic to literary critics who are interested in originality and complexity, formula is grist for the cultural anthropologist. As they gather around the campfire, or at the checkout counter, the mass audience essentially votes certain stories in — and certain stories out. What they like is stories they have already heard.

Genre, or what is now called "category publishing," presents a unique pattern of how our culture expresses its preoccupations in narrative form. Until recently, the dominant genres were the western, the romance, and the mystery. They began their modern lives in pulp, were re-formed in celluloid, and are now omnipresent in various mutations in all media. Since the western is considered the most American, and is historically the most popular mass-market paperback genre, it unfolds and resolves much of what makes us anxious. The western is essentially a three-sided game played out on a field where the middle is the frontier; one side is the settled town, and the other side is the savage wilderness filled with villains. The good townspeople want law and order; the villains reject this, whether Indian or desperado. Enter the hero, who has ties to both sides. The object of this game is to win the white hat's attention and to get him to use his force to destroy the black hats. There are various rules. For example, the hero cannot use force unless provoked, someone must win (until recently, the hero), and a final resolution must be achieved. As we all know, the formula includes the attendant stereotypes: the barroom brawl, the shootout, and the box canyon, as well as supporting characters like a schoolmarm from the East, a dance hall girl, a slick gambler, a crooked banker, a seedy doctor, and the cowboy's horse. That Louis L'Amour can retell this story to hundreds of thousands of repeat readers demonstrates that our appointment at the frontier is still being met.

The romance is an adventure story for women complete with mystery, threat, and fulfillment. The theme centers on bringing potential lovers together, then pulling them apart, and finally marrying them off. The genre has its roots in eighteenth-century etiquette books and the gothic novel. The formula was developed in the art novel, then recast in the pulp novel, and traveled back and forth throughout the nineteenth century. These are the dangerous books so beloved by Flaubert's Madame Bovary:

> They were full of love and lovers, persecuted damsels swooning in deserted pavilions, postillions slaughtered at every turn, horses ridden to death on every page, gloomy forests, romantic intrigue, vows, sobs, embraces and tears, moonlit crossings, nightingales in woodland groves, noblemen brave as lions, gentle as lambs, impossibly virtuous, always well dressed and who wept like fountains on all occasions.

As with the western, the romance centers around some barrier that must be overcome to affirm not peace so much as domesticity. Until a few years ago, the tale of lovers meeting, being separated, meeting, separating, and finally reuniting accounted for almost 40 percent of total paperbacks.

In the mystery genre, the focus is an investigation and discovery of something hidden, which will benefit someone with whom the reader identifies. The print myth remained relatively elegant from Poe's classic detective story to the ratiocinations of Arthur Conan Doyle, to Christie, Sayers, and Simenon. A generation ago, because of the influence of radio and the movies, a hard-boiled detective appeared. The story soon centered on the exploits of a Sam Spade, Nick Charles, or Philip Marlowe. The paperback mystery, in contrast to its high-culture counterpart, is held together by the rapid actions of one of these characters. Detective confronts mystery with violence.

Women are victims. Heroes are tough and lonely. They live on the margin. They have ordinary tastes. The law is hopeless. Language is masculine. Sentences short and punchy. Plotting is precise. The rich are evil. The violent villain is discovered, and brutal resolution forthcoming. Mickey Spillane is "everybody's supreme embodiment of the tasteless, vulgar, obsessive sadistic and unredeemable dregs of popular formula literature" (Cawelti 1976:162). Such oft-repeated conventions of violent men on the edge of control, crossing the line, then pulling back in the nick of time has sold over forty million books. Television, with its predominantly female audience, has mellowed this character. From Peter Gunn, 77 *Sunset Strip, Call Surfside 666,* Cannon, Barnaby Jones, Mannix . . . to the more current crime-busting heartbreakers Thomas Magnum and Sonny Crockett—all are examples of the private eye from Vulgaria. Male problem-resolution still drives the plot, but the males on the small screen are certainly more sympathetic than their brethren in pulp.

These popular genres are not corruptions of ancient genres like tragedy, comedy, picaresque, pastoral, and satire. They are essentially the adaptation of folklore configurations to modern show business. The western, the romance, and the detective story are written to entertain, and if they resolve social anxieties, so much the better. They are sentimentalizations, cartoons, perhaps closer to the primitive originals than the complex versions we have received via the art tradition. The modern reading audience of paperbacks has, in a sense, demanded that print behave more like moving pictures than like static tableaus. They don't want to be told how to feel; they want to be forced to feel. The sensationalizing force they crave is melodrama. Ever since Dickens kept Little Nell in serial limbo (and well before), successful authors have learned how to attenuate and broaden scenes to increase the readers' thrills. Like the music added to intensify the film and television experience, melodrama has been a characteristic of these genres, but there is a problem. Melodrama ages quickly. After all, musical tastes change with new instruments, orchestrations, and amplification. We now have a hard time responding to the print compositions of E. D. E. N. Southworth, Susan Warner, Harold Bell Wright, or Winston Churchill with anything like the excitement felt by our grandparents. Still, every once in a while a melodrama will achieve an enduring power almost in spite of itself, as did *Uncle Tom's Cabin* or *Gone with the Wind.*

The current crop of category fiction promises more of the "what sells." "Target books," as they are now called, make up between 25 to 30 percent of mass-market publishing and are increasing their hold. Clearly, we are moving back to the days of the pulp magazine when books were commissioned by publishers at so much per word, and produced by formula. The common reader, if any such reader exists, is lining up to read a number of new genres like (1) the psychobiography (as Joyce Carol Oates calls it) with motifs of social dysfunction, failed careers, and failed promise. We have seen such biographies of Ernest Hemingway, John Berryman, Dylan Thomas, Katherine Anne Porter, Tennessee Williams, John Cheever, Shirley Jackson, Truman Capote, John Lennon, Pablo Picasso, all of which direct us to look on the mighty and not despair. This category has decayed further, to what has been called the trash biography, practiced by Kitty Kelley on Frank Sinatra and mastered on Nancy Reagan. (2) The techno-thriller, such as Tom Clancy's *The Hunt for Red October*, *Patriot Games*, *Clear and Present Danger* and Stephen Coonts' *Final Flight* and *Flight of the Intruder*, which are little more than ordnance magazines spliced with "Us vs. Them" espionage. (3) Gruesome crime stories from *Helter Skelter* to *Blind Faith* to *Silence of the Lambs*, which are really updates of the Newgate Calendars of the eighteenth century. And, most interesting, (4) the super-macho adventure story dubbed Action-Adventure, and (5) epic fantasy cycles. These last two categories, which now account for more than 15 percent of paperback sales, are the most recent manufactured genre. When an emerging trend in adventure or fantasy suddenly attains huge and unexpected success (e.g., *Rocky*, the Rambo series, *Lord of the Rings*, *Star Wars*), then a "packager" develops and refines the sequences with an eye to the market, devises an outline, and hires a stable of writers to turn out a volume every month.

The secret to all category publishing, as in profitable television programming and movie-making, is to sell the product like fast food. They are franchise entertainments — McGenres — books aspiring to the condition of hamburgers. This drive for repeating the known, for avoiding the unique or different, for taking few chances has been the legacy of the most recent generation of conglomerated publishers. This "comestibilization" of print can even be seen in so-called high-culture advertising. In an advertisement in the *New York Times Book Review* for a recently published novel, Liz Smith called it "a great read," Jerry Tallmer said it was "a sheer truth-telling wildfire read," but Erica Jong gave it the plug it needed: "a rich, yeasty read." Not to put too fine a point on it, no one felt comfortable calling it a book.

Action-adventure novels are hamburger fiction for the male working classes—Rambo for readers. Although with antecedents in Victorian pulp, action-adventure books have most recently been brought to market by Zebra press. This is boys' literature for men. Zebra knows that market and has the shady past to prove it. For a time, it was connected to Pinnacle and later to Grove Press where it had some success in publishing pornography. Zebra is now a division of Kensington Publishing Corporation and specializes in publishing interchangeable titles of the same tale. Kensington clearly hopes that while the missus is in the bedroom devouring the latest romance, Buck will turn off *The A-Team* and pick up a—gasp!—book. By all accounts he has. Once hawked on Victorian street corners, the action-adventure novel is now sold at truck stops, drugstores, and service stations.

The typical novel, with a title like *The Avenger, The Cutthroat Cannibals,* or *Cody's Army,* tells the story of a war between a small group of good guys with good war records and an army of bad guys with bad reputations and no (or dishonorable) war records. The good guys are paramilitary types, usually Vietnam vets, modern-day guerrillas, survivalists, and the baddies are Mafia types, foreigners, politicians, corrupt career army types, drug dealers. As in the romance, the interaction is simple. Instead of the woman getting the man of her dreams, in the male action-adventure stories the heroes get the self-respect of their dreams. As Don Pendleton, an author of this genre, says, "The idea is that you are really larger than you realize. You're able to take command of things, sort of like the male role. You're able to make things happen. This is a very romantic idea because we really don't live in that kind of world" (Mehren 1988). It is also a very profitable idea. In 1987, Gold Eagle Books, a division of Harlequin, shipped 500 million copies of its "Executioner" series. Predictably, they were joined by other series: Warner Books' "Cody's Army," Pinnacle's "Midnight Lightning," Bantam's "Overload" (centered around 18-wheelers), and NAL's "The Destroyer." Although 2 percent are sold to women, at last men between twenty-two and fifty have their own hard-hat lunch-hour reading.

While the Harlequin romance is target publishing for working-class women and action-adventure novels for working-class men, fantasy publishing attracts their children. After Missy graduates from Sweet Valley High and Junior from Dungeons and Dragons, they may be ready for a little escape of their own. Fantasy fiction has found an enduring audience of adolescents since the eighteenth century. Its history can be traced from William Beckford's *Vathek* in the Age of Reason, to Victorian children's stories of reason gone mad (as in *Alice's Adventures in Wonderland*), to the modern-day parallel worlds of *The Book of the Three Dragons* by Kenneth Morris and *A Wizard of Earthsea* by Ursula K. Le Guin. Often the genre dips into pulp, as it does in magazines like *Unknown*, *Fantastic Adventures*, and *The Magazine of Fantasy & Science Fiction*, and from there down into comics. Rescued by middlebrow culture with J. R. R. Tolkien's *Lord of the Rings* trilogy and the works of H. P. Lovecraft, what is called "adult fantasy" now accounts for a startling 10 percent of paperback sales. With richly colorful Frank Frazetta covers, from specialized imprints like Ballantine Books' Del Rey, these novels often come in packs like Stephen R. Donaldson's series of *The Chronicles of Thomas Covenant* or the best-selling trilogies of Piers Anthony or Anne McCaffrey. The story they tell almost always begins in the "real" world, then plunges into an imaginary one. In this second world the moral coordinates are extrapolated from reality. The major character is an Everyman, who, like the young reader, is caught in a struggle between good and evil. Unlike the reader, however, he resolves the dilemma just in time to move on to the next book in the series. When they are inventive, as are C. S. Lewis' Narnia chronicles or Peter S. Beagle's sentimental fantasy *The Last Unicorn*, the genre clearly has high-culture aspirations, but when they are cartoonish, as is Robert E. Howard's *Conan the Barbarian* series, they leave print and play out their fables in electrons and pixels.

What all these genres have in common is a dedication to portraying action. In fact, the most striking aspect of modern best-selling fiction is the exaggeration of action — the cartooning of violence. To be sure, this is one influence of the movies and television on print. In a recent national study, the National Conference on Television Violence found a 61 percent increase in so-called antisocial or proviolence themes in fiction from 1966 to 1988. The NCTV based their findings on formulae derived from television studies applied to books chosen at random from B. Dalton and Waldenbooks, as well as from the best-selling books of 1980s. More startling, a whopping 300 percent increase in gratuitous violence was noted when the bestsellers of the 1980s were compared to those in the first half of the century. In the last decade 72 percent of the best sellers featured violence, and 78 percent of all paperbacks sensationalized violence. Furthermore, spy novels, crime and detective stories, horror, war, fantasy and science fiction, and cowboy genres are now essentially dedicated to transporting scenes of exaggerated violence. Only the romance, a genre for women, had predominately nonviolent and prosocial themes. Assuming that chain-store sales accurately represent the tastes of the burgeoning audience in print entertainment, then the story most people want to hear is of "Us" against "Them." The "Us" (at present) includes the United States, Great Britain, and Israel, and the "Them" are the Nazis, Arabs, and, until recently, the Russians. This theme accounts for 20 percent of bestsellers since 1964, while it is found in only 1 percent of all novels prior to 1959. Almost all the blockbuster writers—Robert Ludlum, Frederick Forsyth, Mario Puzo, James Clavell, Helen MacInnes, Stephen King, Leon Uris, Harold Robbins, Ken Follett, Sidney Sheldon—manage to weave concussive scenes into the unravelling of national and personal paranoia.

According to the NCTV study, the change of subject matter started in 1949; prior to this date 41 percent of bestsellers had prosocial themes. But from 1949 to 1965 this figure droped 27 percent, and since 1966 it has dropped another 18. The study concludes:

> In the past 20 years violent books have been more intensely sadistic and gruesome than anything ever making the bestseller list in American history. Satanic and horror themes have become commonplace after being non-existent before the 1960s. It is clear that modern readers of popular fiction are entertaining themselves with more hate-filled, sadistic and gruesome material than any previous generation of human beings in world history. (Radecki 1988:3)

The NCTV comes to no conclusion as to causality. Doubtless such distortion is an influence of both cold war anxieties and the electronic media. But it also reflects a different reading audience, a younger audience, which wants to hear different stories. Is it a coincidence that the increase in violence corresponds to the shifting of control from hardcover to paperback, from editor to agent, from gatekeeper to barker, from verbal to visual culture?

With the history of the last twenty or so years of publishing in mind, one can make sense of the 1991 *cause célèbre* in publishing circles — the case of Bret Easton Ellis' novel, *American Psycho*. Here we have a misogynistic book, a powerful agent, a writer of marketable talent, two conglomerated publishing houses, an entertainment media eager to latch onto an easy-to-tell story, and publishing decisions based on shifting predictions of the bottom line. The story is simple and apt.

Simon & Schuster paid Mr. Ellis $300,000 for a hyperviolent novel about a Wall Street investment banker who prefers murders and executions to mergers and acquisitions. Simon & Schuster knew what they were buying: Ellis' first novel, *Less Than Zero*, was smarmy as was his second novel, *The Rules of Attraction*. S&S is owned by Paramount Communications, whose movie subsidiary, Paramount Pictures, earned millions in the 1980s portraying a stalk-and-slash maniac named Jason Vorhees in the interminable *Friday the 13th* series. But to the people who worked on the Ellis manuscript, the pathological Patrick Bateman was too much Jason Vorhees, too much a slice-and-dice movie villain, not enough a book villain. They complained, some even refusing to work on the project, and *Time* and *Spy* published excerpts, agreeing that this was indeed a very nasty book. Crucifixion by nail gun, breasts exploded by jumper cables, and starved rat shoved into vagina are just three of more than twenty murders committed by the debonair Mr. Bateman. And it gets worse, much worse. Martin Davis, chairman of Paramount Communications, asked Richard Snyder, CEO of Simon & Schuster, to rethink the publishing decision. Snyder did. After reading the bound galleys, he issued a press release in which he said he made the decision alone, and "on the basis of taste." (Remember that this is the same company now publishing works by V. C. Andrews that are not by V. C. Andrews). Still, Snyder refused the book. The $300,000 advance was forfeited.

Had the story ended here it might have been a typical publishing tale from the 1940s, except that the financial numbers were so huge. But Binky Urban, Ellis' agent, knew what she had in *American Psycho*. She knew this from the first time she read the manuscript. It was so unremittingly violent that she actually hid the typescript from her two-year-old daughter (Hoban 1990:34). Urban quickly tried to sell the book again and, within a few days, she did. Sonny Mehta, the head of Knopf and Vintage, bought it. How could a book that was in such "bad taste" that even Mr. Snyder would sacrifice $300,000 not to print it be worth some $75,000 to Mr. Mehta? Clearly, it was no longer a book; it was a show-business event. As Mr. Mehta told Roger Cohen of the *New York Times*, "Profit is one way that you can take pride in the way you publish things and insure that you can go on doing it" (Hoban 1990:37). Not to be overlooked in this parable of modern publishing-as-showbiz is the format Mehta chose for *American Psycho:* it was brought out by Vintage Press, the paperback division of Knopf. *American Psycho* will have no hardcover life. For a few weeks it was on the paperback bestseller lists.

While this is not the way most books are sold, it is the way many movies and television shows make it to production. "Buying on turnaround" is common in the electronic media. Shifting "hype" rearranges perceived value. No one really cares about the artistic integrity of a "property"; they care about the "deal," the box office, the stars, the playdates, the sequel, the points. . . . In a telling comment, Tammy Bruce, president of the Los Angeles chapter of NOW, explained the L.A. boycott of *American Psycho*, "You won't see books being burned or fireworks when the novel is published. What you *will* see is our attempt to show the gatekeepers of this culture that the women of this country will no longer tolerate gratuitous violence for the sake of profit and entertainment" (O'Brien 1990:34). Finding those gatekeepers, let alone convincing them, is easier said than done. While publisher Roger Straus feigned naïveté ("I think it is sad that a publishing house like Knopf/Vintage, so distinguished in the past, should see fit to publish this book. Their motive escapes me, but it seems unusual that they are putting it out in a hurry, in paperback, at a cheap price in order to cash in on its notoriety and what we know about its content"), Robert Massie of the Author's Guild knew exactly what had happened: "If you step back from the picture you see a perfect example of the conglomeration of the publishing business as more and more power over publishing ends up in the hands of people who are not publishers" (Reuter, November 30, 1990).

The fact of the matter is that conglomerated book publishers are behaving more like movie distributors: making their decisions about profitability first and last. "Don't tell us how good it it is," they say. "Tell us who is going to buy it." In some ways, of course, this is refreshing and revitalizing. In contrast to the studios, however, the transformation has been traumatic for those caught in the middle. As Eco's *Name of the Rose* predicts by implication, the opening of the modern library means the overturning of the old order, and today's abbots have good reason to be concerned. In a special issue of the

Voice Literary Supplement in 1990, appropriately titled "Books & Bucks," Morris Philipson reminisced about being caught as the forces were shifting — at the moment when candles were becoming shoes:

> In the history of American commercial publishing, people who cared a great deal about what books contain (ideas, arguments, feelings, guidelines, ideals, for example) invested their capital, their taste, their willingness to gamble, and their ability for hard work in gaining the pleasures taken from association with books and their authors; this is thought of as the glamour of publishing. Then, incidentally, they were satisfied to make a decent profit. I was at an editorial meeting when one of the stepson-executives actually said, "Since 90 percent of our income is derived from 15 percent of our list — why do we publish the remaining 85 percent?" I got out while the getting was good. That was twenty-five years ago. (1990:16)

Mr. Philipson went on to become director of the University of Chicago Press. Doubtless the stepson-executive went on to Hollywood. For what we will now see, as we turn to the film industry, is a dedication to blockbusters that makes publishing look as if it is still being managed by monks.

three

Peepshow America: Hollywood and Popular Taste

There can be no easier way to feeling culturally disenfranchised than to insist on seeing the most popular film in the nation each week, whatever it may be. Reading everything on the fiction best-seller list might offer a comparable shock, but it could never match the immediacy of a really bad (as is so often the case) hit film. Much of the time this week's biggest moneymaker is an action or horror picture; sometimes it's an Arnold Schwarzenegger vehicle, which is to say both.
—Janet Maslin, "To Look at the Hits Is Often to See the Misses"

The studios no longer make movies primarily to attract and please moviegoers; they make movies in such a way as to get as much as possible from the prearranged and anticipated deals. Every picture (allowing for a few exceptions) is cast and planned in terms of those deals. . . . Part of what has deranged American life in this past decade is the change in book publishing and in magazines and newspapers and in the movies as they have passed out of the control of those whose lives were bound up in them and into the control of conglomerates, financiers, and managers who treat them as ordinary commodities.
—Pauline Kael, "Why Are Movies So Bad?"

It is not hard for readers of the *New York Times* and the *New Yorker* to be sympathetic to Maslin and Kael, to shake their clenched fists and demand, "Give us back our movies, you money-grubbing conglomerates." But, alas, their cries will not be heard. Not because those nasty conglomerates are deaf; they have a most acute and developed hearing — "the radar of bats," says Aljean Harmetz of the *New York Times* — but because the criers are spending entirely too much money buying high-culture newspapers and magazines, and not nearly enough at the box office. The only fists the studios recognize are those clutching greenbacks. Studios segment audiences into male, female, children, teenagers, then the 20 to 30,

30 to 40, and over forty age groups. They do not divide them by degrees of intelligence. The first rule of Hollywood has always been the same; whether in the days of the moguls and the studio system, or in the days of the independent producers, or now in the current days of the conglomerate: make movies to make money.

The production of images on film is first and foremost a business, and secondarily (and then only perhaps — if ever) an art. Actors know this. As Charlie Chaplin said after accepting an Academy Award in 1972, "I went into the business for money and the art grew out of it. If people are disillusioned by that remark, I can't help it. It's the truth." Studio executives certainly know money-making as the first principle of survival. Andy Albeck, onetime president of United Artists, explains what is known to everyone in the "industry": "Critics have lots of ways of telling us what is a good movie. They have stars or cherries, or other ways to tell us. But, as businessmen, we have only one gauge for a good movie. How much money did it make?" (Lees 1981:frontispiece). Studio production vice presidents are also aware, as Richard Zimbert, vice president of Paramount, comments: "Since the movie business boils down to one thing, *money*, everything in the deal revolves around that. The effort is to achieve agreement on the basics: who will do what for how much; what the options, rights, or opportunities of each party are as the project develops and their cost levels; and finally the accounting for and division of receipts from the distribution of the picture, if it's made" (Lees 1981:177).

Every day at Twentieth-Century Fox, Richard Zanuck took his place at the head of his private luncheon table outside the studio commissary. On his plate was a piece of paper listing the closing price of Twentieth-Century Fox stock on the New York Stock Exchange and the number of shares traded. Independent producers also know the iron truth of profit and loss. You must give the people not only what they want, but what they want enough to pay for. Maslin and Kael are not "the people." The people, as Alfred Hitchcock once said, want "a piece of cake, not a slice of life."

The moviemaker is paid a great deal of money to make the confection, but only if there is a sizable audience willing to pay for a taste of it. George Romero tells why he makes horror movies: "I've always loved the genre. But the real appeal of it is it's what people want to hire me to do. That holds a great deal of appeal" (Van Gelder 1989:19). The Los Angeles town fathers have never been fooled as to what is made in Hollywood. Concerning a matter of studio land development, the city's Film Development Council reports, "There was much concern among committee members, who cited their purpose as being a business and economic one, with no cultural significance attached" (Lees 1981:frontispiece). Nor is the Bank of America in doubt as to the purpose of movie-making. According to Peter Geiger of the bank's special movie-financing branch:

> We look at [providing capital] as an interim advance, like a real estate construction loan, but there must be someone else responsible for the long-term risk. After all, the movie business is one of the riskiest businesses there is; we cannot foretell by any stretch of the imagination whether a given project is even going to be completed, much less if it will be acceptable in the marketplace. In addition, we cannot have realistic market studies done, such as those that define what types of cars or microwave ovens the public want to buy next year. It's totally speculative. We must evaluate a motion picture company using the same guidelines we have on other industrial concerns seeking loans, by looking at the financial statement and making projections. The one distinct factor is the unusual risk involved. (1983:109–110)

The Supreme Court also has always known how to categorize what Hollywood makes. In 1915, in the famous *Mutual Film Corporation v. Ohio* case, they held that, "the exhibition of moving pictures is a business pure and simple, originated and conducted for profit." Even high-culture authors know. Vladimir Nabokov wrote to his American publisher about putting *Lolita* on film: "My supreme, and in fact only, interest in these motion picture contracts is money. I don't give a damn for what they call 'art' " (Lehmann-Haupt 1989:16). In a venerable Hollywood story, Samuel Goldwyn tried to convince George Bernard Shaw that he could film one of his plays "artistically." "Forget it," Shaw said. "You are after art while I am only after money" (Mitgang 1989:14). Ben Hecht, one of the greatest screen writers, once told a reviewer, "There was no art to the film. There never was, any more than there is to making toilet seats or socks or sausages. It's a commodity for mass consumption. . . . They're platitudes strung together, repetition of plots" (Gabler 1988:326). Hecht even celebrated his part in the movies-as-sausage industry with a backhanded verse he sent to Hollywood executives as a Christmas card:

Good gentleman who overpay
Me fifty times for every fart,
Who hand me statues when I bray

And hail my whinnying as Art—
I pick your pockets every day
   But how you bastards break my heart.

Knee deep in butlers, smothered help
In horse-shit splendors, soft and fat
And worshiping the Golden Calf
I mutter through my new plush hat
"Why did you steal my pilgrim's Staff?
Why do you make me write like that?" (Schatz 1988:190)

If the truth be known, while print critics may complain along with Maslin and Kael that what we see on film is insulting to *our* intelligence, and that the industry should make better films, they know better. Said Vincent Canby, éminence grise at the *New York Times:* "The true business of movies is business, the making of a buck (the faster the better) and not the expression of any so-called art. Only by understanding this truism can one get a fix on the chaos that's sometimes known as the art-industry, or even on why certain movies are made" (1987:31). From time to time even an academic critic will admit, as does John Izod in *Hollywood and the Box Office,* that

> Profits have always, from the earliest days, been the primary objective of the American film industry. However it may appear from the outside, Hollywood has always been first and foremost a business; and although occasional exceptions have been made of movies that were thought likely to enhance a studio's corporate image, few films are released in the certain knowledge that they will lose money. This is not to say that all American features do make profit—but almost all are intended to do so. (1988:ix)

I have ridden this dim-witted economic hobbyhorse into a lather because most print critics prefer to pretend the subject doesn't exist, or to insist it is not really important. Jealousies aside, print critics have struggled mightily to make word-sense of film. The natural assumption that one can interpret the stories of one medium with the vocabulary of the other, and the almost-as-natural assumption that celluloid should aspire to print, have proven feckless. Going to the movies has little in common with opening a book and reading a line of print. Movies offered the first new way to tell a story since the invention of the printing press, yet criticism was still constructed around linear principles, line following line, introduction, body, conclusion. Print abominates collage; celluloid revels in it. The people who made successful movies were not articulate verbalizers, nor are they today. Their business was, and is, as close to carnival as this culture gets. Their business is show business, and they show what the audience wants or they go out of business. Their vulgarity is purposeful.

H. L. Mencken once described the movies accurately enough as "entertainment for the moron majority." While the exchange of temporary escape for money is central to all show business, what separates film is that the entertainment is done in flickering images — shapes projected in light to an audience sitting in darkness. Film and the carnival are by nature primitive, even savage, in that they "speak" with little or no dependence on the language of any formal culture. They excite with illustration, image, movement, not with contemplation, reflection, or words. The cash is the same, however. By no means was it a happenstance that movie storytelling was developed by men who "knew only one word of two syllables, and that word was 'fillium.' " Louis B. Mayer did not decide to make a movie by reading a script. He listened to a storyteller tell him a tale. His aide de camp, Irving Thalberg, knew that the best writers for the movies were journalists who not only "saw" stories, but were accustomed to having them substantially rewritten. To the bafflement of print critics, successful producers still make up their minds on the basis of story conferences in which someone "pitches a concept," rather than by reading an outline. Moviemakers can read all right, but they have to see first.

Since film is first visual, and then only perhaps laden with intellectual content, the art form it most nearly seems to resemble is painting. But since movies are moving pictures, perhaps sculpture is a better analogy or, since objects are perceived as moving in three dimensions, maybe architecture is better still. When Morris Lapidus, architect extraodinaire of Miami Beach and Las Vegas, was asked how he developed his style, he responded, "People are looking for illustrations; they don't want the world's realities. And, I asked, where do I find this world of illusion? Where are their tastes formulated? Do they study it in school? Do they go to museums? Do they travel in Europe? Only one place — the movies. They go to the movies. The hell with everything else" (Venturi 1977:80).

If movies end as architectural objects in motion, they begin as construction projects. Making a movie is more like constructing a building on a vacant lot than like writing a book. The literary property is the lot. The movie is the building. The screenwriter is the architect, the director is the contractor, and the producer is theoretically the owner. The major studio (if one is involved) can represent the lending institution, the equity partner, and/or the leasing agent for the finished building. The artist, if we need to believe one is involved, is likely to be the lawyer. Comparing movies to buildings is not the standard trope: books, yes; paintings, perhaps; but Las Vegas or Miami Beach hotels? Hardly.

Orson Welles once observed that if a poet needs a pen and a painter a brush, then a filmmaker needs an army. The analogy is accurate in an offhand way. The director is not the author, nor is the screenwriter. Movie-making is a collaborative effort, and the act of making one is rather like a war, with the battle waged for the box office. Again, this is not the standard analogy — Clausewitz as auteur. The study of film needs such inelegant, even rude, metaphors. Yet, to be discussed inside the *New Yorker* and not inside *Popular Mechanics*, film reviewers had to treat the entertainment as a "literary text" and not as a construction project.

Until the late 1980s, academic criticism of the movies came under the rubric of "cinema studies" and aspired to be part of an English curriculum, or perhaps an aspect of art history, or, as a last resort, maybe a course in journalism. Never, however, did it appear in building construction or in ROTC departments. To be "teachable," movies *had* to become art. Fanzines had to be sneered at, and "scholarly periodicals" with names like *Cinema Journal* (the official organ of "The Society for Cinema Studies"), *Screen*, and best yet, *Camera Obscura* had to appear. The professor of English literature cannot walk in and say, "Let's study something we all can observe." She has to say, "There is something very important but subtle that you need to know, and it is over here behind this gate, and there is only one key and I have it." The gatekeeper is nothing without a gate, and no gate is worth opening unless it can be locked. A generation ago, English teachers refused to teach "20th Century Lit" because it was too recent. Two decades ago, no subject existed that could be called African-American literature, much less feminist literature, third world literature, or gay literature. Critics need to legitimate the object of study whether by James Joyce, women, blacks, Hispanics, or homosexuals. In the academy, the legitimizing word is always "art." If you want to teach a course in popular music, the first thing you do is call it "The Poetry of Rock Lyrics." Surely, it is a sign of our vulgarian times that today anyone with a spray can and a subway car, or a typewriter and an NEA application form, is an artist and that whatever they do is called art.

Teachers have to impose a framework so that the business of scholarship can begin. There have been two frames in studying film: contemporary film theory and classical film theory, essentially pre- and post-semiology. Of all the contemporary theories of the last decade (Althusserian-derived Marxism, Barthesian textual criticism, Lacanian psychoanalysis, and now feminism) the most influential and wrongheaded was auteurism. This is not much of a theory, but rather an excuse for connoisseurship first proposed by the French and later promoted by *Village Voice* critic Andrew Sarris. Its attraction was that it cast the studio boss as the heavy and elevated the director to artist. Such an elevation appeals to teachers of literature because it validates close reading of film as literature. Once we have an author we can use terms of Lit. Crit., teach classes for academic credit, and publish scholarly articles. The industry loves it too, of course. Apotheosis is a powerful marketing tool. Like the little boy who cried "Wolf!" publicists now cry "Art!" So an interview with Kevin Costner about his *Dances With Wolves* carries the tag "Costner Makes His Masterpiece," and we think nothing is amiss. As Thomas Schatz has written in *The Genius of the System: Hollywood Filmmaking in the Studio Era*, "Auteurism itself would not be worth bothering with if it hadn't been so influential, effectively stalling film history and criticism in a prolonged state of adolescent romanticism" (1988:5).

Other modern theories, adapted from Freud, Marx, Barthes, Lacan, and feminism, also have proved more revelatory of the state of the professoriat than insightful about the nature of the medium. Countless journal articles and conference papers have argued that movies are like dreaming, like stages of infantile growth, like this or that, and there is plenty of talk about fetishism, voyeurism, gender-based narrative frames. Most of this is uninformative about what the entertainment is, namely, show *business*. As Noel Carroll aptly concludes his *Mystifying Movies:*

> For the last decade, film studies in America have been dominated by an established theory, the psychoanalytic-Marxist theory. And, moreover, this period of domination corresponds to a time in which the academic study of film has grown dramatically. The establishment theory has, as a result, become, effectively, the lingua franca of a new academic field. It provides a common medium of discourse for an entire generation of

film scholars. The problem with this language, however, is that it says virtually nothing. It has impeded research and reduced film analysis to the repetition of fashionable slogans and unexamined assumptions. (1988:234)

Print critics have tended to overlook what F. Scott Fitzgerald meant when he wrote that only a few people in Hollywood really understand that movie-making is a business. David O. Selznick was furious when he learned that Sergei Eisenstein had been hired to direct an adaptation of a Dreiser novel. "The advancement of the art is not the business of this organization," he roared at a subordinate (Schatz 1988:77). Print critics need to be reminded that the "Ars Gratia Artis" motto for MGM was as pure public relations hokum as Leo the Lion. Samuel Goldwyn, who used it first, had no idea what the Latin motto implied in art history.

As film studies have become more entrenched in the curriculum, the need to see "movies" as "the cinema" has become more pressing. The First New York International Festival of the Arts was held in 1988. It was appropriately sponsored by the Tisch School of the Arts at NYU and considered the question, "Has the Cinema Fulfilled Its Promise as the Art of the Twentieth Century?" The roundtable discussion evoked this response from the people — chiefly men — who really produce the product. Sidney Lumet snarled, "I call them 'movies.' I won't even use the word 'film.' I'm in such protest against it. And the word 'cinema' won't pass my throat." He continued by stating that the whole conference was a farce because the "movies were conceived of as a money-making machine," not as an art form. Arthur Penn continued, "Someone decided they'd lay a curse on us, and said, 'Here's the art form of the twentieth century; do something with it.' Who laid this malediction on us?" Lumet yelled, "Pauline Kael!" (James, June 23, 1988).[1]

In the last few years, movies have occasionally been approached by a few academics and reviewers as the products of an industry that has making money as its primary purpose. To be sure, this approach was

1. Lumet was not far off the mark. For just as academic cinema studies came of age with the necessity of finding "texts" to teach students who were bored with print, so film criticism came of age with the retirement of Bosley Crowther as film critic at the *New York Times* and Pauline Kael's first article in the *New Yorker*. The final mark of this consolidation came a few years later when the *New York Times Book Review* front-paged Pauline Kael's fourth collection of movie reviews. For better or worse, the movies have labored under the terrible, ill-fitting, and heavy yoke: Art.

first stated in the 1950s with books like Hortense Powdermaker's *Hollywood, the Dream Factory* and in later articles like David Gordon's "Why the Movie Majors Are Major." Gordon explains the economic approach to the industry:

> Movie buffs tend to be as ignorant about the movie industry as they are knowledgeable about its products. The very word "product" is one they find distasteful, reminding them as it does of a manufacturing process churning out items for mass consumption. People who love films seem to need to bless the object of their affection with the sacred title of art. In so doing, they set up a whole mythology of how films come to be made which rests on a supposed opposition between art and industry. The directors and writers are the artists, the genuine film maker, the creators, and they are all on one side of the fence; the movie tycoons, the faceless executives, the studios, capriciously open and shut the golden gate and allow the artists to enter, forcing them to bend their talents to the philistine dictates of the money men. It is commonly assumed that good films are made in spite of the system, by some kind of a trick on a particularly good, or gullible, guard at the golden gate." (1973:194)

This view, which seems so déclassé to those who want to call motion pictures *cinema;* to call directors *auteurs;* to call themselves *cineastes;* to use words like *syntagmatic, diachronic,* and *gestalt;* to compile anthologies on "The Film as Art" or "The Art of Film," has recently been reiterated in a covey of books written by those in the industry.[2]

2. David McClintick's *Indecent Exposure* details the fall and rise of David Begelman of Columbia Studios; Stephen Bach's *Final Cut* shows how an "art" movie (*Heaven's Gate*) ran amok and ruined United Artists; Julia Phillips' *You'll Never Eat Lunch in This Town Again* lobs cherry bombs and insights with equal vigor as she charts her own rise and fall as a producer; Peter Bart's *Fade Out* recounts the calamitous final days of MGM; John Gregory Dunne's *The Studio* chronicles a year in the life of Twentieth-Century Fox; Andrew Yule's *Fast Fade* and Charles Kipps's *Out of Focus* sketches the rise and fall of quixotic David Puttnam, who set out to counter the blockbuster trends at Columbia and found himself soon unemployed; and William Goldman's *Adventures in the Screen Trade* gives a working view of how studio stories are constructed. Such books have made the academic view of moviemakers laboring like so many romantic poets in the Lake District of bucolic Hollywood into the self-serving bunk that it is.

These insights from insiders have not gone unnoticed in the scholarly community. In the last few years, as the studios have sloughed off their archives to university libraries for tax purposes, we are at last seeing how the engines of carnival really operates. In Thomas Schatz's *The Genius of the System* we see a world pieced together by budgets and deals; in Neal Gabler's *An Empire of Their Own* we watch the rise of immigrant Jews as they created and merchandised an America of their dreams; in A. Scott Berg's *Goldwyn: A Biography* we see the producer as creator not only of film but also of a comprehensive mythos centered on profit and loss; in Douglas Gomery's *The Hollywood Studio System,* in Tino Balio's collection

Thanks to research based on fact and not on self-serving whimsy, we can now begin to appreciate how this carnival operates, and why it was inevitable that the Maslins and Kaels were eventually excluded.

In the last twenty years movie-making has become driven by blockbusters not because nasty capitalists have re-waxed their whiplash mustaches and muttered, "Let's give the morons more trash," but because money-making has been more successful with a few expensive movies seen by tens of millions than with cheaper movies seen by a few million. As in conglomerate book publishing, these blockbusters, also called franchise or locomotive movies, are not something studios would like to have; they are something the studios *must* have. Blockbusters are also called "tentpole" movies because if they are strategically placed the entire bigtop is supported. Here are the all-time top 25 "tentpoles" in terms of domestic box-office rentals (the share of the box-office gross, roughly 50 percent, that goes back to the distributor of a movie) expressed in millions of dollars. Those titles produced between 1980 and 1989 are in boldface.

1. *E.T. The Extra-terrestrial* (1982), $228.6
2. *Star Wars* (1977), $193.5
3. **Return of the Jedi** (1983), $168
4. **Batman** (1989), $150
5. **The Empire Strikes Back** (1980), $141.6
6. **Ghostbusters** (1984), $130.2
7. *Jaws* (1975), $129.5
8. **Raiders of the Lost Ark** (1981), $115.6
9. **Indiana Jones and the Temple of Doom** (1984), $109
10. **Beverly Hills Cop** (1984), $108
11. **Back to the Future** (1985), $104.4
12. **Rain Man** (1988), $102
13. *Grease* (1978), $96.6
14. **Tootsie** (1982), $96.3
15. *The Exorcist* (1972), $89
16. *The Godfather* (1972), $86.3
17. *Superman* (1978), $82.8
18. *Close Encounters of the Third Kind* (1977), $82.7

---

of articles in *The American Film Industry*, and in Ethan Mordden's *The Hollywood Studios*, we see how the free-for-all industry evolved into an oligopoly always struggling for vertical integration, always attempting to give the people what they wanted . . . for a price. The best work of fiction about the current Hollywood — in fact, one of the best books on moviemaking since Fitzgerald's *The Last Tycoon* — is Elmore Leonard's *Get Shorty*.

19. *Three Men and a Baby* (1987), $81.3
20. *Beverly Hills Cop II* (1987), $80.9
21. *The Sound of Music* (1965), $79.7
22. *Gremlins* (1984), $79.5
23. *Top Gun* (1986), $79.4
24. *Rambo: First Blood Part II* (1985), $78.9
25. *The Sting* (1973), $78.2

Sixteen of the top 25 films have appeared in the last decade, and it is clear that these new blockbusters make millions in a few weeks. Since *Jaws* in 1975 and *Star Wars* two years later, Hollywood has learned to orchestrate a film "by the numbers." The nascent blockbuster starts with nationally advertised openings on thousands of screens. A media barrage continues until the target audience has been saturated. Bingo! It works, or it doesn't, all within a few weeks. *Batman*, for instance, made $40.49 million between June 23–25 on 2,850 screens. Such films become bona fide cultural events. They may even become "megablockbusters," events independent of theatrical display, existing in the cultural plasma all over the world until superseded by other orchestrated extravaganzas.

Merchandising rights are often the most valuable rights that flow from such a motion picture and can produce, as *Star Wars* first did, a literal bonanza. Spin-off is the ultimate goal of movie-making. When Dawn Steel, onetime production head of Columbia and before that of Paramount, was asked what she really wanted to do, she said her dream was to run Bloomingdale's. After all, her most notable success before the movie business was as a designer of toilet paper. The died-and-gone-to-heaven fate of the successful Hollywood producer is to become a manufacturer of toys. Consider the Batman regalia: the T-shirts, socks, records, lunchboxes, computer games, shoes, toys, hats, posters, candy. . . Mumford High sweatshirts had to be specially manufactured after *Beverly Hills Cop*. Teenage Mutant Ninja Turtles had their day in the shopping aisles. First eat the cereal, then see the picture. Merchandising has progressed from the "Shirley Temple dolls" with dimples in their knees in the 1930s, to the Wizard of Oz coloring books in the 1940s, to the Davy Crockett raccoon-skin hats and Mickey Mouse ears of the 1950s, up to the more recent commercial cross-pollination of Nintendo breakfast cereal, Ghostbusters Proton Pack, Police Academy Loudmouth Bullhorn, Leatherface doll (complete with chainsaw), and Mickey Mouse on the waistband of Pampers. As Steve McBeth, vice president of consumer products for

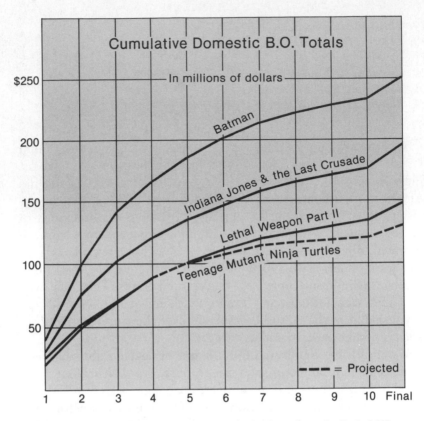

Rapid release of *Batman, Indiana Jones & the Last Crusade, Lethal Weapon: Part II*, and *Teenage Mutant Ninja Turtles* in months of box-office totals (*Variety*, May 2, 1990; permission of *Variety*).

Disney, said of the little rubber replica of the Flounder from *The Little Mermaid* in a McDonald's Happy Meal, "It extends the entertainment experience for the child — it's a way of letting the fun of the movie continue" (Maslin, December 12, 1989). Come back next week for Ursula the Seawitch. The 1989 New Line catalog has thirty-eight different items featuring Freddy Krueger, including a digital watch, a Nintendo game, pajamas, a rap song by the Fat Boys, a 900 number for junior to call to talk personally with Mr. Krueger, and, of course, the Freddy Krueger "Nightmare on Elm Street" glove complete with stiletto fingernails. Freddy, in fact, has his own television show, dedicated to his nightmares as does Jason Vorhees (*Friday the 13th — The Series*). Is it any wonder that Freddy and Jason are better known to

Sample page from Freddy Krueger Catalog of *Nightmare on Elm Street* memorabilia, 1989 (New Line Cinema: Move Inc.).

children between ten and thirteen than George Washington, Abraham Lincoln, or Martin Luther King?

Just as film images can take on a life of their own outside the "text" in popular culture, so too have previously forbidden images from advertising culture been allowed inside the celluloid world. As filmmaking has become more self-consciously commercial and risk-averse, the conglomerates, who control the studios, have been more willing to rent out billboard space. This is called "synergy." So in a typical Hollywood film like *Rocky III* we glimpse products like Coke, Sanyo television, Nike shoes, Wheaties, TWA planes, and Wurlitzers and are treated to outright advertisements for Nikon film, Harley Davidson motorcycles, Budweiser beer, Maserati cars, Gatorade, and the American Express card. A firm called Associated Film Promotions analyzes scripts scene by scene for product placement and so informs the appropriate would-be sponsors.

Sometimes the studio does this on its own as Disney did with *Mr. Destiny*. In a letter to the makers of consumable products, quoted by *Advertising Age* (April 25, 1990), Disney says that for $20,000 your product can appear in the background, for $40,000 it will be mentioned, and for $60,000 it will be consumed on-screen. Disney, one might remember, is the same studio that forbids theater owners to run commercials before any of its own films because advertising demeans the experience. In what is probably the most incredible example of product placement, Philip Morris paid $350,000 to have James Bond smoke Larks in *Licence to Kill*, even including a warning at the film's conclusion informing the kiddies that smoking could be dangerous.[3]

Blockbusters are becoming the sine qua non of the industry for reasons other than product placement inside the movie and after-market merchandising outside of it. In 1973, box-office receipts dominated total returns. Studios made movies for people who "went *out* to the movies." About 85 percent of exhibition revenue was generated at the theater. The three national television networks provided the rest. In 1990, box office will account for less than 40 percent of total revenues. Where will the 60 percent come from? From cable television, videocassette sales, and from foreign markets. Film is much more international than print, for obvious reasons. In each global aftermarket — theater, cable, cassettes, television, and syndication — the blockbuster does not merely dominate: it rules.

"Ancillary market performance" makes or breaks movies, and it makes or breaks them in a matter of months. To remain solvent, a movie should recover 85 percent of its cost of production within fourteen months of release. Doing well at the domestic box office is not enough, but it does ensure that the film can then travel down the golden path through television, videocassette, and global distribution. Like publishing houses, studios need not only "product," but a continuous flow of product. Since they don't know where the be-stseller/blockbuster will come from, they concentrate their efforts at the top of the list. Publishers estimate one bestseller in every 100 books, while studios need one blockbuster every twenty films. In the terms of the trade, this flow is called "having bulk." Bob Shaye of New Line Pictures explains what he learned in the grocery business in Detroit: "I learned that product is everything. If you run out of Domino Sugar in the warehouse, you ask them to send you some more. The worst mistake an independent company can make is not having enough resources to assure itself of a product flow" (Harmetz, July 13, 1989). New Line is one of the few minor studios to survive the 1980s, and it did so solely on the strength of repeating *Nightmare*

3. The record for product placement so far seems to be held by *Days of Thunder*. There are plugs for more than seventy products or corporate names including Winston, Exxon, Chevrolet, Pepsi-Cola, Diet Pepsi, Mello Yello, Coca-Cola, Gatorade, STP, Citgo, Prestone, Quaker State, Super-Flo, Havoline, Budweiser, Busch, Coors, Miller, Champion, Goodyear, Ace Hardware, True Value Hardware, Heinz, Tide, Ford, GMC, Pontiac, Ryder, U-Haul, ESPN, Skoal, Hardee's, Hilton, Levi's, and Lee. The most blatant plug is for Sweet 'n' Low. During a lovemaking pit stop, Tom Cruise's tongue trails two packets of the sugar substitute along Nicole Kidman's bare thigh.

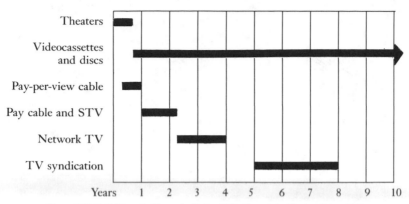

SOURCE: *Channels' Field Guide to the Electronic Media*, 1985. Copyright Marian Chin, 1985.

Geographic Market Share of Theatrical Films — 1980, 1984, and 1988. *Movie Industry Update*(Goldman Sachs Investment Research, March 13, 1989).

on Elm Street's success — that is, until *Teenage Mutant Ninja Turtles* came along.

Studios have realized they are not going to create that blockbuster by making movies for the domestic audience down at the Cineplex 16, even if Maslin and Kael *were* entertained. They must make movies for a worldwide theatrical audience and for a worldwide television audience. The global market today is not only Western Europe, but the Asian Pacific Rim as well. Hollywood has always been aware of this audience, but only recently has it become a central target. Hollywood has been able to control world distribution by a bit of serendipitous good fortune. After World War II, the Justice department allowed the movie industry to do abroad exactly what it had prohibited at home — to act like a cartel. It allowed blind bidding, "cross-collateralizing" (bunching the profits and losses to reduce risk), and the outright dumping of films. Although the Europeans didn't like it, and set limits on repatriated money, the Americans bought foreign studios to shelter their profits. Now the situation is reversed. Ten years ago American releases grossed 45 percent of its revenues abroad; today the gross may be as high as 90 percent.

"Globalization" has implications that promise still more vulgariza-

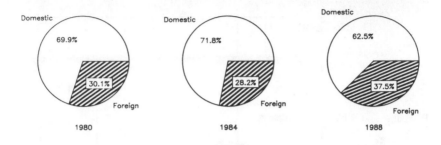

Share of Total Market
Movie Industry Update(Goldman Sachs Investment Research, January 20, 1991).

tion. Since nuances of language and cultural eccentricities impede instant gratification, the studios have moved to a still-lower common denominator — the production of stereotypes. This genre focuses on immediately recognizable international stars (usually men, because they can be typecast as macho longer than women can be cast for sexpots) like Charles Bronson, Sylvester Stallone, Arnold Schwarzenegger, Clint Eastwood, Sean Connery, or Paul Newman in high-speed action. The risk in creating such stereotypes and their astronomical salaries is worth it, usually. Witness the box-office success of Tom Cruise in *Cocktail* or of Eddie Murphy in *Harlem Nights*. These are films that would have flopped without their presence. The emphasis on the predictable explains the huge advances paid to Stephen King and Thomas Clancy. The audience wants the brand name first, then the story. These actors come complete with a thematic bar code optically scanned by the audience. They are sold as packaged products. "Sean Connery is terrific," trumpets the ad, giving no indication as to what the movie is about. Who cares?

To the global audience, *redundant* and *derivative* are terms of praise, not opprobrium. Hence, we have the stream of presold stories as prequels and sequels. "High concept" teen-pic genres like horror and action/adventure find a world audience quickly, while culture-specific genres like screwball comedies or sociological dramas do not. Like category publishing, movie stories now move in contagious rashes. In the last few years, we have had a rash of movies about connubial meltdown (*The War of the Roses* or *She-Devil*), childbearing (*Three Men and a Baby, Parenthood, Baby Boom, Look Who's Talking*, and *She's Having a Baby*), comic-book heroes (*Batman, Superman, Indiana Jones* and *Dick Tracy*), people swapping bodies and ages (*Vice Versa, Like Father Like Son, 18 Again*, and *Big*), and science experiments (*Weird Science, Real Genius*, and *My Science Project*). This is not to mention the sexy-thriller genre which literally plays all over the world all the time. And always, always, the emphasis in these genre products is on special effects, a happy ending, and the hint of a sequel. The movie must *show* something the audience cannot see elsewhere. And this action must be easily decoded. Gratification must be quick. When *Rambo* was shown in the Middle East to Arabs who had no quarrel with the Vietnamese, the enemy was shifted to the Japanese and so dubbed. Globalization is not without risk, however. Paramount Pictures thought the Japanese would not tolerate the Western ending of *Fatal Attraction* (in which the wicked heroine is first nearly drowned then shot by her ex-lover's wife), and so inserted one in which she is first dishonored and then commits ritual suicide. Paramount guessed wrong. The Japanese wanted the same blown-out-of-the-water ending as did the rest of the world. Twentieth-Century Fox had trouble marketing *The Abyss* because moviegoers did not know what an abyss is, or how to pronounce the word.[4]

Just as globalization for movies is beginning to reach an audience around the world, television has allowed a depth of audience penetration into each culture unmatched by any other medium. Although the initial shock of television to movies was felt in the 1950s (to which the movie industry responded with Cinerama, 3-D, the teen-pic at the drive-in, Smellorama, and the like), the threat of the at-home screen has been almost mastered. The television industry has more than an insatiable hunger for movies; it has an addiction. And, thanks to the FCC, the networks cannot behave like studios, at least not yet. In the 1960s only one movie in ten made a profit; by end of the 1970s

---

4. In a sense, the era of the blockbuster came in 1977 when George Lucas carefully released *Star Wars* to theaters that had to meet special technological standards. The special effects were so important that his first-run theaters had to be able to support a soundtrack in Dolby stereo played over an advanced system filled with a newly designed "subwoofer" (that generated sounds you could feel as well as hear), and also had to have projectors geared for the large-frame 70mm format. In a decade Dolby Laboratories and Lucasfilm Inc. changed theaters all over the world and in so doing changed content. As the paperback form shifted mass-market reading, so have projection and audio equipment reformed film treatment and subject matter.

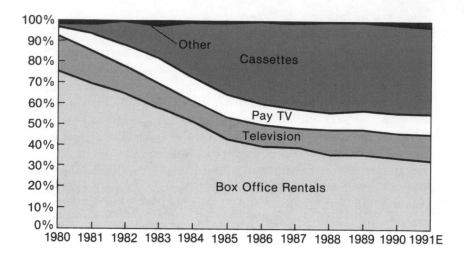

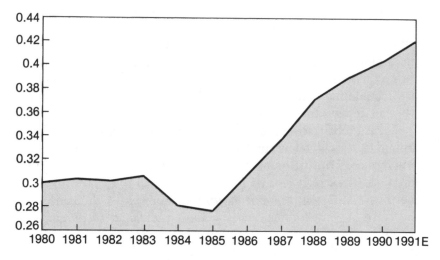

Foreign Theatrical Revenues as a Percent of Total Revenues
Movie Industry Update (Goldman Sachs Investment Research, January 20, 1991).

three in ten, and in 1985, for films with negative costs above $14 million, every second such film was making a profit. Why? Cable television had introduced more buyers, more competition for less programming, and up went prices. Television sales in 1989 rose 30 percent from 1987, from $1.3 billion to $2.3 billion. Currently, pay television like Showtime and HBO accounts for more than 20 percent of movie revenues.

Now there is a newer technology to be mastered. What the paperback book was to the publishing industry, the videocassette is becoming to the movie industry. This little tail is just starting to wag the big dog. More than two-thirds of American homes now have a videocassette recorder (VCR). Home video promises to infantilize film still further, as the audience in the videoaftermarket is demonstrably less and less sophisticated. In 1987, videocassette rentals surpassed ticket sales. The retail market for videocassettes was about $4.6 billion. The math of the future is simple. The studios receive gross receipts of about $1.58 per theater ticket, eighteen to twenty-five cents per cable subscriber, and five cents per broadcast television household. But when they sell the videocassette, they clear about $55.00 for each $79.00 cassette sold. This market is determining which movies get made. In 1986, when Oliver Stone accepted one of the four Academy Awards won by *Platoon*, he unabashedly acknowledged Vestron Video, which had funded the war epic. Vestron took a gamble and bankrolled Stone in exchange for video rights, in very much the same way that New American Library made the deal for the paperback first and then farmed out the hardcover. A few years from now, we may realize that it was not the Paramount decrees to unbundle the theaters in the 1950s, or the introduction of television that changed the movie industry in the 1960s, but rather a hybrid technology in the 1970s — the videocassette — that rearranged the carnival.[5]

The studios do have a problem, however. In the short run, they make quick profits when they sell cassettes to retail outlets. But they lose the profit stream of repeated rentals, which goes to retailers like

5. Video has even changed the way movies are filmed. The television screen is so small that the last thirty years of movie technology necessary to accommodate the big screen has had to be reversed. A pan-and-scan process is used to convert movies to video, which controls some, but not all, the big-screen distortion. When Susan Seidelman shot *She-Devil* she had one eye literally on the video monitor, with bars on it to indicate the television screen. Warren Beatty did not film *Dick Tracy* in Panavision because of the problems in converting the ultrawide format. Occasionally, moviemakers like Woody Allen and Steven Spielberg will demand that their films be shown on television and in videocassettes using the "letterbox" format (blanking off the top and bottom of the TV screen while leaving the middle distortion-free); this allows the full movie screen to be shown, but it is difficult to watch. In terms of content, there is an increased emphasis on close-ups and medium shots that register best on the TV screen, on cutting back and forth between "talking heads," and on using long shots only to establish locale. Often the movie you see on video is substantially different: *Batman* was lightened for video, Brian DePalma made more than 1,200 changes to *The Untouchables* before he was willing to release it, and in *The War of the Roses* a multisecond scene of the family dog (still alive) was added to make the wife seem a bit more sympathetic.

Paramount Video sell-through advertisement, 1990.

Blockbuster Video, National Video, Video World, and the thousands of "mom and pop" operations. Hence, the studios do not share in 80 to 90 percent of the film's profit. Worse still, the studios sell to retailers who rent the units and then, months later, put them up for sale. Because of the antitrust decisions about controlling exhibition, the studios cannot own the video stores, and because of the "first sale" legal doctrine, once the retailers buy the cassette from a studio they can rent it out repeatedly without any compensation to the studio. Although the studios now realize they should have pushed pay-per-view television harder, they also realize the only solution is to sell the videos directly to the consumer, thus bypassing the video store. Direct selling is what book publishers learned to do in the nineteenth century, bypassing the lending library, but it only works if production costs fall. "Sell-through" (as it is called), rather than rental, is beginning to influence which stories will be told, which movies will be made. As book publishers still attempt to circumvent the retail link and reach the customer via book clubs, so too do the studios.[6]

6. In the late 1980s, a two-tier pricing system was in effect: rental stores paid from $59.95 to $89.95, and "sell-through" to individuals was around $29.95 (but sometimes as low as $12.98). They are having some success. From 1987 to the end of 1989, video sales

The videocassette blockbuster, like the mass-market paperback, is especially rewarding in sell-through. A film with the potential of selling 400,000 cassettes at $89.95 generates $22 million for the studio, but a $24.95 cassette that sells three or four million copies puts the total between $42 and $58 million, even with the extra duplication costs and extra promotion. In 1988 studio revenues from videocassette sales increased by 27 percent, to $2.3 billion, with *ET* and *Cinderella* accounting for about 30 percent of this gain. The studios predict that as prices fall even further, consumers will turn from rental to purchase. While the price of the cassette is relatively inelastic at around $20.00, the studios found with *Top Gun* and *ET* that they could "cross-promote" products — that is, sell advertising space on the tape, and so reduce production costs to around $8.00. Industry observers guess that we will soon see "super-discounted" cassettes at about $10.00.

But now comes the kicker, and the reason why critics Kael and Maslin can only look forward to more disappointment. In 1988 the top 10 percent of theatrical releases captured almost 50 percent of total box-office receipts. The rental of cassettes does not always mirror box office (in fact, except in the large cities, certain video genres like the X-rated video has all but destroyed "porn theaters" or "art houses," depending on your point of view), but the purchase does. Customers are not interested in owning 95 percent of the films released. But they do want to buy the hits. And the hits that are really popular are children's films, animated or otherwise, and action-adventure films like *Indiana Jones and the Last Crusade* or *Total Recall*.[7]

The desire to own a cassette of a popular movie is hard for book buyers to understand, but it seems that, just as many people like to

climbed from $115 million to $195 million, about a 70 percent gain. Sales in 1989 were projected to be about $2.5 billion or about 22 percent of the $11.5 billion video market. In 1990, for the first time, sell-through revenues were greater than rental releases.

7. *Batman* changed the thinking about how to sell video. The Batman's forte was not that he could befuddle the Joker, but that his "sell-through" was so powerful that in less than six months after release, and without going first through pay cable, Warner Bros. was able to ship ten million cassettes wholesaling for $14.00. At the same time, *Batman* earned $140 million in rentals.

While cassette sales approximated box-office receipts, Warner Bros. kept about 55 percent of the cassette price. Once hundreds of thousands of cassettes had been sold at about $19.00 apiece, the industry learned that indeed there is a "magic" price point. The demand was so intense that the *Batman* tape was sold without the Macrovision anti-piracy codes (which make a videotape difficult to copy). Customers did not want a "copy." They wanted the "real thing."

build libraries of books, there are millions of people who do the same with videocassettes. Paul Keagan Associates, which collects such data for the industry, estimates that the average video household spent $120 on rentals in 1990 and about $42 on sell-through (Berman 1991:30). Of the more than four hundred films released in 1990, most of the readers of this page probably cannot think of more than ten they would like to own, or even rent, but they would be in the minority. They might rent the film once or twice, but it is doubtful that they would pay to own the "original." It is not a happenstance that most hardcover books cost about the same as the sell-through cassette. Video clubs sell cassettes the way record and book clubs sell records and books, even using identical advertising copy.

A few more figures, and the concerns of Kael and Maslin will be put into even more melancholy perspective. Imagine three films. Film A has domestic rentals (box-office gross less exhibitors' costs) that are 400 percent of negative costs (the producer's cost to create the actual celluloid). Film B is a profitable film with domestic rentals 125 percent of negative costs; and Film C is a loss product with domestic rentals 25 percent of negative costs. Assume all variables such as advertising, overhead, distribution, and participation costs are equal.

Although the movie industry is reluctant to release all its figures for non-box-office sales, the same top 10 percent of theatrical releases that captures almost 50 percent of the total box-office receipts continues to reap equally vast rewards as these move through the ancillary markets in global release. The movie that has a line of eager customers at the Cinema 16 maintains that appeal in television sales, and especially in videocassette sales. This is not to mention what happens if megablockbusterhood is achieved and the movie's images can be merchandised and licensed. However, the smaller or more modest film, like the midlist book, is usually doomed.

In the studio days, when the studio owned its own theaters, "product" could be protected by moving it from first-run houses to second- and third-run houses until it found an audience. The B-movies were essentially made to tide the studio over, ways to exploit otherwise wasted assets like studio space, stars, directors, and screenwriters while major projects were mounted. These "programmers" also functioned as testing grounds to try out new configurations of personnel, equipment, and stories. But no longer. By reducing supply, and promoting certain "A" films intensely, studios are willing to suffer a loss on the slow-moving movies in order to concentrate on the hits.

Ironically, television has aided and abetted this process. Between 1950 and 1970 the number of homes with television jumped from 10 to 95 percent. In the same twenty years, movie-theater audiences dropped from sixty million customers a week to fewer than twenty million. In 1940, 500 domestic films were produced; today 250 is an average yearly production. Television removed the "B" picture from the downtown theater and provided it "free" to viewers at home. In the immortal words of Sam Goldwyn, "Why should people go out and pay to see bad pictures when they can stay at home and see them for nothing?" Not only did television reduce the market for secondary movies, it also provided the means to promote blockbusters by national advertising, encouraged their production by paying to rebroadcast them, and, coupled with the VCR, gave them yet another access to a mass audience.

If a film is now going to make big money, it must travel through

Film A
(Millions)

TIME	1–4 Months			4–8 Months			8–12 Months		
	Revs	Cost	Profit	Revs	Cost	Profit	Revs	Cost	Profit
Domestic rental	$80	39	41						
Foreign rental				40	20	20			
Domestic cassettes				20	13	7			
Foreign cassettes							15	10	5
Domestic pay TV							10	3	7
Foreign pay TV									
Network									
For TV									
US syndication									
TOTAL	$80	39	41	60	33	27	25	13	12

Observations
(1) Total profits are $90 million on revenues of $182 million (Box office was about $180 million).
(2) 90% of revenues are realized in first year.
(3) Margins are about the same in the major markets.

Film B
(Millions)

TIME	1–4 Months			4–8 Months			8–12 Months		
	Revs	Cost	Profit	Revs	Cost	Profit	Revs	Cost	Profit
Domestic rental	$25	22	3						
Foreign rental				15	13	2			
Domestic cassettes				3	2	1			
Foreign cassettes							2	2	0
Domestic pay TV							3	2	1
Foreign pay TV									
Network									
For TV									
US syndication									
TOTAL	$25	22	3	18	15	3	5	4	1

Observations
(1) Total profits are 11% of Film A's with revenues of 30% of Film A's (box office $55 million).
(2) 87% of revenues are realized in the first year.

Film C
(Millions)

TIME	1–4 Months			4–8 Months			8–12 Months		
	Revs	Cost	Profit	Revs	Cost	Profit	Revs	Cost	Profit
Domestic rental	$5	21	−16						
Foreign rental				2	4	−2			
Domestic cassettes				NM		—			
Foreign cassettes							NM		—
Domestic pay TV							1	1	0
Foreign pay TV									
Network									
For TV									
US syndication									
TOTAL	$5	21	−16	2	4	−2	1	1	0

Observations
(1) Total amount to $18 million with 89% absorbed during the domestic release (box office is about $11 million).
(2) One failure is detected advertising budgets are cut.
(3) There are essentially no ancillary market revenues.

12–16 Months			16–20 Months			20 Months +			TOTAL		
Revs	Cost	Profit	Revs	Cost	Profit	Revs	Cost	Profit	Revs	Cost	Profit
									80	39	41
									40	20	20
									20	13	7
									15	10	5
									10	3	7
3	1	2							3	1	2
			7	3	4				7	3	4
3	1	2							3	1	2
						4	2	2	4	2	2
6	2	4	7	3	4	4	2	2	182	92	90

12–16 Months			16–20 Months			20 Months +			TOTAL		
Revs	Cost	Profit	Revs	Cost	Profit	Revs	Cost	Profit	Revs	Cost	Profit
									25	22	3
									15	13	2
									3	2	1
									2	2	0
									3	2	1
1	1	0							1	1	0
			3	1	2				3	1	2
1	1	0							1	1	0
						2	1	1	2	1	1
2	2	0	3	1	2	2	1	1	55	45	10

12–16 Months			16–20 Months			20 Months +			TOTAL		
Revs	Cost	Profit	Revs	Cost	Profit	Revs	Cost	Profit	Revs	Cost	Profit
									5	21	−16
									2	4	−2
									NM	0	NM
									NM	0	NM
									1	1	0
NM		—							NM	0	NM
1		—	NM		—				1	0	0
NM		—							NM	0	NM
						1		—	1	0	0
1	0	—	0	0	0	1	0	—	7	25	−18

Marketing of Films A, B, and C
Goldman Sachs Investment Research, March 13, 1989, and September 21, 1988.

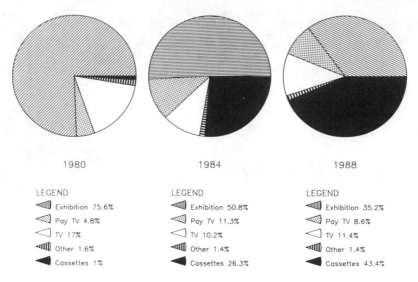

Revenue Mix of Theatrical Films — 1980, 1984, and 1988
Goldman Sachs Investment Research, March 13, 1989, and September 21, 1988.

the ancillary market until it is finally merchandised and sequelized and sent through again. The industry is candid about this. In the publicity material for *Back to the Future Part II*, Universal says: "Future II was made because in its initial release *Back to the Future* earned over $350 million world wide, and emerged as the top-grossing film of 1985" (Kael 1989:139). However, *Future III* was shot at the same time as *II*, so the decision was really made to make two sequels. Enough said.

Films are made to imitate films that made money. This is, after all, the attraction of genre from the storyteller's point of view. A clone is as good as a sequel. In theory, cable and video should be encouraging more adventurous filmmaking, but this is not the case. More profits are made by exploiting across all the media outlets than by narrow casting through only one or two. As Goldman Sachs' Richard Simon, one of the most knowledgeable observers of the industry, has commented on this multimarket release, "The beneficiaries will be the hits, and the tie-ins will not create interest for the B and lower titles. Now, more than ever, the non-A title is slipping" (1989:10).

By and large, only the conglomerated studios have the resources to make "A" titles. Others have tried but, as A. H. Howe of the Bank of America argued a generation ago, the size of the production investment is so large and the risk so great that even in a good year one or two of the major studios will be on the brink of disaster. Now that total box office is $5 billion, the same risk obtains. It just costs more to get into the game. The money to be made, Howe first predicted, is not in movie-making but in movie-distribution. Successful studios are not those that want to make movies, nor are they the ones that make the best movies, they are the ones who distribute movies — often those made by others. The risk is in production, the profits in distribution. The goal of distribution is always to maintain a product shortage. This shortage ensures there will be a dozen blockbusters. As of 1990, each major studio has a target production level of about fifteen films at an average negative (production) cost of about $23.5 million. Each of these fifteen films will have an additional print and advertising cost of about $8 million for a total of $120 million. The studios amortize the negative cost of a film, including the box-office receipts (rentals), cassette sales, pay-TV sales, and television sales in both the domestic and foreign markets. They then deduct a distribution fee (which is equal to about 35 percent of rental income) and profit participation of about 7 percent. Since the top ten films will corner about half the business, each studio drives for those films or is edged out of the market.

If you do the math the conclusion is inescapable. A studio now needs about an 11 percent market share to break even. There are currently eight majors in various conditions: Fox, Warner, Universal, Disney, Orion, MGM/UA, Columbia/Tri-Star, and Paramount. In the same way that just as a handful of publishers control more than 90 percent of what makes it to print, these eight studios control 90 percent of the film market. Even if they accurately forecasted the ancillary-market revenues and budgeted accordingly, there would be no profits *if* all studios were equal. They would all lose. But they don't. Some make money — lots of it. Universal, Warner, Paramount, and Disney have normalized production levels, focusing on "A" films, on potential blockbusters only. Disney, in fact, has done even more. It has added another ministudio, Hollywood Pictures, to Walt Disney Productions and Touchstone Films, putting more pressure on all the others. If the top two studios were ever to capture a 35 percent share, the other nine would average about 6 percent of the market and go under. The iron law of modern movie-making is the iron law of the carnival. If the audience doesn't increase, some of the exhibitors will fail. Therefore, some studios — Columbia, Tri-Star, and Fox — are

MEGAHIT/MEGABUCK FILM

(modeled after WB's "Batman")

	Costs	Revenues
	(in $ millions)	
Negative cost	50	—
Market:		
Domestic theatrical	25	150
Foreign theatrical	15	90
Other foreign	10	30
Domestic video	20	90
Paycable	0	20
Syndication	0	10
Network tv	0	10
Subtotal	120	400
Less 30% dist. fee		– 120
Less 20% gross participations		– 80
Recoupment	120 vs.	200
Net profit	80	

MODEST-BUDGET THEATRICAL FLOP

(modeled after BV's "Gross Anatomy")

	Costs	Revenues
	(in $ millions)	
Negative cost	12	—
Market:		
Domestic theatrical	8	4.5
Foreign theatrical	1	0.5
Other foreign	0	1
Domestic video	1	4
Paycable	0	3
Syndication	0	1
Subtotal	22	14
Less 30% dist. fee		– 4
Recoupment	22 vs.	10
Net loss	12	

Release of Four Films: Megahit, Barely Released, Modest-Budget Flop, and Foreign Hit (*Variety*, February 21, 1990; permission of *Variety*).

BARELY RELEASED

(modeled after Par's "The Experts")

	Costs	Revenues
	(in $ millions)	
Negative cost	12	—
Market:		
Domestic theatrical	0	0
Foreign theatrical	0	0
Other foreign	0	1
Domestic video	1	2
Paycable	0	3
Syndication	0	1
Subtotal	13	7
Less 30% dist. fee		− 2
Recoupment	13 vs.	5
Net loss	7	

FOREIGN HIT

(modeled after Col's "Karate Kid Part III")

	Costs	Revenues
	(in $ millions)	
Negative cost	18	—
Market:		
Domestic theatrical	12	19
Foreign theatrical	6	30
Other foreign	2	10
Domestic video	2	10
Paycable	0	5
Syndication	0	2
Network tv	0	4
Subtotal	40	80
Less 30% dist. fee		− 24
Less 10% gross participation		− 8
Recoupment	40 vs.	48
Net profit	8	

NORTH AMERICAN THEATRICAL FILM RENTAL MARKET SHARES: 1970-1990

By A.D. MURPHY

Feature film rentals from U.S. and Canadian theaters, expressed in percentages of total industry rentals (including those of minor distributors). This data table summarizes all earlier published annual distributor market share rankings. Although much boxoffice data is recently available, film rentals — the distributors' share of boxoffice gross — are preferable in measuring distributor performance. For convenient reference, each year's largest market share percentage is shown in a box. Percentages do not add to 100% in any year; the residual amount is accounted for by smaller and/or defunct distributors.

See notes (1) through (10) below for important information on certain newer, minor or defunct distributors.

YEAR	COL (3)	FOX	MGM/UA (1)	PAR	UNIV	WB (8)	BV (9)	ORI (2)	TRI (3)
1990	5%	14%	3%	15%	14%	13%	16%	6%	8%
1989	8%	6%	6%	14%	17%	19%	14%	4%	7%
1988	3%	11%	10%	16%	10%	11%	20%	7%	6%
1987	4%	9%	4%	20%	8%	13%	14%	10%	5%
1986	9%	8%	4%	22%	9%	12%	10%	7%	7%
1985	10%	11%	9%	10%	16%	18%	3%	5%	10%
1984	16%	10%	7%	21%	8%	19%	4%	5%	5%
1983	14%	21%	10%	14%	13%	17%	3%	4%	—
1982	10%	14%	11%	14%	30%	10%	4%	3%	—
1981	13%	13%	9%	15%	14%	18%	3%	1%	—
1980	14%	16%	7%	16%	20%	14%	4%	2%	—
1979	11%	9%	15%	15%	15%	20%	4%	5%	—
1978	11%	13%	11%	24%	17%	13%	5%	4%	—
1977	12%	20%	18%	10%	12%	14%	6%	4%	—
1976	8%	13%	16%	10%	13%	18%	7%	5%	—
1975	13%	14%	11%	11%	25%	9%	6%	5%	—
1974	7%	11%	9%	10%	19%	23%	7%	4%	—
1973	7%	19%	11%	9%	10%	16%	7%	3%	—
1972	9%	9%	15%	22%	5%	18%	5%	3%	—
1971	10%	12%	7%	17%	5%	9%	8%	3%	—
1970	14%	19%	9%	12%	13%	5%	9%	3%	—

North American Theatrical Film Rental Market Shares, 1970–1989 (*Variety*, January 17, 1990; permission of *Variety*).

trying to increase production, while others like MGM/UA and Orion are being divided up or are slipping away into bankruptcy.

This level of risk explains why the surviving studios have become conglomerated. Most independents are perpetually in trouble. New World, DeLaurentiis Entertainment, Atlantic, Weintraub Entertainment, Cannon (now absorbed by Pathé), Vista, Vestron, New Vision, Avenue, and Spectrafilm all face tough times and will probably not make it through the 1990s in their present forms. New Line, which makes niche movies at the low end of the market, and Carolco, which does the same at the high end, have survived. But they have often been only one flop away from Chapter 11.

About thirty years ago, the process of "diversify or die" began. To spread risk, Warner moved into books and camera equipment, Columbia into records, Disney into theme parks, Fox into resorts, and MGM into Las Vegas hotels. For a while, each studio seemed to own a soft-drink bottler. But after the moguls had all died in the 1960s, the gobbling-up process happened in reverse. Diversified companies bought studios. Universal fell to MCA in 1962, Paramount to Gulf + Western in 1966, United Artists to Transamerica in 1967, and Warner Bros./Seven Arts to Kinney National Service, later to become Warner Communications. The shifting into bigger and bigger units is continuing. Rupert Murdoch snapped up Twentieth-Century Fox to get a beachhead for satellite-beamed Sky TV, and Warner merged with Time, Inc., lest either one be swallowed by Paramount Communications. Matsushita in 1991 purchased MCA for some $6 billion. As in book publishing, such conglomeration betokens still greater concentration on the bottom line. And this concern translates into the creation of entertainments for which the only standard of judgment is financial.[8]

8. To understand the current allure of the studios, we might look at Sony and Columbia Pictures. Columbia was a moribund studio in the late 1980s, yet the Japanese paid a shade less than $5 billion to buy it. To get "product" to distribute, Sony next bought the Guber/Peters production company for $200 million, paying the coproducers a $2.75 million salary for five years, a share of profits, a one time $50 million bonus, plus 8 percent of the appreciation in Columbia's assessed value. However, Sony did not count on Guber/Peters' contract with Warner Bros., which cost it another $500 million to buy them out (plus granting Warner a half-interest in Columbia's book club and cable distribution rights to Columbia's television productions). All of this added an estimated cost of $400 to $600 million to the deal, but Sony was still pleased. Why?

Because, as Willie Sutton said of robbing banks, that is where the money was. In the past decade we have come to accept the fact that a baseball star is paid $50,000 per homerun. We may even accept an executive who pockets $50 million as a leveraged-buyout incentive to leave town. But are production heads of Columbia Pictures really fifty times as valuable as other dealmakers? To be sure, Peter Guber and Jon Peters did produce two megablockbusters — *Batman* and *Rain Man* — as well as such fine movies as *Missing*, *The Color Purple*, *Flashdance*, *The Witches of Eastwick*, and *Gorillas in the Mist*, but they also kenneled such dogs as *Caddyshack II*, *Vision Quest*, and *Clue*. Clearly, Sony was interested in more than production. They wanted Columbia's 2,700 film library with movies like *Lawrence of Arabia* and television programs like "Designing Women" and "Jeopardy."

The real power in Hollywood poker is announced as the credits first roll — in the presentation of the studio logo. That power is located geographically just south of Central Park in a half-mile radius of the corner of 59th Street and Fifth Avenue and now also in downtown Tokyo. On almost the exact spot where P. T. Barnum's American Museum once stood in midtown Manhattan is the Time Warner headquarters (which also houses parts of HBO and Little, Brown & Company), the Paramount building (inside which is Showtime and part of Simon & Schuster), the network headquarters of ABC (a subsidiary of Capital Cities Communications), "Black Rock" at elegant "51W52nd" (which houses CBS), and Rockefeller Center (inside which is NBC, part of General Electric). The offices of record companies' affiliates are also within five blocks of each other on Sixth Avenue (as New Yorkers still call the Avenue of the Americas). The headquarters of International Creative Management (ICM) are on Fifth and Seventh Avenues, while rival agency William Morris is just around the corner. Not far away are various large law firms such as Weil, Gotshal & Manges; Paul, Weiss; and Cravath, Swain. Downtown are the bankrollers — Goldman Sachs, Lazard Frères & Company, Salomon Brothers, Lehman Brothers, Allan & Company, and nearby are Chase Manhattan and Morgan Guaranty. On the horizon, peering in, are the robber barons who have replaced the moguls. Eyeing the pot are the leveraged buyout kings: Kirk Kerkorian, Saul Steinberg, Herbert Allen, Rupert Murdoch, Giancarlo Parretti, Ted Turner, and even Akio Morito and Akio Tanii.

How ironic that the old-time moguls who went west to get away from the dreaded "Trust," the Motion Picture Patent Company, have themselves evolved into near-monopolistic behemoths. They have had to, so they say. Movies are wildly expensive and too risky. To film on location costs from $30,000 to $50,000 a day, or about $5,000 an hour — more than the average advance for most first novels, more in fact than most first novels ever make, and almost more than the average novelist makes in a year. There is no movie counterpart for a

---

But even more, Sony wanted to control the "software" first before introducing their new 8mm videocassete system. They remembered how their Betamax system was pushed aside by Matsushita's VHS. Still, to pay so much for the producers of blockbusters shows that the movie industry, like the book publishing industry, passionately believes that the only way to survive at the carnival is not only to sell the most tickets, but to bankrupt some of the other players. Like high-stakes poker, success is not always determined by what you have in your hand, but what it takes to stay in the game. Sony raised the ante.

North Point Press, or an Algonquin Press (although Orion may be giving it a try), and certainly no equivalent to the university presses. With some very rare exceptions, no one in this business is "subviened" by the national endowments. Decisions here are made on the basis of market research, tax laws, demographic trends, and the spreading of financial risk. Everyone watches the box office. MBAs and CPAs in pinstripes call the shots, not cigar chompers in jodhpurs. As an understandably wistful Otto Preminger observed a few years ago, "Picture-making itself had a better shot under the old moguls. They were basically movie guys. Not conglomerate or bank-endorsed people. There were giants in the industry. Now it is an era of midgets and conglomerates" (Litwak 1986:97). However, from a macroeconomic point of view, although the Paramount decrees and the tax laws have had pronounced effects, the industry in the 1990s is more and more resembling the industry of the 1940s.

The Reagan decade of hands-off regulation allowed the conglomerate-housed studios to reassert the drive for vertical integration. One could argue that the current obsession with blockbusters really started when the theaters were taken away from the producers in the 1950s. With the loss of controllable screens, the balance of supply and demand was settled by controlling supply. With no guarantee of exhibition, fewer movies were made. Risk-taking was not rewarded. Pictures could not be protected in studio-owned theaters. The stars took off on their own, clutching their agents. The studios had to break up backlots. "Runaway production" saw the abandonment of Los Angeles soundstages for cheaper locations. Now, however, because of the video aftermarket and globalization, the studios are recovering the movie theater audience. And, thanks to a lenient Reagan Justice Department, they are also being allowed to re-purchase theatrical outlets. In 1948, just before the Paramount decree took effect, the studios controlled 17 percent of 18,000 theaters. Since 1985, cocooned inside conglomerates, the studios have acquired more than 3,500 of the nation's 22,000 screens.[9] The studios now own about the same percentage of outlets as they did in 1938 when the Sherman Antitrust Act was passed. In addition, the Reagan

9. Among current holdings, MCA (Matsushita) owns more than 40 percent of Cineplex Odeon, or about 1,880 screens. Columbia Pictures Entertainment owns Loews Theater Management with 839 screens, and Paramount Communications is a 50 percent partner with Time Warner in Cineamerica L.P., controlling 466 screens each.

years were also kind to the industry by repealing tax shelters, which dried up money for independent production.

Although the ingredients are a little different, movies are now being made according to the same show business recipe. The main ingredient is money. And the money all comes to, and goes out of, New York. Although we tend to think that the major decisions are made on the West Coast, this has never been the case. The young hustling junk dealers, furriers, and glove salesmen may have become the first moguls, but they only ran the factory floor. The front office, in Manhattan, always ran the shop.

While anecdote after anecdote is told about the power of Louis B. Mayer, Jack Warner, Harry Cohn, and Darryl Zanuck (in his early career), and how they controlled theater screens and/or dealt ruthlessly with stars, the real power was always in the East. Every day the theater divisions gave information to the CPAs in Manhattan, and they reported to the CEO. Men like Marcus Loew, Nicholas Schenck and Joseph Schenck, Abe and Harry Warner, Barney Balaban, Frank Freeman, and Darryl Zanuck (in his later career) signed the checks. In pseudo-Darwinian style, John Huston reminisced about life at MGM:

> L. B. Mayer guards the jungle like a lion. But the very top rulers of the jungle are here in New York. Nick Schenck, the president of Loew's Inc., the ruler of the rulers, stays here in New York and smiles, watching from afar, from behind the scenes, but he's the real power, watching the pack close in on one or another of the lesser rulers — close in, ready to pounce! Nick Schenck never gets his picture in the papers, and he doesn't go to parties, and he avoids going out in public, but he is the *real* king of the pack. And he does it all from New York! God, are they tough! (Ross 1952:11–12)

Depending on where the greatest profits had been made, the New York office communicated its wishes to the factory. Make more Chevrolets, fewer Cadillacs, too many convertibles, more station wagons. So, for instance, every year the Warner brothers in New York cabled their projected outlays to Darryl Zanuck, when he was head of production. Zanuck then sat down with a list of the stars and directors under contract, and matched them with the stories he owned. "OK, we want three Bette Davises, four Cagneys, four Eddie Robinsons, three Bogarts, two Errol Flynns. Who's got a good story for Bogart — anything we can put Bogart in?" (Mosley 1984:393). In a few days, Zanuck had outlined the entire production schedule for next year. The studio chief then hired producers who would be responsible for six to eight features. These producers were responsible for all writing, shooting, and editing within a New York-ordered budget. The studio chief was also responsible for organizing the music departments, newsreels, stars, short subjects, and cartoons. If General Motors provided the production ideal, Woolworth and Sears developed the distribution pattern. This centralized producer system was perfected by Irving Thalberg and Louis Mayer at MGM, and was what F. Scott Fitzgerald meant when he said that only a few people could understand "the whole equation of pictures."

Putting images on celluloid is only a small part of the process. From the first prospectuses for underwriting capital (prepared by investment houses like Halsey, Stuart; J.& W. Seligman; Bankers Trust Company; Kuhn, Loeb & Company; Goldman, Sachs; Hayden, Stone; and Dillon Read), the film industry was not touted for artistic expression, but for its assembly-line production, worldwide distribution system, air-conditioned exhibition halls, conservative accounting practices, and especially for its vertically integrated structure.

The mission of the New York office was to wring the most money out of each entertainment by means of efficient promotion and distribution. The only industry with a higher marketing-to-revenue ratio is cosmetics. In New York, an elaborate distribution scheme evolved whereby the "product" circulated through discrete exhibitions so as to maximize profit at each cycle. The majors all followed the same pattern. In fact, the industry was like a quarrelsome but closely knit family. On the West Coast moguls pooled and exchanged stars, as well as lots, stories, and personnel. On the East Coast they determined whose films would play where and for how long. By the 1930s, a three-tier system was in place. "Presentation" houses, which often seated thousands and charged the highest prices, were owned by the studios and were the first to show a film. Next came the neighborhood theaters, often independently owned. And, third, the small run-down houses called "dumps," never owned by the studio and always treated with disdain and financial chicanery.

Films circulated through these "zones" governed by fixed "clearances" of fourteen days, then twenty-eight days, and finally forty-two days, each time finding a new audience at a lower price. Just as garments in the fashion industry were first sold uptown in exclusive shops, then moved to department stores, and ended their lives at the close-out shops downtown, so too did the system of runs, zones, and clearances lock up the cycle of exhibition. The chain held together even after the Paramount decrees because, as David McClintick observes,

> To many producers, the process of marketing the average movie (they believed there was such a thing) was very simple: You opened it at Loew's Tower East on the East Side of Manhattan, Loew's Astor Plaza in Times Square, the Bruin in the affluent Westwood area of Los Angeles, and the Chinese on Hollywood Boulevard. You took full-page ads in the *New York Times* and the *Los Angeles Times* beginning a few days before the movie opened and extending a week into its run. If the movie did poorly, you doubled the ad budget. No motion picture was so bad that it could not be sold to the public by an aggressive studio advertising department. (1982:109–110)

A movie might have more than ten runs in some cities and take more than a year to exhaust different audiences. All along the way, the distributor in New York set the admission prices.

Competition with nonaffiliated theaters was controlled with block booking and blind buying, which forced the independent theaters to guarantee a base figure, and so shifted the financial risk to the powerless exhibitors. To be sure, the distributor did more than provide the film. He arranged exhibition, prepared marketing, publicity, advertising, and negotiated terms and arranged delivery of print. (As a vestige of carnival days when the carnies often skipped town before paying their bills, newspapers still charge higher rates for "amusement advertising" than for other products.) For his services, the distributor collected, and still collects, his fee of some 30 percent of box-office gross, which is appropriately called the "first position." Every seven days a box-office statement is due from each theater and if any irregularities are suspected a watchdog service is called in to stand outside the theater and check the traffic flow.

The relationship between distributor and exhibitor has always been based on mutual distrust and occasional hate. In the game between distributor and exhibitor, the exhibitor is Wile E. Coyote and the distributor is the Roadrunner. As compared to bookselling where the bookstore owner can return unsold merchandise, the theater owner is stuck. Many theaters, in fact, have to guarantee to show a film *x* number of weeks in order to play it at all, which is why many big-budget "flops" like *Days of Thunder* hang around so long. Even when he has a hit, the exhibitor has no control. As Samuel Marx has reminisced, "Theaters are stores where customers buy entertainment, but unlike most merchandising outlets, the buyer doesn't take his purchase away. He pays for it and looks at it, then leaves with only the memory of it. When the last customer has paid and looked and left, the material that was bought still belongs to the man who sold it" (1975:14).

The *process* of movie distribution, however, is like that of book distribution. The print product cycles through hardcover, then trade paper, then mass market, just as the movie changes venues. The movie industry could keep far greater control over its outlets. The only power independent exhibitors have is to exaggerate the house expenses (called the "nut"), to bid unfairly, to be cantankerous about reporting box-office receipts, and to be dilatory with payments. Even then, New York has the upper hand — no payment, no product. The ability to collect money is still why the large studios control the industry, and they do it by controlling distribution. An independent producer can "four-wall" his product (rent the theater and do his own ticket collecting), but he will almost always lose if he expects the independents to report receipts honestly. Money reporting could become computerized with EDP POS terminals, as has happened in the chain bookstores, but independent exhibitors have steadfastly refused. It is their only trump card.

One cannot overestimate the importance of this distribution hegemony. The major studios did, and still do, control 95 percent of all the bookings. Any studio that cannot direct agents in major American outlet cities, and in the population centers of the world, will suffer. Distribution fees, for instance, saved United Artists when Samuel Goldwyn was making their only profitable pictures. However, distribution without a notable product is not enough, as demonstrated by the fate of RKO. The studio's logo is really the distributor's name. In the early days, the header film showed no credits, no stars, but only the name of the company, called an "exchange." This company consisted of salesmen, brokers, and cashiers. Films were literally exchanged. They still are. Although films were originally sold by the foot, they are now licensed, never sold. The distributor owns the product, and the theater operator is the licensee whose rights are limited by contract. The distributor determines how the picture is released, and for a number of reasons that have to do with generating blockbusters, they have come to prefer fast distribution.

Once an "average" picture is "locked in," prints are struck, dubbed, checked, and made ready for release. The films open on about five hundred screens in the first few days. Does it have legs? Movie viewing is considered a weekend, Christmas, and summertime pastime, and if certain key theaters in places like Phoenix, Arizona, and Madison, Wisconsin, are filled, the distributor will rush more prints around the country into open dates. If not, he will pull the prints and go straight to video. The average novel has a shelf life between that of milk and yogurt, the movie that of cut flowers. Since 40 percent of a film's income is in the first fifty markets, and since ten circuits contribute 50 percent of the majors' income, the studios often prefer to saturate these markets by playing a thousand screens at a time. For this type of movie, often a sequel to a blockbuster, the distributor will receive up to 90 percent of the box office. Admittedly, market saturation increases advertising expenses, since it short-circuits the much-vaunted "word of mouth." But it also "buys the gross." On such films, the studio takes the distribution fee out of gross (while filmmakers share in net profits), so the additional advertising expenditure helps the studio, often at the expense of the net participators. The exhibitor goes along; after all, the film has become the loss-leader used to sell popcorn.

Not only did the New York office control admission price, zone, run, and clearance, which minimized the number of theaters needed to control the market, they also established the so-called Production Codes which served to stabilize competition. Contrary to common opinion, the codes were not forced on the industry by church, government, or irate audience. Hollywood was more than happy to control content as a way to control access to markets. If you wanted a rating for your film so that exhibitors would show it, you had to join the Motion Picture Producers and Distributors of America (MP-PDA). From the 1920s until the 1950s, the "big five and little three" had to submit scripts and films for approval. Since the majors controlled theaters, nonapproved films were denied access and, in all but a few cases, this disapproval guaranteed box-office failure. So, in a sense, the industry exercised prior restraint over itself in exchange for production control.

This control sometimes broke down, not only as the Paramount decrees forced the big five corporations to relinquish most of their theaters, but also when the Supreme Court in a landmark 1952 case said that the First Amendment extended to filmmaking just as it did to newspapers, magazines, and books. You could count the months on your fingers until Otto Preminger released his silly *The Moon is Blue* (UA 1953), complete with those forbidden words *virgin* and *mistress*, and a new audience was ushered into the theater and a new code was called forth. Until the 1950s, however, these codes were a sturdy fence not to keep the taboo out as much as to keep the competition from getting in.

One of the most interesting aspects of the various codes is how each new code forbade exactly what the industry would produce a generation later. Once the gate was built and the gatekeeper installed, the gate was opened. Don't let *that* through, the studios said, as bit by bit that was exactly what was let through. Although the early codes were a public-relations coup stabilizing oligopolistic control under the stern eye of postmaster Will Hays, in 1925 the "Don'ts and Be Carefuls" were printed and promulgated. Eleven items were not to be shown at all, such as white slavery, miscegenation, sexual perversion, and ridicule of the clergy. There were twenty-six subjects to "be careful" of, such as arson, murder techniques, rape, first-night sex, drugs, and excessive and lustful kissing. Once this document was out, the 1930s had its marching orders. "Step this way, folks. See just a bit of what should not be seen." Soon it was necessary for the next code to announce what was to be prohibited and then to be shown.

The 1934 Production Code was the motion picture industry's Magna Carta of official decency, and hence a centerpiece of the vulgarizing process. The word "moral" or its derivatives appear twenty-six times; "sin," "evil," "bad," "right" and "good" appear frequently. Along with special sections on "Crimes against the Law" and "Sex," a section expressly devoted to an aesthetic category appears for the first time. Here it is:

> III Vulgarity
>   The treatment of low, disgusting, unpleasant, though not necessarily evil, subjects should be guided always by the dictates of good taste and a proper regard for the sensibilities of the audience.

The general sections continue, dedicated to Obscenity, Profanity, Costume, Dances, Religion, Locations, National Feelings, Titles, and Repellent Subjects (such as actual hangings, brandings, sale of women, and surgical operations). To make sure its gates were secured, the 1934 code added enforcement power. No film could be distributed or screened by a member of MPPDA unless it carried the Production Code Administration (PCA) seal. Violators could be fined $25,000. None was.

Every censoring code—from the Production Code of 1908, through the publication of "Don'ts and Be Carefuls" and the edicts of the Hays office in the 1930s, past the Catholic church's Legion of Decency and the PCA rules of the 1940s and 1950s, to the current self-registered G, PG, PG-13, R, and NC-17 rating system—has attempted to prescribe patterns of sex, and also of violence. Each has promised that vulgarity of all kinds will be avoided. "Not at this carnival, you don't," says the self-righteous code. And every code has failed. Vulgarity has been victorious. The carnival has prevailed. Six months after the Supreme Court's 1968 decision in *Interstate Circuit v. Dallas*, which allowed local-option censorship, the industry announced its new "self-regulation."

The current ratings system continues the industry's history of attempting to gain the largest possible audience while not alerting the police. What separates the present code from earlier attempts is that it is blatantly self-serving. Essentially this code says: Make any picture you want, just put it into one of these categories, originally: G (all ages admitted), M (mature audiences suggested), R (restricted to over sixteen or with a parent), and X (no one under sixteen). No sooner said than hedged. The age limit for R and X was moved to seventeen; then M became GP, and from GP to PG (general public to parental guidance); and finally a new category, PG-13, was added. PG-13 is an especially interesting rating because it says specific parental guidance is suggested for those under thirteen but establishes no prohibitions. PG-13 can supposedly be invoked by a single "gratuitous" drug scene (i.e., without bad consequences) or a single "sexually derived word." But what it usually means, as critics were quick to point out, is that the "soft R" summer movie blends in with the PG-13. Thus PG-13 films now have *more* violence, but less sex and drugs. The newest rating, NC-17, is an attempt to retrieve the audience lost to the X. The X was not copyrighted and was used (often gleefully, as in XXX) by the Pussycat Theaters and trenchcoat crowd, much to the chagrin of the industry. Even more important, many theater chains had contracts with mall developers *not* to show X-rated movies in cineplexes, and many newspapers would not carry X-rated movie advertisements. The NC-17 allows the chains to recapture that audience without violating their contracts. In addition, many of the national video chains, which would not carry X-rated cassettes for fear of violating local zoning ordinances, will carry those rated NC-17, thereby increasing studio sales in the aftermarket. Any student of ratings should not overlook the fact that, after much bickering, the first film to carry this rating was *Henry and June* (1990) from Universal Studios, a subsidiary of MCA, which also controls the Cineplex Odeon theater chain.

The gist of all these shifts is to make obvious what was always clear to the moviemakers. Since the adolescent audience is between the PG and R ratings, these are the best ratings to acquire for the largest box-office receipts. Movies are made for the ratings; ratings are not made to categorize the movie. This upside-down system has produced some telling ironies. For instance, in *Student Bodies*, an otherwise forgettable send-up of the stalk-and-slash genre, a genial narrator intrudes with some foul language saying that this ought to be enough to assure an R (he was correct). Sometimes the system has been grossly inappropriate. In 1968, 32 percent of the pictures produced by majors and minors were G; by 1984 it had dropped to 2 percent. During that same period, R-rated films rose from 22 to 45 percent of all releases. PG films were relatively stable — about 40 to 50 percent of the total production. In 1989, *Variety* reported that 559 films were rated: the R rating was given to 67 percent; PG-13, 17 percent; PG, 15 percent; G has 1 percent; and X less than 1 percent. G and X were supposedly box-office poison: G because of television and X because of videotape rental. The X rating, formerly given for violence (*Midnight Cowboy* and *A Clockwork Orange* both had X ratings), became synonymous with pornography. Although the MPPDA's Production Code said of the depiction of murder on-screen, "The basic dignity and value of human life shall be respected and upheld. Restraint shall be exercised in portraying the taking of life," Brian DePalma's *Scarface* (1983) showed what was really meant. This ballet of gore worked its way up from X to R. Violence was (and is) acceptable as R; only sex was prohibited as X. The main reason it took twenty years for theater owners to accept the NC-17 rating is that they did not want to have to take time away from selling popcorn and candy to check the age of patrons.

The trend is toward more sex and violence, more exaggerated action, more special effects, more vulgarity. Blockbuster movies are cartoons, literally and figuratively. Read the advertising copy for

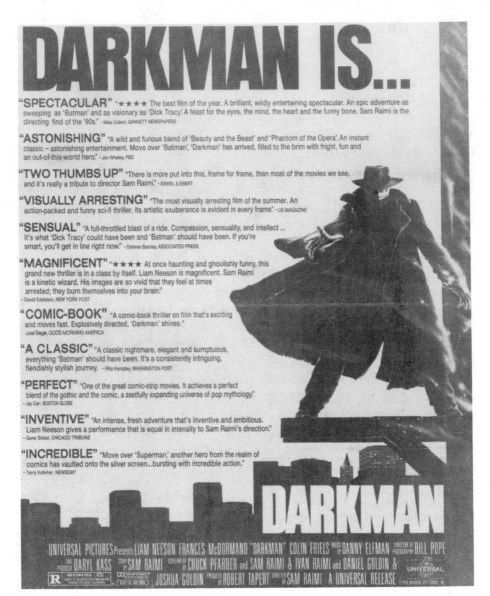

Universal Studios' *Darkman* advertisement, 1990.

Darkman and it becomes clear that the adjectival panegyric of the 1990s is "comicbook." In this sense, one could argue that of all the modern media the movies have really changed the least. They started by competing with burlesque and have ended by competing with television. The shift from nickelodeon to studio-made movies took about thirty years, followed by an era of studio domination, with a short hiatus after the Paramount decrees for "independent" productions and studio realignments, and now there is a return to studio control of nickelodeon movies.

The second coming of the studio system has already begun, and the trend is likely to continue with the consolidation of studios into a few colossal worldwide entertainment conglomerates. Certainly, the technology has continually evolved ever since the introduction of sound in 1927, the development of incandescent lamps, new electrical cables, new lenses, faster film, color, larger screens, air conditioning, increased portability of equipment, Dolby sound, computer-driven optical advances, digitalized sound, the large-frame 70mm format. . . And certainly the production codes of what constitutes acceptable "morality" have changed. But the process of production/distribution/exhibition has changed very little. "The new Hollywood is very much like the old Hollywood," David Chasman, ex-vice president of MGM, has said (McClintick 1982:frontispiece). Studios still generate cash from their control of distribution which they reinvest in production.[10]

While the New York offices of the movie industry were all similar, all dedicated to wringing the last drop of profit from distributing and exhibiting the product, the factory had a distinct personality. This "house style" is really what has disappeared in the vulgarization of film as it has almost disappeared in publishing. When Knopf publishes *Miss Piggy's Guide to Life* and Warner Bros. distributes Akira Kurosawa's *Dreams*, the concept of a unified corporate personality has been blurred. One blockbuster looks just like another: that's the purpose.

10. The term *independent producer* has always been a misnomer, even in the 1950s, and essentially refers to how studios were able to spread risk-participation by exploiting tax laws. The so-called independent producer really isn't. George Lucas had Twentieth-Century Fox money for *Star Wars*. Steven Spielberg had funding with Universal for *Jaws* and with Columbia for *Close Encounters of the Third Kind*. Francis Ford Coppola made *Apocalypse Now* with United Artists' money.

The few truly "independent producers" soon find that the only thing worse than being involved with a major studio is not being involved with a major studio. As long as the studios control distribution they will also control production. Just as in book publishing, there may be new ways to "presell product," to exploit "ancillary markets," and "control downside risk," but the bottom-line prize will go to those who can distribute effectively, not to those who can produce the best product. Samuel Goldwyn and David Selznick were exceptions. A great movie "in the can" loses to a mediocre movie on the screen. Algonquin Press published wonderful books that often never made it to the store.

In the first studio era, the men who crafted the house style were like editors at publishing houses in the 1940s. They chose what to publish, how to publish, and when to publish. The editors in movie-land were the producers and, although they now act like their print colleagues traveling from house to house, they often spent their entire career with one studio. As Leo Rosten said of this old Hollywood: "Each studio had a personality; each studio's product showed special emphases and values. And in the final analysis, the sum total of a studio's personality, the aggregate pattern of its choices and its tastes, may be traced to its producers. For it was the producers who established the preferences, the prejudices, and the predispositions of the organization and, therefore, of the movies which it turned out" (Schatz 1988:7). Billy Wilder agreed: "Studios had faces then. They had their own style. They could bring you blindfolded into a movie house and you opened it and looked up and you knew. 'Hey, this is an RKO picture. This is a Paramount Picture. This is an MGM picture.' They had a certain handwriting, like publishing houses" (Gabler 1988:187).

The men who made that style were often criticized as "carnies" and to an extent, of course, they were. These middle-European Jews — Zukor, Lasky, Mayer, Thalberg, Goldwyn, Selznick, the Warners (the exception being Darryl Zanuck from the midwest) — simply did not know the New England Protestant Northeast. They were indifferent to the high-culture heritage of Emerson, Thoreau, and the Boston Brahmins. *The Education of Henry Adams* was not on their summer reading lists. They never had a stake in that mythology, so instead they created a carnival of their own exhibits, perforce "vulgar" to America's logocentric and Anglophile elite. The men who produced (not directed!) movies uniformly would have preferred Busby Berkeley to Howard Hawks. Doubtless they would be chuckling over the current high-culture huffing about colorizing their movies.

On the subject of Samuel Goldwyn and his "Goldwyn Girls," Robert Sherwood reportedly told Anita Loos, "You can't really resent Sam's vulgarity when he himself never learned the meaning of the word" (Dunne 1989:29). In fact, Goldwyn's feelings would have been hurt had he known in what low esteem vulgarity was held. One could say the same about Louis B. Mayer at MGM, Jack Warner and Hal Wallis at Warner Bros., Darryl Zanuck at Fox, Harry Cohn at Columbia; and independents like David Selznick. The only exception — and this the result more of reminiscential folklore than actual fact — was

Irving Thalberg. These men were not "unit" producers who worked inside a studio, as Robert Altman does with Lion's Gate, Ron Howard with Imagine, Spielberg with Amblin, George Lucas with Lucasfilm Limited, or (now no more) Francis Ford Coppola with Zeotrope. These men controlled an entire studio. They could do this because each studio had its own writers, designers, and editors, all the way down the line to its own filmcutters and scorers. Before the Paramount decrees, each studio even knew what its audience was like, and in which theaters its movie would play. Studios had distinctive styles forced on them by the exigencies of who worked there and the properties they owned.

These distinctive styles were also the result of who *didn't* work there and what they didn't own. Warner Bros., which did not then have high-priced stars (true, Bogart, Cagney, Muni, Flynn, Robinson, and Bette Davis *became* stars) or an eagerness to spend money, produced blunt, tough, fast (even speeding-up the film to give it pace), cynical movies — rather like their cartoon hero Bugs Bunny. Warner did remakes of everything on the cheap until the audience tired and went elsewhere. Titles were rewritten, recast, and refilmed. Warner Bros. exhaled characters at the margin, characters just like Jack Warner.

Meanwhile, across the way at Columbia, Harry Cohn ran a cheap, dingy, and heartless studio, "a riffraff of a place" said Frank Capra, Cohn's most famous director. Cohn had no money bosses in the East, and so let his staff make pictures freely as long as the pictures made money. What made money was the earnest populism of Frank Capra and Robert Riskin in the 1930s, and moral comedies in the 1940s. So that was what Columbia produced. Cohn was a dictator to be sure, but he also had the knack of understanding vigor in any form. He knew that moving pictures must move.

Paramount, under Adolph Zukor, had directors like Ernst Lubitsch, Mitchell Leisen, Preston Sturges, and later Billy Wilder, who created a world of surfaces and sex and abandon in which virtue was not always triumphant, but style certainly was. Universal did not have the economy and speed of Warner, the screwballness of Columbia, the continental sheen of Paramount, but had instead westerns (which Carl Laemmle liked to read as a kid) and horror movies assembled by the Europeans he imported. Universal's motto might well have been "A Good Cast is Worth Repeating" for, especially in the horror genre, the same faces appeared again and again, often cast in contradictory roles. So, for instance, Lon Chaney, Jr., plays the mad doctor, then the werewolf; the Frankenstein monster, then the son of Dr. Frankenstein. One couldn't blame Abbott and Costello for finally making fun of the whole entourage in the late 1940s. The Fox studio was essentially two operations — one started by William Fox with medium budgets and second-rank stars (which was forgettable), and the other one run by Darryl Zanuck with big budgets and plenty of daring.

But the premier studio for distinctive style was MGM. Under Louis Mayer and Irving Thalberg, MGM became the Tiffany of the industry with its stable of glamorous stars, its production units, its writers, choreographers, and composers nonpareil. The MGM producer was king, the director was subordinate, technical values the highest, and stories edifying (but not too edifying). MGM was able to produce and sell prestige items because of its tie to the Loew's theater empire which, before the divestiture, had to show MGM product, and did so for top dollar. Even in the 1950s, long after television had captured most of its audience, MGM continued to produce a version of America in spangles so distinctive that it can be recognized after a few frames. Ironically, this culture also caused MGM's downfall.[11]

These studio styles were the result of having a factory with an assembly line, of having the same machines, same personnel, same raw materials, and the same exhibition halls. Oldsmobiles and Pontiacs have always looked like each other, as have Plymouths and Dodges, Mercurys and Lincolns. We call what we see in the movies before the 1950s "studio style," but aesthetics were not on the list of "must haves." However, as contrasted to the current conglomeration of the industry in which the money men are in almost total control, the moguls and their central producers had a sense of responsibility and tradition, a sense of themselves, albeit exaggerated, and of their audience. To be sure, they were mostly first-generation Americans

11. RKO was the anomaly. Founded in part by RCA as a way to put their audio systems in competition with Western Electric (the "R" was for "Radio" as in Radio Corporation of America, and the "KO" for the Keith-Orpheum theater chain into which the system was installed), this was the only studio without a guiding presence. True, David Selznick was there for a while, as well as Pandro Berman and Dore Schary, but RKO had no lasting stylist, no guiding presence. Although RKO produced some uptown sophisticated screwballers like *Bringing Up Baby* and many of the Astaire-Rogers films, its success came not from production but from distribution. RKO handled Walt Disney Productions, Samuel Goldwyn Films, John Ford's Argosy Pictures, and Frank Capra's Liberty Films, to name a few. Howard Hughes finally took it apart to sell for scrap.

who wanted assimilation quick. The Jews who created Hollywood were not from Middle Europe with a taste for finance and art, but instead were poor immigrants from Poland, Russia, and Hungary. They were working-class Jews who had come from the world of selling coats, suits, gloves, furs, and dresses. Their economic future lay in knowing what the *goyim* wanted.

Making "flickers" was a suspect business, an entertainment descended from the nickelodeon, itself one step removed from the carnival. As compared to book publishers, the moguls really did not know what they were doing because they were often doing it for the first time, but they knew for whom they were doing it. Their rapidly expanding audience was primarily working-class with tastes derided by the critics from high culture. Yet almost to a man, each of the soon-to-be moguls had a sense of responsibility. They saw themselves as gatekeepers, even if they didn't always act that way. In contrast to current studio executives, they were carnival barkers, yes, but they believed they could show something enlightening in the dark.

So here is Jack Warner, cynical, smarty, smarmy, smirky, addressing the troops: "I do not mean we should strive for so-called intellectual films, but we should strive for pictures that provide something more than a mere idle hour or two of entertainment." Here his New York-based brother, Harry: "The motion picture presents right and wrong, as the Bible does. By showing both right and wrong, we teach the right" (Gabler 1988:195, 196). Self-serving comments, certainly, but the Warners did feel that they had a role in the transmission of culture, even if they weren't sure whose it was. Part of the reason why Warner Bros. took the chance in converting to sound was not to improve plot, but rather to provide high-culture music. Darryl Zanuck recalls Harry Warner saying: "Do you know what sound means? From now on we can give every small town in America, and every movie house, its own 110-piece orchestra" (Schatz 1988:59).

At Columbia studios, Harry Cohn, who was not committed to much besides making money (and about whom Rabbi Magnin, when asked to say something nice about the deceased, said, "He's dead"), supported Capra's movies showing the common man fighting for his beliefs, even when the films were not profitable. True, no one had more contempt for "culture" than Cohn (his motto was "Let Rembrandt make character studies not Columbia"). But if one looks at pictures made by Columbia, one senses the self-conscious posturing of the chronically insecure. Cohn was a smart man petrified of being mistaken for an uneducated man.

Meanwhile, Adolph Zukor, resident mogul at Paramount, "was surprised when anybody criticized his gestures for improving the social tone of the cinema as publicity schemes" (Busch 1929:29). "We were always trying to lift public taste a little bit," Walter Wanger, a Paramount executive by way of Dartmouth and Oxford, reminisced: "Zukor and Lasky [in the New York office] were dedicated men who would produce pictures that they thought should be done, even though they weren't going to be profitable" (Rosenberg and Silverstein 1970:84). William Fox recalls:

> When I entered, actively, the producing field of motion pictures I was actuated by a double motive. The so-called features that I had been selecting with all the care possible for my theaters did not fill my ideals of the highest standard possible in motion pictures. Therefore, I was fairly driven, in the interest of my patrons, and also as a secondary consideration in the belief that there was an immense demand of really good pictures, into the manufacturing end of the business. . . . I decided to carry out, in my motion picture producing career, the same ideals as I had introduced at the Academy of Music. That is to say . . . that the public insistently demands photoplay features by great and world-famous authors, featuring celebrated dramatic stars. (Gabler 1988:69)

That same desire for respectability is echoed in Irene Selznick's memory of her father: "Even when I was a very little girl my father spoke of the importance of what was being shown to the public. He deplored the way show business was being run; he thought everyone in it had an obligation to help make it respectable and then keep it so. . . . He became evangelistic about show business, most particularly movies" (1983:27). No one talks that way about movies any more.[12]

12. To observe the mechanisms of cultivation at work, consider MGM under Louis Mayer. MGM made a fetish of noblesse oblige. As Mayer said as he opened the studio, "From a production standpoint, you can count on it that Metro-Goldwyn-Mayer will reach a point of perfection never approached by any other company. If there is one thing that I insist on, it is quality" (*Motion Picture News*, July 19, 1924:321). Ars Gratia Artis ("Art for Art's sake") became MGM's highfalutin' motto, its implications hardly understood, but its spirit appreciated.

"Ars Gratia America" would have been more appropriate, as Mayer took his newly acquired nationalism seriously. Andy Hardy was a favorite of Mayer's, in fact, a reflection of what he himself yearned to be. One story has it that Mayer saw Mickey Rooney

Having moguls at the gates to fend off the barbarians occasionally produced some rather ludicrous results. When MGM director Mickey Neilan turned in what he thought was a completed cut of a silent film adaptation of *Tess of the D'Urbervilles*, Mayer demanded a happy ending in which Tess is saved by a last-minute reprieve. MGM owned the rights to the story and could adapt it as it pleased, stated Mayer, who was convinced that he understood the sentiments and tastes of movie audiences better than either Neilan or Hardy. Or, what of the Sam Goldwyn ending to *Wuthering Heights* in which Cathy and Heathcliff are seen climbing into the clouds up transparent stairs to become etherealized in vaporous schlock. Still, the moguls sought out high-culture literature not only for accepted, market-tested stories, but because they believed that high culture existed and was somehow better for us. So what if it had to be revised? Paramount and RKO devoured literary tomes. MGM worshiped them. Universal ignored the printed word except for the gothics which it improved on. Even Warner Bros., probably against its better judgment, went to print for celluloid ideas.

Whereas today we might think of exceptions to the iron rule of bottom-line moviemaking, as with Spike Lee's *Do the Right Thing* or Martin Scorsese's *The Last Temptation of Christ*, such risks were far more common during the first studio period. Consider RKO's adaptations of classics like *Little Women*, or its risky ventures like Maxwell Anderson's *Winterset*, or of importing the Abbey Theater production of *The Plough and the Stars*, or of producing *Mourning Becomes Electra*, which the studio knew would lose money. Twentieth-Century Fox allowed Zanuck to adapt *The Ox-Bow Incident*, which no one else would touch, and supported his treatment of *The Grapes of Wrath* as a family melodrama, not as an economic fable of oppression. When

---

roughhousing about the lot and exclaimed: "You're Andy Hardy! You're the United States! You're the Stars and Stripes. Behave yourself! You're a symbol!" In an MGM picture children always learn from their parents to avoid the vulgar and aspire to the elite. Not Mayer, but Irving Thalberg, resident perfectionist, translated this passion into profitable pictures. In his words: "Idealism is profitable. That is the reason I retain my conviction that it is the thing. Quality pictures pay. We're in this business to make money, naturally, but the quality production, which is more often than not the expensive production, is the one that pays the big returns" (*Los Angeles Times*, August 19, 1933:32). Thalberg propounded the notion — heresy today — that the studio should make a worthy film or two without expecting any profit. This notion held true even after his death, and was the oft-proffered reason Mervyn LeRoy was allowed to continue with *The Wizard of Oz* in 1939 with a prohibitively expensive budget.

King Vidor wanted to film *The Crowd*, Irving Thalberg gave permission, although both men knew the political and economic risks.

Perhaps Samuel Goldwyn's Eminent Authors Project was the high point of reaching into high culture. Authors even had control of the adaptation of their work, something almost unheard of before or since. Goldwyn signed up Elmer Rice, Maxwell Anderson, Lillian Hellman, Rachel Crothers, Ben Hecht, Charles MacArthur, and Preston Sturges, all of whom must have been dumbfounded. And when Goldwyn thought Jascha Heifetz would be good for those who couldn't afford a ticket to Carnegie Hall, he made *They Shall Have Music*. "Next time," he said, "I'm putting Toscanini and Stokowski together" (Berg 1989:330). That Hollywood felt compelled to sugar-coat its productions reflected anxieties about its own self-image, but it also paid tribute to the perception of a higher culture. What an irony that Walt Disney's *Fantasia*, which became a head trip for the psychedelic generation of the 1960s, was originally conceived as a plan to bring high culture to the lowly in the 1940s.

The movie industry, ever since the 1920s, has both epitomized and abhorred vulgarity with equal sincerity. On the one hand, the moguls yearned for respectability, and on the other they had to keep making entertainments in a suspect medium. These men were not young bucks, but middle-aged businessmen seeking new fairgrounds. They wanted to improve public taste, yes. They also wanted to slough off the peephole carnival image of nickelodeon days. In fact, most of them had not even wanted to make movies. They made movies because they needed product for their outlets. The early moguls moved from exhibition to distribution to production out of need, not desire. As Neal Gabler has written in *An Empire of Their Own*, the moguls "understood public taste and were masters at gauging market swings, at merchandising, at pirating away customers and beating the competition [but] as immigrants themselves, they had a peculiar sensitivity to the dreams and aspirations of other immigrants and working-class families, two overlapping groups that made up a significant portion of the early movie-going audience" (1988:5). As long as they owned the theaters, they needed the Hollywood factory. And Hollywood needed respectability. Little wonder that the Fatty Arbuckle scandal was so important to control, that Wallace Reid's drug-related death was so quickly covered up, or that so many in Tinsel Town were willing to cooperate with the blacklists and Joseph McCarthy's witch hunts.

Part of that respectability could be achieved in the theater. When sound became profitable, Warner Bros. signed up the New York Philharmonic to record for feature films. By August 1926, the brothers had mounted a touring show with music from Wagner's *Tannhäser* played by the Philharmonic, followed by six acts of stage show, of which five were classical music including tenor Martinelli singing arias from *I Pagliacci*. Then, finally, came the feature film: *Don Juan* with John Barrymore. A decade later high culture was still being touted, this time by big-city exhibitors, who attempted to outdo their Hollywood colleagues in avoiding the vulgar by imitating what they took to be old-world elegance. Although he was an exaggeration of what exhibitors aspired to be, Samuel Rothapfel, known better as "Roxy," personified what happened at the end of the distribution chain. The epynomic Roxy, who was to give his name to the Manhattan theater, was the grand impresario of high culture. "Don't give the people what they want — give them something better," he repeatedly urged (Izod 1988:43). Roxy would go the Warners one better. On either side of the main cinematic attraction, he included classical music together with instruction in how to appreciate it. With typical American middle-class optimism, he promised to "give the movies a college education." In the coup of a lifetime of extravaganzas, he assembled the entire Metropolitan Opera Company to perform with the main attraction. Take that, Warner Bros.

When the movie industry lost its theaters in the 1950s, the balance shifted. There is no better way to see its transformation than to observe what happened when the theaters were cut loose. Movie theaters were no longer palaces. They became peep shows again.[13] As

13. The Nickelodeon, which followed the cabinet-sized peep shows, or Kinetoscopes, was approximately twenty feet wide and eighty feet deep, divided by a single aisle. Developments in lens technology and the introduction of air conditioning allowed the exhibition halls to grow like the Gothic cathedral. In the studio era the size exploded into such "cathedrals of motion pictures" as the Roxy (1927) and Radio City Music Hall (1932) in New York, Grauman's Chinese (1927) in Los Angeles, the Majestic (1922) in Houston, and the Riviera and Rivoli (1920s) in Chicago.

These imitation opera houses could seat about five thousand viewers in a confectionery fantasy of ersatz opulence. Since the 1960s the opposite trend has been just as strong. Once the studios were forced to divest themselves of their theaters, and once television had captured a huge share of their audience, big theaters were not being built — they were being razed. Most are parking garages today. In 1948 there were eighteen thousand theaters; in 1958 only twelve thousand. Add to this the impact of the drive-ins, which grew from eight hundred to four thousand in the decade of the 1950s. But even then the promise of darkness and privacy was delivered better elsewhere.

theaters contracted into multiplexes, seating space shrank and screens proliferated. In the 1950s the average theater had more than five hundred seats; in the 1980s, just over two hundred. These shopping-mall theaters, really movie dens, have been able to exploit the economies of mass production by targeting specific audiences. Just as book publishers have turned to category publishing to locate niche audiences, so too have moviemakers and movie exhibitors. In a sense, demographics and technology have returned us to pulp fiction and nickelodeon movies, the very vulgarities abhorred by the aspirants to high culture a generation ago.

One could make the case that the contemporary theater, and hence contemporary movie fare, was the invention of Stanley Durwood. Just as Robert de Graff realized he could cut the size and the price of hardcover books and put them into millions of pockets, in 1963 Durwood had the cost-accountant's happy inspiration that one could show many movies in the same space to many more patrons. Since the fixed costs of exhibition (the house costs, or the "nut") are almost 50 percent of total projection expenditures, why not show two movies at the same time? Durwood opened a "twin" theater in Kansas City. The twin grew, and soon these multiplexes gobbled up the market. Although "twins" are only 10 percent of all indoor theaters, they command more than 50 percent of the screens.

So if you think "They're not making movies like they used to," you're right. If you think, and wish to be grammatically correct, that, "They're not making movies or showing movies as they used to," you are doubly right. Motion pictures today are neither like those of thirty years ago, nor are they made as they used to be, nor are they shown in the same way. We still go into the dark to see moving pictures, and they still move at twenty-four frames a second, but the pictures themselves — the way they are written, photographed, exhibited, and controlled — have changed. Ironically, however, the industry resembles what it was sixty years ago — seven or eight vertically organized oligopolies. With the breakup of the studio system all the parts of the carnival have scattered.

Today the parts are coming back together with some important realignments.[14] Most important is that everything and everyone

14. At last glance, this is what the business looks like. "Uncle Carl" Laemmle's Horror and Western factory, which had a history of close calls with Chapter 11, was taken over by agents Lew Wasserman and Jules Stein and made part of the Music Corporation of America (MCA). Universal, now a minor subsidiary of the Matsushita Electric Industrial Com-

"above the line" (story writer, producer, director, cast) as well as everything and everyone "below the line" (laborers, sets, costume,

pany, relies on various "independent" producers such as the Mirisch Corporation, Ron Howard's Imagine, Steven Spielberg's Amblin Productions, as well as on the team of Richard Zanuck and David Brown.

The Walt Disney Company broke with faltering RKO in 1953 and made it big by allying with the upstart American Broadcasting Corporation. In the prototype of media conglomeration, complete with interactive merchandising, Disney needed capital and ABC needed product. While the Disney television show provided only 8 percent of Disney gross, it proved to be a key in the promotion and merchandising of products that were soon expanded into entire theme parks of commodified myth. Disney is now running three film units: Walt Disney Pictures, Touchstone Pictures, and Hollywood Pictures. If any current studio can be said still to have a "style," Disney might·be it. Disney has produced blockbusters the old-fashioned way: it keeps writers under contract and follows through on projects with relatively low-priced actors. Paramount emerged in the fall of 1966 under the control of Gulf + Western (the "Engulf and Devour" of Mel Brooks' *Silent Movie*) with its sister companies in auto parts, zinc mining, cigars, and meat packing. The company is now called Paramount Communications and has had success with blockbuster movies: the Indiana Joneses, Crocodile Dundees, Star Treks, Friday the 13ths, and, it seems, any movie with Eddie Murphy.

Warner Bros., which went through hard times in the 1960s, merged with Seven Arts Productions of Canada and then merging with Kinney National (which started with funeral parlors), is now part of the largest media conglomerate in the United States — Time Warner. Warner also pays fealty to the blockbuster mentality and has been successful with *Batman* and *Lethal Weapon II*. However, Warner's greatest advantage is its worldwide distribution system. Not so for Twentieth-Century Fox which is currently controlled by Murdoch's News Corporation, having previously been shuttled between private and public corporations. Fox hasn't the clout to last as a studio. Murdoch may not mind. What he really needs is a feeder of programming to his Fox American television network and his European, twenty-four-hours-a-day, satellite-delivered, pay-TV Sky Cable (or whatever it turns out to be called). And Columbia/Tri-Star would certainly be floundering had Sony not come shopping for software.

Orion is an object lesson in the problems of *not* being conglomerated. Started by a defection of executives from United Artists (itself started by a defection of artists — a sign of changing times), Orion is respected for "taste." If any studio can survive by not producing blockbusters, Orion will be it. The Woody Allen franchise belongs to Orion Pictures and, although it is dearly beloved by buffs, it is a money loser. Over the last decade, Allen has cranked out eleven films for Orion costing well in excess of $100 million which have returned less than $60 million in domestic rentals. As with UA, Orion usually finances and distributes films rather than producing them; in fact, a library of Orion Classics (chiefly of foreign-language films) may protect it during the globalization of the 1990s.

Probably nothing, however, can protect MGM/UA. This husk of two of the old-guard studios has been more raped and pillaged than Helen of Troy. After Mayer, MGM went through the hands of liquor magnate Edgar Bronfman, then to cowboy Kerk Kerkorian, now to Giancarlo Parretti and his French bankers. UA went from Mary Pickford and Charles Chaplin to Transamerica Corporation, to join MGM as its distributor. Although both studios now are reliquaries (having sold or rented off most of their libraries), MGM/UA still controls certain rights to *Gone with the Wind, The Wizard of Oz, Doctor Zhivago, 2001: A Space Odyssey,* and has about one thousand films in UA's library and home video rights to three thousand MGM films.

makeup, hair styling, optical and special effects) are negotiable. The aftermarket has become so important that no picture can be made for domestic release alone but instead must be "factored": so much for television, for pay-television, for cable, for cassettes, for the global market, for merchandising. Movie-making has become a business of ancillary rights, foreign-distribution advances, tax benefits, the laying-off risk on investment groups, "participation points," "step deals" with "pay or play" stipulations, "negative pickups," and other arcana concocted by lawyers. Always the focus is on how to presell around downside risk and to maximize profits.

The real art of Hollywood today is the art of putting the pieces together; "making the deal." The role of the mogul has fallen to the lawyer and the agent. The agent, who often represents all the creative parties, does what used to be studio work by packaging the above-the-line talent. After Lew Wasserman exploited the tax advantages of "participation," in which the star incorporated himself and traded salary income for a percent of the gross (the tax rate is less for capital gains than for straight income), the power shifted. Once Wasserman put together James Stewart's revolutionary contract for *Winchester 73* (in which Stewart got 50 percent of the profits in lieu of salary) studio control of actors was over. When Wasserman took the next step, essentially packaging the *Pillow Talk* movies of Rock Hudson and Doris Day for Universal, studio control of entire projects was called into question. Wasserman's Music Corporation of America, a onetime talent agency, became so successful that it soon ate up the very organizations it had served. MCA sold off its talent agency and took over Universal Studio.

Other agents soon stepped into the vacuum between creative talent and studio distribution. Ted Loeff set up Literary Projects to tie in the various aspects of show business: books, records, tapes, toys, and the host of products linked to modern storytelling. The most powerful man in Hollywood today supposedly is Michael Ovitz, president of Creative Artists Agency. What separates CAA from other agencies is that it not only arranges the aftermarket, but also provides the premarket. CAA generates ideas, hires readers to find new stories, employs writers, and even arranges financing in what are called "PFD" agreements — production, financing, and distribution. Ironically, this is a job the studios don't want, though this is exactly what they used to do. Twentieth-Century Fox, a second-echelon studio, receives some ten thousand screenplays, books, and "treatments" each year, of which seventy to a hundred make it into development,

and from which only twelve movies are ever made. The conglomerates are happy to let agents do this sifting work for them. Ovitz earns
a mogul's salary, does a mogul's work, and has twice been offered a
mogul's job as studio chief. He has refused. What does he need a
studio for? In fact, Ovitz was the broker who brought MCA and
Matsushita together; he is a mogul-making mogul. Needless to say,
the current agency-packaged movie is market-driven. What the agency pitches is the television Q-ratings of their stars, the presold and
audience-accepted nature of their stories, and their ability to deliver
every part at the proper time for a percentage. As one agent working
for CAA said of the job, the motto of such agencies is "don't smell
'em, sell 'em" (Litwak 1986:58).

As the agent has replaced the studio chief, the role of studio production has fallen to the execution of what is called the "deal memo."
As opposed to the book contract with its standard boilerplate, the
"deal memo" is like a modernist poem — inexplicable, inexhaustible
to interpretation, and purposefully obscure.[15] The land around Cen-

---

15. What the participants and observers say about it tells much about the triumph of
vulgarity in the Hollywood carnival. Joan Didion has written of the omnipresent "memo":
"The spirit of actually making a picture [is] a spirit not of collaboration but of armed
conflict in which one antagonist has a contract assuring him nuclear capability. Some
reviewers make a point of trying to understand whose picture it is by 'looking at the script';
to understand whose picture it is one needs to look not particularly at the script but at the
deal memo" (1979:210). Her husband John Gregory Dunne, in his book on life inside
Twentieth-Century Fox, elaborates, " 'The deal, that's what all this business is about,' a
Studio producer told me over lunch in the commissary. 'Who's available, when can you get
him, start date, stop date, percentages — the deal, it's the only thing that matters. Listen, if
Paul Newman comes in and says he wants to play Gertrude Lawrence in *Star*, you do it,
that's the nature of the business' "(1985:100).

Richard Zimbert, a vice president of Paramount, explains the interaction from his side
of the equation: "Since the movie business boils down to one thing, *money*, everything in
the deal revolves around that. The effort is to achieve agreement on the basics: who will do
what for how much; what the options, rights, or opportunities of each party are as the
project develops and their cost levels; and finally the accounting for and division of receipts
from the distribution of the picture, if it's made" (1983:177). Agent Marty Hurwitz explains
the operation from his side, "The object is for one side to be guaranteed as much as
possible and the other side to be guaranteed as little as possible, because people don't trust
each other. People are always sure they're going to get fucked" (Litwak 1986:158). Those
who actually make the movie would agree. Here is Danny Rissner, a line producer: "It's not
about whether it's a piece of shit or it's not a piece of shit. It's about whether we want to
make a goddamn deal" (Bach 1985:63). And William Goldman, the screenwriter of such
hits as *Butch Cassidy and the Sundance Kid* and *All the President's Men*, observes, "Often in this
scramble for hot material, 'Fellas, this book is a piece of shit!' becomes lost in the frenzy
over 'Can we make the deal?' " Goldman's first rule of Hollywood, in his own caps:
"NOBODY KNOWS ANYTHING" (Bach 1985:71). Over on the midway, the only thing
the carnie knows is how long the line is.

tury City in Los Angeles that was once back lots and soundstages is now filled with skyscrapers filled with lawyers and dealmakers. The studios, however, are hidden, squeezed into cramped quarters around L.A. Now that the directors have had a crack at being auteurs, and the studio producers have had their chance, it may be time for the lawyer as auteur to become de rigueur. Legal complexities are the norm. In the delivery of the screenplay alone there is a "treatment," a "story outline," a "first draft," "second draft," "revised second draft," and a "polish," all of which are discrete forms and for which each writer is paid in "steps," and around which litigation can cling. So much is paid for each format, with each format clearly marked on script for future litigation. In addition, there is a "coverage," or a reader's synopsis (that is, an objective retelling of the story in two to twelve pages with the reader's comments), and there is a "selling synopsis" presented to director, stars, or network which emphasizes the exploitable aspects. Until the current rash of million-dollar screenplays, the writer was rarely singled out and given artistic control.

Directors are not exempt from the legal clutch. A director has a minimum number of days to deliver his cut, a certain number of days to edit, contractual rights for the producer to receive a "scratch print" for sound and music, and an "optical print" which, once joined, is called an "answer print," and then finally, after more tinkering under contract, the "release print." The contract often stipulates what rating the entertainment is to carry. Pity the poor director who has to make his product more violent and vulgar to achieve the R or NC-17, but not the dreaded X. And he usually has to do it in no more than 120 minutes. There is more legal work per dollar spent in the motion picture industry than in any other industry in the world. Little wonder that the oligopoly, rent asunder in the 1950s, is reconstituting itself.

From time to time, just as the swallows return to Capistrano, studio heads inform their underlings that they have had enough bloat and glut, and it is now time to return to their primary calling — "good stories, well-executed." Usually this happens after some blockbusters have failed to explode. So on January 11, 1991, after some hard thinking about his $100 million *Dick Tracy* which barely made money, Disney chairman Jeffrey Katzenberg circulated a twenty-eight-page memo to his staffers. The memo was filled with "morning after" resolutions and promises to reform.

> The time has come to get back to our roots. If we remain on our
> present course, there will be the certainty of calamitous failure, as we

will inevitably come to produce our own *Havana* or *Bonfire of the Vanities* . . . and then have to dig ourselves out from under the rubble. . . .

And the seeds were planted by the "blockbuster mentality" that has gripped our industry. Because of this homerun thinking, every studio has increasingly been out to have the biggest weekend opening and the biggest first week gross and the earliest $100 million total. . . .

It seems that, like lemmings, we are all racing faster and faster into the sea, each of us trying to outrun and outspend and out earn the other in a mad sprint toward the mirage of making the next blockbuster. . . .

Especially during these economic hard times, *we must not fool with the public's expectations . . . we must deliver on them.* (1991:5, 24)

One could almost hear the fax machines as they whirred into action at studios, agencies, and production companies around the country. Paramount's Barry London had been saying the same thing to his staff. So had Warner's Bob Daly. But what did they have moving through the pipeline? More $50 million movies. As *Variety* headlined its article on the memo: "Studios put their money where their mouths aren't."

The real wonder of Hollywood today is not which movies get made but that any movies get made at all. The risks are so great, and the process so complicated, that a good story is never enough. The emphasis in moviemaking is on finding something already tested and presold like a star, a name writer, a director, a sequel, a best-selling book — anything to provide "bankablity." Ironically, this desire to cut risk only drives the cost up. In the early 1980s a comedy or a drama could be made for $10–14 million. Now this has doubled. Stars' salaries are in the range of $3–12 million a picture. Directors are not far behind. A goodly number of directors command $2 million, creating what Mel Brooks calls "the Green Awning Syndrome." He explains:

After Mike Nichols made *The Graduate*, I said, "If Mike Nichols went to Joe Levine and said, 'I want to do *The Green Awning*,' the answer would be, 'The what?' '*The Green Awning*.' 'What is it?' 'It's a movie about a green awning.' 'Does any famous star walk under the green awning?' 'No, all unknowns.' 'Are there any naked women near the green awning?' 'No, no naked women.' 'Are people talking and eating sandwiches and scrambled eggs on outdoor tables under the green awning?' 'No, it's just a green awning.' 'Panavision?' 'Just a green awning. It doesn't move.' 'How long would it be?' 'Two hours, nothing

but a green awning on the screen. No talking, no dialogue, nothing.'
'All right, we'll do it.' That's the Green Awning Syndrome." (1983:34)

With two stars and a "green awning" director, the above-the-line expenses start at $20 million. With that much money tied up, the film will probably "cost out" at $40 million. The CPA rule of thumb is that a film must make 2.5 times its production cost at the box office before there is any profit. So *only* a blockbuster will repay the investment.

Clearly, high risk also encourages the production of films that are, by nature and design, renditions of what already exists and has found an audience. Risk rewards repetition, up to a point. It is all well and good to take a chance when the entertainment costs $15,000, as does a first novel, but something else again when it costs more than the gross national product of some countries. With a day on location costing $5,000 an hour, making film demands more capital in a few hours than an entire book produces over its lifetime. In the years before the Paramount Decree some two-thirds of films were original screenplays, 5 to 6 percent were stage plays, and 15 to 20 percent were based on published novels. Today, the figures are reversed, not only because of vanishing scriptwriting departments, but because of the need for presold, market-tested entertainment. As long as the hundred or so "players" — the top studio executives, producers, and agents — have "packages" to sell, and are rewarded by their "cut," the desire to innovate will be minimal.

The same marketing that sells Oreo cookies, Stephen King novels, Madonna, and Marlboro cigarettes also sells movies. In a business where an estimated 25 to 35 percent of studio films are bought on "turnaround" (i.e., projects that have been passed over before and are now making another round through appraisal), brand-name loyalty is crucial. This is a business of repeat consumption. It is not unusual for teenagers to see the same film ten times. Then they line up for the sequel. They even pride themselves on multiple viewings as if it were a sign of commitment to a mythic ideal. Moviemakers not only tell the same story again and again, but evaluate new stories in terms of already-existing ones. As the director Jim Jarmusch reports, "A script was sent to me that was a teenage sex comedy that sort of summed up Hollywood attitudes for me. There was a cover letter which said, 'We realize this story reads a little like *Risky Business*, but when our rewrite is done it will read much more like *The Graduate*.' Which I thought was pretty hilarious. Everything had to be related to some other film. The idea of being original is probably terrifying to them" (Litwak 1986:270). It should be. Why be original when the audience wants repetition? Why be "artistic" when one *Heaven's Gate* can destroy an entire studio? *Thelma & Louise* was sold to MGM as a feminist version of *Butch Cassidy and the Sundance Kid* and *Easy Rider*, which is exactly they way they sold it to the audience. The studios, as someone once said, are barreling down a highway with their eyes fixed on the rear-view mirror.

So we have been treated to (so far) three Rambos, five Rockys, four Supermen, two Beverly Hills Cops, a number of Star Wars, Back to the Futures, Sergio Leone westerns, James Bonds, Aliens, Karate Kids, Toxic Avengers. . . Now playing: *Robocop 2, Gremlins 2, Die Hard 2, Another 48 Hours, Back to the Future Part III*. As I write this the following sequels are in various stages of production: "The Understudy: Graveyard Shift II," "Bedroom Eyes II," "Delta Force Commando 2," "Manic Cop 2," "Scanners II: The New Order," "Aliens III," "The Exorcist III," "Maniac 2," "Young Guns II," "Alligator 2," "Eddie and The Cruisers II," "Toxic Avenger III: The Last Temptation of Toxie," "Xtro II," and "Bride of Re-Animator." The titles betray not only the prime moviegoing audience, but also its carnival tastes.

As can be seen from the above list, the "franchise movies" of the 1970s and 1980s were horror movies. Just as teenagers stand for hours to ride the latest loop-the-loop at the fair, the youthful movie audience makes household names out of Freddy Krueger (*Nightmare on Elm Street*), Jason Vorhrees (*Friday the Thirteenth*), Leatherface (*Texas Chainsaw Massacre*), and Michael Myers (*Halloween*). The ancient desire, serviced by every carnival, to confront and subdue one's fears, to transgress the bounds of the normal, is sought out and temporarily satisfied — for a price.

Repetition has become a central attraction of all modern show business. "Show it to me. Cowabunga! Now show it again," is the audience call. The attraction of "the same but different" removes audience doubt and anxiety. Hollywood has always banked on this desire, not only with horror films or matinee serials, but with such long-lasting cycles as those featuring Andy Hardy, Dr. Kildare, Charlie Chan, Sherlock Holmes, and Nick and Nora Charles in the *Thin Man* series.

There is nothing innately problematic about sequels. We don't complain about Sophocles' Oedipus trilogy, Shakespeare's two parts of Henry IV, Dos Passos' *USA* trilogy, or Updike's Rabbit novels. What characterizes contemporary film, however, is that repetition has become the price of success. Movies are not made in terms of individuality, but in terms of likeness. Play it again, Sam. And again. So too, Stephen King, Tom Clancy, and Danielle Steel have sold two-thirds of the best-selling books in the 1980s by writing essentially the same book over and over. It is news only when Paul Hogan says, "No more *Crocodile Dundee*," or George Lucas says, "No more *Star Wars*." We expect them back at the trough. We want them there. It is more nearly the norm to hire an Alexandra Ripley to write a sequel to *Gone with the Wind*, or a John Gardner to continue the James Bond saga. Or, better yet, hire someone to write using the name of someone already famous, as with the posthumous novels of V. C. Andrews, Louis L'Amour, or L. Ron Hubbard. The ultimate Hollywood movie is the complete lookalike of the original lookalike. The retread is not only the reward of success, it is the goal of the enterprise. In a wonderful "what goes around, comes around" irony, the studios are even planning to remake the shows of their old adversary, television. Full-length movie versions of *The Addams Family, The Beverly Hillbillies, Car 54, Where Are You, The Flintstones, The Fugitive*, and *The Saint* are already in the works.

Harry Cohn saw the future coming: "They're mechanical bastards," he said of the new crop of moviemakers. "All they care about is what sold last year" (Thomas 1967:174). So too, his fictional counterpart Sammy Glick knew that power had shifted: "Now, these aren't men who know pictures. They've got ticker tape in their brains" (Schulberg 1941:265). As I. A. L. Diamond, Billy Wilder's co-writer/producer, has lamented: "The people who run the studios today come from Harvard Law School or the Wharton School of Business. They think they already have class. All they give a shit about is money. I mean they want the Rolls, the Mercedes and to be able to serve a better brand than the record producer that lives next door. They don't care. They care about the bottom line, the downside risk. That's what they learned at business school. If *Porky's* makes money, then *Porky's* is what we get. And *Porky's IV* and *Rocky IV* and all the rest" (Litwak 1986:309).

These sentiments, like the melancholy of Maslin and Kael, are common to those who were once the target audience of a medium and have been pushed aside. There is no feeling so hopeless as the loss of mythic nurture. "They don't want my stories. I can't hear my stories. No one is paying proper attention to me." The next generation's stories often seem repetitive rather than original, dynamic rather than dramatic, overwhelmed by special effects, cartoonic parodies of once-central concerns. To some degree, this is a modern condition caused by the tension between highbrow and lowbrow entertainments competing for finite exhibition space. To some degree, it is generational. What is truly modern, however, is that the appearance of the previous generation's myth almost sounds the leper's bell to the carny master. Stories are either quickly repeated or quickly forgotten. As the current generation of adolescents who "run the show" finds itself making way for the next audience, they may feel even greater loss and nostalgia. For book readers this nostalgia translates into a sense of a lost tradition stretching back to the Renaissance — Western Civilization. For the movie audience the loss is less global and is usually expressed in terms of a missing American heritage.

We now turn to the medium that is "eating everyone's lunch," the medium whose "golden age" was over in a glimmer, where nostalgia is commodified but never felt, a medium that ceaselessly must re-create itself every minute of every day, a medium whose impact is so profound and so resolutely banal that it has almost single-handedly removed vulgarity from modern culture by making it the norm: television.

four

Programming Television: Reflections on the Electronic Midway

As I write this I am in Ann Arbor, Michigan, for a semester. We have rented a house from a professor of art history, who has the full-channel cable television — nearly forty channels. There are so many channels that you hold a switchboard in your lap and punch buttons and flip toggles to change channels. The buttons snap and the toggle clicks when pressed. I am in the living room with my computer keyboard; my daughter is a room away watching the set with her television keyboard. I have asked her to turn down the television volume, and so what I now hear is the incessant snapping and clicking. This is how she watches television, ceaselessly prospecting for images that astonish her. She watches television with her thumb. This is how I watch TV too, except that at home I have fewer channels and I do it with a noiseless remote-control wand. The constant noise, however, makes me realize how active watching the "boob tube" has become in the last decade. Her activity also makes me realize that in spite of (more probably, because of) its irrepressible vulgarity, television is also a continually recording meter of desire. Call it what you will — "idiot box," "American dada," "Charles Dickens on LSD," "the greatest parody of European culture since the *Dunciad*," "wallpaper," "child molester," "plug-in drug," "thief of time," "pain killer," "chewing gum for the eyes," "the bland leading the bland," "summer stock in an iron lung," "Hollywood films for the blind," "dream killer," "dream machine," "vast waste-land," "white noise for the brain," "a toaster with pictures" — this electronic midway is the carnival culture of modern life.

In the fall of 1954, my parents bought a television set. It was a maroon Zenith "portable," and it weighed a ton. It appeared one day in the corner of the livingroom. When I first saw it a piece of paper was taped across the glass screen. On the paper was a drawing of a cemetery. Over the grave of a book was a cross. "Requiescat in Pacem" was written on it. The note had been left by a professor friend of my parents who had dropped by as the servicemen were lugging the Zenith into place. My parents were embarrassed that they had capitulated. They tried to pretend it wasn't there. They were not alone. In those days television sets were often disguised as expensive pieces of furniture with folding doors so the thing could be hidden. I wasn't ashamed. I loved it. They rationed my viewing time. But it didn't work. Whenever they were out of the house I would make a beeline for the tiny screen. They moved it to the cellar. I followed, pulling up my chair close to the set so that I could continuously change channels while keeping the volume low enough so they wouldn't notice I was watching.

Little did I realize that my style of viewing would be passed on to my children and that, in fact, it would become the dominant viewing style. Television culture — the phrase has not only a wonderful oxy-moronic ring but also a sense of bacterial growth — is my culture. I know how to watch it. I've watched it all my life. I was weaned on that Zenith. Whereas generations ago maturation was defined by a pro-gression of books, then for my parents by movies seen, for those of us born since World War II, it has been marked by a progression of television shows. Print took about two centuries to gain currency as communal memory; photography was in general use after 1900; the telephone took half a century to become part of everyday life; radio was absorbed in thirty-five years, and the cinema in twenty. Television happened overnight. At some mysterious point in the 1950s, television ceased to be just an odd-looking gizmo — a radio running a picture track — and entered the bloodstream. It became us. It is who we are.

Any study of television begins with the recognition that in our culture most people watch it most of the time. After sleeping and working, watching images on a video tube is what we do with consciousness. It is our favorite way to pass time. More than 95 percent of American households have at least one television set, and it is on more than six hours a day. We spend the equivalent of a day a week watching it. Well over eighty million households have this thing as part of their lives, and asked if they would give up the thing or a family member, most respond that the thing stays.

More American households have televisions than have indoor plumbing. The New York legislature passed a bill stating that television is a "utensil necessary for a family." On any given evening as many as fifty million people are observing this "utensil." The experience of watching has become the social and intellectual glue that holds us together, our "core curriculum." Television has co-opted many of the ceremonies of American life. Religion, politics, and sports have gone into the box. "Did you see . . . ?" has replaced "Do you know . . . ?," "Did you read . . . ?," or "Have you heard . . . ?" Television displays most of what we know and much of what we believe. Television is such a force that the only comparable analogy from the past is not the movies, certainly not books, but rather the medieval church *and* the carnival.

We do not "watch" television programs; we sample, taste, choose, reject, and consume in bits and pieces. A never-ending flow crosses the screen, and we dip from one flow to another, often watching two or three different "programs" at once. The English call television "the two-minute culture" — the usual time they spend changing channels. The golden section of our attention span is now measured in seconds, not minutes. Young watchers even have a "nesting channel" from which they start their diurnal migration. Programmers refer to this activity as "video grazing" or "video surfing." In a two-year observation of two hundred families in Seattle, the R. D. Perry Company concluded: "Most of us simply snap on the set rather than select

The channel for today's "grazing" generation.

Let's face it. In today's era of remote-control TV, viewers are constantly looking for greener pastures. They're "zapping" commercials and "grazing" through up to 70 different channels.
In fact:

- 75% of TV households now have remote controls
- More than half of TV households with remotes "graze" frequently
- "Grazing" will increase as even more remotes go into use

Well, finally there's a channel designed for the way people watch TV today —

and you can be a part of it. It's THE COMEDY CHANNEL — featuring a format that's unlike any udder! Fast-paced. Immediately accessible. Specially made to capture the grazer's attention, and keep it captured, with:

- The universal appeal of comedy (hey, everybody needs a laugh!)
- 25% fewer commercials per hour than the average cable network
- Shorter breaks (most national spot pods are under 90 seconds)

So for an upbeat ad environment that's easy for today's audience to get into, get

onto THE COMEDY CHANNEL— **the best way to round up the "grazing" generation!**

THERE WHEN YOU NEED US, 24 HOURS A DAY

Comedy Channel advertisement, 1990.

a show. The first five minutes are spent *prospecting* channels, looking for gripping images" (Chagall 1981:48). Even when we find those images, many of us don't stay for long. A *TV Guide* (January 20, 1990) report on "What You Want to See in the New Decade" concludes: "Only a quarter of the people in our survey say they don't have a remote control. Of those who do, 30 percent say they try to watch two or more shows at once — either occasionally or most of the time. While a majority of Americans (54 percent) say they have a specific program in mind when they turn on the TV, a significant number (37 percent) say they just like to flip around the dial" (Lipton 1990:13).

Setmakers understand that viewers meander through the fields of stations rather than watch one "show," and have now made sets that display two and sometimes three channels at once (shown in "windows" on the TV screen). Perhaps within a generation such split screens may remove the need to change channels. Except for gripping events such as the Kennedy assassination, certain rocket launches, or Watergate-esque debauches, there is rarely the will to watch a specific show. We usually do not prepare to watch TV in the same way we plan to go to the movies, or to read a section of the paper, or quiet down to read a book. Instead, we turn on the machine when we want whatever it is that television provides, and turn it off when we are finished.

The experience of watching television is like listening to the radio while driving a car. In the early days, one had to turn the radio's station selector knob, and in the 1960s you pressed a preset button. Now you hit "scan" or "search" and wait for "your" music to come up. "Hurry up and choose," the machine says, but many of us just let it continually "search." The pre-TV generation is a "one thing at a time" generation, a "you can't do two things at once" generation. The TV generation, by contrast, does "multitasking": homework, talk on the phone, watch a number of TV programs, and listen to the radio all at once. As contrasted with reading, television almost requires us to do something else while we are choosing what to watch. You can eat (the TV dinner and the TV tray showed almost from the first what the medium was for). You can recline; you can walk around. An entire generation has raised its children with the machine on, still in perfect contact with the medium, still changing channels. Most of us use peripheral vision to consume most television.

One of the most significant developments in household furniture was the construction of the BarcaLounger in the 1940s. This chair allowed one to assume the proper supine position for viewing. More than 25 percent of American homes have either a BarcaLounger or its brother the La-Z-Boy. Beer consumption has increased dramatically since the 1950s, and it seems to be the favorite substance for lowering the viewer into the lazyboy viewing mode. In spite of what the advertisement says, "Miller Time" is really television-watching time. Since the activity which follows 90 percent of television viewing is sleep, many sets come equipped with "sleep control," which turns off the set

This is not the way we watch TV. DuMont advertisement for the 1949 DuMont Bradford (National Museum of American History, Archive Center).

after consciousness has been lowered sufficiently. As Isaac Newton said, "A body at rest tends to remain at rest." Television reads us to sleep, and reads us awake. Did I see that on television, or did I dream it? "Do I sleep or view?" asks the modern Keats.

The producers of television flow know this intuitively. That is why so much is made of being the sleepy viewer's comforting friend. "Welcome to . . . " "Good evening, folks." "We'll be right back." "See you next week." "Stay tuned." "Don't touch that dial." "You wouldn't turn your back on a friend, would you?" the machine almost whines, aware that nothing will overcome the channel-turning impulse. "Stay with me a bit longer. By the way, did you hear the story of . . . ?" "Yep," we say, punching the key. "Already heard it." Formula and fungibility are the hallmarks of television fare. As the television semiologists say, shows are "homologues" of each other, and "semilogues" of those in the genre; entertainments share diachronic and syn-

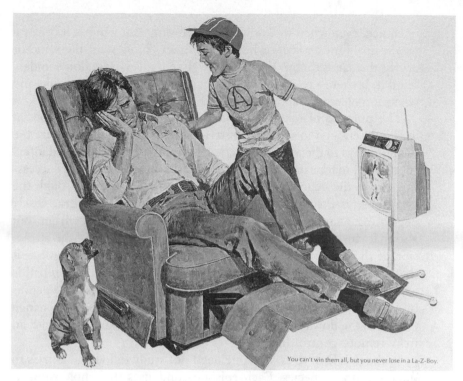

You can't win them all, but you never lose in a La-Z-Boy.

La-Z-Boy Recliner — illustration for yearly calender "The Twelve Months of La-Z-Boy": "September" 1977 (La-Z-Boy Chair Company).

chronic similarities; they refer both to individual texts as well as to all precursors and successors. What the academics mean is that repetition and redundancy are what viewers want. We want choice among equals. Media reformers have found this out to their dismay. The availability of three channels or thirty channels does not change the product differentiation. All networks ultimately behave as one, as do all shows inside a genre.

The television generation is not overwhelmed by this charade of choice, rather, the absorption of superfluous choice is what we do best. A decade ago, grocery stores carried about 9,000 items; they now stock about 24,000. Revlon makes 158 shades of lipstick. Crest toothpaste comes in 36 sizes and shapes and flavors. We are even eager to be offered choice where there is really none to speak of. AT&T offers "the right choice"; Wendy's, "there is no better choice"; Pepsi, "the choice of a new generation"; Coke, "the real choice"; "Taster's Choice is the choice for taste." We'll settle for the promise of choice, even when we know it is a delusion. But why? Is it because we do not want choice, or because so many of us want the same or nearly the same thing? Who knows? Even advertisers don't understand it. Is there a relationship between the number of soft drinks and television channels (about 27.7)?[1]

The purpose of television is to keep you watching television, at least long enough to see the advertisements. Choice is the tribute the medium pays to the attention span. Programs are the scheduled interruptions of marketing bulletins, and marketing bulletins are successful only to the degree that people see them. "We break through the clutter," says the promotion campaign of a major network, wisely neglecting to mention not only where the clutter comes from, but also that clutter is what we watch television to see. Part of the attraction of the Super Bowl, television's most-watched sporting event, is the promise of a glut of clutter. In a four-hour show, the football is actually moved and in play for only about seven minutes. The genius of MTV is that it is so cluttered that one does not need to change channels; the flow is endlessly shifted for us by a programmer with an itchy remote-control finger.

In the jungle of television one need not study individual entries to understand the species. Each episode condenses the whole show as well as the entire series, as well as the entire medium. In television phylum, ontogeny recapitulates phylogeny. So too does each commercial seek to sell its own product while acting out principles formulated over generations of other commercials. Like a language made up entirely of idioms, we never need pay attention to the phonemes. Television is an "eternal void" that must be refilled each

---

1. Economists explain the concentration of choice with the theory of "spatial competition." Imagine a town evenly strung out along a single avenue of twenty blocks with only two grocery stores. The most efficient placement of stores for public service will be on 5th and 14th streets. But the smart grocer on 5th will soon realize he should move to 13th Street if he wants to maximize his market share. He will then get three-fourths of the shoppers. When the 14th Street grocer recognizes the same fact, he will move to 12th Street. Chances are that the final placement will be side by side on 10th street. Hence, the law of "excessive sameness" limits competition.

But what happens when lots of grocery stores arrive started by Wharton MBAs who realize that specialty stores are the way to "counter-program" the large grocery stores? Shouldn't that increase choice? Not necessarily. Just as Paul Klein, chief programmer at NBC in the 1970s predicted, the "least objectionable program" will survive. The 7-Eleven will push out S. S. Pierce. The Beverly Hillbillies will have their way over the Boston Brahmins.

day from beginning to end. Watch it once, you've watched it a hundred times. And that is precisely its attraction.

Every programmer's worst fear is that we might turn the set off. Especially fearsome are the "edges" of shows where, after watching twenty-two or fifty-five minutes of sequences, we are moved through the boundary rituals of changing channels. Here choice is most likely and viewers tend to go prospecting as pods of commercials are broadcast. These commercials are built on ten-second blocks (30, 60, 120 seconds) inherited from radio days when they were split around station identification. Each program is thus under stress not only to keep the audience from drifting to other channels, but especially from drifting away from the set. Television shows are chosen in part for how well they "deliver" an audience across the half-hour breaks (called "flowthrough"). Since this hiatus is the riskiest time for programmers, here we often find the "newsbreak," a conflation of a "break" in programming with the "breaking" of an urgent story. We hear the newsmusic and see the newscaster at the newsdesk telling us to stay there for the news — complete story at 11:00. So too, the opening credits of each show are punchy with the promise of pleasure to come and are contrived to hold us through the next commercial pod and past the impulse to choose again.

Television is where we go to be hooked. It's our carnival. If this exhibit doesn't astonish us, we change channels. This barker promises all manner of forbidden sights, of strange exchanges, of freaks, of bizarre behavior, and it parades them before us again, and again, and again. Of course, television is "vulgar" to those who have already tuned in and seen where the edges are, and it is "irredeemably vulgar" to those who have lost interest in the sideshow. To Newton Minow at fifty-seven years of age it was a "vast wastcland"; to me in my teens it was a vast midway. The closer to prime time — the so-called family hours — the calmer the carnival. The closer to the bigtop, the more acceptable the entertainment. Non-prime-time television, however, is out by the fence where the *real* action is, the really great wasteland. At the end of this chapter, I intend to visit that part of the carnival by looking at the edge of the programming day and examining such wasteland habitats as professional wrestling, reality-based tabloids, afternoon talkshows, televangelism, and program-length commercials.

Considering television as carnival may seem too forgiving even to

Bakhtinians. If you need a reminder of the carnivalistic atmosphere of modern television, consider this: at the end of the 1980s, *TV Guide* (December 9, 1989), the Baedeker of television travelers, listed "The Top 20 Television Personalities of the Decade." They were, in order: Bill Cosby, Larry Hagman, Oprah Winfrey, Ronald Reagan, Joan Collins, Ted Koppel, Vanna White, David Letterman, Michael J. Fox, Tom Selleck, the California Raisins, Sam Donaldson, John Madden, Hulk Hogan, Don Johnson, Roseanne Barr, Dan Rather, Mort Downey, Jr., Alf, and Pee-Wee Herman.

Every one of these "personalities" is a sideshow exhibit of sorts. Bill Cosby plays a doctor married to a successful lawyer, which, considering their race in a white-dominated culture, is as unlikely as the amount of money this family spends on sweaters, or its ability to resolve every dilemma in a half hour. Likewise, Oprah Winfrey is extraordinary for her ability to reverse color-line expectations. (In a sense, Cosby and Winfrey are twentieth-century wishful resolutions to P. T. Barnum's questioning title of liberated blackness in our culture: "What is it?" They are what whites like to think African-Americans would like to be.) Larry Hagman, Joan Collins, Michael J. Fox, Tom Selleck, Don Johnson, and Roseanne Barr all play or have played characters whose attraction is also a distortion of norms. Ditto Vanna White, who may, or may not, be doing it on purpose. Ted Koppel, Sam Donaldson, and Dan Rather are news personalities with either an exaggerated head or mouth, or both. Mort Downey, Jr., is an exaggeration of this exaggeration. The logo that opened the credits of his show was a bellowing mouth. David Letterman and John Madden are subversions of television types, the former a send-up of the latenight talkshow host, and the latter a send-up of the sports announcer. The California Raisins, Hulk Hogan, Alf, Pee-Wee Herman are all literal or figurative cartoons, and one might also say the same about Ronald Reagan. In the geography of Roger Rabbit, these characters are all from Toontown.

It is not a happenstance that some of the most popular personalities on the electronic midway are from groups that make the majority feel anxious, and are themselves not visually normal. For instance, the roles of blacks are either hypernormal, as is Bill Cosby with his family problems, or Oprah and her diet, or literally distorted, like Mr. T who is huge, or Gary Coleman who is tiny. Like religion, television addresses our deepest concerns by first distorting them. So sex therapists like Dr. Ruth Westheimer can mention the unmentionable because she is not only the stereotype of the Jewish mother, but she is tiny as well. Jiminy Cricket can tell us things we would never accept from someone "normal." Although it is doubtful they understood the context, when ABC cast Chris Burke, who really has Down's Syndrome, to play Corky Thacher (a character with Down's Syndrome) on *Life Goes On*, they were addressing an audience desire that motivates much watching.

The sideshow delivers what the bigtop promises: it lives on the boundary of embarrassment. At the edge of the Centennial City is Dinkeytown. The simulacrum of television is not "real life," but television life. The subject of carnival is carnival. Television continually points to itself. It is its self-referential quality that best defines the medium — autocanonization. "Look at me," it insists. Fred Allen came close to the truth when he quipped that "Television is called a medium because anything good on it is rare." The medium never struggles to be good, only to be watched. Television is most revealing when it admits this. From George Schlatter's *Rowan and Martin's Laugh-In*, to the Monty Python segue "And now for something completely different," to the signature opening sequence of *SCTV* (with tens of television sets being thrown out a window), to the self-ironizing of latenight shows like David Letterman, Arsenio Hall, Gary Shandling, and especially *Saturday Night Live*, television preempts derision by deriding itself first. How else can one explain the tongue-in-cheek antics of characters like Hulk Hogan, "Sledge Hammer," Joe Isuzu, J. R. Ewing, Madonna, Pee-Wee Herman, Alf, Mort Downey, Jr., Alexis, inter alia. Wink-wink, says television. Grrrr, say the critics. Let's go watch some TV, say the rest of us.

I make this point because the criticism of television has almost always centered on content — what is it that is "on" television — instead of the experience "of" television.[2] In this experience, espe-

---

2. What separates television criticism from that of earlier media is that it is so wrong so much of the time. Never before have so many had so much to say about which they knew so little. The closest competition was at the turn of the twentieth century when teachers criticized eraser-topped pencils, claiming the rubber tip would encourage mistakes. As we see Eastern Europe opening up before us partly because of the globalization of television, and as we see fascist dictators brought down by the very medium they attempt to exploit, it is instructive to reread John Gould's "What Is Television Doing to Us" in the *New York Times Magazine* (June 12, 1949) to hear the famous theologian Reinhold Niebuhr promise that "much of what is still wholesome in our lives will perish under the impact of this visual

cially since the advent of the remote-control operation, the viewer essentially makes up his own show out of a potpourri of sequences. Most critics don't understand this because they don't consume television as an ever-shifting carnival. They watch shows, not flow. Critical matters are changing, largely because professors need what are now called "texts" to comment on, and (conveniently) they have been assured by the French that a "text" can be anything from a breadbasket to a billboard. It helps if one can find "texts" that your students are also interested in so — poof! — in the 1980s the movies became "texts," and books were published on "The Transcendent Art of Republic Studios," and in the 1990s television is going to have its day.

Teletheory: Grammatology in the Age of Video is already out; the lead article of the Arts and Leisure section of the *New York Times* (October 7, 1990) trumpets, "Yesterday's Boob Tube Is Today's High Art;" and *The Art and Artifice of "Gilligan's Island"* is probably in press. Five books on MTV already have been published. Eager to play catch-up, museums are now paying large sums for videotape, monitors, and computer controls to showcase the works of the usual postmodern suspects: Jenny Holzer, Jeff Koons, Sherrie Levine, and Richard

---

aid," or to read Mahonri Sharp Young in the *American Scholar* (Spring 1948) assure us that the electronic media are deadly opiates sapping the strength and imagination of the young and resulting in social chaos.

These early critics had the good fortune to have it both ways — television stirs us up while it also calms us down. The debate, hardly two-sided (for no intellectual attempted to defend the "idiot box") raged on through the 1950s. Clement Greenberg pronounced it the medium of kitsch, not so bad in itself until you realize "the precondition of kitsch is the availability close at hand of a fully matured cultural tradition, whose discoveries, acquisitions, and perfected self-consciousness kitsch can take advantage of for its own ends" (99). Followers of this vampire theory were in the ascendancy, the most famous being Dwight Macdonald. "Mass culture," he contended, "began as, and to some extent still is a parasitic, a cancerous growth on High Culture. The relationship between popular and high culture was not between leaf and branch, but the caterpillar and leaf" (59). C. Wright Mills joined in from the Left in the name of democracy, attacking those degenerate elites who control the production of culture.

The academic institutionalization of this view of television as debasement was held by the Marxists, more specifically by the Frankfurt school. The argument of the Left was, and is, relatively simple. What we see in mass media is the result of manipulation of the many for the profit of the few; the last gasp of capitalism; the result of "the culture industry" attempting to enlarge its hegemony, to establish its ideological base in the hearts and minds and pocketbooks of the mindless by creating a "false consciousness" driven by material desire. The emphasis is usually on how the critic is the adult, and the audience is infantile. The Frankfurt school is still alive (witness the publication of *American Media and Mass Culture: Left Perspectives* by the University of California Press in 1987), but not taken seriously by many in the industry or in the audience.

Prince. Of course, Robert Rauschenberg, Roy Lichtenstein, and Andy Warhol paved the way, but video installations in high-art galleries may be elevating the medium too much too soon. In 1989 there were two major shows of "video art" in Manhattan — "Image World: Art and Media Culture" — at the Whitney Museum of American Art and a more interesting and less contrived one, "Graphic Design in America: A Visual Language History," at the Walker Art Center. A more certain sign of high-culture acceptance: there are at least five major museums of broadcasting in cities around the country, the two most important being in New York.

The innovative study of television is not being done by leftward-leaning grouches from the humanities, but by semiologists, sociologists, psychologists, cliometricians, and psycholinguists. Perhaps the moment that announced the change was on one of the last episodes of the *Mary Tyler Moore Show* (a favorite show for those who hated television), in which one of these academic Eeyores, who has complained once too often about how television does not entertain him, gets a cream pie in the face. Now Methuen has its New Accent series announcing works on the Semiotics of Theater and Drama, Structuralism and Semiotics, Deconstruction, Metafiction, etc., all of which will include television. And although no one knows what postmodernism will produce in scholarship, it will certainly take television seriously. Fiction already has, as Thomas Pynchon's *Vineland*, Oscar Hijuelos's Pulitzer Prize-winning *Mambo Kings Play Songs of Love*, and numerous other works attest. We have at last moved beyond the McLuhan clones who celebrated the global village, echoed by industry toadies on the take, as well as the descendants of Dwight Macdonald who condemned the medium they suspected was robbing them of their audience. Critics have almost admitted that television watching is pleasurable to many of us, at least some of the time.

All mass media are audience reflectors and magnifiers. If they were not, they would cease to exist. When they stop reflecting and magnifying, they stop entertaining. Since they usually reflect the commonest of concerns, the most fundamental anxieties, the wish-fulfillment fantasies of the mass of people with (or with access to) disposable income, they are usually condemned by the elite as mindless, or even worse, as dangerous. The Marxists are certainly correct: what we watch/read/hear is an aspect of struggle. However, it is more a struggle of audience maturity than of economic class. Fables promulgated by electronic mass media, consumed by the populace, and criticized by intellectuals are some of the most dependable registers not only of social, but of species, concern. Although the critical cant of the Left is that the media are manipulated by a few powerful business interests, the reverse is far more accurate. In no other industry are the promulgators manipulated so completely by the seeming whimsy of so many.

In television, for instance, we blame the programmers and think nothing is amiss when *TV Guide* headlines its perennial story on the "new season" "SO THESE ARE THE PERPETRATORS!" and then goes on to profile Brandon Stoddard, Kim LeMasters, and Brandon Tartikoff as if they were the heirs of Rasputin, de Sade, and Goebbels. Contrary to such mythology (as the 70 percent failure rate for prime-time television shows attest), there is nothing so difficult to exploit as popular taste. It has been estimated that of every three thousand ideas pitched to a network, twenty-five get made into pilots, eight get on the air, and two last long enough to go into syndication. Leslie Fiedler has often said, "Predicting popular taste is the modern equivalent of riding a tiger." If it were not, we would still be driving Edsels, wearing Corfam shoes, listening to eight-track tapes, watching the Betamax, and drinking "new" Coca-Cola.

The not-so-hidden agenda of fairy tales and television is social conditioning. The television network doesn't care which stories it broadcasts because its reward is not in the telling, but in how many people it can persuade to listen and how long it can keep their attention. In a relatively free communications' market in which no government agency tells the network what stories to tell, the programmers attempt to tell whatever attracts the largest target audience. Audience share is the commodity that ABC, CBS, and NBC sell — not the shows. Or, seen another way, production companies sell video sequences to the networks, which broadcast them in order to sell the attention of the audience to advertisers.

Robert Niles, vice president of marketing for NBC, puts the matter like this: "We're in the business of selling audiences to advertisers. They [the sponsors] come to us asking for women 18 to 49 and adults 25 to 54 and we try to deliver" (Harmetz, June 2, 1986). Mr. Niles' predecessor, Sonny Fox, now an independent producer, makes the point more politely at a lecture series sponsored by the Annenberg School at USC: "The salient fact is that commercial television is primarily a marketing medium and secondarily an entertainment medium" (Andrews 1980:64). And Roger King, in charge of syndication for King Brothers (*Wheel of Fortune, Jeopardy*) contends, "The people are the boss. We listen to the audience, see what they want, and try to accommodate them. I know it sounds simplistic, but that's exactly what it is" (Dunkel 1989:80). Or here is Arnold Becker, CBS's vice president for research: "I'm not interested in culture. I'm not interested in pro-social values. I have only one interest. That's whether people watch the program. That's my definition of good, that's my definition of bad" (Andrews 1980:64). No one except a critic ever pretends otherwise. Does the parent while telling the child the fairy tale concern himself more with the story or with the child? Without the child's attention there is no story. "What do you want to see tonight?" the parent/programmer asks, hoping to get in his "plug." The carnival barker doesn't care what is behind the curtain. He cares only how long the line is in front of the curtain. Even he may not know what the "What Is It?" is.

From the first narrow broadcast, television was commercial. The prophetic Philo T. Farnsworth presented a dollar sign for sixty seconds in the first public demonstration of his television system in 1927. Once Hazel Bishop became a million-dollar company based solely on advertising, the direction of the medium was set. In a free-enterprise culture a sponsor says to the advertising agency: "Buy me a sequence of images that people who might want my product will watch. We will pay to broadcast that sequence providing we can insert certain images of our own in and around the story. If you can't get the right story we'll go somewhere else to find a story that will work." The agency goes to the network which goes to the production company to find that story. The story is *always* secondary. The audience comes first. The network finds the audience for the story and the advertiser pays for the broadcast. This quid pro quo is the dynamic that critics pass en route to more interesting matters like plot, character, and social content. No one in television or advertising cares about such matters; they care about market share, the line in front of the tent. The viewer is, in fact, even sold to advertisers in round lots of a thousand. If twelve million people wanted to watch goldfish racing, that is what would be broadcast. The only bad show is one not seen. The only bad story is an unpopular one.[3]

3. Advertisers buy CPM, or cost per thousands, not the shows. So, for example, if an advertiser pays $5.25 CPM for access to women between the ages of twenty-five and fifty-four, this means that for each one thousand women in the network audience who are twenty-five to fifty-four he is paying $5.25. When advertisers talk of "a good show," they

The largest audience will always manage to have its stories told, first by patronizing its favorite storytellers, and second by influencing the legislative bodies that "police" existing programming. The current view of the Federal Communications Commission is that television is a business, and not a charitable enterprise or an extension of education. The high-sounding, but unrealistic, mandate of the Communications Act of 1934 that broadcasters serve the public "interest, convenience and necessity" has been replaced by laissez-faire economics under the five-year reign of Mark Fowler. The public interest, Mr. Fowler has said, should be determined by the "public's interest." This view has created what Fred Friendly has called "an electronic midway," which is exactly what most people want. But how do we know what most people want, especially when critics are claiming that viewers are being short-changed? How do we know which stories are most in demand? How are the network barkers informed as to which myths are the ones to tell?

Since the network cannot depend on copies sold, or on gross receipts at the box office, programmers have to guess how long the line is. In radio days, AT&T noted that calls dropped 50 percent during *Amos 'n' Andy*, and water departments found that pressure decreased in the evening on the half hour, but these were hardly sophisticated counters. More accurate guesses were developed, misnamed "ratings." The ratings are generated today, as they were with radio, by statistical probabilities. To find the "probable" viewers, the network and advertising agencies agree on an independent calculator. Since these calculations are so central in determining what is broadcast, one would expect that they would be continually consulted in any interpretation of mass culture. After all, here at last, we have data on who is really consuming what. Yet these audience profiles, produced at considerable expense (currently almost $5 million per year per network), are usually passed over en route to more provocative matters like content.[4] Finally, after generations of guessing, we may at last have a verifiable estimate of who is actually watching what.

---

are referring not to aesthetics but to how much of their target audience they are delivering to the sponsor. In programming, sheer numbers, called tonnage, are less important than demographics. For instance, *St. Elsewhere*, even though it got a 23 share, was sold to advertisers as a 32 because it reached a young urban audience.

4. Dun & Bradstreet, which now owns Nielsen, tells me that they are rarely asked for their data by scholars even though they would be happy to furnish it free on request to "responsible parties."

In the mid-1930s two professors at MIT developed an ingenious device called the "Audimeter," which measured where and when the dial on a radio was moved. Each time the dial was turned, a mark appeared on a moving spool of paper so a history of specific listening habits could be constructed. Not only could the Audimeter provide a quantitative measure of audience, it could also tell who was listening to what. Hooking the meter up to Junior's set, or to Grandmother's set, would produce a different chart and let a station know what percentage of its audience was working-class, male or female, adolescent, retired, or whatever profile they wanted. In 1936, A. C. Nielsen purchased the Audimeter, and the history of broadcasting was forever changed. Nielsen gathered and sold audience profiles. Since broadcasters are in the business of selling the attention of an audience to advertisers, here was a way to tell where the audience was and how long it would pay attention.

Nielsen was soon able to determine precise audiences using what still seems a ridiculously small sample. The Nielsen rationale: imagine 100,000 beads in a washtub; 30,000 are red and 70,000 are white. Mix them thoroughly, then scoop out a sample of 1,000. Even before counting, you are sure that not all beads in the sample will be red. Nor would you expect the sample to divide exactly at 300 red and 700 white. The mathematical odds are about 20 to 1 that the count for red beads will be between 270 and 330 (27 percent to 33 percent of the sample). This is called a "rating" of 30, plus or minus 3 with a 20 to 1 assurance of statistical reliability. Nielsen deals with two sets of numbers: ratings and shares. A *rating* is the percentage of the total television households in an area that are tuned in, while the *share* indicates the percentage of viewers already watching who are tuned to a particular program.[5]

5. The A. C. Nielsen Company always makes clear that it does not provide a "rating" but rather a "statistical estimate." Nielsen also makes clear that the process is not at all like polling, which requires prediction. Nielsen has no interest in how an audience plans to act, or expects to act, or pretends to act; it wants only to calculate the act itself.

The networks have five age categories in their demographic analysis: (1) up to eleven years of age, (2) between twelve and seventeen years of age, (3) eighteen to thirty-four, (4) thirty-five to fifty-five, and (5) over fifty-five. The heaviest watchers are in 1 and 5, but unfortunately for TV critics, they are the smallest consumers. Those with the most disposable income are in 4, but those who are most willing to part with it are in 3. In the 1950s only 4 and 5 had access to sets, and so programming was for them. Essentially, the history of TV has been the shifting downward of demographic clusters (until the 1970s when the medium was omnipresent), and now there is a gradual rise, as the population of aging baby boomers passes like a rabbit through a python and promises more "mature" programming in the future.

These basic sampling laws wouldn't change even if you drew your sample of 1,000 from 80 million beads instead of 100,000 — assuming that the 80 million beads had the same ratio of red to white. In many ways measuring a television audience is like counting beads. With advances in computer technology, sampling became an overnight inquisition. "Is the set turned on or not?" "If on, is it turned to channel 2 . . . or 4 . . . or 7?" These questions are just as simple as asking if the bead is red or white. The answer in each case is a simple yes or no. Producers can now know within an hour how large their audience was. While the idea that a sample of 3,000 families represents 200 million viewers is hard for some to accept, statisticians respond that the next time your doctor wants to do a blood test, don't let her take only that smear — make her take all of it.

To measure the television "acts" the Nielsen company started using two systems. First, it installed a Storage Instantaneous Audimeter, a box the size of a cigar box, in 1,700 homes. This device measures dial switching as an electrical impulse sent over telephone lines to a computer in Dunedin, Florida. This system, however, does not record *who* is watching, so a separate sample is taken by asking up to 2,600 respondents to fill out a diary of their week's viewing. This group is chosen at random and one third is shifted each week. This diary is the weak link. Having filled it in for a week myself, I can understand the industry's concern. Not only was it hard to enter data because of space considerations and the number of variables, it is also susceptible to subterfuge. In most families one person is chosen to fill it out. That person is usually an adult female and too often, say the ad agencies, she constructs a diary of what she would like to have seen, or what she would like to keep on the air. While watching the thirty-seventh rerun of Gomer Pyle, there is an understandable temptation to put down the Carnegie Hall Special. This "halo effect" protected many family shows, such as the *Cosby Show*. The advent of cable, and the complexity caused by having almost 50 percent of households able to receive more than twenty channels, proved to networks, ad agencies, and sponsors that the system would have to change.

The English, who have produced such dystopian masterpieces as *1984* and *Brave New World*, provided the solution — a passive mechanical eavesdropper. (After all, the English have a history of elegant snooping.) BBC radio introduced audience-counting first with its Listener Research Department. In the early 1980s, a small corporation called Audits of Great Britain (AGB) introduced the dreaded and ballyhooed "Peoplemeter." The Peoplemeter device combines the functions of the Audimeter and the diary in yet another little cigar box which sits atop the set like a religious icon. The Peoplemeter is operated by a handheld remote-control wand. The metering function acts as it did under the Nielsen system, but the diary function is activated when each family member enters a number on the wand whenever he or she is watching the set. The Peoplemeter is now in 4,000 demographically profiled households, and these 4,000 essentially control what stories the rest of us will see. To be sure, this system has its quirks. It favors those who are not intimidated by electronic gadgetry — the young and urban — and it can be neglected and abused. Junior may enter Mom's number to preserve his professional wrestling, and Mom may want to preserve reruns of *Family Ties*. So the R. D. Percy Company of Seattle is promoting still another solution. Their "Voxbox" is a totally passive system that records the number of people in the room on the basis of body heat and body mass. One turns on the television, and the Voxbox records. If someone leaves the room a message on the screen asks who is still there. Supposedly whoever's left will tattle.

A new generation of passive meters is on the horizon. The new model has a cameralike recorder programmed to recognize faces and to note which members of the family are watching. Called "smart-sensing technology," this is the method used by the military to distinguish between warplanes. Every seven seconds the infrared sensor scans the space in front of the television looking for patterns of light and dark, the shine of nose, the line of mouth, and if any new object is noted it then makes more detailed scans at higher and higher resolution and compares this information with stored data. The unfamiliar would be scored as "visitor." When a match is made, the information is instantaneously sent over phone lines to the Nielsen computer. No one in the media seems particularly concerned about Big Brother. With $26 billion in advertising per year, the stakes are too high.[6]

6. Ironically, after more than thirty-five years of cooperation between the networks and the advertisers in the use of the Nielsen system, it was the networks that balked at the Peoplemeter. No wonder. One of the most glaring facts the Peoplemeter revealed was how much market share the networks have lost to the independents in the cable networks. In the first three months of use the Peoplemeter showed a still more startling trend: millions of viewers were abandoning not just the networks for cable or for rented videocassettes, but were simply shutting their sets off for the sake of other pursuits. ABC threatened to drop the Nielsen altogether as did a half-hearted CBS. Why pay millions of dollars a year to be told that their carnival was not being attended? CBS was especially concerned because it

Once we realize that the images we see on television are not the result of conspiratorial foreign forces, not the subterfuges of the networks, not the worn-out schlock of Hollywood producers, not the exploitation and imperialism by which the dominant culture preys on the weaker, not the nefarious tricks of advertisers nor the brainwashing of the captains of industry, we will begin to appreciate the profound and utter mindlessness of the medium. Here, at last, is vulgarity victorious — vulgarity not by design but by necessity. Certainly there is nothing unique about blaming the medium for the message. The publishing empires of Lloyd in the nineteenth century and of Murdoch in our own century have been vilified, as have been the Hollywood studios. Blaming commercial television is easy and satisfying. It is just so omnipresent and so resolutely trashy. Who but fools and toadies have ever risen to its support? But has criticism ever had less impact on a medium? Is television getting better? Most critics would say no. It is only getting better at what it does badly. There is precious little on commercial television to appeal to people who read books, even less to those who write them, and for a reason.

At about the same time that publishing and movie-making were becoming conglomerated, the networks were being folded into larger entities. Supposedly the "webs" were the ideal market-driven money machines whose "synergies" would allow them to pump money into larger and larger coffers. In the glory days of the late 1970s these expectations were not inappropriate. At the peak of network power, say, February 11, 1979, here is what was "on." CBS showed *Gone with the Wind*, NBC debuted *One Flew Over the Cuckoo's Nest*, and ABC hyped its made-for-TV movie *Elvis!*. In a then-typical example of three-way programming hara-kiri, *Elvis!* got a 40 percent share, *GWTW* received a 36 share, and *Cuckoo* did a 32 share. Yes, this is more than 100 percent! Some households had two sets on. With a market like this no wonder that Capital Cities Communications purchased the American Broadcasting Company, that General Electric

uses a system of "make-goods" which guarantees to provide free advertising time on other programs if the contracted market share is not delivered.

To make matters still worse, women aged twenty-five to fifty-four (an audience CBS prided itself on entertaining), were wandering away to other campfires. The advertisers didn't care about the networks' problems. With thirty-second spots costing from $80,000 to $400,000, who could be concerned about the digestive problems of network executives? The real alliance is no longer between network and sponsor, as it was in the days of the *Firestone Hour* or *Kraft Theater*, but between worldwide sponsor and worldwide advertising agency.

subsumed the National Broadcasting Company, or that Lawrence Tisch and the Loews Corporation took a controlling interest in the Columbia Broadcasting System.

Like the conglomerated publishing houses and the conglomerated studios, the conglomerated networks are remarkably similar in their desire to control as many vertical operations as possible. Each of the big three "webs" has about 205 affiliates with exclusive contracts. The FCC allows each network to own and operate up to 12 stations, called O&Os, as long as they do not comprise more than 25 percent of the U.S. total. The networks pay their affiliates a fee to run their programs just as they did in the days of radio. In return, the network gets a generally agreed-upon "commercial load" of about seven minutes per hour of commercial time, which it then sells. That seven minutes an hour is worth the trade. In 1960 advertising revenue for the three webs was $820 million; in 1989 it increased twelve-fold to $10 billion. What sets the networks apart from publishing and movie-making, however, is that, until 1991, they had no hands-on control of the product. Publishers own books, studios own movies, but television networks could only rent shows. Since the 1970s, as the result of antitrust lawsuits brought against them by studios and the Justice Department, the networks signed consent decrees that took effect in 1980 and limited in-house production and ownership positions in shows. Under the new FCC regulations, the networks are limited to owning a total of 40 percent prime-time hours a week. None has even approached that limit, at least not yet.

Since a network could not derive a "financial interest" from a show, it contracted with a production company for "product." The network pays a licensing fee of from $270,000 to $600,000 to the production company per half-hour episode for two showings. If the show is a success, the fee will be raised after the first year. Sometimes the production becomes so expensive that the production company sells parts of the show to other producers. As with film production, the "laying-off of risk" is the art form. Once the "product" has been shown twice, ownership reverts to the producer, who may use it in the "aftermarket."

That aftermarket is called *syndication*, and it is the real profit engine of television production. The profit in syndication is so alluring that production companies practice "deficit financing," losing money on renting the shows in order to be sure they are broadcast in the hope that they can later be syndicated. Currently the average deficit for a half-hour sitcom is $100,000, and for an hour show it runs from $150,000 to $500,000. Once a sufficient number of shows have been exhibited and rerun (usually about four years' worth) the producer can re-rent them to independent stations. Especially lucrative is "strip syndication," in which the program that originally ran once a week is "stripped" across the week and shown daily. Hence, as the drives the publishing industry, as the platinum record drives the recording industry, and as the blockbuster drives the movie studio, so the television show that can make it into "strips" is the goal of all producers and programmers.

By the late 1970s, the networks seemed to have a lock on broadcast entertainment. But then as a way to improve their penetration into still more households, a technical development transformed not only the networks but also all popular culture, and made it inevitable that vulgarity would prevail. At about the time CBS, NBC, and ABC were engulfed and devoured into conglomerates, an old method of improving reception was given a new application. Community Access Television, originally a technology developed by retailers to sell more sets by building one receiver to draw down a signal and then cable it into a community of viewers, found a new application. Instead of capturing the frequencies of a few stations transmitted from ground transmitters, CATV became the ground station that received signals beamed from satellites in perpetual geosynchronous orbit 22,300 miles above the equator. All manner of alphabet mutations were worked out — MSO, MDS, SMATV, STV, DBS — but they all started with the relatively simple concept of CATV, a shared access to television signals. The satellite transponder could receive and send hundreds of channels, and the coaxial cable could carry most of them from the antenna to the individual set.

In 1970, 7 percent of American homes were so wired; today, more than 55 percent. There are now some seventy-two basic cable MSOs (Multiple System Operator) charging from $14 to $17 a month for a basic service reaching fifty million of the ninety million television viewers. The largest cable systems, owned by Time Warner and Tele-Communication Inc., now have well in excess of twelve million homes wired and can make or break a program service. In 1989 Americans spent $14 billion to receive cable, almost double the amount spent on movies and video rentals. Of all utility bills the cable television bill is the most promptly paid and has the lowest default rate. Americans would rather be without power than images.

Ted Turner was the first to realize he could create a national station, WTBS, using this new technology, and compete with the networks for audience attention and hence for dollars. So too did the Christian Broadcasting Network which exchanged programming for donations, and Time Inc.'s Home Box Office went directly to the viewer for a subscription. In eleven years HBO was making a bigger profit than NBC. Thanks to the transponder and the cable, we recognize the alphabet soup that characterizes American television and will soon characterize the whole Western world. Just as a generation ago everyone knew what Henry Holt or Charles Scribner's Sons published, most of us now know exactly what ABC, NBC, CBS, PBS, CBN, WTBS, CNN, HBO, MTV, C-Span, ESPN, A&E, et al., broadcast. What is not so easily recognized is that the one thing that was expected did not happen.

Almost everyone in broadcasting believed that an increase in the number of channels would result in a concomitant increase in diversity, maybe even in quality. Previously closed-out audiences would demand and pay for their kind of entertainment. Consider what happened to the demise and/or decay of *Life*, *Look*, the *Saturday Evening Post*: the rise of specific-audience magazines like *Apartment Life*, *Byte*, and *Runner's World*. Where there is a market niche, there is money. Mass media was dead; specialized media was the future. This happened up to a point. ESPN is dedicated to sports, MTV to music videos, CNN to news, HBO to movies, but what of high culture? Cable was supposed to serve upper-taste cultures too. But subscription television (STV) did not prosper. And the high-culture channels, like ARTS, founded by ABC and Hearst, and Bravo, supported by CBS, not only did not flourish — they were out-and-out flops. Cable television has shown students of carnival that the audience that claims to want stimulating programming is really watching the same four or five shows as the rest of us.[7]

---

7. More than any other development, the rise of the satellite and the coaxial cable spelled the end of network dominance in programming. Together the networks now hold about 68 percent of the prime-time audience, down from 80 percent only five years ago, and could slide to 55 percent. Little wonder that the FCC is finally (1991) repealing the "finsyn" rules that for twenty-one years have kept the "webs" out of the back-end profits. Although the new rules do allow for some participation in syndication, the procedures are so byzantine that they will enrich only the lawyers.

The networks are still in deep trouble. Most new shows are doomed unless they open next to an established hit. Of twenty-two network series introduced in the fall of 1988, only two wound up in the season's top 30. A decade ago it was not uncommon for two shows

The nationally subsidized network, the Public Broadcasting System, instead of elevating its fare, actually has had to settle for more common entertainment to survive. PBS did two things well — it imported shows from the BBC like *Masterpiece Theatre*, and it aped commercial television with such shows as *Sesame Street*. Too much of its audience pretended to watch, and then pretended to donate, all the time decrying the sorry state of commercial television. With its own productions, like *American Playhouse*, PBS lost audience. When PBS wants money, it knows where the audience is. During beg-athon "pledge" weeks, *Masterpiece Theatre* and *American Playhouse* are banished to the cellar, along with any series on American poetry and Bill Moyers. Classic movies, specials on Bing Crosby, Lerner and Loewe, Grace Kelly and Marilyn Monroe, as well as retrospectives on the Beatles, Elvis, and rock 'n' roll tributes like "Shake, Rattle and Roll," come front and center. Then people watch. Alas, although Ken Burns' *Civil War* received massive media attention and the highest ratings of any PBS series, its actual audience share was that of a mediocre sitcom.

Most of public broadcasting is looking increasingly like network television. In fact, PBS is now buying advertising time on network television to hype its own ratings. WTTW in Chicago, "the nation's most-watched PBS station," no longer refers to itself on the air, or on its stationery, as a public television station. Why should it? WTTW is doing what more than 71 of the 319 public stations are doing: broadcasting syndicated programs like *I Spy* and *I Love Lucy*. When *Lassie* outdraws Bill Moyers, and when the "best shows" PBS has to offer, like *The Jewel in the Crown*, trail even the worst shows the

---

opposite each other to be in the top 10. Now the networks are behaving like AM radio. They are not doing anything wrong; there is just too much to choose from on cable. The networks have had to go from broad-casting to narrow-casting. As with radio, in which each station now has a single daylong program that is congruent with its identity — top 40, C&W, all AOR (album-oriented rock), all MOR (middle of the road), all Muzak ("easy listening"), all classical, all jazz, all news, all talk — so, too, television is specializing. The all-news station, the all-weather station, the all-movie station, the all-shopping station, the all-music video station. . . . In 1980–81, twenty-eight network shows got a 20 rating or better; in 1989 only nine did, and for many weeks no network show even cracked the 20 rating. In the 1970s, a 30 share was a success, but now a 20 to 22 share is enough to get a series renewed and even a 12 share can survive. Syndicated reruns on cable are so successful that the ABC and CBS flagship stations in New York had to shift evening newcasts from 7:00 P.M. to 6:30 P.M. to make way for game shows. The cable networks not only eroded the market share of the webs, but of the market itself, and has led to the intense carnivalization of broadcast entertainment.

networks have to offer, the dilemma is clear. While PBS has allowed "enhanced underwriting" (a euphemism for commercials) for shows like *Wall Street Week* or *MacNeil/Lehrer*, the advertiser-supported channels like A&E or Discovery have bid up the prices for documentaries, nature shows, and the very British series historically associated with public television. Cable stations, hungry for product, can pay well in excess of the $125,000 to $150,000 per hour that Mobil pays for *Masterpiece Theatre*.

We have not been alone. Although most Americans think of British television as endless *Jewels in the Crown* or *Rumpoles of the Bailey*, such is not the case. Once the English opened up their airwaves, their programming plummeted in taste. There are four networks in England — two run by the BBC, another made up of a private consortium of some sixteen independent producers called ITV, and then Channel 4, a specialized channel to promote quality and "ethnic variability." The amount of American programming is arbitrarily set at 14 percent overall, including BBC and ITV. What is the quality of British television now that ITV has captured 42 percent of the audience? In the top 20 shows of British ratings on BBC-2 are *Golden Girls*, *Lost in Space*, the *Waltons*, *St. Elsewhere*, and *Oprah Winfrey*. At the very top of BBC-1 and ITV ratings are soap operas: *Eastenders*, *Neighbors*, and *Coronation Street*. According to Paul Johnson, writing in the *Spectator:* "Most of what the duopoly produces is of revoltingly inferior confection — endless quiz-shows and sport, cheap imports (often, nowadays, pap from Australia), lackluster situation comedies and old B-movies without end. There is often no choice. By contrast, U.S. televison (including cable) is rich in both quality and variety"; or Daphne Lockyer in *Today:* "You can sound off endlessly about 'quality' British television. But the truth is that the four best series on British TV at the moment are all American imports — *L.A. Law*, *thirtysomething*, *Cheers* and *Roseanne*" (Whitney 1989:C24).[8]

Before cable, the American networks had been gatekeepers, in part because they feared for their licenses, in part because they wanted to

8. What makes English television especially interesting is that this was the gatekeeper medium nonpareil. In 1927, Lord Reith said at the founding of BBC radio, "He who prides himself on giving what he thinks the people want is creating a fictitious demand for lower standards which he will then satisfy." Aim high, improve standards, speak the proper BBC language, have your radio newsreader wear formal attire, noblesse oblige. Compare this to Rupert Murdoch, whose direct broadcast Sky Cable will usher in the next generation of British entertainment, "Anybody who, within the law of the land, provides a service which the public wants at a price it can afford is providing a public service" (Whitney 1989:C24).

ensure their advertisers an unblemished medium. Each network was willing to establish departments of "broadcast standards" costing more than a million dollars a year. Admittedly, these standards were often more interesting as concepts than as practices. For instance, Rob and Laura Petrie of the *Dick Van Dyke Show* still slept in separate beds as Ozzie and Harriet Nelson had done a generation earlier. Verbal threats were tabooed as violent acts, but destruction of property was acceptable. ("I'm going to spread your guts out" is unacceptable, but car chase sequences and brutal fistfights in which bodies are mangled is acceptable.) And certain acts like smashing glass, placing a weapon at a human head, or showing the impact of a bullet entering a body were simply forbidden regardless of context. Language was proscribed: "ass" passed the censors, "tush" did not. "Seek protection" could be used, but not "prophylactic" or "condom." At their peak between 1975–1980, each department of standards had between 60 and 80 full-time employees whose sole purpose was to scour programs for possible libel and lapses of taste. By the end of the 1980s, NBC had axed the entire department, CBS cut its unit in half, and ABC (never much in the standards department to begin with) continued with its skeleton crew of 35. In 1989, *Saturday Night Live* celebrated the demise of the censor. In a skit at a nude beach club, cast members gathered around a bar and said the word "penis" in every sentence. After about five minutes of such nonsense, a performer delivered a soliloquy on the joys of being released from uptight network censors. When asked why the program was so tasteless, Lorne Michaels, executive producer of *Saturday Night Live*, explained, "My competition isn't *The Late Show* any more. It's cable and VCRs" (Polskin 1989:21).

Censorship is now in the hands of the viewer at home with a finger on the "off" button. If viewers do not want to hear Darlene Connor on *Roseanne* brag to her sister about how she was "felt up"; or Rosie O'Neill on *The Trials of . . .* tell a friend, "I'm thinking of having my tits done" to cope with a divorce; or Grace van Owen on *L.A. Law* saying that she is upset because her former boss is "pissed at me"; or the endless series of jokes on *Golden Girls* about Sophia's gas, Blanche's promiscuity, and Dorothy's celibacy, let them censor such vulgarity in the only way the networks understand: change channels. Censorship is also being left to pressure groups like Christian Leaders for Responsible Television (known as Clear-TV), with its own fundamentalist agenda, and with outraged individuals like Terry

Rakolta, the Michigan housewife who temporarily toned down Fox Television's *Married . . . with Children* by appealing to advertisers, not to the Fox network. However, if no one complains loudly enough about Geraldo Rivera doing a show on cross-dressing transsexuals from a topless doughnut shop in Colorado, so be it.

Not so, however, for advertisements, television's raison d'être. They have their own ever-alert watchdogs, whose job is not to protect the viewer but the sponsor. The Advertising Information Service, which is owned by twenty-one large advertising agencies, employs twenty people to screen shows for problems. Examples of what they do: A scene in which wild dogs chase a girl on an episode of *Little House on the Prairie* was cut because one of the sponsors was Puppy Chow. No cat food commercials appeared on *Alf* because the alien threatens to eat the family cat. General Motors wants to be sure that none of its commercials are in the neighborhood when Michael Moore is touting his anti-GM movie *Roger and Me*. The Advertising Information Service is not in the least concerned about the steady infiltration of product placement into prime-time television. Quite the contrary. They check to be sure that Coca-Cola has a red coke machine in the series *TV 101*, that Alf is eating only Hershey bars, that Oneida silverware is identifiable on the tables of *Dynasty* and *Dallas*, and that Budweiser beer is drunk at Roseanne's house while Stroh's is served over at Cheers.

If the business of America is business, as Calvin Coolidge put it, then television is the art of business, and programming is the practice of that art. The triumph of vulgarity is essentially the goal of programming. It entails finding what the largest audience wants to see, and then repeating that entertainment until the audience is worn out. Each show has a distinct "entropy curve," a life span that ends when ratings no longer justify its broadcast and it can pass into syndication Valhalla. The life of any series forms a bell curve in which time is the only variable. However, decay can be slowed down by shifting variables like characters, plot, script, or, especially, time of broadcast. While there are vice presidents for comedy development, current comedy, drama development, current drama, miniseries, made-for-television movies, specials, daytime shows, and children's shows, there are only a handful of programmers. They run the prime-time bigtop and the fringe-time sideshow. These men fit together the parts of the television day, and their choices have a profound cultural effect. The great programmers like Fred Silverman, Paul Klein,

Harvey Shepard, Michael Dann, and Brandon Tartikoff have every bit as much power as the movie moguls of the 1940s or the book editors of the 1930s. In fact, they have far more.[9]

Programming is the art of telling the right story to the right audience at the right time. Television is a consensual medium. Just as bookstores are divided into sections, and movies are shown at different times at different prices, so television "airtime" is broken down into salable segments called "dayparts." The most well-known daypart is called "prime time" and covers 8:00 P.M. to 11:00 P.M. (EST) Monday through Saturday and from 7:00 to 11:00 on Sunday evening. "Daytime" is 10:00 A.M. to 4:00 P.M. Monday through Friday, and "latenight" is after 11:30 P.M. seven days a week. The hours surrounding prime time are called "fringe time" and are, as we shall see, where the carnival thrives. The first fringe hour is called "access time." The FCC has designated this slot for local stations to make their contribution to local culture. They are to complete the day's contribution in "late access," from 11:00 P.M. to 11:30 P.M..

Each daypart has a characteristic audience and we all know the

9. In the early days of television (the "golden age"), programming was done by the advertiser, who not only made the show but determined when it was going to be shown. Advertisers initially treated this exchange as a gratuity, occasionally sponsoring shows as "thanks for just thinking of our product." A vestige of this early control inheres in the programs' names: *Kraft TV Theater*, the *Hallmark Hall of Fame*, *GE Theater*, the *Bell Telephone Hour*, the *U.S. Steel Hour*, *Westinghouse Studio One*, *Goodyear Television Playhouse*, *Philco Television Playhouse*, and the like.

But, as they had learned in radio, the networks realized the advantage of controlling *all* the airtime, and so started to sell segments of time, and hence audience-share, to advertisers. The networks provided the shows and sold the time. As cable has shrunk the network audience by some 25 percent, as production costs have climbed, and as advertisers can participate in the syndication aftermarket, sponsors are returning to produce and distribute their own shows. Procter & Gamble never stopped packaging *Another World*, *As the World Turns*, and *The Guiding Light*. But companies like Coca-Cola are experimenting in Europe with self-contained programs on American music which they plan to use in the domestic market if successful abroad. For commercial television at its purest, and hence its least self-conscious, look into the Saturday morning ghetto. All pretense is discarded. The *Adventures of the Gummi Bears* is a program commercial for jellied candy; *The Game Master* is based on a Nintendo video game; and the *California Raisins* is a half-hour commercial for another commercial. Experiments in commercialization are happening elsewhere.

Recently, CBS and K-Mart, and NBC and Sears, attempted to work together to "synergize" marketing approaches. Sears offered prizes to shoppers who would watch CBS's new shows, and NBC claimed 5 billion "gross viewer impressions" by combining in-store displays with on-screen promotions. Clearly, the next step to be taken is when the sponsor and the network coproduce the entertainment and cross-market it. NBC and McDonald's came close. They cosponsored "the McMillion campaign" in which you had to watch NBC to see if you had won a prize at McDonald's. The FCC seems willing, and the audience doesn't care.

parts because passing through them is one of the central aspects of maturation. The early morning is for soft news, happy talk, and to hype upcoming shows. When Sylvester "Pat" Weaver imaged the prototype of the *Today Show*, he saw a Norman Rockwell family eating breakfast and getting ready for work. He was right. Morning television is to be glanced at while eating, not read like the newspaper, and this accounts for the indomitable success of the three undistinguished and indistinguishable morning shows. Then, after 9:00 A.M., it's off to the children's shows and the syndicated encounter interviews of Geraldo, Oprah, Donahue, Sally Jesse, and whomever; then to the supposedly female entertainment of the soap operas; to the "kidvids" of late afternoon and the reruns; and then to the attenuated news hour. The "newshour" starts with tabloid strips like *A Current Affair*, *Inside Edition*, and *Hard Copy* mixed in with the local news, and the ubiquitous *Entertainment Tonight*, all of which are essentially the autocanonizing promos of the medium — "entfotainment." Somewhere within this TV mix of self-serving news about itself is a half-hour of network "news of the world."

Then on to the predictable genre-driven, much-studied and much-watched, but rarely interesting, prime time, which the FCC considers the "family hours" of Victorian lore. The half-hour between 10:30 P.M. and 11:00 P.M., however, is often dedicated to jarring audience expectations, and shows like *thirtysomething* and *L.A. Law* usually test the visual and verbal limits. (The "Venus butterfly" references, for instance, could only have appeared during the last acts of *L.A. Law*, also the discussion of breast cancer and homosexuality on *thirtysomething*.) Then on to the once-standard late news, which now is being replaced by such strip syndication encounter television as Mort Downey, Jr. Here the audience fragments. Broadcasting from Upper Vulgaria can begin in earnest, especially on weekends. Those of us who have grown up with television know the dayparts so well that we can tell the time of day just by seeing what is being broadcast.

The programmer's job is to exploit each audience as these dayparts pass. As Brandon Tartikoff says, "We are in the business of trying to achieve a mass audience wherever we can at each minute" (Gerard 1988:28). The problem is that as the medium flows, so too does the audience. The goal of programmers is "flowthrough": to keep the audience in place as the shows change across the half-hour margins. Since motivating viewers to turn on the set is difficult, programmers focus on keeping them from turning it off, or worse still, from changing channels. Programming should produce "flow," not only through commercials but from show to show. About 86 percent of the audience stays put if the next show is the same program continued; 68 percent, if a new program of a similar type comes on in the next half hour, but only 50 percent if the show is of a different type. Thus the lead-in shows in access time should deliver audience from "early fringe" into what is now about an hour and a half of "news." The reason that *Jeopardy* is omnipresent in the late afternoon and early evening is that it delivers 70 percent of its audience to the next show. *People's Court* funnels about 60 percent, while *Oprah*, *Geraldo*, and *A Current Affair* do about 50 percent. The *Cosby Show*, which set price records for syndication, proved to be difficult to program because it let too many young viewers flow into the news audience.

Programming strategies are like chess gambits. "Counterprogramming," or mixing daypart genres, tries to separate parts of the same audience. So professional wrestling is counterprogrammed with a Sunday televised church service because it competes for the same audience. Other programming techniques: "block programming" interconnects shows; "hammocking" places a weak show in between two established shows; "tentpoling" is the reverse strategy with the established show between two untested ones; and "stunting" shifts programs at the last minute so they cannot be counterprogrammed. P. T. Barnum would have understood "crossover," or "spin-off," programming in which shows expand laterally to ease out the competition. So, like paramecia, the *Colbys* splits from *Dynasty*; *Knots Landing* from *Dallas*, *Maude* and *The Jeffersons* from *All in the Family*; *Laverne and Shirley* from *Happy Days*; *Trapper John* from *M*A*S*H*; and *Rhoda*, the *Betty White Show*, and *Lou Grant*, all from the *Mary Tyler Moore Show*. In programming the cardinal rule is always: Don't predict and innovate, rather react and imitate. As Ernie Kovacs once said on his eerily prescient show, "There's a standard formula for success in the entertainment medium, and that is: Beat it to death if it succeeds."

In programming, as on the midway, the secret in three words is: location, location, location. As Michael Dann, veteran programmer, recently said, "What is fundamental, and has never changed, is that where a show is placed is infinitely more important than the content of the show" (Kleinfield 1989:42). And never is that location more important than during the four "sweep weeks" in November, February, May, and July (especially the first two), during which Nielsen collects its data. A miniseries adaptation of a bestseller or a made-for-television movie on the disease of the week is usually reserved for sweeps, as are the various prime-time "specials." These genres are usually money losers since they are too timely to be rerun but are staples of the sweeps because they can be hyped with advertising. Decades ago, television had distinct seasons: fall premiere, winter second season, spring tryouts for new short runs, and summer reruns (including pilots of shows that didn't make it). But no more. Competition has gradually forced programming into one never-ending season of tryouts.

When a show is a hit it can control an entire daypart and also influence the entire network. The impact of a runaway bestseller on a publishing house, a platinum record for a music publisher, or a megahit for a movie studio pales when compared to a television smash. For instance, this is what the *Cosby Show* has done for NBC *before* syndication: First, *Cosby* does about 12 rating points better than the average show. Each point is worth about $8,000 of advertising revenue per thirty-second spot. Thus, a commercial on *Cosby* brings in about $100,000 more than an ad on another show. Since there are seven spots in each half-hour, this means $700,000 more per week. The show appears about forty-five times a year, so the differential from the average will be about $30 million. But the impact is not over. Shows that follow *Cosby* will draw larger audiences, and it is not unreasonable to assume that a half-hour runaway success could mean about $80 million in additional revenues for the network. Worse news is in store for the competition. With a steady-state audience, a hit on a competing network means a nightlong loss of audience. Not only did *Cosby* make NBC profitable, it clobbered CBS for all of Thursday night. To say that CBS (and ABC, as well) rue the day they passed *Cosby* by when it was offered hardly describes the sentiment.

The key to understanding programming is to accept the fact that no one really knows what will work.[10] The risks of failure are over-

10. Programming has been likened to a blind man depending on other people's vision, most of whom are also blind, except that he can't tell which ones. Hence the importance of the "*f*-scores" and "*q*-scores" for those entertainers who measure high on familiarity and affection independent of context. As the bestseller lists are dominated by Stephen King, Tom Clancy, and Danielle Steel; as movies are vehicles for Sylvester Stallone, Tom Cruise, or Jane Fonda, so television is filled with the likes of Bill Cosby, Alan Alda, and Loni Anderson. The "*f*" and "*q*" scores are one of the few quantitative predictors in the medium. Fine actors who rate low (like Jack Nicholson or Jon Voight) are passed over en route to

whelming. A general rule of thumb is that no network can be successful if it has to replace more than seven series in a season (even though NBC in 1983 canceled all its new series). The networks now cancel about 15 percent of new shows. Warren Littlefield, vice president of series at NBC, reports that for every ten ideas the network hears, only one script is ordered. Out of every five scripts ordered, only one makes it to pilot. One of every three pilots eventually becomes a series, and only two of every ten new series return for a second season. The ratio of ideas to shows that eventually make it to series is 150 to 1, and the chances of having a hit with one of those ideas (a series that makes it to second season) is 750 to 1 (1986:39).

Because vulgarity thrives at the sideshow, and since the sideshow of television is on the margin between the various dayparts, it might be instructive to examine some of the recent representative displays. What separates television from the other endeavors like moviemaking and book publishing is that very often what is being vulgarized is not an external reality, but television itself — a subversion of a simulacrum, an ironizing of a satire. Additionally, what makes non-prime-time television intriguing is that in the compressed and competitive world of programming one can witness how the sideshow inches in on the midway and little by little changes the bigtop. Here we can see the history of modern taste going down the tube, see how the vulgar has come to dominate as the audience has grown younger and less sophisticated, while also growing more powerful in the marketplace. The end of the twentieth century promises to reverse what the nineteenth century had separated as high culture and low culture.

---

attractive images. The series hero must be able to be our pal, someone whom we might be like, or be able to like — a brand name on feet.

Because programmers abhor risk, almost every new show is screened by a "live" audience. This occurs in a nondescript building on Sunset Boulevard known as Preview House. Promised free entertainment and door prizes, viewers line up in the afternoon and fill out information forms. About four hundred people will finally be chosen. They take assigned seats. The operators of the Stanton-Lazarsfeld Program Analyzer know that, for instance, the occupant of seat 12A is in the eighteen to twenty-five-year-old group, has two children, and makes between $11,000 and $14,000 a year. If the production is a sitcom, the audience is first shown a *Mr. Magoo* cartoon (called "the magoo" in the trade), which has a pretested level of "laughs." There is a point in the cartoon when Mr. Magoo falls off a mountain which has "tested funny," and reaction to this moment has more to do with what America watches on television than anything else. If the preview audience does not meet the laugh levels of "the magoo," then the evening is scrapped, and the data discarded. Once accepted as a test audience, the viewer twists a dial that measures likes and dislikes, and he or she is asked to respond to each joke on a 1 to 100 scale. Questionnaires follow as well as discussion groups. This information is coded and computerized.

Where the elite threatened to exile the vulgar, now the vulgar threatens to suffocate the elite.

Although one could find any number of genres and dayparts to study, I have chosen five examples from these central categories: sports, news, interviews, religion, and, what is unique to television — advertising itself. The mutations of these showbusiness phyla have produced species now existing only in the television jungle. I am going to focus on "sports" like professional wrestling and confected combat; on reality-based news where reality itself is fantasy; on conversation made confrontainment; on religious programming so powerful that it supports its own network; and on a new development that is essentially what all television aspires to be — the pure-advertising advertisement, the "infomercial."

Sports have always had special sway on television in large part because it is the only genre that guarantees a male audience. Television has taken over football at the yearly cost of a billion dollars because it is the only way to assure advertisers male demographics. The major sports, however, had a life before television and outside of television. But professional wrestling, the roller derby (in its modern incarnation, *RollerGames*), and a self-conscious exploitation of the "decline and fall" of modern culture called *American Gladiators* exist primarily on television. This genre, called "crash TV," is usually shown on weekend mornings where it is consumed in bulk by adolescent males all over the world.[11]

The paterfamilias of all imitation sports is, of course, professional wrestling. Although critics of modern culture bemoan the absence of herocs, and although it might seem ludicrous to compare the Macho Man and Hulk Hogan with Beowulf and the Redcrosse Knight, nevertheless the Hulkster and his crowd do represent an ancient yearning of a particular audience for larger-than-life figures with simple problem-solving techniques. Professional wrestling is a bizarre varia-

11. *RollerGames*, for instance, is a combination of the roller derby, MTV, and Crocodile Dundee. Inside a NASA hanger, coed skating teams (with names like Bad Attitude, the Violators, and the Rockers) race around a mammoth figure-eight track containing the "Wall of Death" — a fourteen-foot-high curve rimmed with Plexiglas (so that the cameras on the other side can capture the splattering bodies) — while in the center is a pit of live alligators for sudden-death overtime. Complete with "the Commissioner," who appears in the control booth in a blazer with WAR (an acronym for World Alliance of Rollersports) on his breast pocket, promises of "heated rivalries of professional athletes" with "danger at every corner," and an abundance of rock music, this is a cheery send-up and homage to the Roman circus.

American Gladiators, 1990 (The Samuel Goldwyn Company).

tion on the medieval tournament with its own pomp and circum-
stance. It is the wrestling match of giants at the carnival as celebrated
by Rabelais. In this contest without real competition, this hagiogra-
phy of battle, we see the vulgarizing process as it transforms violent
action into symbolic gesture — a ritual confrontation complete with
freeze frame and instant replay. Television depends on such easy-to-
decode rituals, and none is easier than this burlesque of knights-at-
joust and giants tossing each other about. True, the knights and giants
have been democratized and unionized. They no longer play the
parts of princes-in-training and ersatz giants but are street-smart
working men, bellowing braggarts, trend-setting macho fashion
plates, and greedy capitalists — all images drawn from the day-to-day
world of the audience.

Unlike such modern hybrid sports as the roller derby or kick boxing, professional wrestling has always pitted clearly recognizable good against equally recognizable evil. This is the kind of entertainment that can be profitably broadcast precisely because it unfolds in such easy-to-recognize pictures. The "fights," both on and off the mat, explode in short, photogenic scenes that verge on primitive psychodrama. Still, it was not until the advent of cable television that an adolescent (and not just in age) audience could be assembled. (The audience that attends the actual bouts is not at all the audience that watches at home. The standard joke among wrestlers used to be: "What has fourteen teeth and an IQ of 50? *Answer:* The first ten rows at a wrestling match.") The home audience, however, is every advertising man's dream — predominately, males between twelve and sixty years old. Little wonder that ESPN, the male sports network nonpareil, has taken to broadcasting its own brand of wrestling under the guise of "sports entertainment." And little wonder that shaving cream companies, chainsaw companies, motorcycle companies, and beer companies lined up to sponsor it. On February 5, 1988, professional wrestling achieved the ultimate integration. NBC broadcast a live "Main Event" featuring Hulk Hogan and André the Giant in the most prime of prime time, 8:00 to 9:00 Friday evening. Call it what you will, "that's entertainment."

That entertainment has depended almost entirely on non-network television to broadcast its fables. In the 1970s Vince McMahon, who had inherited the World Wrestling Federation (WWF) from his father, transformed a loose confederation of southern New England carnivals held in high school gyms into an international multimillion-dollar enterprise. He did this by first contracting with the USA Cable Network and then with Ted Turner's WTBS until he had essentially created his own national network. With the kind of quid pro quo that characterizes entertainment ventures in a world of CPAs and tax schedules, McMahon provided the stations with carefully edited videotape footage of each week's matches. In return, the stations ran WWF promotional advertising. The stations made their profit (and it soon became huge) by selling the remaining commercial time.

This relationship proved so successful that the WWF "network" soon penetrated almost 90 percent of American TV households. McMahon even developed a parallel talkshow format to promote his promotional video clips. Called *Wrestling TNT,* this surreal parody of Johnny Carson's *Tonight Show* consisted of McMahon interviewing his own carnival acrobats. Making sure to include supposedly hostile

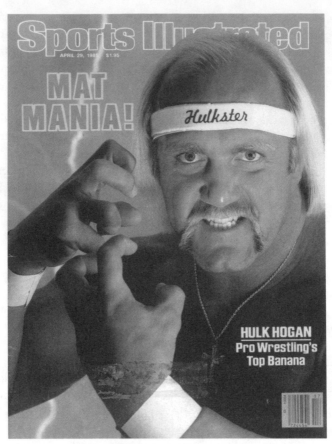

Sports Illustrated cover of Hulk Hogan, April 25, 1985.

guests, McMahon sat back calmly and watched in mock outrage while these behemoths proceeded first to squabble and then, on cue, to pummel each other, and finally to destroy the set à la rock musicians. Just before the last commercial, Mr. McMahon always managed to express disgust that this was happening in front of millions of impressionable youngsters, then announced the sites for the upcoming week's events and promised to be back next week. His viewers were there: *TNT* was the most popular program on USA cable and the number one cable show in sophisticated Manhattan.

Wrestling did not become overtly professional (i.e., "fixed") until the vaudeville and saloon shows of the early nineteenth century. By 1908 the ring size had been set at the "squared circle" of eighteen feet, the parody of Greco-Roman holds had become standardized, and the establishment of regional organizations with high-sounding names like the National Wrestling Alliance organized the hijinks and supplied the itinerant stunt men. Under the influence of hustlers like P. T. Barnum, wrestling, an ancient heroic sport, became 'rassling and then became, with the advent of television, "professional wrestling." Television allowed the ritual to be seen in private, safe from censorious eyes. Newspapers and radio had always mocked the event, in part because they could not supply much commentary, in part because they knew it was sham. In some states, such as New York, professional wrestling cannot even be called a "sporting event," but must be plainly labeled an "exhibition," while in other states like Texas, professional wrestling is legally a "burlesque." Only when threatened with regulation do promoters ever admit the truth. Faced down by the New Jersey Senate, the WWF petitioned that "professional wrestling be defined as an activity in which participants struggle hand-in-hand primarily for the purpose of providing entertainment to spectators rather than conducting a bona fide athletic contest." Professional wrestling is, after all, a charade — "a male soap opera with sweat." However, television lives on such charades, on "let's pretend," on make-believe.

In the last forty years one can see an almost Darwinian struggle between boxing and wrestling on the television airwaves as carnival violence has forced out real violence. (Real wrestling has never been a contender for attention since it is a test of balance, skill, and grace — hence boring.) Boxing is athletic, pugilistic, violent: working-class brutality. Professional wrestling is theatrical, histrionic, gesticulatory: blue-collar circus. Boxing, the first sport to be successfully broadcast on television, is now relegated to occasional showings, largely on cable. Professional wrestling, however, called "studio wrestling" in the late 1950s, was conducted on a soundstage in order to advertise upcoming events. It has now become one of the most popular televised genres of "crash TV." In the land of Vulgaria, kinetic ritual displaces "real" life.[12]

12. The French critic Roland Barthes unfolds the semiotic distinction between the two events:

> The audience knows very well the distinction between [professional] wrestling and boxing; it knows that boxing is a Jansenist sport, based on a demonstration of excellence. One can bet on the outcome of a boxing-match: with wrestling, it would make no sense. A boxing-match is a story which is constructed before the eyes of the spectator; in wrestling, on the contrary, it is each moment which is intelligible, not

Like the bullfight, whose routines it dimly resembles, the wrestling "match" depends on a host of subsidiary characters and routines. Although there can be variations and ambiguities, the battle itself has a preestablished ending: a pin, a disqualification of one or both wrestlers, a draw, or the increasingly popular "outside interference." By no means will good always win. Evil often triumphs. But the playlet is constructed so that multiple contests are occurring. Since this is teletheater, a narrative voice preinterprets the action like a Greek chorus and explains these various contests. This announcer is always a rigid moralist, usually mildly anemic, who uses our habitual trust in the on-site observer (even though he himself is often watching a videotaped replay and adding the "voice-over"), plus his power of naming ("a figure-four leglock," "a back suplex," "a flying dropkick") to establish the illusion of intense combat on a number of levels.

In the first act the spieler outlines the order of events. He names the participants, and in so doing he unfolds their identities. So there is the "Junkyard Dog," a black who wears the chains of slavery around his neck; there is "Sergeant Slaughter," a turncoat drill instructor who now supports the Iraqis; there is Jake "The Snake" Roberts, who appears dragging a you-know-what in a burlap bag; there is André the Giant, the affable and absurd behemoth. There are also characters like the Iron Sheik, Nikolai Volkov, Saddam, and Mr. Fugi, whose names need no explanation since the crowd's xenophobia fills in the motivation. Also, Swede Hansen, the British Bulldogs, Pedro Morales, Orient Express, and Hillbilly Jim need no gloss as to geography. So too Tugboat, Barbarian, Earthquake, and Brutus Beefcake need no explanation as to size and technique. The names, however, are not enough. To make sure that his "humor" is properly understood, the villain is often accompanied by a manager. The manager is usually a superannuated wrestler who — like Bobby "the Brain" Heenan, Jimmy "Mouth of the South" Hart (he is never without an electronic megaphone), or "Classy" Freddie Blassie (who refers to the crowd as

---

the passage of time. The spectator is not interested in the rise and fall of fortunes; he expects the transient image of certain passions. Wrestling therefore demands an immediate reading of the juxtaposed meanings, so that there is no need to connect them. The logical conclusion of the contest does not interest the wrestling-fan, while on the contrary a boxing-match always implies a science of the future. In other words, wrestling is a sum of spectacles, of which no single one is a function: each moment imposes the total knowledge of a passion which raised erect and alone, without ever extending to the crowning moment of a result. (1972:15–16) "pencil-necked geeks") — often tricks the hero so the villain can win. Having a manager in tow clearly announces dependence on others, and a willingness not to fight "the American way" — that is, alone. In addition, both contestants may wear carnival costumes over their spandex tights — the more outrageously narcissistic the outfit, the more villainous. Much is made of the undraping of the robes, whether the languorous uncaping of villains or the over-eager shedding by the hero.

Heroes are always enthusiastic about the bouts while villains are condescending. Hulk Hogan, who comes in a sling-shot T-shirt with "Hulkamania" writ large, is so eager to get to the fighting that he literally tears his shirt off and throws it to an adoring crowd. The rock star throwing his sweaty bandanna, the matador tossing the trophy ear, or the knight-at-arms wearing the colors of his lady love — the exchange of favors announces a solidarity, a dedication to the ritual and to the audience. Villains exchange nothing but boos. Wrestling heroes have taken to entering the arena accompanied by loud popular music to reinforce the symbolism, as well as to show values shared with the crowd. The hero usually is the second to enter the auditorium, and he approaches the ring with a gladiatorial flourish. Mr. Hogan strutted to the tune of "Eye of the Tiger," the Junkyard Dog to "Another One Bites the Dust," and Jesse "The Body" Ventura to "My Body Rules." The concept of theme song is yet another reinforcement of the recognition code. Before he sold out to the enemy, Sgt. Slaughter used to lead the crowd in a rendition of "The Battle Hymn of the Republic," while Nikolai Volkoff drones through what the announcer assures us is the Russian national anthem.

After the entry onto the fighting surface, which is as prescribed as Japanese Noh drama, the second act can begin. This is the "parade and pose," during which the combatants strut like roosters, snarl like tigers, howl like mad dogs, and often even climb the ring ropes like apes to show their personae. In the 1950s Gorgeous George set the tone for this act by having his valet come to disinfect the corner, set up a tea service, and prepare George's little throne. Since television demands immediate action, such elaborate ceremonies have been cut short. The referee checks the wrestlers' bodies for the infamous "foreign object," while the television announcer fills us in on what is at stake: the reputation of the Free World, the dignity of the family, the ancient unresolved grudges of races. We are always given a clear signal as to which side is personifying our hopes and, should we ever doubt, the villain will often announce his role by attempting a premature or an unsportsmanlike initiation of hostilities: he will not shake hands like a gentleman; he attacks before the bell; he tries to throttle our hero while our hero is still getting out of his costume. The announcer is outraged. "My goodness — it's just like Pearl Harbor up there." "This is most unsportsmanlike." "I'm shocked by this behavior." "Really, something should be done." "It looks like payback time coming up." "If this happens again we'll have to notify the Commissioner." The breach of conduct and the mandate for vengeance are established.

In the last act the action begins in earnest, culminating in the villain's near-victory and the hero's "reaching down deeper than ever before" to repel this attack and deliver his own. The villain often achieves this near-victory by virtue of the referee, who always has his back turned when deceits are performed. In professional wrestling, Fate, the referee, is a stooge. Hair-pulling, having an arm or a leg outside the ring ropes, using the "foreign object," choking, and general misbehavior all occur while the crowd is imploring the referee to please look behind him and see what is happening! Our announcer will say something like, "I hate to say this but really this disgusts me. Why won't he look? Something is going to have to be done." If the referee, perchance, does notice, a warning recognized by all as thoroughly insincere is issued. Only one person can reset the scales of justice.

This redress occurs as the hero, realizing now that he has been liberated from the laws of good sportsmanship, can become, *must* become, violent. The crowd has always known this. When violence is the only alternative, violence must out. Now is the time for villainy to suffer. "Give it to him," they yell, "make him suffer. Make him pay." "Yes indeed, it looks like payback time," says the television announcer as he launches into a litany of venerable clichés delivered like ancient kennings. The hero "unloads the heavy artillery," "administers punishment," "makes the challenger go to school," "powers out of submission holds," "has a ring savvy well beyond his age," and "drives the oxygen from the opponent's body."

The final retribution is achieved through what is called a "hold" or a "move." All the movements of both wrestlers require collusion and often not-so-subtle illusion. The "forearm smash," for instance, requires stamping the foot to provide acoustic emphasis, as well as the backward hurl of the head to heighten the effect of impact. The "hold" is still more subtle. For instance, there are villains' holds like the "sleeper," in which the recipient nods off limply while the announcer says something like, "I hope he [the villain] knows that he is legally responsible to revive his victim." Meanwhile the victim's body is experiencing rigor mortis, jittering about in death throes. After the audience gasps, the villain not-so-gently wakes the victim, who behaves as if he has had a full night's sleep. He is often amazed to find he has lost the match. Other villainous favorites are the "pile-driver," in which one man is jack-hammered headfirst into the canvas, and the self-explanatory "heart-punch," "head-butt," and abdominal "claw." Of more recent vintage is the "figure-four leglock," a submission hold, in which the combatant's feet are pretzeled together and which can only be applied by our hero after first having been introduced by the heavy. The announcer opines, "This can do permanent damage. He will never walk normal again." Since the rise of gymnastics in the 1970s, the final coup de grace often requires the victor to fly through the air, sometimes having leapt from the turnbuckle, and landing, *thud!* on his patiently waiting opponent.

Another recent development, again thanks to television, is that the field of battle is no longer the "squared circle," but has been extended to encompass the walkway around the ring. After waiting for the cameraman with the handheld Steadicam to get into place for the best shot, the wrestlers regularly hurl each other out of the ring into this perimeter and then continue pummeling, while the camera comes in for the close-ups. The hapless referee proceeds first to cajole, then warn, then count out the disqualifying "ten" count. Although the announcer assures us the combatants are being "thrown to the hard cement floor," here the wrestlers are especially careful. Many arenas spread gray gymnastic mats around the ring, just in case. Breakaway chairs from the first rows are conveniently empty so that they can be used first by the villain, and then by the hero.

Should the match end in a pinfall, the all-American victor (if such is the case) will have his hand raised by the referee and then make a triumphal tour of the ring. Matadors have been accorded this passage for centuries; before them, knights, and still earlier, gladiators. Doubtless the ancient victors of the hunt paraded around their slain conquest with whoops of exhilaration. If the match is for a championship — and on most wrestling cards there is such a championship, even though it be for the "Northeast Intercontinental Title of Georgia" — the victor will raise the trophy belt high above his head and bray. As with all other visual effects of this cartoon ritual, the belt is sparkling hyperbole. Twice the size of the belts won in boxing, these slabs of leather with their oversized medallions are continually referred to as the objects of intense desire. They are the holy grails of combat, the holy sepulchers. In a sense they represent what is missing — displaced female attention. Wrestlers may even squabble in the ring like children on a playground over who is entitled to the belt. In regional matches and those televised in the studio, the victor often stops by the announcer's table after combat to express thanksgiving for having the belt, as well as to set up the context for the next battle for the belt.

The postmatch and especially the prematch interview have become, again because of television, a central part of the drama. The successful " 'rassler" is not always the best stunt man, but rather the best projector of his humor character. So figures like "Rowdy" Roddy Piper, who plays the part of miles gloriosus; Adrian Adonis, the underhanded sissy; Kevin Sullivan, the diabolic brat; Dusty ("the American Dream") Rhodes, the corn-fed Texas plowboy; and George ("the Animal") Steele, the evolutionary throwback, are mediocre tumblers but coherent television personalities. Each has a particular presence and never violates the unity of his character. Their foil is the anemic announcer, whose cravenness in the presence of their characters provides the internal norm. We see in the announcer's fawning affect how threatening their violence really is, while at the same time imagining that we might be able to confront it.

Just as professional wrestling carnivalized sport as "crash TV," so reality-based programming has vulgarized the news as "trash TV." The original template of television news was the nightly network news from New York. This format, in turn, had descended from the newspaper via the radio. It consisted of a "front page" at the top of the segment, with varying in-depth reports, followed by a back section of general interest, or what is now called the "life-style" or "relax" sections. The history of television news, and of print news as well, is that the back section has moved frontward in much the same way that the sideshow moved into the bigtop. Although *USA Today* has borne the brunt of highbrow criticism, change at the once-staid *New York Times* has been far more revolutionary. Compare the lower half of the front page of the *Times* with that of ten years ago and you will recognize the influence of the tabloids. Mark the fact that the second section of the national edition is dedicated to popular-culture entertainment, complete with a gossip column called "Chronicle," a celebrity showcase called "Pop Life," the weekly Nielsen numbers and television hype — just like the "enfotainment" shows on television or *People* magazine. The New York Times Company, a holding company of numerous magazines and television stations, is in the same business as Gannett or NBC; it trades its shares on a national exchange, is beholden to shareholders, and is out — first and last — to make a profit. All the news that's fit to print comes in between.

In the 1950s, television news consisted of a newsreader reading the wire-service news with a clacking teletype machine (lifted directly from radio sound effects) in the background. The newsreader was often a radio announcer put in front of the camera and, with the advent of filmed reports from the field, renamed "anchorman." Thus did the radio voices of Howard K. Smith, John Chancellor, and Walter Cronkite become the avuncular presences we all recognize. The English and French, slower than we to realize that the news is, in a business sense, only a form of entertainment, have never resorted to the anchor personality and instead use "linkmen," "hosts," or "presenters" to read the news. What separates electronic news from print is that while a newspaper reader can browse from story to story and section to section, a television show must carry the viewer along. While television has always given the impression that it is a news medium, it really abominates hard news. What it loves is the "newsbreak." Here, between commercials, when the remote-control finger is most itchy, the newscaster sitting at his news desk alerts us to some startling event that is just happening. "Details at 11:00," we are told as we segue into the next commercial.

In September 1963, during the glory days of network dominance, CBS and NBC expanded their national news from fifteen to thirty minutes. Four years later, the then-habitual laggard ABC followed. This expansion in time was hotly contested by local stations since they had been able to earn more advertising revenue with the local news. They feared the network would expand to an hour. But this was not to be. Instead, the national news became too expensive even for the networks. ABC felt the pinch first and started the shift from giving the public "what it needed" to "what it wanted."

In 1977, Roone Arledge was transferred from ABC Sports to ABC News, bringing with him all the computer graphics and hocus-pocus *Wide World of Sports* had developed. ABC News prospered. Technology dominated: the satellites, the videocam, and the miniaturizing of all aspects of remote broadcasting made television news for the first time demonstrably different from radio or print news. Van Gordon Sauter became head of CBS News. The old-style radio reader was out. The clanking teletype machine was replaced by banks of video monitors. Symphonic intros and promo music were added. And the cordial but mildly smarty-pants anchor was in. Tom Snyder, Dan Rather, and, to a lesser extent, Peter Jennings and Tom Brokaw, practiced the art of eyebrow-arching. The tele-smirk of Sam Donaldson is, like the ironizing humor of Arsenio Hall or David Letterman, dependent on knowing that what is being sent up is the medium itself. TV news is delivered in the way gangster movies used to treat newspaper headlines. We hear the latest dispatch hawked by the urchin at the newstand and see the whirling headlines as copies ripple off the presses. There is no inside story; there are only images. A forty-second soundbite in the 1960s was the average; now one lasts for ten seconds.

While "delivering the news" is the pervasive illusion of television from sign-on to sign-off, from the two-hour early morning intimacy of the "Good Morning, America" shows, through the innumerable newsbreaks, to the halfhour of news from New York, and finally to the late-fringe local news, the reality is different. The information load is minuscule. The nightly news from any network would fill perhaps four of the eight columns on the front page of the *New York Times*; four-fifths of the stories covered by all three networks have very little variation in presentation. Like political conventions, most of them have been arranged for television news, and picture news will always be show business because the brain does not have to translate the information.

So it is interesting that the "news hour," while becoming an entire network at CNN, or a full hour on the *MacNeil/Lehrer* show on PBS, has become a two- to three-hour block on commercial television. From 5:00 to the beginning of prime time at 8:00, the back end of the news has not only come front and center, but has spread out to become independent of any network news organization. Like *People* magazine (which was the bloating of the "People" section of *Time* magazine), syndicators have spun off more news shows from the networks' half-hour shows. "Entfotainment" – the autocanonization of the medium, or show business about show business — has now institutionalized gossip as news. Already broadcasting is *E!*, which stands for Entertainment Television (and which used to be the Movietime network). This incarnation of entfotainment to the videomax narrowcasts twenty-four hours of gossip, celebrity interviews, and entertainment news. Ironically, the networks showed the way. If ABC changed the face of network news, CBS changed the face of tabloid news.

In the 1950s, CBS started to present reality-based news by using real actors in *You Are There*, and in the 1970s developed the multiseg-ment newsmagazine *60 Minutes*. Both were criticized as tabloid televi-sion, but one could not deny their appeal or influence. The future was clear: Ted Koppel had his highest ratings when interviewing Jim Bakker as did Barbara Walters with Fawn Hall. Tabloid clones like *A Current Affair, Inside Edition, Hard Copy*, and *Inside Report*, and "you are there" shows like *Crimewatch Tonight, Unsolved Mysteries*, and *America's Most Wanted* have carnivalized the original CBS entries, not only increasing the pace of delivery, but hyping the importance of the events as if they were the news. ABC even attempted "reenactments" on its nightly news. The real "news," however, is how such shows have affected the bottom line. *A Current Affair*, for instance, grosses $850,000 a week with production costs of about $260,000. Little wonder that network anchors now wink at the viewers and sign-off with such totally inane comments as, "Courage."

Entfotainment is clearly also influenced by the sitcom. Maury Pov-ich, who used to be an anchor on a Washington D.C., station, did a stint as anchor of *A Current Affair* (Rupert Murdoch's entry into televised tabloid journalism). He combined the priggishness of *Mary Tyler Moore*'s Ted Baxter, the testiness of *Murphy Brown*'s Jim Dial, and the enthusiasm of *Howdy Doody*'s Buffalo Bob. Povich would gleefully call forth the next scandal, then express sardonic contempt. "Still ahead: the horrible obscene phone calls kept coming . . . and coming . . . no one would have ever guessed they were coming from . . . a university president."

While the TV tabloids dispatch reporters to the scene to interview the participants just like the real news shows, on the reality-based crime shows the anchor-host walks and talks us through the lurid events. These crime shows enact a crime — the more heinous the better — but are essentially made up of replays of the same scene shown from numerous angles. We see everything in super-slow mo-tion narrated by an Orson Welles clone who is full of sunshine. "Right this way, folks. See where the knife went in and got stuck." While the tabloid shows are admittedly gossip punctuated by a wink-ing and sardonic anchorman who continually assures us that this is

National Enquirer stuff and not to be taken seriously, the reality-based programming never loses a chance to tout "real people, real cases, real life." The allure of a show like ABC's popular *Crimes of the Century* depends on blurring the line between street action and street theater. In other reality-based entertainment we get actual footage from actual trials in shows like *On Trial*, while in *Judge* and *Divorce Court*, actors perform from scripts based on real events. Soon to come: two entire networks designed for legal buffs — *In Court* and the *American Trial Network* — which will carry live courtroom proceedings from interesting (and no doubt notorious) trials around the country.

When reality-based programming is crossed with the game show, the result is *People's Court* with Judge Joseph Wapner. Here jurisprudence is carnivalized: a gruff snowy-haired judge with just the right mix of Mike Wallace and Mayberry RFD, Rusty the ever-obedient bailiff, and anxious litigants eager to prove Andy Warhol's observation about transitory fame. In cases with appropriate titles like "The Case of the Disappearing Dachshund," Judge Wapner hears the litigants, then retires to chambers (allowing time for a commercial and for us to play the game), after which he returns to lay down the law. Who should be rewarded from the special fund of game money? If the defendant wins, both litigants split $500; if the plaintiff wins, the program pays the judgment, and the defendant gets what's left. Whose presentation was better? Unlike professional wrestling (which it resembles in many ways), the law must prevail, with never a hint of chaos. Learn to like it or lump it. Do we know the California Legal Code, or not? Outside the courtroom, smarmy Doug Llewelyn, in a blue blazer and plastic hair, stands ready to make sure we understand this. If we don't like someone, take him to court — and once we get there, toughen up. Not everyone knows the code. (Llewelyn is such a compelling presence that he now earns considerable extra income doing commercials for personal-injury law firms.) This lip-synch justice is surface truth without the consequences — the only penalty perhaps being embarrassment.

If the sideshow has influenced sports and the news, it has overwhelmed the TV studio-interview show. Here, truly, is the land that taste forgot. The genre certainly did not start out like this when "Pat" Weaver, then a programmer at NBC in the late 1940s, launched the first latenight talk show. Watching chatty people chatting was such a success that he inserted it into the morning news. Maybe one could

Dave Garroway, first anchor of *Today*, and J. Fred Muggs, another regular, 1957 (National Broadcasting Company).

argue that once Dave Garroway introduced J. Fred Muggs into the chatting context, the die was cast. However, when Weaver tried talking heads in midafternoon on the *Home Show*, there was no interest — at least not yet. Talk is not only popular, it is cheap, and until recently was relatively polite. From Les Crane, Mike Douglas, Merv Griffin, and Joey Bishop to Dick Cavett and William Buckley, the ideal was parodied by Dinah Shore's kaffeeklatsches. To be sure, J. Fred Muggs was not entirely out of sight. The mid-1960s brought the blunt *Joe Pyne Show*, syndicated from Los Angeles, and the abrasive *Alan Burke Show* from New York. Like the campus food fight, these shows started innocently enough but then predictably degenerated into monkey business by the numbers.

In the 1970s, a new syndicated "homemaker" entertainment found the audience Weaver was looking for. The *Phil Donahue Show* from out-of-the-way Dayton, Ohio, had no desk and no monologue but instead a peripatetic "sensitive man" host, a hyperactive audience, and controversial subjects like Madalyn Murray O'Hare, childbirth, an anatomically correct male doll, not to mention real homosexuals, bisexuals, cross-dressers, and wife-swappers. By the time the then-President's mother Lillian Carter was invited on the show, everyone knew what to expect. "I don't wear an IUD, I'm not a homosexual and I don't smoke pot — just what am I going to talk about?" Miss Lillian asked her host. If Phil was ever at a loss for words, he could always answer the telephones. The *Phil Donahue Show* soon moved to Chicago and was syndicated into two hundred markets. As we have seen, no success in show business goes unimitated for long. Soon Chicago's own Oprah Winfrey was making a big splash with discussions on penis size, vaginal orgasm, and porn queens — and Oprah beget Geraldo Rivera and Geraldo beget Mort, and the spirit of Joe Pyne and Alan Burke had another chance.

The latest and most irrepressibly vulgar barker has been Morton Downey, Jr. The resemblance to Mr. Muggs is uncanny. Mr. Downey's rise, shining, evaporation, and fall show where the outer limits of the sideshow really are (so far). In the world of "confrontainment," "garbage and guts TV," it is instructive to compare the two bad boys, Geraldo and Mort. After a seemingly never-ending series on humans who prefer anything a little out of the ordinary, Geraldo backed into a brawl with the NAACP's Roy Innis and members of the White Aryan Resistance. He got a broken nose and the cover of *Newsweek*. A week later he did a show on devil worship for NBC, garnering such reviews as "An exercise in hysteria" (*Village Voice*) and "dirty-minded teleporn" (*Washington Post*), as well as the highest Nielsens ever for a two-hour documentary. The allure of life on the margin, experience at the edge is powerful indeed, as Geraldo knows: "I have every ratings record there is on documentaries and nothing but scathing reviews. When you get 50 million viewers, that is not a cult, that's not a fringe audience, that's the *people*. So, are these handful of critics from a relatively narrow slice of American society right and all those 50 million people wrong? I mean what the hell is going on?" (Waters 1988:78).

Morton Downey, Jr., however, was not so lucky. He fell over the edge. The carny master closed him down after fifteen months on the national electronic midway. Downey did the unforgivable. He forgot the difference between subject and object. When Mort applied a swastika to his face and claimed he had been attacked by San Francisco skinheads, his story was so ludicrous that the independent stations finally yelled "uncle." As contrasted with Geraldo, Mort was not acted upon but was actor. But until that moment of "enough, already," everyone had had a chance to see Mort out-geraldo Geraldo.

The *Mort Downey Jr. Show* was a talkshow on steroids that had jumped its afternoon time slot and moved into late fringe. Mort's audience was predominantly young urban male, and its geographical locus was not the Middle West, but middle New Jersey, somewhere around Secaucus. After a signature montage of Mort's mouth screaming, the show began with Mort high-fiving the studio audience, all set for a little bearbaiting. Tossing away his jacket, rolling up his sleeves, and chain-smoking, Mort resembled nothing so much as a jumpy wolverine. Bring on the lumbering bear. Not only did Mort engage the audience in affronting his guests, Mort himself was a freak of bad behavior. "If it moves, scream at it," was Mort's modus operandi. "Zip it, puke breath," he would yell after first lining up with the camera. Or, lifting his arm to a guest, he would snarl, "Suck my armpit." Downey, eyes bulging, chin jutting, fists clenched to an angry woman: "Shut up, you old hag," or, to a Libertarian: "If I had a slime like you in the White House, I'd puke on you." His solution to criminals? "An animal who drools needs his lips wiped, all right? And you wipe his damn lips right off his face." Someone breaks into your house? "Just make sure you shoot him inside the house; if not drag him back in and then blast him." To each eruption of "pabulum puker" or "fathead," the crowd, straight from the Roman circus, would chant, "Mort! Mort! Mort!" "Step right this way, folks. See the wonder of bad taste."

The critics also chanted, but this kitchen match of a man was not snuffed out. He flamed out. Even Time Warner's *People* was outraged, which is a little like Rupert Murdoch giving lectures on journalistic ethics.

> [Mort] is lowering TV's standards. Worse, it is lowering America's standards of civilization. We should be ashamed of ourselves for watching — but so far we are not. We tune in this junk in big numbers and the producers use that to justify making more junk. We should call the leaders of this mob just what they are: the pimps and pushers of television programming. Then perhaps their egos — if not their ethics — will stop them. At the same time the good guys in television news and entertainment must set standards and police themselves. Don't join the mob. Don't watch these shows. Don't appear on them. Don't tolerate them. Tabloid TV is not funny. It is dangerous. It is a disease. (Jarvis 1989:11)

Morton Downey, Jr., 1990 TitanSports (photo: Tom Buchanan).

Mort had his defenders. Van Gordon Sauter, himself responsible for making CBS News frolicsome, defended Morton in *TV Guide* against the "Turgid Triangle of Imperial Journalism, a spiritual and geographical locus embracing the District of Columbia, the West Side of Manhattan and Cambridge, Mass." (1989:4). But Sauter himself was rebuffed in the *New York Times*'s "Critic's Notebook" by Walter Goodman, who knows a thing or two about the carnival:

> Everybody has a right to be on television if their programming commands an audience and the content doesn't, as they said in a prior century, frighten the horses. If a program frightens the horses, rest assured the audience and advertisers will vanish. As will the program itself. That is the immutable logic, perhaps the sole saving grace. (1989:C22)

During a special panel on "Trash TV" at the annual convention of the American Society of Newspaper Editors, Phil Donahue explained the dynamics of "confrontainment": "I do not apologize for wanting to draw a crowd. I am as interested in ratings as the people in this room are interested in circulation" (Jones 1989:18). Morton was just too vulgar, too crude, but he has not disappeared. He has gone to a smaller sideshow on cable. He now works for CNBC, the Consumer and Business Channel, where he hosts a sit-at-a-table-and-talk-politely show.

Just as television in the past decade has foregrounded tomfool sports, and just as the news has become overwhelmed by entfotainment, so too has religious programming become a station on the sideshow, a booth on the midway. National anxiety and the promise of salvation elsewhere is a powerful combination to begin with, and television has been party to the resurgence of fundamental Protestantism, which has a sizable stake in both creating unease and providing the palliative. Since radio days, American culture has supported two electronic churches. One has reflected the established institutions and has acted as a loss-leader in the marketing of a conservative Christian dogma. The other has existed over the airwaves primarily for the purpose of marketing guilt and redemption.

In the 1920s, the former approach was represented by the National Radio Pulpit with prominent Protestants Harry Emerson Fosdick, Ralph Sockman, and Joseph. F. Newton, who promoted ethical values and social responsibility rather than conversion. The show titles tell the tale. The earliest was "National Vespers," then in the 1930s came "The Catholic Hour" and "The Lutheran Hour." In the Great Depression, however, a new strain of muscular, exclusionary, and self-aggrandizing Christianity took to the airwaves. "The Old Fashioned Revival Hour," presided over by Charles Fuller, wanted to reach the "unconverted" and show them the "way." The "way" usually entailed writing a check. When the networks refused to carry his show, Fuller pulled together his own network of individual stations. His "suck and blow" delivery was heard by the unconverted as well as by entrepreneurs like Oral Roberts and A. A. Allen, who realized that the mass audience would support a steady stream of salvation. When the FCC looked askance at single-theme stations, the fundamentalists went south to Mexico to set up their transmitters. By the late 1940s, radio was a religious zoo, with each animal in a separate cage. However, some animals had larger cages and were better fed than others.

Soon it was network television's turn, and to a considerable degree it again repeated the history of radio. In the early days, Sunday morning air time was offered gratis by individual stations to the major church denominations and was duly recorded on the yearly FCC reports as community service. In 1952 the DuMont network, eager for programming and respectability, introduced Bishop Fulton J. Sheen to prime time on Tuesdays at 8:00 P.M.. Sheen continued until 1955 when he jumped the sinking pulpit to board ABC, first at 8:00 P.M. on Thursdays and finally an hour later on Mondays. By the time he retired in 1957, this "Loretta Young of the sacristy" had won an Emmy as the Most Outstanding Personality, a sponsor (the Admiral Company, which paid a million dollars a year just to have its name associated with Christianity), and the envy of entertainers throughout show business. When the archbishop went head to head with the king of early television, Milton Berle, Berle quipped that he didn't take the archbishop's often larger audience as an affront since, "We both work for the same boss, Sky Chief." Sheen's kindly manner and gentle remonstrances were a box-office success, not so much for the Catholic church as for Christian goodwill, and this strain continued through such preachers as Norman Vincent Peale and today's Robert Schuller.

The other sex, so to speak of Christianity, was not long in asserting itself. The feminine side, the compassionate side, the forgiving side was certainly more presentable in a medium that was struggling to be noninflammatory and nonjudgmental. After all, if you want to sell radios or television sets, you do not also want to sell anxiety but its relief. However, there was another side of Christianity, the masculine side, the combative side, the "sinners in the hands of an angry God" side, and that side came to television, as it had to radio, through the southern branches. Although Billy Graham shared with Sheen a paternalistic attitude toward his flock, and a general willingness to offer the carrot rather than the stick, his brand of premillenialism was too potent for any network to sponsor. So Mr. Graham did what independent movie producers did when no studio would distribute their films, and what the "suck and blow" Baptists had done in radio. He "four-walled" his *Hour of Decision* by purchasing prime time, usually from ABC affiliates. Under the rubric "Good News" was the implied "bad news": If you are not saved *now*, tonight, it will be too late. Time is running out.[13]

13. Only two interest groups in America have been able to sustain their own national networks. The upper-middle class has been able to convince Congress to support their own

As this message has moved from pitched-tent revivalism in the nineteenth century to radio waves in the mid-twentieth century and the electronic midway of television, it has riled the sensitivities of less exclusionary Protestants. Detractors who have not joined the 700 Club, or matriculated at Liberty Baptist College, have never been far from the scene. But Elmer Gantry still rides the carnival circuit because so many are comforted by his presence. Let Carl Sandburg rail against the ever-popular Billy Sunday as he did in "To a Contemporary Bunkshooter"; as long as Mr. Sunday could gain a convert at two dollars a head, the market will out. The electronic church changed nothing but the cash flow. The economies of scale make salvation in pixels big business indeed. In 1987 there were 221 television and 1,370 radio stations dedicated to soul-saving. Some thirty-nine distinct teleministries were able, in the glory days of the late 1970s, to beam messages of hope to more than seven million households. Admittedly, this figure plummeted when it was disclosed that Jimmy Swaggart had paid a prostitute to pose naked, that Oral Roberts was not spirited away by God when he failed to meet his fund-raising goals and had to close the City of Faith hospital in Tulsa, and that Jim Bakker had been convicted of twenty-four fraud and conspiracy charges. Down perhaps, but certainly not out. The religious Right may be neither moral nor a majority, but they are certainly still part of show business and yet another example that the low carnival is never far from the High Church.

If romantic art struggles for the condition of opera, and if Newtonian science aspires to pure mathematics, then television — all modern free-market commercial television — seeks the state of pure advertisement. The struggle has had moments of unparalleled success. In 1969 executives at the Mattel Company in Southern California had a brilliant idea. Instead of sponsoring kiddie entertainment with

---

"Public" Broadcasting System, and the Christians have been able to support the "Christian" Broadcasting Network. Both are currently in financial distress. Historically, at least, the odds favor the Christians.

Evangelical programming offers considerable choice. There are the "manly supersavers" in darkblue suits (like Graham, Roberts, Rex Humbard, and Jerry Falwell); the "mainliners" in the tradition of Sheen (like Robert Schuller; the "baby-faced spielers" like the recent Jim Bakker, Pat Robertson, and Paul Crough); the "sweating brow-beaters" (like Jimmy Swaggart and Ross Bagley); the "schoolmarms" (like Richard DeHaan and Paul van Gorder); the "rising youngsters" (Kenneth Copeland and Jack van Impe); and the simply crazed, like Ernest Angley. But the message is the same: The present is miserable. No one appreciates you. There is a way to be saved. Our ministry is also in trouble. They're forcing us off the air. Pay up.

their advertising monies, why not create their own television show around their toys and then get someone else to buy the advertising? Since the commercials on children's shows had always been more entertaining than the programs, and since the audience didn't know the difference, why not quit pretending? Make the entire show into a commercial. Mattel's show, based on their toy tricycle, was to be called *Hot Wheels*. But just as *Hot Wheels* was about to air, the Tonka Corporation, which had its own big wheels spinning, cried "foul" to the FCC. The rules of the television road were being violated. The FCC agreed with Tonka, decreeing that *Hot Wheels* "subordinated programming in the interest of the public to programming in the intent of salability." *Hot Wheels* was garaged.

The doors remained closed for the next decade. The FCC, worried about the intrusion of advertising into programming, was especially cautious when such programming was directed toward children. But in 1981 Marc Fowler, a Reagan campaign stalwart whose fame rested primarily on his famous definition of television as "just another appliance — a toaster with pictures," was appointed to the chairmanship of the FCC. Within two years the garage doors swung open and "hot wheels" spun out onto the tarmac of television. With it came such toy-based shows as *He-Man, GI Joe, Thundarr the Barbarian, Blackstar, Mr. T*, and a host of other plasticine vigilantes who literally pound good sense and manners into evil villains while all the time selling toys. The days of Bugs Bunny, Woody Woodpecker, Mighty Mouse, Popeye, and even the Road Runner were over. Gone also were such shows as *Captain Kangaroo, Kids Are People Too*, and children's specials. There was to be no protection from the ratings, and the ratings clearly showed that animated toys in action were what made the youngsters stop turning the dial and watch.

Once the advertising restrictions were lifted, the airwaves were overrun with toy-based shows. Not only did the cartoon ghetto of Saturday morning turn hyperactive, but weekday afternoon programming, the once-docile afterschool time slots, were quickly co-opted by what are essentially cartoons advertising war toys. There are now almost thirty different shows. Before Fowler's FCC decision there was only one. These shows are broadcast from one to five times a week in a never-ending loop of reruns. While such cartoons consumed an hour and a half in 1982, they now account for more than forty-three hours of weekday programming.

The toys that sponsor the shows that sponsor the toys are not from

Barbie and Ken's neighborhood. They are more likely to be from the thunder-and-lightning world of Zeus and Hercules. Here are the "Transformers," from Hasbro Inc., which includes the evil Decepticons — like Shockwave (the inscription on the package informs us that Shockwave is "a military operations commando with a cold brutal scientific approach to war . . . using nuclear energy [and] can be manipulated from a laser gun to a robot"). Or the old standby, "GI Joe," also from Hasbro, who comes with a cadre of thirty-four different good and bad troopers, all of whom can be purchased individually, as can their mines, mortars, laser rifles, AK-47 attack rifles, missiles, flying submarines (!), and whatever else is necessary "to protect democracy from the evil enemy." Needless to say, all "troopers" are male except Lady Jayne, a U.S. covert operations' spy. The *GI Joe* cartoon series, which shows the squad in heroic action, is seen five days a week in almost 45 percent of the country, achieving, as Hasbro touts proudly, "penetration into 90 percent of the cabled nation." With a life span of a little over two years, these "concept toys" appear in easy-to-purchase "separates" which Junior can collect. Just as he is about to complete the collection, another new entourage appears and he'll be encouraged to start anew. There are many other such "concept toys" in the trade, like "Manteck," "Omni Force," "Starriors," "Super Powers," "Beast Machines," "Gobots," "Thundercats," and "RoboForce."

The progenitor of these modern-day bash-'em-up storm troopers is Prince Adam, aka He-Man, who, together with the Masters of the Universe, is continually at war. He-Man did what Hot Wheels was forbidden to do. He opened up both the airwaves and the shopping aisles. In the early 1980s, when Mr. Fowler and the FCC first allowed commercially based programs to leak into public view, He-Man existed as a minor-league plastic figurine protecting his natal Castle Grayskull from the evil Skeletor. In a merchandising coup, "Filmation Associates," a subsidiary of Westinghouse, animated a fantasy around this 5½-inch warrior and tried to sell it to the networks. *He-Man and the Masters of the Universe* was a crude, poorly crafted cartoon, but it was full of screen-bursting violence. The networks, still cautious about the relationship between advertising and entertainment, were timid. However, hundreds of independent stations on the cable were desperate for "filler" shows to put into the local-access air before the profitable evening prime time. The number of independents had tripled between 1972 and 1980, and most of them were unable to afford the prices of the afternoon syndicated reruns that the majors ran primarily to cover the midafternoon doldrums. The independent stations bought *He-Man* and in so doing essentially allowed the toy companies to create their own temporary networks.

Filmation syndicated sixty-five half-hour shows to these independents through the prototype of what is now called "barter syndication." Essentially, the toy company or animator exchanges the video sequences advertising its toy in return for airtime. The station then sells part or all of the commercial time and pockets the proceeds. Professional wrestling had also used this tax-free system to barter video footage for "promotional consideration" (i.e., advertising of upcoming matches). Financial arrangements could become Byzantine as licensees joined the melee, selling rights to incorporate the toy's logo or image on everything from bubblegum to bedsheets. By the time *Thundercats* came to the market in the mid-1980s, Lorimar Telepictures had cut a deal whereby they paid a percentage return to the station based on how well the toys were selling in the broadcast area. In order to maximize its return, the television station saturated its audience with specific toy-driven cartoons. The more toys sold, the larger the station's cut.

Keeping up with the "kidvid" deals was enough to tax the endurance of Voltron CPAs and Gobot lawyers. But, clearly, success was worth the effort. Since He-Man made his television debut in 1983, Mattel has sold almost 170 million Masters of the Universe figurines at $4.50 apiece. Lined up two by two, the 5½-inch figures would stretch from Los Angeles to New York and back. No wonder that Cannon films and Mattel invested almost $20 million to have Dolph Lundgren, the evil Russian boxer of *Rocky IV* fame, play He-Man in the movie version, or that there are several different He-Man magazines and books, or that Mattel has a Stanford University psychologist on the payroll (as well as on the credit run) to insert prosocial messages, or that He-Man now has a sister, Adora, aka She-Ra, Princess of Power, who rides a unicorn with a "groomable mane."

Each month of the last decade seems to bring a new concept to the fore: the *Adventures of the Gummi Bears* features characters who were first candies, now a half-hour show of candies sponsoring candies sponsoring a show. Likewise, the California Raisins — first a food, then a commercial, then a television show, and now a toy. And what of the Teenage Mutant Ninja Turtles, which are not really just a toy, or a comic, or a food, or a program, or a movie with a sequel, but a way of life. Yo, dude! We're not talking concept here; we're talking money pump.

Although children are the prime audience for program-length commercials, they are not entirely alone. In 1984 the FCC ruled that local television stations had exclusive rights to the programs they were broadcasting. This situation may sound illogical, but with cable in place it is not. Often a local station may carry a third-tier rerun like *Gilligan's Island*, which is also carried by another station far away but available on the cable system. In such a case the local station can bar the interloper and the interloper can then show anything it wants, irrespective of time limitations on commercials. Hence, usually late at night and early in the morning, while the cheapie syndication shows are in full bloom, the innocent viewer may come across a show that seems to be acting like a recognizable genre, but is instead a full-hour advertisement.

These "infomercials" look so much like real programs that it is often only in the last few minutes that you realize that the *cine noir* you have been watching, which is making you feel afraid to go out on the street, is really trying to sell you a stun gun. Or that the instructional exercise show is really trying to sell you a home gymnasium in umpteen easy payments. One of the most often-shown infomercials is the Soloflex ad in which godlike young men and women work themselves into an almost sexual lather while the voice-over suggests reverently that such bodies could also be possible for us couch potatoes at home. We potatoes, if we watch television long enough, can also learn how to inhibit baldness, become rich in real estate, become thin with body creams, quit smoking without using will power, and learn to dance. The snake-oil salesmen of carnival days are alive and well, with E. G. Marshall, John Davidson, Robert Vaughn, Joseph Campanella, Monty Hall, Richard Simmons, and Michael Reagan enthusing us on to shell out $39.95 for hair cream, $297 for real estate hints, $69.95 for learning to quit smoking, or $59.95 for a "food substitute." To show that there really *are* some standards, the FTC disallowed an infomercial hosted by Lyle Waggoner extolling the virtues of Y-Bron Homeopathic Formulation as a sexual stimulant and impotency cure. Usually there is nothing particularly objectionable about these "infomercials" other than that they are being passed off as documentaries or spontaneous talk shows. After all, it may be entertaining to have Barbi Benton assure you that you can "Play the Piano Overnight," Dick Clark answer the question "Is There Love

After Marriage?," Morgan Fairchild tell "How to Raise Drug-Free Kids," Fran Tarkenton help with "Personal Power, 30 Days to Unlimited Success," and, of course, Brenda Vacarro on how to "Light His Fire." But in each of these cases a study-in-the-privacy-of-your-own-home (and-pay-a-lot-of-money) course is being shilled.

Arguably, professional wrestling, tabloid news, confrontainment, televangelism, and infomercials are about as low-culture as this medium can go. In each case we have seen how a shift in audience maturity has trivialized a genre (sports, news, talkshows, religion, and even commercials), increasing the level of visual activity and decreasing the level of reflection. While it may be willfully perverse to turn critical language on its head, to consider judgments like mediocre, cultural wasteland, schlock, imitation, junk, spin-off, mindless, and even "terrifying," not as opprobrium, but as accurate indicators of a centuries-old conflict over audience taste, television has shown what happens when a free market is let loose on a culture's mythology. Gatekeepers run for cover. Yet, why blame the messenger when so many of us seem to want the message? The concerns of many television critics today are the same as they were for the Victorian critics of popular print, to wit: the medium corrupts consciousness, the work ethic, natural desires, concentration, and culture itself. Somehow the dreck of the masses is changing the quality of an otherwise benign culture. The concerns of Matthew Arnold, Ortega y Gasset, T. S. Eliot, F. R. Leavis, and all other protectors of our high-culture heritage still come through loud and clear: the Philistines are coming.[14]

I have tried to argue that "Philistine" is often, but not always, synonymous with "adolescent." Indeed, the words you will find in the vocabulary of television critics are reiterations of Victorian anxiety about what teenagers, mainly boys, are reading. So television dulls perception, flattens consciousness, manipulates desire, breeds decadence, fosters escapism, insulates the senses, rebarbarizes, infantilizes, is a narcotic or a plug-in drug, mediates experience, colonizes, pollutes, encourages commodity fetishism, leads to psychic privatization, makes us narcissistic, passive, and superficial, and also increases aggression.

14. See, for example, Stanley Aronowitz (*False Promises*), Daniel Boorstin (*The Image*), Christopher Lasch (*The Culture of Narcissism*), Jerry Mander (*Four Arguments for the Elimination of Television*), John M. Phelan (*Disenchantment*), Neil Postman (*Amusing Ourselves to Death*), Richard Sennett (*The Fall of Public Man*), Milton Shulman (*The Ravenous Eye*), or Marie Winn (*The Plug-in Drug*). You will find few good words for the medium, but plenty of melancholy.

There can be no gainsaying television's triumphant sway over the electronic media, or its impact on the adolescent audience. But does this "visitor in the corner" produce juvenile offenders (as contended by some of the more pessimistic social scientists), or merely more vidiots such as Chauncey Gardiner in Jerzy Kosinski's fable *Being There*? Who knows for sure? But this much is certain. As the English humorist Alan Coren has said, "Television is simply more interesting than people. If it were not, we should have people standing in the corners of our rooms" (Metcalf:249). As much as we claim not to like the electronic interloper, we spend a considerable part of our day being entertained by it. No one makes us buy a television receiver. No one makes us watch. If "mediaocracy" is in full bloom, it is because it has been nurtured by many hands.

What the electronic media do is not as Panglossian as Marshal McLuhan promised, nor as apocalyptic as the Jeremiahs warn. At a fundamental level, television transmits stories that the masses of consuming viewers will stop to watch. The medium has insinuated itself into everything; in fact, most of us spend our lives within yards of a video screen of some sort. Like the Blob of cinematic lore, television has not only arrived on the planet, it has oozed everywhere. Like all mass media it has adjusted to us before most of us could adjust to it. We can flip it on with the touch of a finger and so can our children. Once it is on, we are never more than a few channels away from some cartoon of human behavior, some carnival of ritual affairs, some ephemeral banality. As with all the "trivial" diversions on the sideshow of culture, they are sustained by audience desire and are often the most revelatory when they are the most mindlessly repeated.

When a population becomes distracted by trivia, when cultural life is redefined as a perpetual round of entertainments, when serious public conversation becomes a form of baby-talk, when, in short, a people become an audience and their public business a vaudeville act, then a nation finds itself at risk; culture-death is a clear possibility. —Neil Postman, *Amusing Ourselves to Death*

No longer, certainly, could you assume that your lit classes would recognize, say, Donne's Holy Sonnet XIII, or the Houyhnhnms, or the first sentence of *Pride and Prejudice*, or any of the other fragments that had once been common knowledge among English majors. Many majors had been thus ill-educated since the mid-Sixties. By the mid-Seventies, however, I could not even expect my undergraduates (except for a pale few) to catch broad allusions to *Citizen Kane* or *Dr. Strangelove*, or to recall the last scene of *Sunset Boulevard*, or to know who Frank Capra was. And yet, while a roomful of students might just sit there, mute and wondering, at the quotation of any film or novel, they could also, without pausing, and in one firm voice, recite any advertising slogan, or hymn the last half of any jingle: "You dee—?" "—ZERVE A BREAK TOO-DAY!"
—Mark Crispin Miller, *Boxed-In: The Culture of TV*

five

Vulgarity Victorious: The Collapse of Cultural Hierarchy in Postmodern America

Messrs. Postman, a professor of media ecology at NYU, and Miller, who heads the film study program at Johns Hopkins, are clearly aware that something rather dreadful has happened. Someone is not taking them, and what they profess, seriously. What they profess is, of course, cultural literacy, a faith in a body of material that has been canonized, sacramentalized, into high culture. All the terms of priestly anxiety are present in Postman: "distracted by trivia," "baby-talk," "public business," and, most revealing of all, "culture-death." We are being infantilized by the low culture of narcissism, says the schoolmaster brandishing the ruler. What we really need is maturity. What is maturity? Miller names names and, like E. D. Hirsch and Cultural Literacy Inc., tells us precisely what it is in the high-culture repertoire that we should know lest we regress. Hamburger jingles are not on the list. But the jig was already up. While we might expect "media ecology" in the NYU curriculum, the fact that film, albeit "the classic cinema," is taken seriously at Hopkins is like finding out that when the Supreme Court justices convene in chambers they don't invoke the Constitution, but instead discuss the classic scenes from *Dragnet* and "Police Gazette."

Still, there is an interesting epistemological problem that Miller doesn't address. Why was or is it so important to know Donne, or Austen, or later, *Citizen Kane* and *Dr. Strangelove*? They were important, that is self-evident. We studied them because they were a serious part of our cultural past. They were the stuff being ferried back and forth by the librarians/gatekeepers in our modern Name of the Rose. But *why* were they important? Were they important because they were markers of truth, or because by knowing them we shared in a community called "cultured"? How did they get into the secret cell in the dark room on the top floor of the monastery? And how can we be so sure that the seeming drivel of advertising is not also important? How can we be sure that the forbidden text of carnival should not "be there too"?

Or to put the matter another way: how can cultural junk be so vapid, nay, noxious, that it will result in "culture-death" and *not* be worthy of study? More perplexing: recall that John Donne was also the author of scandalous love poems, that Swift's "houyhnhnms" were a brutal satire on archcritics of contemporary mores, and that Jane Austen was writing in a genre highly suspect as a corrupter of youth. Many of their contemporaries believed that Donne, Swift, and Austen were not to be treated as reliable guides. They were carnies. Now, while both you and I agree that the McDonald's corporation is a merchandiser par excellence, we surely think there is something more important to store in finite brain space than this stupid appeal to our supposed deserved reward of a meat patty. No one would argue that we can compare Ronald McDonald with Jane Austen. Still, the fact that so many people know the jingle and so few know the first sentence of *Pride and Prejudice* must mean something about their current relative importance. As the gatekeeping professors, we don't have to know what is so important about Donne, Swift, Austen, et al. Their work to us is what Kant's Categorical Imperative is to philosophy, or the Constitution to the law, or even the Bible to fundamentalist

Christianity. They are part of the body of material that we just accept as worth knowing, as the revealed Word of high culture. Nor do we have to know what is so reprehensible about knowing a commercial jingle; if it comes from low-culture advertising it is, ipso facto, not worth knowing. To paraphrase the pigs of *Animal Farm:* Written in print, good; seen on television, bad.[1]

The carnival culture of show business has overthrown our faith in this hierarchy of communication forms over the last two decades. The Great Chain of (media) Being is no more. One sees this in the Miller paragraph. He values print: do these students know their Norton Anthology of famous excerpts? Then, a little lower, do they even know their art movies? Nope. They only know stuff from, ugh, television. Is that a "culture-death" I hear a-knocking? The pecking order is clear: that which is in print is most important; what is on celluloid is next; and finally, the worst is whatever is in pixels. The Triumph of Vulgarity is, as I hope I have shown, that these distinctions have been blurred almost beyond recognition. Consider books and movies in relation to television, for instance. Here is Leonard Goldenson, one of the founding fathers of network television (ABC) and broadcaster of *Charlie's Angels* and *Love Boat:*

> Of course there are lousy programs — perhaps 40 percent of what's on the schedule at any given time is junk. . . . Moreover, no one claims that more than 60 percent of all the books published in America are wonderful, enlightening, inspiring works of art. Many, including many bestsellers, are worse trash than anything on television. Yet that's what

---

1. To appreciate the depth of videophobia, one might note the introductions of print-centered critics when they approach television. Here, for instance, is the beginning of a piece on daytime television called "TV: A Day in the Life," published in the *New York Review of Books:*

> Some years ago, I fell seriously ill and had to go to a hospital, where I was fitted out with catheters and intravenous tubing on both arms and could read only with great difficulty. I tried to divert myself with an enormous book on the several generations of a distinguished southern slaveholding family that had passed through various trials during the Civil War, but the weight of the book proved so unmanageable that it constantly fell from my hands. (Lieberson 1989:15)

What more can the poor professor do? He has tried so manfully to be good. He turns on the television with predictable results. So, too, William Styron has to be clinically depressed before he is willing to flick the switch. He can be forgiven too. He was in a mental hospital for three weeks unavoidably exposed to "its constant flow." He finds most television is "immeasurably vulgar" and provides the prescription for health: no transmissions during morning hours, then only documentaries like *Nova*, nature shows, and a few classic sitcoms (Townley 1989:13).

people want to read, so publishers give it to them. Television is no better and no worse than book publishing. (1991:123)

Mr. Goldenson may be too hard on himself. Jeff Jarvis, then an editor of *People*, actually compared the bestsellers with the most-watched television shows:

> By my count, there were seven great shows [in the 1987 top 10 Nielsens], two good ones, and one that's merely mediocre. Compare those shows to the books on a recent *New York Times* list of best-sellers, filled with trashers and romancers by the likes of Danielle Steel, Sidney Sheldon and Stephen King. The obvious conclusion: TV viewers have better taste than readers. (1987:9)

And here is John J. O'Connor, TV critic for the *New York Times*, comparing movie blockbusters to television:

> For decades, some of the more patronizing and printable catch phrases have been reserved for television. The pecking order of popular culture over the years settled into a widely accepted hierarchy. At the bottom, there was television entertainment — formula-ridden, silly, pointless, and forgettable. Far above, there was the art of film, occasionally called cinema — probing, elevated, provocative, memorable. Those distinctions never did hold up very well under close scrutiny. Now as television entertainment enters the nineties growing both more adventurous, and pointed, they are being obliterated. . . . One thing would seem certain. A significant sea change has taken place in popular culture. It is now the typical Hollywood film that is becoming pointless and forgettable. And it is television that is showing distinct signs of being provocative and, on occasion, memorable. The old pecking order is very much on the verge of collapse. (1990:1, 27)

All the mass media are behaving like one vast carnival, each "delivery system" behaving like the others, all striving to program images for whatever finds the largest audience. The fact that the Ralph Lauren and Calvin Klein advertisements at the opening of the *New York Times Magazine* do not use words, only pictures, is worth setting into this context. So, too, the fact that today's movie scripts are some 25 percent shorter than those of the 1940s, even though the movies last as long. One picture may well be worth a thousand words, especially if the audience doesn't understand many words. The average number of words in the written vocabulary of a six- to fourteen-year-old American child in 1945 was twenty-five thousand; the average number today: ten thousand.

In the modern world, sequences flow through the print/cellu-loid/electron loop pushed by conglomerated industries, pulled by audience demand, and invariably condemned by whatever gatekeeper has recently been removed from his post. I have no interest in eval-uating these media. They appeal to different audiences at different maturity levels at different times of day. And just as clearly the domi-nance of first print and then of film has yielded to the worldwide influence of television.

The ascendancy of television happened almost in a wink. An exam-ple: the games humans play always tell more about their priorities than what the pundits say. In 1948 WNBT, a New York television station, produced a half-hour quiz show called *Americana* (patterned after radio shows like "Information Please," "Professor Quiz," and "Dr. IQ and the Quiz Kids"). Print critic John Mason Brown moder-ated print guests like Merle Miller and Bennett Cerf, asking them logocentric tidbits of high culture like, "What was the first sentence of *Pride and Prejudice?*" Copies of John Gunther's *Inside USA* were given as prizes to those sending in questions. The grand prize for really good questions was the complete *Encyclopedia Americana*. Pro-fessor Bergen Evans of Northwestern had a show called *The Last Word*, and even Fred Allen and Groucho Marx played games with words, literally and figuratively. The ultimate in this genre was *Twenty-One*, and Charles van Doren was, for a while at least, the very personification of a culturally literate man. What do we watch for games now? On *Hollywood Squares* contestants match "wits" with nit-wit celebrities. (The celebrities find their answers on the Teleprompt-er.) And on *Family Feud* two families guess answers to questions based on what a hundred people chosen at random have said. Ques-tions like: name the best-tasting cookie; name a famous fairy; name an animal with three letters in its name, or list three states with "new" in their names ("Newbraska" was not correct). The right answer is not the one mentioned in the encyclopedia, but is the one mentioned by the most people in the control group.

Such dreck may indeed make us more sympathetic toward Post-man and Miller. Supposedly there was a sign in quizmaster Monty Hall's office that read: "You can learn more about America by watch-ing a half-hour of *Let's Make a Deal* than you can from watching Walter Cronkite for a month." Awful, perhaps, but possibly true. Television is not, however, the medium that deserves the bashing that Postman, Miller, Lash, Bloom, Yardley, Bennett, and others wish to administer, but rather the political system that allows such discourse. That system is Democracy, the supposed will of the majority. Show business, like politics, is an expression of that will. As Clive Barnes wrote decades ago, "Television is the first truly democratic culture — the first culture available to everybody and entirely governed by what the people want. The most terrifying thing is what the people do want" (Metcalf 1986:248). Here, as elsewhere, de Tocqueville saw it coming. The bourgeois audience has no taste for ideal beauties; it is not entertained by the sublime. Given time, democracies ultimately "depopulate heaven" and fill it with the stuff of earth. What he could not have appreciated is the incredible efficiency of the modern delivery systems of the unsublime.

Let me belabor the obvious: sooner or later, if they are to survive, all mass media become audience reflectors and magnifiers of the here and now. If they were not they would cease to exist. When they stop reflecting and magnifying, they stop entertaining. Of all media, television has the most powerful lens. The Germans call it *Das Fernsehen*, "the thing to see far with." And what we see, if we are properly focused, is into the commonest of concerns, the most fundamental anxieties, the wish-fulfillment of the mass of people with (or with access to) disposable income. These concerns are usually condemned by the elite as mindless, or even worse, as dangerous. Miller is certainly correct when he says, "Television has become our native language." Language is how we share concerns, communicate experience. Who in my generation cannot sing the M-i-c-k-e-y M-o-u-s-e song, does not know that when Columbo pauses at the doorway he will say, "Oh, just one more thing," or imitate Jack Lord ("Book 'em, Danno")? Of course this knowledge is crass. We may not know Donne's Holy Sonnet XIII, but we do know that Tina Turner drives a Plymouth, Michael J. Fox drinks Diet Pepsi, Sheena Easton pumps iron at Jack LaLanne's, Bill Cosby eats Jell-O and drinks Coke, Tip O'Neill carries the American Express card, and that both Ronald Reagan and GE believe in "progress."

The future holds more of the same. The jargon of American televison culture already has become the lingua franca of the world. All around the globe youngsters understand "U Can't Touch This," can lip-synch with Milli Vanilli, and dance like Paula Abdul. Next month new words will be added, new images flashed. Mass media are languages filled with shared experiences. It is simple-minded to say, as do many critics, that television represents the co-opting of a language by industry without first realizing that this language, this medium, is a consensual interaction between numerous speakers, each trying to get his or her story told. And also of numerous listeners, each lining up to hear. Such jostling is also typical of high culture, but it is much more pronounced with television. Monks are quieter but, as Eco knows, just as viciously insistent. The results of these interchanges is what we share, our "core curriculum."

As George Bernard Shaw saw in the 1890s, the public theaters are a replacement for churches. Entertainment becomes its own liturgy. George Gerbner, Dean of the Annenberg School of Communication, writes, "Television is the universal curriculum of young and old, the common symbolic environment in which we all live. Its true predecessor is not any other medium but religion — the organic pattern of explanatory symbolism that once animated total communities' sense of reality and value." (Alley 1982:93). And Martin Esslin, erstwhile head of the BBC Radio, continues this transcendental argument of electronic *communitas*, "We may not be conscious of it, but television culture is the religion by which most of us actually live, whatever our more consciously and explicitly held beliefs and religious persuasions may be. This is the actual religion that is being absorbed by our children from almost the day of their birth" (1982:271). But the surest sign of overlap is that show business has replaced religion as the perceived opiate of the masses.

Television did not create this body of shared desire; it made it visible. We much prefer the notion that "they" — the culture industry, the press lords, the networks, the advertising agencies — are sending this vulgar stuff our way uninvited. "We" certainly never *asked* for it. Yet, what we have seen in the history of modern mass entertainment is that when a particular audience, primarily a younger audience, gains access to a medium and can therefore influence the stories told, the stories will become progressively more sensational. This has happened with a vengeance in the last two decades. The process of shifting control of the established medium, however, has always occurred with the introduction of a new one. When technological or economic advances make a medium consumable in bulk by teenagers, a kind of Gresham's law of myth sets in. Sensational fables force out gentler ones. The paperback book (especially the comic), the movie matinee, Saturday morning programming, and MTV are all the result of the arrival of this previously excluded audience. Their arrival is no recent phenomenon, although each generation thinks it is. What is different about today is that the process of audience exchange is happening all around the world and that the entertainments demanded are decidedly American in construction and transmission. In the 1990s the biggest tourist attraction in Europe will not be the Eiffel Tower, or the Sistine Chapel, or even the Swiss Alps. It will be the Euro Disney Resort.

In ancient days the Roman audience, from the relatively small Flavian Amphitheater to the massive Circus Maximus, was divided into wedges (*cunei*) whose shouts of approval or disapproval determined the course of show business. The shows in the big Coliseum were always more violent since more than half its quarter-million spectators were young males. The wedges of enthusiastic young men literally drove out the old entertainments and replaced them with their own spectacles. "If we are forced, at every hour, to watch or listen to horrible events, this constant stream of ghastly impressions will deprive even the most delicate among us of all respect for humanity," said Cicero, predicting "culture-death" (O'Connor 1989:16). If he could have viewed the future he would have also noted how the commedia dell'arte was made into Grand Guignol; marionette farces made into hand-puppet Punch and Judy; the gothic novel made into the penny dreadful; the illustrated story made into the comic; the *film noir* made into stalk-and-slash. The cartooning of action, the introduction of vivid and hyperbolic scenes, not only generates its own sensational context but penetrates older stories with concussive hyperbole.

The history of all modern media has been similar. As the economies of mass production give greater access to those previously excluded — the young, the unsophisticated, and the aggressive — the stories demanded and produced become progressively more crude and "vulgar." Show business shows what gets the business. To those who originally patronized the medium it will appear that the "golden age" is over. Carnival time starts. The sideshow moves closer to the center. Intellectual distress — currently expressed as, "They are not making movies for us any longer"; "You just can't read a good novel any more"; or "The networks are only interested in producing junk" — was first articulated in the early modern world by the Augustans as a reaction against the newly literate. What was Sir William Temple's plaint in the "Battle of the Books" but that the modern dreck obscures great ancient works. What is today's cry against the "Closing of the American Mind" and the necessity for "Cultural Literacy" but an attempt to reestablish a stable body of accepted knowledge? But popular culture, which depends on reproducibility, is continually in flux, sifting through audiences. English professors now talk about "expanding the canon" as if this awareness was recent and radical. The democratizing of myth has been occurring with gusto since the French Revolution and with now-manic speed since World War II. Theories blaming the "lowest common denominator," "cultural relativity," or "least objectionable programming" are explanations advanced to explain what happens when one audience captures the delivery systems and starts telling its own stories.

What is unique in our time, however, is television. Television culture is no oxymoron. It is rapidly becoming the species culture, the nervous system of the animal, just as print had been for generations before. Everything is behaving like television: books, movies, even entertainment parks. Invariably the newest medium, the freshest language so to speak, is the one undergoing the most intense audience shift, and so is the one most nostalgically remembered, and the one most vehemently pilloried. To be sure, the modern scapegoat is television, but the paperback book — especially the illustrated comic book — was more censoriously treated only a generation ago. Who would now burn a television set? But, then again, remember that Plato criticized the written language for despoiling the spoken. The printing press was not welcomed with enthusiasm by the monks whose illuminated manuscripts it rapidly rendered obsolete. Even the rise of literacy and the advent of publishing were hardly welcomed as an advance. Many eminent Victorian critics considered both a disaster. First, the novel was ruining literature; then the serial throwaway was ruining the novel; then the paperback was ruining the novel. Electronic media only accelerated the process. Radio was excoriated because it carried the mass-marketed fantasies of soap operas, and detective and western violence, to a popular audience. And if cheap novels and radio drama were not enough to dilute Western culture, just look at how Hollywood was ruining what was left. Lucky for the studios that the television networks came along to shoulder the blame. "Television is making a mess of things," we say as we turn on the set. "You dee-serve a break today."

Televison is unique in that once we turn it on, we cannot turn it off. Every minute thousands more sets are turned on. Eyes turn to see "what's on." Television is such an immediate language — a visual esperanto, a punch in the nose — it respects no frontiers. There is no intermediary between the glass screen and the eye. There is no way to stop this electronic flame from coming in. Radio can be jammed, not so satellite-beamed television. This is the true Star Wars. The Evil Empire has fallen. The Video Empire strikes back. In every country in which a commercial channel exists, American programming has pushed out the indigenous culture. Although France and Italy have attempted to limit the amount of foreign material, such limits will prove impossible to enforce. In 1992, not only will Western Europe have opened up its broadcast boundaries to some 340 million viewers, but by then the worldwide satellite systems will be on line. The image of the radio antenna sending its waves around the world, which announced an "RKO Picture," will be replaced by a big trashcan of hardware orbiting the earth, receiving and returning thousands of discrete signals carrying American spectacle. A new generation of direct broadcasting satellite (DBS), transmitting 108 channels to a 2x4-foot screen in your window, will make it impossible to contain what comes in. Fiber optics promises a still greater multiplicity of channels than the conventional "twisted cable." Together with the telephone and computer lines, hundreds of channels will flow through what are now being called "information pipes."

And who will be providing the global programming, the software for the pipes and satellites? The usual suspects: Time Warner, Murdoch, Sony, Maxwell, Paramount, Disney, Silvio Berlusconi of Italy, Bertelsmann A.G. What will be the operating code? Return on investment. What will be seen? John Perriss, director of the worldwide advertising concern Saatchi & Saatchi, claims, "The idea that American television will vulgarize the high temple of European culture is nonsense and dreadful snobbery" (Lohr 1989:39). But if we have learned anything from the collision of American popular culture with other cultures, it is that such "nonsense and snobbery" is true. Rather, as William Styron has said, "The export of our vulgarity is the hallmark of our greatness. I don't necessarily mean to be derogatory . . . but at least it's vital" (Bernstein 1990:59).

Witness the vitality of the "music video." A decade ago Warner Amex Satellite Entertainment Company (now owned by a consortium of conglomerates — the usual suspects) started a nonstop, twenty-four-hour, commercial channel beamed via satellite across the United States. The content seemed harmless enough. Musicians had made performance films of their acts since the 1940s so why not show them along with advertising? The impact of these "videos" was immediate, transforming not only the recording industry but show business as well. Performers who could sing as well as project a slightly outrageous persona (called "great visuals") like Boy George, Prince, Cyndi Lauper, Billy Idol, Tina Turner, and especially Michael Jackson and Madonna, became "recording artists." Mainline television programs like *Miami Vice* and *Hollywood Beat* were specially formatted to capitalize on the new imagery and pacing. (A perhaps apocryphal story has it that *Miami Vice* was conceived by Brandon Tartikoff, who scribbled a simple note to Tony Yerkovich: "MTV Cops.") Even news shows like *West 57th* were organized around musical scenarios. *Flashdance* and *Beverly Hills Cop* adapted the stop-and-go modular techniques to film. This staccato, telegraphic "style" has even been translated into print. The fast and furious, intense and surreal works of Mark Leyner (*I Smell Esther Williams* and *My Cousin, My Gastroenterologist*) depend on a reader's being familiar with the juxtaposition techniques of MTV.

For a while even the advertisers, who had introduced the music video, were the recipients of their own frantic styles. Coke, Levis, and Ford "spots" were almost interchangeable with what could be seen on MTV, except that these clips were in thirty-second segments. In fact, the advertisement and the music video occasionally interpenetrated. Michael Jackson promoted Pepsi in his videos and made Pepsi commercials that were "knock-offs" of these videos. Even mainline advertisements have been affected. A case in point: a recent American Express commercial for travelers' checks opens with a burglar breaking into a hotel room while the occupant is in the shower. As the thief rummages, a newscast playing on the TV shifts to a commercial. It is Karl Malden warning, "Don't leave home without them!" As the burglar absconds with the tourist's wallet, the camera zooms in on Malden repeating his caveat. On MTV, as on television itself, the entertainment is the advertisement and the advertisement is the show.

If the art of television is such advertising, then MTV is an entire network dedicated to this art. Quick cutting, slow dissolves, computer-generated images, animation, wild angles, multiple-image montages, hallucinatory special effects, Chromakey, magnified close-ups, masked screens — everything that is implied in that portmanteau term "state of the art" is involved. No wonder that Brian DePalma,

Martin Scorsese, John Sayles, John Landis, and even Andy Warhol lined up to try the viewfinder. Here was a chance to make your own *Andalusian Dog, Entr'acte,* or *Ballet Mecanique* and be paid for it.

Television must make everything visual, even music. MTV is what we have for opera. Forget the bizarre plots; the experience sends all information to the eye and ear and from there straight to the nervous system. Old-fashioned purists, and even some legislators, are distraught that many of the most popular performers charge what seem to be outrageous prices for concert performances and then never sing a note. They lip-synch instead. But the fans of Milli Vanilli, New Kids on the Block, Janet Jackson, Paula Abdul, M. C. Hammer, and even Madonna, don't care. They want to hear exactly what is on their $14.00 CD at home and see a show that duplicates the video. Milli Vanilli simply took image-driven pop a step farther. They didn't even use their own voices. A decade ago Liza Minnelli was excoriated for "synching" during strenuous song and dance numbers in a Broadway show. And, more recently, playgoers were upset to learn that a few bars of *Phantom of the Opera* came out of a computer. But if the new crop of MTV performers really did sing in their concerts, the audience might have a legitimate grievance. Since the original was manufactured, shouldn't the "live" replica be likewise? "Is it live or is it Memorex?" Who cares?

The bloom is now off the video rose, yet its budding and fading show in almost time-lapse images what occurs in the entertainment garden of Vulgaria. While shifts in print content took generations, and shifts in filmic subjects took decades, shifts in television fashions happen in months. While no one was really looking except the kids, two strains of music video turned sensational. As if reflecting the concerns of affirmative action elsewhere, one strain was white, Western European, and visual; the other black, Caribbean, and verbal. Both, however, were hebephrenic. And both proved so powerful that they have helped make the fastest-growing segment of the music business not the sale of records, but the sale of the music videos. The audiences for these kinds of entertainment are not satisfied to hear the sound or see the action, they want to own the sequences on videotape. No longer is the music video a promotional tool, now it is the grown-up product.

This white music was "heavy metal," appropriately named for its reliance on the amplification of metallic instruments which produces a harsh metallic sound. This distinctly urban sound resembled an amplified traffic jam. The accompanying imagery on video was rife with stilettos, chains, leathers, tortured women, monsters, dirty streets, male-strutting, gang warfare, and all the trappings of urban male aggression. This aggression was not new. After all, Wayne Cochrane in the 1950s and Peter Townshend of The Who in the 1960s were breaking furniture and smashing guitars. What *was* new was the style. The onstage violence became so stylized that one could distinguish the "punk" routines of a Sid Vicious or a Johnny Rotten of the Sex Pistols from the cosmic storm-trooper show of KISS, from the bash-'em-up show of Twisted Sister. Still, what remains constant is the overwhelming maleness of such entertainment. Almost without exception these are all-male groups, in an almost all-male industry, playing to an almost all-adolescent male audience.

As one would expect given such components, the behavior is bizarre because the real anxiety is focused on what is missing — namely, women. Metal lyrics were all but obliterated. This was *West Side Story* not as high romance, but as punk mating calls. No one ever argued that "heavy metal" was the music to sooth the savage breast — quite the opposite. This was the music of stage-diving, slam-dancing, and, in the self-descriptive term of praise, head-banging. Groups with mediocre talent but an arresting presentation of rage (such as Twisted Sister, Ozzy Osbourne, Judas Priest, AC/DC, Ronnie Dio, Motley Crue, Def Leppard, Ratt, KISS, Iron Maiden, Stray Cats, Quiet Riot), as well as groups of almost no talent but even more pugnacious affect (like the Dead Kennedys, 3 Teens Kill 4, Sadistic Faction, Savage Republic, Pseudo Sadists, Alien Sex Fiend, and Rash of Stabbings), soon commandeered almost a third of MTV clips. They also attracted adult attention, predictable censure, and, in true carnival style, wore themselves out. Their audience went elsewhere, leaving only the diehards behind.

If "heavy metal" was the Anglo-American contribution to low culture, then "rap" was the African-American donation. And if "metal" came from the garage where Junior had been sent with his guitar and extension cord, then rap came from the street where young blacks played the only instruments they could afford — the mouth organ and the foot drum. Rap is performed in street clothes; metal in elaborate costumes of leather and fringe. In metal, the volume carries the aggression; in rap it is the words. Both are rife with adolescent misogyny, homophobia, and threats of violence. They are rude, bawdy, boastful, with a kind of "in your face" aggression (called "attitude")

W.A.S.P., 1984 Capitol Records (photo: Moshe Brakha).

characteristic of insecure masculinity. Both musical forms were unique, however, in that they produced platinum records with little radio exposure. They found their audience on MTV.

Inside the coded language, mystic monikers, and voodoo-sounding background noises of rap is the entire world of television reconstituted in hip-hop. "Yo! MTV Raps" was seen twice daily and consistently draws the largest worldwide audience for what is essentially a collage of commercial television itself. The remote-control wand is inside the set. The viewing is characterized by abrupt juxtaposing, voiceovers, zapping between stations, breaks for commercials, and whipsawing in and out of context. Language is chopped, repeated, snipped, and bitten. But, most of all, like its host medium television, rap is dedicated to promoting itself—the essence of braggadocio in which nothing is sacred but itself. Everything else is up for grabs. In fact, the rap term for stealing music and lyrics is called "biting someone's style," in the sense of lifting a sound or visual "bite." Very often the text itself has been lifted from actual verbal and visual television kennings. Rappers imitate game shows, take rests called "commercials," and refer to themselves inside the television genealogy. Marvin Young, aka Young M.C., boasts, "I'm rough like Hunter, clever like MacGyver," and raps, "If I'm not on tour, I'm home watching cable." Ice-T, a devotee of police shows, provides close-ups of shootings during his rap then finishes off with "crime doesn't pay" messages, just like his favorite genre. Most of all, of course, the rapper acknowledges what he shares with his audience — the endless supply of brand-name products: Nike, Coke, Addidas, Gucci, Porsche. . . .

Rather like High Church willing to suffer the Carnival, so MTV rides alongside mainstream programming, subverting and reconditioning the tropes of the medium. With no beginnings or endings, in an endless loop, they flash by like video wallpaper. Yet, observed closely, the music video gathers its strength by continually breaking down distinctions. Artificial boundaries, fostered by high culture, such as those between athletics and art, between stand-up comedy and dance, between pop stardom and religion are occluded as a matter of course. Images are indiscriminately drawn from high and low culture, past and present, to create a self-conscious pastiche in which the only rule is to break a few. Even trendy MTV calls itself "Post-Modern MTV."

An aesthetic category may disappear from neglect, like the picturesque, or be co-opted by some political or religious movement, like the sublime and the New Age movement, or be subsumed into the normal as has the vulgar. The vulgar is no longer the low entertainments of "the other"; it is the standard entertainment for all of us. The market-driven conglomerated entertainment industry does just what it says it does; it gives the people what they want. Or, more appropriately, it exchanges what the audience wants for what *it* wants: stories for money. What the best-selling book did to publishing, what the blockbuster did to the movies, what the top-ten Nielsen shows have done to television is to remove the gatekeeper and restore authority to the audience. MTV even has part of its day programmed by its viewers. Viewers may call a 900 telephone number with their requests, and whichever video receives the most ninety-cent calls gets air time. CNN's *Newsnight* also has such a user-friendly approach to the news. Read the menu. Order your entree-entertainment. Finally the ultimate in synergy: the electronic box office uses the telephone as collection agency. We sit at our individual campfires and motion with our fingers on the numeric keypad telling the bard what stories to sing, what stories to tell.

Bardic television, driven by audience desire and supported by a complex of entertainment and merchandising industries, clearly promises a number of cultural sea changes. They are not all to be feared. And they are not all directly caused by show business. But surely the shift from a manufacturing to a service economy, from an economics of scarcity to one of consumption, from a politics of representation to one of individual and group activity, from acceptance of authority to individual freedom of choice, from self-denial to self-indulgence is partly the legacy of modern entertainment. Certainly, for our purposes, the primacy of the image has meant the end of high culture as a preserve of contrived yearning defined for the last two centuries by the romantics and modernists — that "old literature," as Alvin Kernan recently called it in *The Death of Literature*, has run out of audience. How can it live when nearly 60 percent of adult Americans have never read a book and most of the rest read only one book a year? How can it survive when the average postadolescent American spends forty hours and at least thirty dollars a week being entertained by nonprint media? The notion of a solitary artist, bent on expressing a unique truth to an attentive audience, is daily growing less important. The concept of author, of authority, of story possession dissolves when our Homer does not know what to tell except by checking the electronic scoreboard.[2]

As the author has become an agent of audience demand, the role of gatekeeper, of priestly intercessionary, of a professional class of mediators vanishes. In an oral and visual transaction activated by audience attention, critics come after the entertainment, not before. Theories of art, not objects of art, become the subject of study. Although the loss of mediating authority can be witnessed daily in any number of

2. Nowhere will you see this modern view better expressed than in Stephen King's clearly autobiographical gothic novel *Misery*. Paul Sheldon, an injured writer of romances, is trapped by Annie, a crazed nurse, in the Colorado mountains. Now that he sees that his life is short, he determines to do some "serious writing." But she is just as determined to have him provide what she wants. What she wants as his "perfect fan" is that he revive his romance heroine Misery Chastain. When Sheldon refuses, Annie chops off little bits of him. She knows, and he comes to know, that if you want to survive in show business you give the audience what it wants because without an audience an author doesn't exist. As well, the triumph of vulgarity is the triumph of "what Annie wants" because that is what New American Library, subsidiary of the Pearson conglomerate, will publish.

"sites," it can be clearly observed in the current obsession with the curriculum, or the lack of it, in higher education. From Yale to Stanford we see the once-priestly class of the professoriat showing the characteristic confusion of those who don't have much that others want. As with many academic concerns since the 1960s, the squabble can become ferocious because the stakes are so low. Having given up on our students, or more appropriately, our students having realized they have little to learn from us, the "postindustrial" critic claims that Western Civilization depends on what he has to say and then wanders off to the chatty back sections of purposefully obscure journals with pompous names.

Although it is tempting and satisfying to blame the trashing of taste on higher education, the professoriate is hardly to blame. Would that it was still so powerful. No, the triumph of vulgarity is the application of the marketplace to taste. Pay up or be gone. Show biz trumps the Lit. biz. Free enterprise is always lauded by those who are served and satisfied, and condemned by those who are disenfranchised and ignored. And what modern show business has shown is that the higher-education business, as it is currently behaving, has little to offer. It barely has an audience in itself. Of course no one listens to them. Who can understand what they have to say? When the Yale Critics made the national news in the 1980s, it was not because they were interested in educating the public but rather because they had become either infatuated with French philosophy or with hiding past political sympathies. The purposeful obscurity of much contemporary criticism may well prove salutary, may well turn us from the ditzy theories du jour we have hidden behind and return us to what the preprofessional generation (roughly 1890 to 1930) of modern academic gatekeepers did: explain the world around them to the world around them.

Charles Townsend Copeland, who did not have a Ph.D., spent seventeen years as an instructor at Harvard teaching what we would call Freshman Composition and lecturing around the country. *Time* magazine did a cover story on his influence. William Lyon Phelps, Copeland's counterpart at Yale, published books like *What I Like in Poetry* and *What I Like in Prose*, as well as a column in *Scribner's Magazine* called "As I Like It," in which he commented on current affairs. He invited Gene Tunney to address his Shakespeare class, wrote books on marriage, motherhood, and human nature for the general reader, and contributed to the Rotary Club. Wilbur Cross,

Phelps' colleague at Yale, entered politics to become governor of Connecticut. While governor he edited the *Yale Review*. When he returned to New Haven, after four terms in Hartford, he started a radio talk show. These men were not alone. Bliss Perry, Henry van Dyke, Thomas Marc Parrott, John Erskine, and many others saw themselves as public figures whose job was not to mystify but to explain, not to obscure but to make clear.

To many in the academy today (usually older colleagues), the acknowledgment of endless interpretation, of relativistic readings, seems nihilistic, typical of a loss of nerve. Here, for instance, is a recent characterization of literature departments by an American professor as published in the handbook of seminary culture, the *Times Literary Supplement*:

> Ambitious without direction or specific goals, uncertain of its position in the larger culture, unsure of its basic terms — including "theory," "criticism," and even "literature" — the profession of literary criticism finds itself in a kind of trough. After a generation of theoretical and institutional battles, the polemical edge of literary studies has become somewhat blunt and ragged. And while it is not fair to say that the best lack all conviction while the worst are full of passionate intensity, it does appear that many of the best critical minds find the terms of the old debates non-productive or of merely historical interest, and are not opposed to easing into a phase of stock-taking and consolidation, an era of criticism without cause. (Harpham 1990:872)

One obvious reason for this loss of concentration is that to the new generation of professors — the generation raised on the electronic midway — print is not the primary interest in their personal lives.

If one wishes to witness the atrophy of high culture and the triumph of the marketplace as the gatekeepers lose conviction, there is no better text than a recent flyer from St. Martin's Press touting their *Winchester Reader*. Book publishers inundate professors with such advertising as these books can be immensely profitable if adopted in introductory classes. After the requisite introductory pages of puffery announcing the academic importance of the editors and the relevancy of the selections, a foldout graph appears on the last page. Just as we have had audience-driven bestsellers, movies, and television shows, here finally we have audience driven "literature." The column on the far left announces the criteria and the next column under *The Winchester Reader* shows what is currently preferred. These criteria have nothing to do with complexity, profundity or even application.

See how *The Winchester Reader* compares to other large thematic readers.

Donald McQuade
Robert Atwan
The Winchester Reader

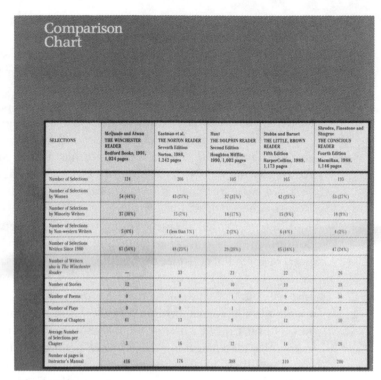

Comparison Chart

SELECTIONS	McQuade and Atwan THE WINCHESTER READER Bedford Books, 1991, 1,024 pages	Eastman et al. THE NORTON READER Seventh Edition Norton, 1988, 1,242 pages	Hunt THE DOLPHIN READER Second Edition Houghton Mifflin, 1990, 1,003 pages	Stubbs and Barnet THE LITTLE, BROWN READER Fifth Edition HarperCollins, 1989, 1,173 pages	Shrodes, Finestone and Shugrue THE CONSCIOUS READER Fourth Edition Macmillan, 1988, 1,146 pages
Number of Selections	124	206	105	165	193
Number of Selections by Women	54 (44%)	43 (21%)	37 (35%)	42 (25%)	53 (27%)
Number of Selections by Minority Writers	37 (30%)	15 (7%)	18 (17%)	15 (9%)	18 (9%)
Number of Selections by Non-western Writers	5 (4%)	1 (less than 1%)	2 (2%)	6 (4%)	4 (2%)
Number of Selections Written Since 1980	67 (54%)	48 (23%)	29 (28%)	45 (34%)	47 (24%)
Number of Writers also in *The Winchester Reader*	—	33	23	22	26
Number of Stories	12	1	10	10	28
Number of Poems	0	0	1	9	36
Number of Plays	0	0	1	0	2
Number of Chapters	41	13	9	12	10
Average Number of Selections per Chapter	3	16	12	14	20
Number of pages in Instructor's Manual	416	176	388	310	200

Back page of *Winchester Reader* circular, 1991 (Bedford Books of St. Martin's Press).

Rather they have to do with gender, race, contemporaneity, and simplicity. Note that having no poetry is clearly an asset — it's too unpopular. The bottom category needs no gloss. The headline on the front page of this glossy flyer announces, "Like Nothing You've Seen — and Just What You'd Expect" and inside we are told that this "is the first of the next generation of large thematic readers, attuned to the needs of the nineties." Indeed.

I have often wished that Frederick Wiseman, who made the cinema vérité movies of life in an insane asylum, in an urban high school, and at a court of law, would do a film inside an English department. It would be curious to see how much time the assistant professors actually spend *reading* Donne, Swift, and Austen (once the tenure articles are written) and how much time they spend "watching the tube." Deconstruction, structuralism, feminism, Marxism, and all the "isms" not yet named have made their way into the monastery, not only because the novitiates have their fingers on the remote-control button, but because the monks do too. It is more entertaining to treat literature as an instrument of Dead White Male domination, or as capitalist hegemony, or middle-class repression than as the revealed word of some great tradition. Small wonder that deconstruction, which elevates the audience, since author and critic have conveniently vanished, should prove so alluring to all parties inside the academy, but is totally unimportant to those outside. In a world of unlimited signs, anyone can be a reader and anything can be read. No wonder the Johns Hopkins University has a Film Studies Program. All is "discourse." No medium can be privileged above others. And best yet, each "reading" is as good as any other reading. Ring the bell. Recess time. At least for a while.

A few years ago, Francis Fukuyama, a state department official, contended in his controversial "The End of History?" that "the ineluctable spread of consumerist Western culture" presages "not just the end of the Cold War, or the passing of a particular period of postwar history, but the end of history as such: that is, the end point of mankind's ideological evolution (1989:3–4). Such predictions are not new. "The End of History (as we know it)" and the "end point of mankind's ideological evolution" have been predicted before by philosophers like Hegel, who claimed it had already happened in 1806 when Napoleon embodied the ideals of the French Revolution, and by Marx, who said the end was coming soon with world communism. What legitimizes this modern claim is that it is demonstrably true. For better or for worse, American culture is already world culture. Certainly one of the unadvertised aspects of the New World Order is the dominance of world-wide conglomerated media and the effacement of culture-specific aesthetic categories like high art.

Yet, the trashing of taste is the triumph of the popular will. Old-style intellectuals may not like what is published, projected, and broadcast, but it is far closer to what most people want most of the time than at any other period of modern history. It would be nice to think that this carnivalization will result in the cosmopolitanism envisioned by the Enlightenment *philosophes*, that universalism would triumph in a crescendo of hosannas. It would be nice to think that show business would "cleanse the doors of perception," release us from racism, sexism, ethnocentricism, and that the apocalypse would come as it did at the end of romanticism in Shelley's *Prometheus Unbound*, leaving us "Sceptreless, free, uncircumscribed . . . Equal, unclassed, tribeless, and nationless . . . Pinnacled dim in the intense inane."

Nancy waves to Ron at Republican National Convention, 1984
(photo: Paul Hosefros/NYT Pictures).

But it is more likely that the globalization of show business will result in the heroic materialism of an ever-increasing, worldwide consumerist culture. Recall that Athens ceased to be a world power around 400 B.C., yet for the next three hundred years Greek culture was the culture of the world. The Age of European Exposition ended in the mid-twentieth century; the Age of American Show Business is already upon us. The untranscendent, banal, sensational, democratic, immediate, trashy, tribalizing, and unifying force of the Vulgar need not result in a Bronze Age of culture. In fact, who knows what it will result in? It is certainly hard not to be of two minds about the outcome, conflicted between democratic ideals and marketplace realities. One matter is certain, however. The future will not produce what Shelley via McLuhan had in mind. We have been in the Global Village a short time, and it is an often scary and melancholy place to be. Whatever it becomes, the mass-mediated world is worthy of our impassioned study lest Oscar Wilde's prediction prove true: "The brotherhood of man is not a mere poet's dream: it is a most depressing and humiliating reality."

Works Cited

Although in the last twenty years there has been voluminous scholarship concerning the mass media, I could not have written this without the flood of entfotainment carried in such newspapers as the *New York Times*, *USA Today*, *Variety*, and the *Wall Street Journal*, as well as in magazines like *Publishers Weekly*, *TV Guide*, *Entertainment Weekly*, and *Advertising Age*. Also, I am indebted to the brokerage houses of Merrill Lynch, Wertheim Schroder, and Goldman Sachs for invaluable information about the conglomerated entertainment industries.

Addison, Joseph. *The Spectator* (No. 447). Vol. 3. Edited by Gregory Smith. New York: Oxford University Press, 1965.

Adorno, Theodor. "On Popular Music." *Studies in Philosophy and Social Science* (1940), 9:17–48.

Alexander, Edward P. *Museum Masters: Their Museums and Their Influence*. Nashville, Tenn.: American Association for State and Local History, 1983.

Allen, Robert C. "Reader-Oriented Criticism and Television." In Robert C. Allen, ed., *Channels of Discourse: Television and Contemporary Criticism*, 74–112. Chapel Hill: University of North Carolina Press, 1987.

Alley, Robert S. "Television Drama." In Horace Newcomb, ed., *Television: The Critical View*, 89–121. New York: Oxford University Press, 1982.

Anderson, Kurt. "Pop Goes the Culture." *Time*, June 16, 1986, pp. 68–74.

Andrews, Peter. "Peddling Prime Time." *Saturday Review*, June 7, 1980, pp. 64–65.

Aronowitz, Stanley. *False Promises: The Shaping of American Working-Class Consciousness*. New York: McGraw-Hill, 1973.

Asahina, Robert. "Blame It on the Tube." *Harper's*, November 1979, pp. 106–109.

Bach, Steven. *Final Cut: Dreams and Disaster in the Making of "Heaven's Gate."* New York: Morrow, 1985.

Bailey, Herbert S., Jr. *The Traditional Book in the Electronic Age*. Bowker Lecture, November 10, 1977. New York: R. R. Bowker, 1978.

Bakhtin, Mikhail. *Rabelais and His World*. Translated by Helene Iswolsky. Bloomington: Indiana University Press, 1984.

Balio, Tino, ed. 1976. *The American Film Industry*. Rev. ed. Madison: University of Wisconsin Press, 1985.

Ballantine, Ian and Betty Ballantine. "From Two-Bit Beginning." *New York Times Book Review*, April 30, 1989, p. 25ff.

Bangs, Lester. *Psychotic Reactions and Carburetor Dung*. Greil Marcus, ed. New York: Knopf, 1987.

Barnouw, Erik. *Tube of Plenty: The Evolution of American Television*. New York: Oxford University Press, 1982.

Bart, Peter. *Fade Out: The Calamitous Final Days of MGM*. New York: Morrow, 1990.

Barthes, Roland. *Mythologies*. Translated by Annette Lavers. New York: Hill & Wang, 1972.

Baudrillard, Jean. *America*. Translated by Chris Turner. New York: Verso, 1989.

Benjamin, Walter. "The Work of Art in the Age of Mechanical Reproduction." In *Illuminations*, 217–251. New York: Harcourt, Brace and World, 1968.

Berg, A. Scott. *Goldwyn: A Biography*. New York: Knopf, 1989.

Berman, Marc. "Sell-Through Revs Up." *Variety*, February 18, 1991, p. 30.

Berman, Russell A. *Modern Culture and Critical Theory: Art, Politics, and the Legacy of the Frankfurt School*. Madison: University of Wisconsin Press, 1989.

Bernstein, Carl. "The Leisure Empire." *Time*, December 24, 1990, pp. 56–59.

Bersani, Leo. *The Culture of Redemption*. Cambridge: Harvard University Press, 1990.

Birch, M. J. "The Popular Fiction Industry: Market Formula, Ideology." *Journal of Popular Culture* (1987), 21(3):79–102.

Bloom, Allan. *The Closing of the American Mind: How Higher Education Has Failed Democracy and Impoverished the Souls of Today's Students*. New York: Simon & Schuster, 1987.

Blum, Richard and Richard D. Lindheim. *Primetime: Network Television Programming*. Boston: Focal Press, 1987.

Boddy, William. "The Studios Move into Prime Time: Hollywood and the Television Industry in the 1950s." *Cinema Journal* (1985), 24(4):23–37.

Bogdan, Robert. *Freak Show: Presenting Human Oddities for Amusement and Profit*. Chicago: University of Chicago Press, 1988.

Bonn, Thomas L. *Heavy Traffic & High Culture: New American Library as Literary Gatekeeper in the Paperback Revolution*. Carbondale: Southern Illinois University Press, 1989.

——*UnderCover: An Illustrated History of American Mass Market Paperbacks*. New York: Penguin, 1982.

Boorstin, Daniel J. *The Image: A Guide to Pseudo-Events in America*. New York: Harper & Row, 1964.

——"The Significance of Broadcasting in Human History." In *Symposium on the Cultural Role of Broadcasting*, 9–23. Tokyo: Hoso-Bunka Foundation, 1978.

Bordwell, David. *Making Meaning: Inference and Rhetoric in the Interpretation of Cinema*. Cambridge: Harvard University Press, 1990.

Bottomore, Tom. *The Frankfurt School*. New York: Tavistock, 1984.

Brantlinger, Patrick. *Bread & Circuses: Theories of Mass Culture as Social Decay*. Ithaca: Cornell University Press, 1983.

Bristol, Michael D. *Carnival and Theater: Plebeian Culture and the Structure of Authority in Renaissance England*. New York: Methuen, 1985.

Brooks, Mel. "My Movies: The Collision of Art and Money." In Jason E. Squire, ed., *The Movie Business Book*, 29–37. New York: Simon & Schuster, 1983.

Brown, Les. *Television: The Business Behind the Box*. New York: Harcourt Brace Jovanovich, 1971.

Burke, Peter. *Popular Culture in Early Modern Europe*. London: Temple Smith, 1978.

Busch, Niven. "Profile" (of Adolph Zukor). *The New Yorker*, September 7, 1929, p. 29ff.

Canby, Vincent. "Real Butter and Big Bucks." *New York Times*, December 13, 1987, p. 31ff.

Carroll, Noel. *Mystifying Movies: Fads & Fallacies in Contemporary Film*. New York: Columbia University Press, 1988.

Carter, Robert A. "A History of Book Marketing II." *Publishers Weekly*, June 10, 1988, pp. 53–55.

——— "A History of Book Marketing – The '40s and '50's." *Publishers Weekly*, January 13, 1989, pp. 54–56.

——— "A History of Book Marketing – The '60s Through the '80s." *Publishers Weekly*, May 26, 1989, pp. 34–37.

——— "'Booming' the Book Through the Years." *Publishers Weekly*, March 11, 1988, pp. 74–76.

Cawelti, John G. *Adventure, Mystery, and Romance: Formula Stories as Art and Popular Culture*. Chicago: University of Chicago Press, 1976.

——— "Concept of Formula in the Study of Popular Literature." *Journal of Popular Culture* (1969), 3(3):381–90.

——— "The Question of Popular Genres." *Journal of Popular Film and Television* (1985) 13(2):55–61.

Cerf, Bennett. *At Random: The Reminiscences of Bennett Cerf*. New York: Random House, 1977.

Chagall, David. "Reading the Viewer's Mind." *TV Guide*, November 7, 1981, pp. 47–49.

Chapple, Steve and Reebee Garofalo. *Rock 'n' Roll Is Here to Pay*. Chicago: Nelson, 1977.

Cohen, Roger. "Ad on Pantheon Leads to a Quarrel Between 2 Publishers." *New York Times*, October 26, 1990, p. C18.

——— "Changing Spirit at Random House." *New York Times*, March 19, 1990, p. C1ff.

——— "Costly Second Thoughts for Some Books." *New York Times*, August 6, 1990, p. D12.

——— "First Novelists, Don't Fret: There's Money in Newness." *New York Times*, April 15, 1991, p. C8.

——— "Publishing World Shaken as Advances for Books Soar." *New York Times*, July 16, 1990, p. D1.

——— "Too Many Books Are Coming Back Unsold." *New York Times*, May 14, 1990, p. C8.

Collins, Jim. *Uncommon Cultures: Popular Culture and Post-Modernism*. New York: Routledge, 1989.

Conant, Michael. "The Paramount Decrees Reconsidered." In Tino Balio, ed., *The American Film Industry*, 537–574. Madison: University of Wisconsin Press, 1985.

Coser, Lewis A., Charles Kadushin and Walter Powell. *Books: The Culture and Commerce of Publishing*. New York: Basic Books, 1982.

Cottom, Daniel. "Taste and the Civilized Imagination." *Journal of Aesthetics and Art Criticism* (1981), 39(4):367–80.

Crocker, Lester G. *Two Diderot Studies: Ethics and Esthetics*. Baltimore: Johns Hopkins University Press, 1952.

Dannen, Fredric. *Hit Men: Power Brokers and Fast Money Inside the Music Business*. New York: Times Books, 1990.

Davis, Kenneth C. *Two-Bit Culture: The Paperbacking of American Culture*. Boston: Houghton Mifflin, 1984.

Davis, L. J. "Hollywood's Most Secret Agent [Michael Ovitz]." *New York Times Magazine*, July 9, 1989, p. 24ff.

De Tocqueville, Alexis. "In What Spirit the Americans Cultivate the Arts." In Bernard Rosenberg and David Manning White, eds., *Mass Culture: The Popular Arts in America*, 27–34. New York: Macmillan, 1964.

Debord, Guy. *Society of the Spectacle*. Detroit: Black & Red, 1970.

Didion, Joan. "In Hollywood." In *The White Album*, 153–167. New York: Simon & Schuster, 1979.

Dunkel, Tom. "Big Bucks, Tough Tactics." *New York Times Magazine*, September 17, 1989, p. 56ff.

Dunne, John Gregory. "Goldwynism." *New York Review of Books*, May 18, 1989, pp. 28–35.

———*The Studio*. New York: Farrar, Straus & Giroux, 1969.

Dystel, Oscar. "Mass-Market Publishing: More Observations, Speculations, and Provocations." Originally the R. R. Bowker Memorial Lecture. In Elizabeth A. Geiser, ed., *The Business of Book Publishing: Papers by Practitioners*, 316–335. Boulder, Colo.: Westview, 1985.

Eco, Umberto. *The Name of the Rose*. Translated by William Weaver. New York: Harcourt Brace Jovanovich, 1983.

Elias, Norbert. *The Civilizing Process: The History of Manners*. Translated by Edmund Jephcott. New York: Urizen Books, 1978.

Eliot, Marc. *Rockonomics: The Money Behind the Music*. New York: Franklin Watts, 1989.

Engelhardt, Tom. "The Shortcake Strategy." In Todd Gitlin, ed., *Watching Television: A Pantheon Guide to Popular Culture*, 68–110. New York: Pantheon, 1986.

Epstein, Joseph. "What Is Vulgar?" In *The Middle of My Tether*, 126–141. New York: Norton, 1983.

"The Era of the Non-B." *Time*, August 22, 1960, pp. 70–71.

Esslin, Martin. "Aristotle on the Advertisers: The Television Commercial Considered as a Form of Drama." In Horace Newcomb, ed., *Television: The Critical View*, 260–275. New York: Oxford University Press, 1982.

Feiffer, Jules. *The Great Comic Book Heroes*. New York: Dial, 1965.

Fiedler, Leslie. *Freaks: Myths and Images of the Secret Self*. New York: Simon & Schuster, 1978.

———*What Was Literature?: Class, Culture and Mass Society*. New York: Simon & Schuster, 1982.

———*The Sociology of Rock*. London: Constable, 1978.

Fiske, John. "British Cultural Studies and Television." In Robert C. Allen, ed., *Channels of Discourse: Television and Contemporary Criticism*, 254–290. Chapel Hill: University of North Carolina Press, 1987.

———*Introduction to Communication Studies*. New York: Methuen, 1982.

———*Reading the Popular*. Boston: Unwin Hyman, 1989.

———*Television Culture*. New York: Methuen, 1987.

Fiske, John and John Hartley. "Bardic Television." In Horace Newcomb, ed., *Television: The Critical View*, 495–509. New York: Oxford University Press, 1982.

Flaubert, Gustave. *Madame Bovary*. Translated by Merloyd Lawrence. Boston: Houghton Mifflin, 1969.

Fowles, Jib. *Television Viewers vs. Media Snobs*. New York: Stein & Day, 1982.

Frank, Jerome. "Book Jackets Go High-Deco in the Display Space War." *Publishers Weekly*, June 2, 1989, p. 60.

———"Graph Expo Offers Exciting New products for Publishers." *Publishers Weekly*, May 20, 1988, p. 59ff.

———"Making Books." *Publishers Weekly*, May, 26, 1989, p. S16ff.

———"Mass Market Covers — Key Weapons in the Rack-Space War." *Publishers Weekly*, January 22, 1988, pp. 78–84.

———"Technology and Fresh Ideas Strengthen Mass Market Covers." *Publishers Weekly*, January 8, 1988, pp. 54–61.

Freedman, Jonathan. "Autocanonization: Tropes of Self-Legitimization in 'Popular Culture.' " *Yale Journal of Criticism* (1987) 1(1):203–217.

Frith, Simon. *Music for Pleasure: Essays in the Sociology of Pop*. New York: Routledge, 1988.

Fukuyama, Francis. "The End of History?" *The National Interest* (1989), 16:3–18.

Fussell, Paul. *Class: A Guide Through the American Status System*. New York: Summit, 1983.

Gabler, Neal. *An Empire of Their Own: How the Jews Invented Hollywood*. New York: Doubleday, 1988.

Gabriel, Trip. "Call My Agent." *New York Times Magazine*, February 19, 1989, p. 45ff.

Gans, Herbert J. *Popular Culture and High Culture: An Analysis and Evaluation of Taste*. New York: Basic Books, 1974.

Garey, Norman H. "Elements of Feature Financing." In Jason E. Squire, ed., *The Movie Business Book*, 95–106. New York: Simon & Schuster, 1983.

Geertz, Clifford. *The Interpretation of Culture*. New York: Basic Books, 1973.

Geiger, Peter W. "The Bank and Feature Financing." In Jason E. Squire, ed., *The Movie Business Book*, 107–112. New York: Simon & Schuster, 1983.

Gerard. Jeremy. "TV Mirrors a New Generation." *New York Times*, October 30, 1988, sec. 2, p. 1ff.

Gitlin, Todd. *Inside Prime Time*. New York: Pantheon, 1983.

Gitlin, Todd, ed. *Watching Television: A Pantheon Guide to Popular Culture*. New York: Pantheon, 1986.

Gold, Richard. "Clamor for Glamor Sparks Media Melee." *Variety*, January 17, 1990, p. 1ff.

Goldenson, Leonard H. *Beating the Odds: The Untold Story Behind the Rise of ABC*. New York: Scribners, 1991.

Goldman, William. "The Screenwriter." In Jason E. Squire, ed., *The Movie Business Book*, 51–62. New York: Simon & Schuster, 1983.

Gomery, Douglas. *The Hollywood Studio System*. New York: St. Martin's, 1986.

——"U.S. Film Exhibition: The Formation of a Big Business." In Tino Balio, ed., *The American Film Industry*, 218–228. Madison: University of Wisconsin Press, 1985.

Goodman, Walter. "Upstart Offerings vs. Elitist of Turgid Triangle." *New York Times*, August 16, 1989, p. C22.

Gordon, David. "Why the Movie Majors Are Major." *Sight and Sound* (1973), 42:194–196.

Gould, John. "What Is Television Doing to Us?" *New York Times Magazine*, June 12, 1949, p. 7ff.

Graff, Gerald. *Professing Literature: An Institutional History*. Chicago: University of Chicago Press, 1987.

Greenberg, Clement. "Avant-Garde and Kitsch." In Bernard Rosenberg and David Manning White, eds., *Mass Culture: The Popular Arts in America*, 98–111. New York: Macmillan, 1964.

Greenblatt, Stephen. "Filthy Rites." *Daedalus* (1982), 111(3):1–16.

Harmetz, Aljean. " 'Amazing Stories' Tries New Tactics." *New York Times*, June 2, 1986, p. 21.

——"Hollywood Pays Court to the Young Adult." *New York Times*, May 13, 1990, sec. 2, p. 17ff.

——"Now Showing: Survival of the Fittest." *New York Times*, October 22, 1989, sec. 2, p. 1ff.

——"Waking from a New 'Nightmare' to New Profits." *New York Times*, July 13, 1989, p. C17.

Harper's New Monthly Magazine, January 1867, p. 261.

Harpham, Geoffrey Galt. "The Triumph of Terminology." *Times Literary Supplement (London)*, August 17–23, 1990, p. 872.

Harris, N. G. E. "The Objects of the Vulgar." *Dialogue* (1985), 24:257–263.

Harris, Neil. *Cultural Excursions: Marketing Appetites and Cultural Tastes in Modern America*. Chicago: University of Chicago Press, 1990.

——*Humbug: The Art of P. T. Barnum*. Chicago: University of Chicago Press, 1973.

Hartwell, David G. "Dollars and Dragons: The Truth About Fantasy." *New York Times Book Review*, April 29, 1990, p. 1ff.

Hawkins, Harriet. *Classics and Trash: Traditions and Taboos in High Literature and Popular Modern Genres*. Toronto: University of Toronto Press, 1991.

Hazlitt, William. "On Vulgarity and Affectation." In *The Complete Works*, 8:156–168. London: J. M. Dent, 1931.

Hebdige, Dick. *Subculture: The Meaning of Style*. New York: Methuen, 1979.

———"Towards a Cartography of Taste." In Bernard Waites, ed., *Popular Culture: Past and Present*, 194–218. London: Routledge, 1982.

Hedges, James S. "Towards Formal Boundaries for the Act in Popular Culture." *Journal of Popular Culture* (1981), 4:9–15.

Heifferman, Marvin and Lisa Phillips. *Image World: Art and Media Culture*. Descriptive catalog to Image World Exhibition, November 8, 1989-February 18, 1990. New York: Whitney Museum of Art, 1989.

Henderson, W. J. "Music." *New York Times Illustrated Magazine*, October 25, 1898, p. 4.

Henry, Tricia. *Break All Rules!: Punk Rock and the Making of a Style*. Ann Arbor, Mich.: UMI Research Press, 1989.

Hijuelos, Oscar. *Mambo Kings Play Songs of Love*. New York: Farrar, Straus & Giroux, 1989.

Hirsch, E. D., Jr. *Cultural Literacy: What Every American Needs to Know*. Boston: Houghton Mifflin, 1987.

Hirsch, Paul. *The Structure of the Popular Music Industry*. Ann Arbor: University of Michigan Press, 1969.

Hoban, Phoebe. " 'Psycho' Drama." *New York*, December 17, 1990, pp. 33–37.

Holden, Stephen. "Strike the Pose: When Music Is Skin Deep." *New York Times*, August 5, 1990, sec. 2, p. 1ff.

Howard, Gerald. "Mistah Perkins — He Dead." *The American Scholar* (1989), 58(3):355–369.

Huxley, Aldous. *Beyond the Mexique Way*. New York: Harper & Row, 1934.

———"Vulgarity in Literature." In *Collected Essays*, 103–115. Edited by Donald Watt. New York: Harper, 1943.

Huyssen, Andreas. *After the Great Divide: Modernism, Mass Culture, Postmodernism*. Bloomington: Indiana University Press, 1986.

Izod, John. *Hollywood and the Box Office, 1895–1986*. New York: Columbia University Press, 1988.

James, Caryn. "4 Directors in a Seminar on Movies." *New York Times*, June 23, 1988, p. 18.

———"Romanticizing the Dream Factory." *New York Times*, November 7, 1989, p. 15.

———"Twice-Told Tales Can Cast a Spell." *New York Times*, August 6, 1989, sec. 2, p. 1ff.

Jameson, Fredric. "Reification and Utopia in Mass Culture." *Social Text* (1979), 1:130–148.

Jarvis, Jeff. "A Pat on Your Back." *People Weekly*, May 11, 1987, p. 9.

———"Conscientious Objection." *People Weekly*, December 3, 1989, p. 11.

Jones, Alex S. " 'Trash TV' Is Debated at Editors' Convention." *New York Times*, April 13, 1989, p. 18.

Jones, Margaret. "Filling the Shelves." *Publishers Weekly*, April 27, 1990, pp. 16–23.

Kael, Pauline. "The Current Cinema." *The New Yorker*, December 11, 1989, pp. 138–139.

——"Why Are Movies So Bad?" In *Taking It All In*, 8–20. New York: Holt, Rinehart & Winston, 1980.

Kant, Immanuel. *Critique of Judgement*. Translated by J. H. Bernard. London: Macmillan, 1931.

Kaplan, E. Ann. *Rocking Around the Clock: Music Television, Postmodernism, and Consumer Culture*. New York: Methuen, 1987.

Karp, Walter. "Where the Media Critics Went Wrong." *American Heritage*, March 1988, pp. 76–79.

Katzenberg, Jeffrey. "The Teaching of Chairman Jeff" (excerpts from the Disney chairman's memo). *Variety*, February 4, 1991, p. 5ff.

Kernan, Alvin. *The Death of Literature*. New Haven: Yale University Press, 1990.

Kipps, Charles. *Out of Focus: Power, Pride, and Prejudice—David Puttnam in Hollywood*. New York: Morrow, 1989.

Kleinfield, N. R. "As Viewers Wander, the Networks Scurry After." *New York Times*, February 26, 1989, sec. 2, p. 1ff.

Kosinski, Jerzy. *Being There*. New York: Harcourt Brace, 1971.

Lane, Michael. *Books and Publishers: Commerce Against Culture in Postwar Britain*. Lexington, Mass.: Lexington Books, 1980.

Lasch, Christopher. *The Culture of Narcissism: American Life in the Age of Diminishing Returns*. New York: Norton, 1978.

Lazere, Donald. *American Media and Mass Culture: Left Perspectives*. Berkeley: University of California Press, 1987.

Leavis, F. R. and Denys Thompson. *Culture and Environment: The Training of Critical Awareness*. London: Chatto & Windus, 1933.

Lees, David and Stan Berkowitz. *The Movie Business: A Primer*. New York: Vintage, 1981.

Leff, Leonard J. and Jerold L. Simmons. *The Dame in the Kimono: Hollywood, Censorship and the Production Code from the 1920s to the 1960s*. New York: Grove Weidenfeld, 1989.

Lehmann-Haupt, Christopher. "A Portrait of Nabokov, Through His Letters." *New York Times*, October 5, 1989, p. 16.

Levine, Lawrence W. *Highbrow/Lowbrow: The Emergence of Cultural Hierarchy*. Cambridge: Harvard University Press, 1988.

Levinson, Richard and William Link. *Off Camera: Conversations with the Makers of Prime-Time Television*. New York: New American Library, 1986.

Lewin, Kurt. *Field Theory in Social Science*. New York: Harper & Row, 1951.

Lewis, George H. "Uncertain Truths: The Promotion of Popular Culture." *Journal of Popular Culture* (1986), 20(3):31–44.

Leyner, Mark. *I Smell Esther Williams*. New York: Fiction Collective, 1983.

——*My Cousin, My Gastroenterologist*. New York: Crown, 1990.

Lieberson, Jonathan. "TV: A Day in the Life." *New York Review of Books*. April 13, 1989, pp. 15–20.

Lipsitz, George. *Time Passages: Collective Memory and American Popular Culture*. Minneapolis: University of Minnesota Press, 1990.

Lipton, Michael A. "What You Want to See in the New Decade." *TV Guide*, January 20, 1990, pp. 11–15.

Littlefield, Warren. "Searching for That 750-to-1 Shot." *Broadcasting*, March 17, 1986, p. 39.

Litwak, Mark. *Reel Power: The Struggle for Influence and Success in the New Hollywood*. New York: Morrow, 1986.

Lohr, Steve. "European TV's Vast Growth: Cultural Effect Stirs Concern." *New York Times*, March 6, 1989, p. 1ff.

Londoner, David J. "The Changing Economics of Entertainment." In Tino Balio, ed., *The American Film Industry*, 603–633. Madison: University of Wisconsin Press, 1985.

Lowell, James Russell. "On a Certain Condescension in Foreigners." In *My Study Windows*, 54–82. Boston: Houghton Mifflin, 1899.

Lynes, Russell. *The Lively Audience: A Social History of the Visual and Performing Arts in America 1890–1950*. New York: Harper & Row, 1985.

MacCabe, Colin, ed. *High Theory/Low Culture: Analyzing Popular Television and Film*. New York: St. Martin's, 1986.

Macdonald, Dwight. "The Theory of Mass Culture." In Bernard Rosenberg and David Manning White, eds., *Mass Culture: The Popular Arts in America*, 59–73. New York: Macmillan, 1964.

Malcolmson, Robert W. *Popular Recreations in English Society 1700–1850*. New York: Cambridge University Press, 1973.

Mander. Jerry. *Four Arguments for the Elimination of Television*. New York: Morrow, 1978.

Marc, David. *Comedy Visions: Television Comedy and American Culture*. Boston: Unwin Hyman, 1989.

———*Demographic Vistas: Television in American Culture*. Philadelphia: University of Pennsylvania Press, 1984.

Marcus, Greil. *Lipstick Traces: A Secret History of the Twentieth Century*. Cambridge: Harvard University Press, 1989.

Marsh, Dave. *The First Rock & Roll Confidential Report: Inside the Real World of Rock & Roll*. New York: Pantheon, 1985.

Marx, Samuel. *Mayer and Thalberg: The Make-Believe Saints*. New York: Random House, 1975.

Maryles, Daisy. "A Decade of Megasellers." *Publishers Weekly*, January 5, 1990, pp. 24–26.

Maslin, Janet. "Is NC-17 an X in a Clean Raincoat?" *New York Times*, October 21, 1990, sec. 2, p. 1ff.

———"Like the Toy? See the Movie." *New York Times*, December 12, 1989, sec. 2, p. 1ff.

———"To Look at the Hits Is Often to See the Misses." *New York Times*, March 19, 1989, sec. 2, p. 15.

McClintick, David. *Indecent Exposure: A True Story of Hollywood and Wall Street*. New York: Morrow, 1982.

McDowell, Edwin. "As Book Companies Grow, They Seem to Become Timid." *New York Times*, August 7, 1989, p. D8.

———"Dell Pays Ken Follett $12.3 Million for 2 Books." *New York Times*, June 28, 1990, p. C13.

———"First Novelists with Six-Figure Contracts." *New York Times*, April 10, 1989, p. 29.

———"Many Houses Find Images Are Blurred." *New York Times*, November 19, 1990, p. C6.

———"Power Behind the Pen: The Book Agent's Rise." *New York Times*, January 19, 1989, p. 18.

———"Publishers Favoring Additional Imprints." *New York Times*, December 11, 1989, p. 37.

———"Sales Rise for Authors Who Perish and Publish." *New York Times*, March 4, 1991, p. C8.

———"The Loyalty of Authors to Publishers has a New Name: It's Spelled M-O-N-E-Y." *New York Times*, January 22, 1981, p. C12.

———"Upbeat Mood as Booksellers Meet." *New York Times*, May, 25, 1987, p. 9.

McLuhan, Marshall. *Understanding Media: The Extensions of Man*. New York: McGraw-Hill, 1964.

Mehren, Elizabeth. "Action-Adventure Novels Invade the Marketplace." *Los Angeles Times*, July 29, 1988, sec. 5, p. 1.

Metcalf, Fred, ed. *Penguin Dictionary of Modern Humorous Quotations*. New York: Viking, 1986.

Miller, Mark Crispin. "Advertising: End of the Story." In Mark Crispin Miller, ed., *Seeing Through Movies: A Pantheon Guide to Popular Culture*, 186–246. New York: Pantheon, 1990.

———*Boxed In: The Culture of TV*. Evanston, Ill.: Northwestern University Press, 1988.

Mitang, Herbert. "Art and Money in a Tug of War for Aldous Huxley." *New York Times*, October 4, 1989, p. 14.

Modleski, Tania, ed. *Studies in Entertainment: Critical Approaches to Mass Culture*. Bloomington: University of Indiana Press, 1986.

Montesquieu, Charles. *An Essay on Taste*. Translated by Alexander Gerard. London: A. Miller, 1759.

Mordden, Ethan. *The Hollywood Studios: Their Unique Styles During the Golden Age of Movies*. New York: Simon & Schuster, 1988.

Mosley, Leonard. *Zanuck: The Rise and Fall of Hollywood's Last Tycoon*. Boston: Little, Brown, 1984.

Motion Picture News, July 19, 1924, p. 321.

Mumford, Lewis. "Megalopolis as Anti-City." *Architectural Record* (1962), 132:101–108.

Murphy, A. D. "Distribution and Exhibition: An Overview." In Jason E. Squire, ed., *The Movie Business Book*, 243–262. New York: Simon & Schuster, 1983.

Myers, Peter S. "The Studio as Distributor." In Jason E. Squire, ed., *The Movie Business Book*, 275–284. New York: Simon & Schuster, 1983.

Newcomb, Horace, ed. *Television: The Critical View*. New York: Oxford University Press, 1982.

Nixon, Will. "Agents and Advances." *Publishers Weekly*, February, 2 1990, pp. 15–21.

Nye, Russell. *The Unembarrassed Muse: The Popular Arts in America*. New York: Dial, 1970.

O'Brien, Maureen. "American Gothic." *Entertainment Weekly*, March 8, 1990, pp. 32–34.

O'Connor, John. "Pop Culture as Insults and Threats of Violence." *New York Times*, March 14, 1989, p. 16.

———"Today TV Outshines the Movies." *New York Times*, July 8, 1990, sec. 2, p. 1ff.

Pareles, Jon. "How Rap Moves to Television's Beat." *New York Times*, January 14, 1990, sec. 2, p. 1ff.

———"In Pop, Whose Song Is It, Anyway?" *New York Times*, August 27, 1989, sec. 2, p. 1ff.

———*The Rolling Stone Encyclopedia of Rock & Roll*. New York: Rolling Stone Press, 1983.

———"When Music Really Means Business." *New York Times*, March 19, 1990, p. B3.

Pattison, Robert. *The Triumph of Vulgarity: Rock Music in the Mirror of Romanticism*. New York: Oxford University Press, 1987.

Peiss, Kathy. *Cheap Amusements*. Philadelphia: Temple University Press, 1986.

Perry, Bliss. *Life and Letters of Henry Lee Higginson*. Boston: Atlantic Monthly Press, 1921.

Phelan, John M. *Disenchantment: Meaning and Morality in the Media*. New York: Hastings House, 1980.

Phillips, Julia. *You'll Never Eat Lunch in This Town Again*. New York: Random House, 1991.

Pittman, Robert W. "We're Talking the Wrong Language to 'TV Babies.' " *New York Times*, January 24, 1990, p. A15.

Plagens, Peter. "Confessions of a Serial Killer. *Newsweek*, March 4, 1991, pp. 58–59.

Polskin, Howard. "TV's Getting Sexier . . . How Far Will It Go?" *TV Guide*, January 7, 1989, pp. 14–21.

Postman, Neil. *Amusing Ourselves to Death: Public Discourse in the Age of Show Business*. New York: Viking, 1985.

Powdermaker, Hortense. *Hollywood, the Dream Factory*. Boston: Little, Brown, 1950.

Powell, Walter W. *Getting Into Print: The Decision-Making Process in Scholarly Publishing*. Chicago: University of Chicago Press, 1985.

Pynchon, Thomas. *Vineland*. Boston: Little, Brown, 1990.

Radecki, Thomas, ed. "Special Bestseller Books Issue." *NCTV News* (1988), 9(5):1–8.

Radway, Janice A. *Reading the Romance: Women, Patriarchy, and Popular Literature*. Chapel Hill: University of North Carolina Press, 1984.

Reuter, Madalynne. "ABA, Michener Join Others in Pantheon Reactions." *Publishers Weekly*, March 30, 1990, pp. 12–13.

———"Vintage to Issue Controversial Ellis Novel After S&S Cancellation." *Publishers Weekly*, November 30, 1990, pp. 8–10.

Roberts, Thomas J. *The Aesthetics of Junk Fiction*. Athens: The University of Georgia Press, 1990.

Rose, Brian G. *TV Genres: A Handbook and Reference Guide*. Westport, Conn.: Greenwood, 1985.

Rosenberg, Bernard and David Manning White, eds. *Mass Culture: The Popular Arts in America*. New York: Macmillan, 1964.

Rosenberg, Bernard and Harry Silverstein, eds. *The Real Tinsel*. New York: Macmillan, 1970.

Rosenblatt, Roger. "Growing Up on Television." In Horace Newcomb, ed., *Television: The Critical View*, 373–386. New York: Oxford University Press, 1982.

Ross, Andrew. *No Respect: Intellectuals & Popular Culture*. New York: Routledge, 1989.

———"Uses of Camp." *Yale Journal of Criticism* (1988), 2(1):1–24.

Ross, Lillian. *Picture*. New York: Rinehart, 1952.

Rostovtzeff, Michael. *The Social and Economic History of the Roman Empire*. New York: Oxford University Press, 1957.

Rothenberg, Randall. "Now, Novels Are Turning Promotional." *New York Times*, January 13, 1989, p. 31.

———"Yesterday's Boob Tube Is Today's High Art." *New York Times*, October 7, 1990, sec. 2, p. 1ff.

Ruskin, John. "Of Vulgarity." In *Complete Works*, 8:343–62. London: George Allen, 1905.

Sauter, Van Gordon. "In Defense of Tabloid TV." *TV Guide*, August 5, 1989, pp. 2–4.

Schatz, Thomas. *The Genius of the System: Hollywood Filmmaking in the Studio Era*. New York: Pantheon, 1988.

Schroeder, Fred E. H. *Outlaw Aesthetics: Arts and the Public Mind*. Bowling Green, Ohio: Bowling Green University Popular Press, 1977.

Schulberg, Budd. *What Makes Sammy Run?*. New York: Random House, 1941.

Schwartz, Tony. "A Publisher Who Sells Books." *New York Times Book Review*, December 9, 1979, p. 9ff.

Seldes, Gilbert. "The Public Arts." In Bernard Rosenberg and David Manning White, eds., *Mass Culture: The Popular Arts in America*, 557–561. New York: Macmillan, 1964.

Selznick, Irene. *A Private View*. New York: Knopf, 1983.

Sennett, Richard. *The Fall of Public Man*. New York: Knopf, 1977.

Shah, Diane K. "The Producers." *New York Times Magazine*, October 22, 1989, p. 27ff.

Shatzkin, Leonard. *In Cold Type: Overcoming the Book Crisis*. Boston: Houghton Mifflin, 1982.

Shaw, Arnold. *The Rock Revolution*. New York: Crowell-Collier, 1969.

Showalter, Dennis E. "Action! Adventure! Sales!" *Publishers Weekly*, May 5, 1989, pp. 20–24.

Shulman, Milton. *The Ravenous Eye: The Impact of the Fifth Factor*. London: Cassell, 1973.

Simon, Richard P. *Movie Industry Update: 1989*. New York: Goldman Sachs, 1989.

Solotaroff, Ted. "The Literary-Industrial Complex." *New Republic*, June 8, 1987, p. 28ff.

Sontag, Susan. "Notes on Camp." In *Against Interpretation*, 275–92. New York: Farrar, Straus & Giroux, 1966.

Sousa, John Philip. *Marching Along: Recollections of Men, Women and Music*. Boston: Hale, Cushman & Flint, 1928.

Squire, Jason E., ed. *The Movie Business Book*. New York: Simon & Schuster, 1983.

Stallybrass, Peter and Allan White. *The Politics and the Poetics of Transgression*. Ithaca, NY: Cornell University Press, 1986.

Stanley, Alessandra. "Romance Novels Discover a Baby Boom." *New York Times*, April 3, 1991, pp. 1ff.

Stanley, Robert H. *The Celluloid Empire: A History of the American Movie Industry*. New York: Hastings House, 1978.

Steinberg, Leo. *The Sexuality of Christ in Renaissance Art and in Modern Oblivion*. New York: Pantheon, 1983.

Stern, Jane and Michael Stern. *The Encyclopedia of Bad Taste*. New York: Harper-Collins, 1990.

Szatmary, David P. *Rockin' in Time: A Social History of Rock and Roll*. Englewood Cliffs, NJ: Prentice-Hall, 1987.

Tebbel, John. *Between Covers: The Rise and Transformation of Book Publishing in America*. New York: Oxford University Press, 1987.

Thomas, Bob. *King Cohn: The Life and Times of Harry Cohn*. New York: Putnam, 1967.

Toll, Robert C. *The Entertainment Machine: American Show Business in the Twentieth Century*. New York: Oxford University Press, 1982.

Townley, Roderick. "Reflections: TV in America." *TV Guide*, March 4, 1989, pp. 13–14.

Ulmer, Greg. *Teletheory: Grammatology in the Age of Video*. New York: Routledge, 1989.

Van Gelder, Lawrence. "At the Movies: Romero Films Poe." *New York Times*, September 1, 1989, p. 19.

Varnedoe, Kirk and Adam Gopik. *High and Low: Popular Culture and Modern Art*. Descriptive Catalog. New York: The Museum of Modern Art, 1990.

Venturi, Robert. *Learning from Las Vegas: The Forgotten Symbolism of Architectural Form*. Cambridge: MIT University Press, 1977.

Vogel, Harold. *Entertainment Industry Economics: A Guide for Financial Analysis*. New York: Cambridge University Press, 1990.

Voice Literary Supplement. "Books & Bucks" (symposium). May 1990, pp. 12–19.

Waters, Harry F. "Trash TV." *Newsweek*, November 14, 1988, pp. 72–78.

Waters, John. *Shock Value: A Tasteful Book About Bad Taste*. New York: Dell, 1981.

Waters, Ray. *Paperback Talk*. Chicago: Academy, 1985.

Whiteside, Thomas. *The Blockbuster Complex: Conglomerates, Show Business, and Book Publishing*. Middletown, Conn.: Wesleyan University Press, 1980.

Whitney, Craig R. "British TV on Eve of Competitive Era." *New York Times*, October 24, 1989, p. C24.

Williams, Lena. "For Advice, the Media as Mom." *New York Times*, August 2, 1989, p. C1ff.

Winn, Marie. *The Plug-in Drug*. New York: Viking, 1977.

Wolfe, Tom. "The Girl of the Year." In *The Kandy-Kolored Tangerine-Flake Streamline Baby*, 204–220. New York: Farrar, Straus & Giroux, 1963.

Wood, Peter. "Television as Dream." In Horace Newcomb, ed., *Television: The Critical View*, 510–528. New York: Oxford University Press, 1982.

Young, Mahonri Sharp. "American Radio: What Is wrong With It?" *The American Scholar* (1948), 17(2):224–227.

Yule, Andrew. *Fast Fade: David Puttnam, Columbia Pictures, and the Battle for Hollywood*. New York: Dell, 1989.

Zimbert, Richard. "Business Affairs and the Production/Financing/Distribution Agreement." In Jason E. Squire, ed., *The Movie Business Book*, 175–188. New York: Simon & Schuster, 1983.

Index

Audience: influence of as gatekeeper, 268–74; *see also* Book publishing, Gatekeeper, Movie making, Television programming
Audits of Great Britain, 210
Auel, Jean, 72–73
Austin, Jane, 254
Auteur (film theory), 137, 139
Avon Books, 92

Bach, Stephen, 139*n*
Back to the Future (movie), 156
Bagdikian, Ben, 118
Bagley, Ross, 245*n*
Bailey, Herbert, 67
Bakhtin, Mikhail, 57
Bakker, Jim, 245
Bakker, Tammy, 14
Baldwin, James, 97
Balio, Tino, 139*n*
Ballantine Books, 90
Ballantine, Ian, 77, 89–90, 98–99
Balzac, Honoré de, 14
Bangs, Lester, 3
Bank of America, 133, 156
Bantam Books, 90, 106, 125
BarcaLounger, 197
Barnes, Clive, 258
Barnes & Noble, 101, 103*n*
Barnum P. T., 14, 31, 60–65, 121, 162, 202, 222, 229; and The American Museum, 60–62; and the carnival, 60–65, illustrated, *61*
Barr, Roseanne, 3, 202–203; and *Roseanne*, 7
Barrymore, John, 181
Barthes, Roland, 229*n*
Bartholomew Fair, 57–59
Bart, Peter, 139*n*
Batman (movie), 141, 151*n*
"Battle of the Books, The" 260
Baudrillard, Jean, 51
B. Dalton (bookstore), 101–102, 126
Beagle, Peter, 126
Beatty, Warren, 149*n*
Becker, Arnold, 207
Beckford, William, 126
Beerbohm, Max, 15
Begelman, David, 139*n*

Bellow, Saul, 106
Benjamin, Walter, 35, 46–48
Bennett, William, 8, 257
Benton, Barbi, 249
Berg, A. Scott, 139*n*
Berkeley, Busby, 174
Berkley Publishing, 92
Berle, Milton, 14, 244
Berlin, Irving, 1
Berlusconi, Silvio, 262
Berman, Pandro, 176*n*
Bernstein, Robert, 74
Bershtel, Sara, 75, *76*
Bertelsmann AG (conglomerate), 6, 90, 100, 102, 262
Bessie, Cornelia and Michael, 117–18
Bestseller list, 2; *see* Book publishing
Bettelheim, Bruno, 50*n*
Bishop, Joey, 239
Blockbuster, 6; *see* Book publishing, Movie making, Television programming
Bloom, Allan, 8, 16, 257
Bobbs-Merrill Incorporated, 84
Book publishing: books as candles or shoes, 67–69, 120; as carnival, 68–130; and cross marketing, 68; and conglomerated ownership, 68, 84–86; economics of, 68, 83; history of, 68, 83; and marketing of "units," 68, 81; recent examples in, 68–69; and graphic revolution, 69–70; role of gatekeeper in, 70, 75, 92, 117, 129; and *The Name of the Rose*, 70–71; recent bestsellers, 71; and video, 71; and Xerox commercial, 71, 72; audience for, 71–72, 80, 102–103; and genres, 75, 101, 121–24; as commodities, 77; like classical music and painting, 80; in nineteenth century, 80; role of blockbuster, 81; and "deal," 81; as show business, 81, 83–84; and electronic typesetting, 82; manufacturing process, 82–83; and returns, 83; and royalties, 83; and software, 83–84; and movies, 84, 86, 129; and synergy, 84; and Authors Guild, 85; as oligopoly, 86; and

chain bookstores, 101–102; and distribution, 101; and EDP POS register, 102; and taste, 102–103; and advances, 103–104, 120; like electronic media, 103; recent flops, 104; and "orphans," 104; three-tier system, 104–105; and backlist, 105; and brand-name authors, 105; example of "Just Killing Time," 105; and author's tour, 106; and posthumous authors, 106–107; and cover art, 107–108; and mall bookstore, 107; and product placement, 112; and aftermarket, 114; and audio tapes, 114–15; new methods of selling, 114–16; and editor self-image, 115–17; and literary-industrial complex, 116; and special imprints, 117–18; and small presses, 118; role of agent, 119–20; role of university presses, 119*n*; bottom-line driven, 121; and Westerns, 121–22; mystery genre, 122–23; and romance, 122; and melodrama, 123–24; and action-adventure genre, 124–26; crime genre in, 124; and fantasy cycles, 124–26; and psychobiography, 124; and "target books," 124–26; and techno-thriller, 124; example of *American Psycho*, 128–29; "buying on turnaround," 129; *see also* Pantheon affair, Paperback book, Bret Easton Ellis

Boorstin, Daniel, 69, 93, 250*n*
Bosch, Hieronymus, 57
Boston Atheneum, 35
Boston, Symphony, 32
Bowdler, Thomas, 9
Bowker, R. R. (publisher), 84
Box-office reports, 2; *see* Movie making
Bradford, Barbara Taylor, 3
Brady, Mathew, 61
Brandewyne, Rebecca, 77
Bravo (cable channel), 215
Breughel, Pieter, 57
Bridge Publications, 107
British Broadcasting Corporation (BBC), 7, 217

Brokaw, Tom, 236
Brooks, Mel, 15, 182*n*; on blockbuster, 87–88
Brown, James Mason, 257
Bruce, Tammy, 129
Buckley, William, 16, 238
Burke, Alan, 239
Burke, Chris, 203
Bush, George, 15

Cable News Network (CNN), 215
Cable Television, 3, 214–18; history of, 214–15; influence of, 214–15; size of, 214–15; and choice, 215; and high culture, 215; like magazines, 215; and networks, 215
Caldwell, Erskine, 97
California Raisins, 202–203, 248
Camera Obscura (periodical), 136
Camp (aesthetic category), 54–56; *see also* Junk, Kitsch, Schlock, Trash, Vulgar
Campanella, Joseph, 249
Canby, Vincent, 134
Canfield, Cass, 77
Canon: creation of, 36–37; *see also* Popular culture, Vulgar
Canon Films, 161
Capital Cities Corporation, 62, 162, 212
Capp, Andy, 3
Capra, Frank, 175
Carnegie, Dale, 88
Carnival: and church, 2, 3, 27–28, 32–33, 259; criticism of, 9–11; and scholarship, 9; repetition in, 10; in nineteenth century, 57–60; in France, 59–60; and work week, 59; and frontier, 60–61; and nineteenth-century America, 60–62; and P. T. Barnum, 60–65; and circus, 53–64; and high culture, 63–65; and capitalism, 65; and electronic midway, 65; and movies, 65; and sideshow, 65; and television, 65, 251, 257; in *The Name of the Rose*, 70–71; and book publishing, 91–92; and movie making, 134–40, 172–78, 184–91; as elec-

Carnival (*Continued*)
tronic church, 245; and talk shows
on television, 240; and cultural literacy, 254, 259; and knowledge,
254, 258; modern influence of, 255;
and literacy, 256–70; and mass media, 256–270; operation of, 256–57;
and gatekeeper, 257; and democracy, 258–59; worldwide, 258–59;
and audience for, 259; and technology, 259–60; as what we share,
259; and cartoon, 260; and curricu-
lum, 269; genres in, 260; and ro-
man amphitheater, 260; and higher
education, 272–74; and globaliza-
tion, 274
Carolco (movie production), 161
Carroll, Noel, 137
Carter Hawley Hale Corporation, 101
Cary Thomas Awards (1988), 118
Cavett, Dick, 239
Centennial City (and Dinkeytown),
203
Centennial Exposition, 63
Cerf, Bennett, 77, 84, 257
Chancellor, John, 235
Chaney, Lon, Jr., 176
Chaplin, Charlie, 132
Chapple, Steve, 4
Chasman, David, 173
Cheers (television show), 7
Cheney, Lynne, 8
Cher, 14
Chesterfield, Lord, 15, 27
Christian Broadcasting Network
(CBN), 215, 244*n*
Christian Leaders for Responsible
Television (Clear-TV), 218–19
Church, Fredric, 14
Churchill, Winston, 123
Cibber, Colley, 29
Cinderella (movie), 151
Cinema Journal (periodical), 136
Circus maximus, 260
Citizen Kane (movie), 254
Clancy, Tom, 72, 73, 104, 124, 146,
190, 223*n*
Clark, Dick, 249–50
Clavell, James, 127

Clay, Andrew Dyce, 3
Coca-Cola Corporation, 7
Cochrane, Wayne, 265
Cohen, Roger, 129
Cohn, Harry, 164, 174, 175, 190; as
gatekeeper, 177–78
Collins, Jackie, 3, 14, 104
Collins, Jim, 3
Collins, Joan, 14, 202–203
Columbia Broadcasting System (CBS),
62, 84, 162, 206, 211*n*, 213, 214,
215, 218, 223, 235
Columbian Exposition, 63–64
Columbia Pictures, 161; style of 175
Comedy channel, *196*
Comic books, 3
Commedia dell'arte, 260
Comedy Channel *196*
Conan the Barbarian, 3
Coney Island, 64–65, *64*
Coonts, Stephen, 124
Copeland, Charles Townsend, 269
Copeland, Kenneth, 245*n*
Coppola, Francis Ford, 173*n*, 175
Corcoran Gallery of Art, 16–17
Coren, Alan, 251
Cosby, Bill, 202–203; and *The Cosby
Show*, 222–23
Costco (bookstore), 103*n*
Costner, Kevin, 105, 137
Coward, Noël, 4
Cowley, Malcolm, 97
Creative Arts Agency (CAA), 184–
85
Crimes of the Century (television
show), 238
Crimewatch Tonight (television show),
237
Cronkite, Walter, 235
Cross, Wilbur, 269–70
Crothers, Rachel, 180
Crough, Paul, 245*n*
Crowther, Bosley, 138*n*
Cruise, Tom, 105, 146, 223*n*
Culture: examples of high and low
culture, 20–65, *20–21*; high culture
defined, 43; *see also* Popular culture,
Vulgar
Curbstone Press, 118

Current Affair. A (television show),
  221, 237
Curtis Circulation Company, 90

Daly, Bob, 187
Dannel, Fredric, 4
Dann, Michael, 220, 222
Darkman (movie), *172*
Dating Game, The, 3
Davidson, John, 249
Davis, Adele, 98
Davis, Martin, 128
Days of Thunder (movie), 144*n*
Dayton-Hudson Incorporated, 101
Deconstruction, 272
Def Leppard (singing group), 265
de Graff, Robert, 86–88, 182
DeHaan, Richard, 245*n*
Delacorte, George T., 90*n*
DeLaurentiis Entertainment, 160
Dell Publishing, 90–91, *91*, 92, 100
Del Rey Books, 118
DePalma, Brian, 149*n*, 171, 263
Diamond, I. A. L., 190
Dickens, Charles, 14
Diderot, Denis, 18
Didion, Joan, 185*n*
"Dinkeytown" (carnival), 63
Direct Broadcasting Satellite (DBS),
  262
Disneyland, 14
Disney, Walt, 24, 68, 161, 262; and
  The Walt Disney Company, 157;
  and status of Disney company,
  182*n*
Divorce Court (television show), 238
Dodd Mead & Co., 94, 104
Donahue, Phil, 221, 239–40
Donaldson, Sam, 202–203, 236
Donaldson, Stephen, 126
Donne, John, 43, 254
"Don'ts and Be Carefuls" (movie pro-
  duction code), 169
Doubleday & Company, 85, 86
Douglas, Mike, 239
Dove Books-on-Tape, 114
Downey, Mort, Jr., 3, 14, 202–203,
  221, 240–43; fall from grace, 240;
  audience of, 241; criticized, 241–

43; and junk, 241; as sideshow, 241;
  and taste, 241; technique of, 241;
  defended, 242
Dr. Strangelove, 254
DuMont Television Network, *198*
Dunne, John Gregory, 139*n*, 185*n*
Durwood, Stanley, 182
Dutton, E. P. (publisher), 98
Dwight, John, 32
Dworkin, Andrea, 16
Dystel, Oscar, 81, 84

Eco, Umberto: *The Name of the Rose*,
  69–71
EDP POS (Electronic Data Process-
  ing Point of Sale) register, 102
Eisenstein, Sergei, 138
Elias, Norbert, 56
Eliot, Charles, 80
Eliot, Marc, 4
Eliot, T. S., 8, 250
Ellis, Bret Easton: *American Psycho*,
  128–29
Ellison, Ralph, 96
Enoch, Kurt, 89–91, 95
Entertainment Sports Programming
  Network (ESPN), 215
Entertainment Tonight, 3, 9, 221
Entertainment Weekly (magazine), 9
Entfotainment, 8–9
Entrekin, Morgan, 118
Enzensberger, Hans, 48*n*
Epstein, Edward Jay, 113
Epstein, Jason, 1, 2, 114
Eridanos Press, 118
Erskine, John, 270
Esslin, Martin, 259
E. T. The Extra-terrestrial (movie),
  112, 151
Evans, Bergen, 257
Evans, Joni, 118

Fairchild, Morgan, 250
Falwell, Jerry, 244*n*
Family Feud (television show), 257
Fantasia (movie), 14, 80
Fantasy genre (publishing), 124–27;
  see also Book publishing
Farnsworth, Philo T., 207

Miller, Merle, 257
Miller v. California, 15–16
Milli Vanilli (singing group), 4, 258, 264
Mills, C. Wright, 203*n*
Minnelli, Liza, 264
Minow, Newton, 201
Mintz, Elliot, 9
Mobile vulgus, 32
Montesquieu, Charles Louis, 18
Monthly Magazine, 26
Monty Python, 203
Mordden, Ethan, 139*n*
Morito, Akio, 162
Morley, Henry, 57
Morris, Kenneth, 126
Motley Crue (singing group), 265
Movie making: as business, 132–35; and supreme court, 133; and carnival, 134–40, 172–78, 191; print criticism of, 134–35; and visuality, 134; and architecture, 135–36; like construction projects, 135–36; and academic criticism, 136–37; and gatekeeper in, 136, 177–78; and art, 136–37; as "cinema," 138; and blockbusters, 140, 186–87; like book publishing, 140, 166–67, 177; and merchandising, 141–44; release of prints, 141, *142, 158–59*; and advertising, 143–45; and synergy, 143; and ancillary markets, 144–46, *148*; and television, 144, 147–48, 153–55, 180; and globalization, 145–49, *146, 148*; "high concept" films, 146; and repetition, 146, 188, 189; and stars, 146; and stereotypes, 146; and genres, 147; and sequels, 147, 189; and special effects, 147; and cable television, 148–49; and pay-per-view, 150; and costs, 153–57; A-titles in, 154–57; and marketing, *154–55*, 165, 188; negative costs in, 154–58; and revenue mix, *156*; distribution of product, 157–59, 165–67; major studios, 157; studio shares in, *160*; diversification in, 161; and book writing, 162–63; Manhattan base for, 162–63; during Reagan presidency, 163–64; and risk management, 163, 187; in days of moguls, 164–68; capital needed for, 165; and saturation marketing, 168; and taste, 168–70; influence of cartoons, 171–73; and independent producers, 173–74; history of, 177–78; moguls as gatekeepers, 177–78; and nickelodeon, 177, 181*n*; and theaters, 181–82; aftermarket in 184; and agents, 184; current status of, 184–91; and the "deal," 184–86; lawyers as moguls, 184; "PFD" agreements, 184–85; and risk avoidance, 184–85; and lawyers, 186; screenwriters in, 186; and brand names, 188; current costs in, 188; as oligopoly, 188; and franchise movies, 189; horror genre of, 189; *see also* Production codes, Movie studios, Videocassette
Movie studios: and audiences, 131–32, 175; as conglomerates, 131, 160–65, 173–75; as oligopoly, 145–46, 182; and B-films, 153; protected product, 153–54; and independents, 160–61; after moguls died, 161–63; control of outlets, 163–64; evolution of, 163–64; and vertical integration, 163–64; and tax shelters, 164; and carnival, 172–78; and distinctive styles, 173; history of, 173–76; and Middle-European Jews, 174–75, 177; moguls like book editors, 174–75; and style, 174; and vulgarity, 174–75; and high culture, 176–79; moguls as carnies, 180–82; current status of, 182–190
Mr. Destiny (movie), 143
Mumford, Lewis, 40
Murdoch, Rupert, 14, 81, 161, 162, 182*n*, 212, 217*n*, 237, 262
Murphy, Eddie, 3, 105, 146
Music Corporation of America (MCA), 6, 85, 92, 161, 182*n*, 184
Music Television (MTV), 49, 204, 215, 259, 262–68; influence on television, 262; and advertisements,

263; as art, 263–64; impact on show business, 263; style of, 263; influence of lip synching, 264; as carnival, 267; as endless loop, 267; as gatekeeper, 267–68; as postmodern, 267; and synergy, 267; *see also* Heavy metal, Rap music
Mutual Film Corporation v. Ohio, 133
Myers, Michael, 189

Nabokov, Vladimir, 133
Napoleon, 272
National Book Awards, 117
National Broadcasting System (NBC), 62, 162, 206, 213, 214, 215, 218, 223, 235
National Conference on Television Violence (NCTV), 126–27
National Endowment for the Arts (NEA), 15, 17
National Enquirer, 3
National Radio Pulpit, 243
National Wrestling Alliance, 229
NC-17 (movie rating), 170–71
Neilan, Mickey, 179
New American Library (NAL), 86, 112, 125, 149; history of, 89–98; motto of, 93; and high-culture publishing, 94; aspirations of founders, 95; and distribution of, 95; and Mentor, 95; and Signet, 95; and vulgarity, 95; and authors, 96–98; and black writers, 96–97; and direct sales, 96; relationship with high-culture writers, 96; and advances, 97; headquarters of, 97; and Irving Wallace, 97; and movies, 97–98, and prizes won, 97; conglomeration of, 98; and Literary Projects, 98; and Times-Mirror Company, 98
Newhouse, S. I., 74
New Kids on the Block (singing group), 3, 264
New Line Cinema, 142–43, 161
News Corporation, 102
Newsweek, 9
Newton, Joseph, 243
New World Pictures, 160

New York International Festival of the Arts (1988), 138
New York Review of Books, 114
New York Times, 9
Nexis (data base): listings of "vulgar," 16
Niebuhr, Reinhold, 203*n*
Nielsen ratings, 2, 208–211; history of, 208–210; defined, 209; how generated, 209; and polling, 209*n*; as opposed to share, 209; and diary, 210; and problems with, 210–211; and network concern, 211*n*; and peoplemeter, 211–212; and "smart-sensing technology, 211; and sweeps, 223
Nightmare on Elm Street (movie), 3, 143–45
Niles, Robert, 206
Nintendo (video game), 7
Nixon, Richard, 84
North Point Press, 85
Norton, Charles Eliot, 37
Norton, W. W. (publisher), 85

Oates, Joyce, Carol, 124
O'Connor, John, 256
On Trial (legal network), 238
Orion Pictures: current status, 182*n*
Ortega y Gasset, José, 250
Osbourne, Ozzy, 265
Outlet Book Company, 103*n*
Ovitz, Michael, 120, 184

Pace Bookstores, 103*n*
Pantheon (affair with Random House), 74–77; characters involved, 74–75; in *New York Review of Books*, 74, 76; editorials about, 75*n*; and Hill & Wang, 75–76; and *Publishers' Weekly*, 77; *see also* Book publishing
Paperback book, 3, 77–130; and dominance in market, 86; history of, 86–89, 98–99; influence of, 86; and vulgarity, 86; distribution of, 88–89, 99; as carnival, 91–92; and magazines, 91–92, 99; Darwinian principles of, 95; gatekeeper in, 99; and movies, 99–100; and advances,

in, 233; television interview, 234; *see also* World Wrestling Federation
Professoriat, role of, 268–74
Public Broadcasting System (PBS), 216–18, 244*n*; begathons for, 215; advertisements on, 216; audience for, 216; competition for, 217; resembles commercial television, 217; *see also* Television programming
Publishers Central Bureau, 103*n*
Publishers Weekly, 77–79, *78*, *79*
Punch and Judy, 260
Punch, Mr., 18
Punk (aesthetic category), 19; *see also* Vulgar
Putnam Berkley Group, 92
Putnam, G. P., 92
Putnam's Magazine, 31
Puttnam, David, 139*n*
Puzo, Mario, 97, 104, 127
Pynchon, Thomas, 205
Pyramid Books, 92

Quiet Riot (musical group), 265

Radecki, Thomas, 16
Radio-Keith-Orpheum (RKO), 167; and style, 176*n*
Rakolta, Terry, 219
Rambo (movie series), 3
Random House, 74–76; *see also* Pantheon
Raphael, Sally Jesse, 221
Rap music, 265–66; concerns of, 265–66; defined, 265; from street culture, 265–6; and language, 266; and brand names, 267
Rap videos, 3
Rather, Dan, 202–203, 236
Rauschenberg, Robert, 49, 205
R. D. Perry Company, 195–96, 211
Readers' Catalog: An Annotated Selection, 114–15, *115*
Reagan, Michael, 249
Reagan, Nancy, *4*, 9, 124, *273*
Reagan, Ronald, 202–203, *273*
Real, Michael, 48*n*
Reform Bill of 1832, 23
Reid, Wallace, 180

Reith, Lord, 217*n*
Rice, Elmer, 180
Riggio, Leonard, 101
Rio, Ronnie, 265
Ripley, Alexandra, 190
Riskin, Robert, 175
Rissner, Danny, 185*n*
Rivera, Geraldo, 3, 7, 14, 219, 221, 222, 240
Rivers, Joan, 14
Rivers, Larry, 45
Robbins, Harold, 127
Robertson, Pat, 245
Roberts, Oral, 243, 245
Rocky (movie series), 143
Rogers, Rosemary, 92
Rohatyn, Felix, frontispiece
Romance, covers illustrated, *110*; *see also* Paperback book
Romero, George, 132
Rosenblatt, Roger, 193
Rosenthal, Arthur, 75, *76*
Ross, Andrew, 3
Rosten, Leo, 174
Rostovtzeff, Michael, 13
Rothapfel, Samuel ("Roxy"), 181
Roth, Philip, 106, 120*n*
Rotten, Johnny, 265
Rushdie, Salman, 73, 74
Ruskin, John, 9, 24–27, 31, 49, 57

Salomon Brothers (investment bankers), 162
Sam's Club (bookseller), 103*n*
Sanburg, Carl, 245
Santayana, George, 22
Sarnoff, William, 86
Sarris, Andrew, 137
Saturday Night Live, 203, 218
Sauter, Van Gordon, 236, 242
Sayles, John, 264
Schary, Dore, 176*n*
Schatz, Thomas, 139*n*
Schiffrin, André, 74
Schiller, Friedrich, 48*n*
Schlattery, George, 203
Schlock (aesthetic category), 54–55; *see also* Camp, Junk, Kitsch, Trash, Vulgar

Swaggart, Jimmy, 3, 245
Swift, Jonathan, 254

Television (*Continued*)
218; and changing tastes, 218, 250–
51; and product placement, 219; as
trash, 243; private networks, 244*n*;
as adolescent entertainment, 250;
videophobia of professoriat, 255*n*;
ascendancy of, 257; game shows on,
257–58; and democracy, 258–59;
globalization of, 258–59; omnipre-
sence of 261; as Esperanto, 261; attraction of American programming,
262; new delivery systems, 262; as
bardic, 268; *see also* Cable television, Federal Communication
Commission, Infomercial, Music
Television, Nielsenratings, Public
Broadcasting Service, Tabloid news,
Talk shows, Televangelism, Television networks, Television programming, Television syndication
Television networks: and advertising,
213–14; defined, 213; and production companies, 213; and programming, 213–17; department of
standards in, 128
Television programming, 201, 206; attraction of American programming,
217–18; on PBS, 217; and entropy
curve, 219; and great programmers,
219–21; and taste, 220; and air time,
220*n*; and cable, 220*n*; history of,
220*n*; and prime time, 220; explained, 221–23; and "flow
through," 221–22; and a hit like
Cosby Show, 222–23; location of
show, 222–23; strategies of, 222;
and sweep weeks, 222–23; and preview audiences, 223*n*; risks in, 223;
and seasons, 223; and taste, 224,
225; and sports, 225; and trash,
234
Television syndication: defined, 213–
14; and financing, 213–15; and networks, 213–14; and bestsellers, 214;
like blockbuster, 214; strip-
syndication explained, 214; and barter syndication, 248
Temple, Sir William, 260

Thalberg, Irving, 165, 174, 175, 176,
180; as gatekeeper, 179*n*
Tharp, Twyla, 49
thirtysomething (television show), 7
Thomas, Theodore, 31
Thorn EMI, 6
Thor Power Tool Case, 101*n*
Thunder's Mouth Press, 118
Time (magazine), 7, 9
Times-Mirror Corporation, 86
Time Warner Incorporated, 61, 62,
68, 77, 86, 92, 102, 113, 162, 214,
262; annual report of, 6–7; interna-
tional reach of, 7–8
Tinker, Grant, 53
Tisch, Lawrence, 213
T, Mr., *4*, 14
Tocqueville, Alexis de, 27, 258
Tolkein, J. R. R, 126
Townshend, Peter 265
Transamerica Corporation, 161
Trash: appreciation of, 53–54; as nov-
els, 53; as television, 53; *see also*
Camp, Junk, Kitsch, Schlock,
Trash, Vulgar
Trump, Donald, 14, 20–22, 112
Trump, Ivana, 20–22
Tunney, Gene, 269
Turner, Ted, 68, 162, 215
Turner, Tina, 263
Twentieth Century Fox, 21, 161; and
studio style, 176; current status of,
182*n*
Twisted Sister (singing group), 265
2-Live Crew (rap group), 2
Tyler, Anne, 106
Tyndall Report, 8

United Artists, 161, 167; current sta-
tus of, 182*n*
United News Company, *96*
United Parcel Service (UPS), 114
Universal Studios, 161, 171; and studio
style, 175–76; current status of, 182*n*
Unsolved Mysteries (television show), 237
Urban, Binky, 128
Uris, Leon, 127
USA Today, 3, 9, 14

Vacarro, Brenda, 250
Van Dyck, Anthony: *Thomas de Savoi-Carignan*, 24–26, *26*
van Dyke, Henry, 270
Van Impe, Jack, 245*n*
Vaughn, Robert, 249
Vendex International, 101
Vernet, Horace: *Carlo Alberto*, 24–26, *24*
Venturi, Robert, 40–43
Vicious, Sid, 256
Videocassette, 2–3; influence of on movies, 149; problems caused Hollywood, 149; sale of, 149; and advertising, 150; and pricing, 150; and sell-through, 150–51; and blockbusters, 151; like paperback book, 151 and clubs, *152*
Vidor, King, 180
Viking Penguin Incorporated, 104
Villard Books, 117
Vitale, Alberto, 74
Vohrees, Jason, 189
Voltaire, 18
Vulgar, 8–11; and art, 2–11, 45; and canon, 2–11, 55; as word, 2, 16; in music, 4–6; questions about, 10–11; as aesthetic category, 13–65, 267–74; examples of, 13–15; and taste, 15; as lost term, 15; andfashion, 16; and food, 16; in geology, 16; and Marxism, 16; and performance art, 17; and pornography, 16–17; triumph of, 19; and wheat, 16; as nineteenth-century aesthetic category, 24–28; as used by John Ruskin, 24–27; in the eighteenth century, 27–28, 56; and mob, 27; victims of, 27; and marginality, 44, 55; and repetition, 46–47, 52; and high culture, 48; and postmodernism, 48–49; and genres, 49; and machines, 50–51; and adolescence, 51, 52, 56; and Frankfurt school, 51; and escapism, 52; and risk, 52; since the 1960s, 52; and emotions, 53; and academic categories, 54; and romanticism, 54; and

audience, 55; and guilt, 55–56; and homosexuals, 55; and Jews, 55; and delicacy, 56; and scatology, 56; and shame, 56–57; and carnival, 57–59; specifically prohibited in the movies, 168–70; *see also* Camp, Freaks, Frankfurt school, Kitsch, Junk, Las Vegas, Schlock, Trash

Waggoner, Lyle, 249
Wagner, Richard, 14
Waldenbooks, 101–102, 126
Wallis, Hal, 174
Wall Street Journal, 9
Walters, Barbara, 237
Wanger, Walter, 178
Wapner, Judge, 238
Warhol, Andy, 18, 19, 105, 264; and popular culture, 44–45; and *Absolut Warhol* advertisement, *46* and *Campbell Soup*, *47*
Warner Books, 77, 92, 120
Warner, Bros., 161, 173; style of, 175; and high culture, 181–82; current status of, 182*n*
Warner, Harry: as gatekeeper, 177
Warner, Jack, 164, 174, 175; as gatekeeper, 177
Warner Records, 6
Warner, Susan, 123
Washington, George, 15
W.A.S.P (singing group), *266*
Wasserman, Lew, 184
Weaver, Sylvester "Pat," 221, 238
Weidenfeld & Nicolson, 104
Weintraub Entertainment, 160
Welles, Orson, 136
Westheimer, Ruth, 203
Weybright, Victor, 77, 89–98; and Alfred Knopf, 97
"What Is It" (Barnum exhibit), *62*, *63*, 121
Wheeler, A. C., 29
Whiteside, Thomas, 118
White, Vanna, 202–203
Whitman, Walt, 37, 65
Whittle Communications, 112–14; and "controlled-circulation adver-